Indian Placenames in America

Indian Placenames in America

Volume 1: Cities, Towns and Villages

Sandy Nestor

McFarland & Company, Inc., Publishers
Jefferson, North Carolina, and London

Library of Congress Cataloguing-in-Publication Data

Nestor, Sandy.
Indian placenames in America, volume 1 : cities,
towns and villages / Sandy Nestor.
p. cm.
Includes bibliographical references and index.

ISBN 0-7864-1654-8 (illustrated case binding : 50# alkaline paper) 

1. Names, Indian — United States. 2. Names, Geographical —
United States. 3. United States— History, Local. I. Title.
E98.N2N47 2003 917.3'001'4 — dc21 2003011417

British Library cataloguing data are available

Manufactured in the United States of America

McFarland & Company, Inc., Publishers
Box 611, Jefferson, North Carolina 28640
www.mcfarlandpub.com

To the Indians of America
May their names forever grace this great land

Acknowledgments

This book could not have been written but for all the libraries that generously sent me thousands of pages of documentation during my years of research. I am most grateful for their interest in my pursuits. I encourage the residents of their respective towns to support their libraries.

I had the pleasure of corresponding and or talking to the following people, and want to thank them for all their help and continued support: Roy Matsuno, for Ugashik, Alaska; Douglas Preston, author of *Cities of Gold*; Gene Serr, Tehama Genealogical & Historical Society, Tehama, California; Lila Bowman, for Aripeka, Florida; Elaine Poole, for Menan, Idaho; Bud Purdy, for Picabo, Idaho; Odell Walker, author of *Profiles of the Past*, Kuttawa, Kentucky; Louis Diggs, author of *In Our Voices*, for Chattalonee, Maryland; Don D'Amato, for Conimicut, Rhode Island; Sandy Drake, for Waka Texas; John Harder, for Kahlotus, Washington; William Stark, author of *Pine Lake* (Wisconsin); and Mayor Thelma Collins of Itta Bena, Mississippi. In 1996, Thelma became the first African-American female mayor of a once-segregated town.

Special thanks to Richard Staehler, along with Ryan Smith (high-school students) who conducted research on the little town of Yalaha, Florida, for a school project. Richard, you were so gracious to share your findings with me. You two should have received a higher grade than you did on your report!

Contents

Preface

"Ye say they have all passed away,
That noble race and brave;
That their light canoes have vanished
From off the crystal wave;
That 'mid the forest where they roamed,
There rings no hunter's shout;
But their name is on your waters,
And ye cannot wash it out."

— *Lydia Sigourney,* 1791–1865

The American Indians may have lost much of their land, but our forefathers continued their legacy (perhaps inadvertently) by giving many of our cities, towns, villages, and hamlets Indian names.

Unfortunately, countless names have been corrupted over time. It is sort of like the parlor game where a dozen people line up and the first person whispers a phrase to the second, which is repeated on down the line. The last person speaks the phrase, and nine times out of ten it is completely different from the original. And so we have the same problem with Indian names.

It was suggested that Pasadena (California) means "crown of the valley," but Alfred Kroeber disputed it, writing, "No unsophisticated and very few civilized Indians would think of calling any place the 'crown of the valley.' The phrase has all the appearance of having been coined by an American out of Indian or imaginary Indian terms."

When French fur traders married Indian women, their languages were interchanged, further corrupting the Indian words. White men were unable to pronounce the guttural words of the Indian language and in their ignorance spelled them they way they sounded. Some people simply made up names that sounded like Indian words. For example, W.W. Tooker wrote about placenames in New York, and although he got a lot of them right, many were guesses. However, his book became a benchmark for future historians. Henry Schoolcraft was an explorer and scholar who named towns in the Great Lakes area. He also coined words and syllables, adding more uncertainty.

There are places with similar spellings. Take, for example, two native villages in Alaska: Napakiak and Napaskiak. They're both Yu'pik Eskimo words. One means "wood pole" (or post) and the other was interpreted as "wood people." Similar spellings, similar interpretations, but one letter slightly changed the definition.

Muddled as they may be, it is still important to preserve what is known for history's sake. Since some tribes no longer exist, we cannot go back to them for a proper explanation of their names. Years ago the last Lenape Indian, Nora "Touching Leaves" Dean, who could still speak the language, died, but she did pass on the proper definitions of some of the names of northeastern towns (mainly in New Jersey and Pennsylvania). The Lenape names she translated are defined in this book, and no other derivations are noted from other sources in order to preserve the correct name origin. Dr. Herbert C. Kraft, chairman of the Anthropology Department at Seton Hall University in South Orange, New Jersey, wrote *The Lenape or Delaware Indians*, in which he included Touching Leaves' correctly identified Lenape place names. Lenni Lenape is often used to describe the Indians, but it is redundant. Their correct name is simply Lenape.

There are entries with no known name origin, but they are included because they are still historically important. Other entries do not name the tribe from which the name was derived. Settlers frequently gave their new communities aboriginal names from their former homes, or selected a name from nomadic tribes, so it was not assumed a name originated from an indigenous tribe from any specific area.

In certain regions, a tribe's name was spelled differently, e.g., Potawatomi was spelled Pottawatomie and Potowatomi. Other examples are Abneki and Abnaki, Athabascan and Athapascan, and the like. In this book, they are spelled one way for the sake of consistency. Some tribes were called by different names, e.g., Delaware/Lenape. Many bands (or sub-tribes) exist under main tribes. The Apaches had the Mescaleros and Chiricahuas. The Sioux included the Dakota, Oglala, Sisseton and Yankton, to name a few. It is not within the scope of this book to break down individual bands within the main tribal designations.

Counties and populations are in parentheses (Alaska has no counties; Louisiana has parishes). Populations in italics were taken from informal statistics of town halls, chambers of commerce, etc., since they were not listed in the U.S. Census. Many of the villages and hamlets (especially in the Eastern states) are part of other towns and their numbers were included in the dominant town's census.

The U.S. Census Bureau was supposed to count everyone in 2000, but it did not. I wrote to the Census Bureau and asked why Bylas was not included in the Census, when the community has a population of more than 1,000 people. Their response was that Bylas was not recognized as a Census Designated Place for the 2000 census. A CDP is a statistical entity, comprising a densely settled concentration of population that is not within an incorporated place, but is locally identified by a name. Beginning with the 2000 Census there were no size limits, but Bylas was not counted. So it seems some Indians not only lost their land, but were not even counted as part of the United States population.

The community of Supai in Arizona (located at the bottom of the Grand Canyon) is another prime example of American Indians not being counted as part of the population. According to the census, no one lives there, but in fact more than 400 people reside at Supai and the mail is delivered to them twice a week by mule. The U.S. Census commented, "There was an error in the census for the Supai CDP. We are hopeful that the Havasupai Reservation folks will write to the Census Bureau to inquire ... as that seems to be the only way the CQR (Count Question Resolution) folks will deal with it."

This book is not complete by any means. It will continue to be an ongoing project. There are scores of towns, villages and hamlets with Indian names that painstaking research will hopefully turn up their name origins and brief histories.

A number of years ago an historian advised me to not to accept at face value the information I received, because an appalling amount of misinformation abounds, and without historical documentation the names would be perpetuated as false definitions. Easy enough to say, but quite difficult to adhere to that premise. There are hundreds of thousands of books out there with numerous definitions for any given community. Which is correct? We will probably never know. It has been too many centuries since the settlers gave our towns Indian names that have been so erroneously corrupted. We can only disseminate what we discover in our research.

A Note about This Book's Title

Although anyone who is born in the United States is a native American, the U.S. Government (and others) decided some time ago to apply the term "Native American" specifically to the Indians, perhaps in a politically correct effort to find a nice, modern, bias-free way to refer to an ethnic group. In my ignorance, a few years ago I used that identifier in my book *Our Native American Legacy*, believing the term was a sign of respect. My communications since then with a number of Indian tribes on the subject brought out some interesting differences. Some do not feel insulted, but find the title amusing. On the other end of the spectrum, one tribe had a resolution approved by their tribal council in 1978, which resolved that they deplored the use of the term "Native American." They officially requested that federally recognized tribes be referred to as "American Indians" or "Indians." Other tribes said they preferred to be called simply "Indian." Therefore, in deference to the often expressed wishes of American Indians themselves, I have used the term "Indian" in the title of this book.

Sandy Nestor
Summer 2003

ALABAMA

ARBACOOCHEE (Cleburne/0)* This former community was founded in 1835 as a gold-boom town boasting a population of more than 5,000. It took its name from Abihkuchi, an old Creek Indian village, meaning "a pile at the base." The region around the Arbacoochee Mining District was one of the richest placer mining sites in the state. When the gold rush began in California in 1849, most of the miners abandoned this site.

ATTALA (Etowah/6,592) Attala occupies the site of an old Indian village and was founded in 1870 as Newton. By 1879, the Alabama Great Southern Railroad had established its line. When the post office was established, Newton was disallowed because of duplication. It was renamed Attala, a derivation of atali, a Cherokee word for "my home," or for Chief Otali, otali meaning "mountain." The first hydroelectric generator in the world was built at Attala in 1903, which made it the first city in the U.S. to be entirely powered by water.

AUTAUGAVILLE (Autauga/820) Located about 20 miles west of Montgomery, this town came into existence in 1820 when Captain William Thompson built a grist mill and saw mill on Swift Creek. A few years later, the Planters Cotton Factory was organized by Reverend D.B. Smedley. Autaugaville Methodist Sunday School was established in 1825, and is the oldest evergreen (year-round) Sunday School in the United States. Autauga means "land of plenty," or "border," derived from the Creek word, atigi.

COOSADA (Elmore/1,382) Situated on the west bank of the Alabama River, this site was home to a tribe of Koasati Indians who named their village Koasati, meaning "white cane," from where Coosada is derived. When Tecumseh started his rebellion against the U.S. in 1812, the chief of the Koasati village refused to join him, and as a result the village was burned down. Coosada was surveyed and laid out in 1816, followed by establishment of the post office in 1821 with Jonas B. Clopton as the postmaster.

EUFAULA (Barbour/13,908) The Creek Tribe of Eufaula Indians from the Muscogee

**County name/population. Italicized figures are from sources other than U.S. Census.*

Nation had occupied this site along the Chattahoochee River since 1733. After General William Irwin received a land grant, he built a wharf for steamboats and began Eufaula's life as a shipping and trading point. Residents named the community Irwinton in his honor. After the Creek Indians were removed to Oklahoma, the town was renamed Eufaula, for "high bluff," descriptive of the river embankments. Another interpretation was "beech tree."

LOACHAPOKA (Lee/165) Early residents were the Creek Indians about 1796. The land was open to white settlement after the Treaty of Cusseta was signed in 1832, forcing the Indians to be removed to Oklahoma. When Square Talley took up a homestead in 1836 the site was called Ball's Fork. Granite used to build the Atlanta Terminal Station in the 1890s was supplied by a local quarry. During the Civil War, thousands of Federal troops stormed the town, raiding and burning the train depot. Loachapoka is derived from the Creek words locha and polga, which mean "turtle killing (or gathering) place."

OHATCHEE (Calhoun/1,215) Ohatchee was established along the Coosa River, and took its name from the Creek word oh-hachi, meaning "upper creek." In 1863, Alfred Janney built a furnace just north of town using slave labor. The Confederate Army hoped to use the furnace to make bullets, but Yankee troops blew up a section of the structure. Ohatchee was home to Tom Sims, who created the comic strip character, Popeye, patterned after his father who was a riverboat captain.

OPELIKA (Lee/23,498) Once the area was open for settlement, wealthy planters established their cotton plantations at Opelika. The post office opened in 1840 (Wesley William, postmaster) as Opelikan, but the spelling was not corrected until 1851. It is derived from Creek words meaning "large lake" or "big swamp." After the Civil War, Opelika suffered through Reconstruction, since homes were burned and industries no longer functioned. By 1881, the Montgomery and West Point Railroad had built it tracks and a depot, adding to Opelika's stability.

SYLACAUGA (Talladega/12,616) This town was once a Shawnee settlement called Chalakagay. Dr. Edward Gantt discovered veins of the purest white marble in the world during the early 1800s. The Herd brothers, stone masons from Scotland, opened quarries and developed the marble industry. The marble from their quarries was used to build the U.S. Supreme Court Building and the Lincoln Memorial. Sylacauga was derived from the Muskogean words, chalak and ge, for "resting place of the Chalaka Tribe." It was also interpreted as "buzzard roost."

TALLADEGA (Talladega/15,143) Talladega is one of the oldest settlements in the state. John Bruner, a half-breed Indian and interpreter, received a land grant and built a fort called Leslie's Station. In 1813, Andrew Jackson defeated the Creek Indians at the Battle of Talladega, destroying the Confederation. After the fighting, many of Jackson's men stayed here and took up homesteads. The name comes from a Creek word for "border town."

TUSCALOOSA (Tuscaloosa/77,906) Tuscaloosa's history dates back to 1809 when Creek Chief Occechemolta received permission from the U.S. government to establish a village. The site was surveyed and platted by Collin Finnell in 1821. Five years later Tuscaloosa became the state capital. Since the town was considered too far from the center of the state, the capitol was moved to Montgomery in 1846. On

April 4, 1865, General Croxton and his army came to Tuscaloosa and burned all but four buildings of the University of Alabama. The town takes its name from Creek Chief Tuscaloosa, which means "black warrior."

TUSCUMBIA (Colbert/7,856) General John Coffee founded and platted the site in 1817. Originally called Big Spring, the name was changed about 1822 to Tuscumbia, derived from a Cherokee Indian named Tashka Ambi for "warrior who kills." The town became an important river port when a canal was built around nearby Muscle Shoals. As a result a railroad was built between town and the boat landing which served the river boats. Tuscumbia was the birthplace of Helen Keller.

TUSKEGEE (Macon/11,846) The first white people to settle in the region were French traders. This was the birthplace of Ussa Yoholo or Black Drink, more commonly known as Osceola. The Western of Alabama Railway was built through town and was one of the oldest railroads in the South. Tuskegee was home to the 99th Pursuit Squadron, composed of Black men, which became the most decorated unit in the U.S. Air Force. In August of 2001, one of the few remaining Black pilots, Louis R. Purnell, Sr., died at the age of 81. Tuskegee is Creek for "one who received a war name," or "warrior."

WEDOWEE (Randolph/818) Before white settlement, the site was home to a Creek Indian named Wahdowwee. Settlers named the community after him, which means "old water." It was changed to McDonald in 1840, but reverted to its original name in 1844. J.C. Swan was a doctor at Wedowee until President Theodore Roosevelt appointed him as first physician inspector to the Atlanta Federal Penetentiary.

WETUMPKA (Elmore/5,726) Encouraging settlement was the first general store established by Theoderick Johnson. With its proximity to the Coosa River, Wetumpka's economy was tied, in part, to the flatboat trade, precipitating building of hotels and boarding houses. Cotton was a mainstay for Wetumpka until 1839 when crops were destroyed by a drought, which also disabled river transport because of low water. Wetumpka means "rumbling (or roaring) waters" from the Muscogee word, wa-wau-tum-cau, descriptive of a succession of shoals on the Coosa River.

ALASKA

ADAK (316) Located on the Andreanof Islands in the Aleutian Chain, Adak comes from the Aleut word adaq, which means "father." The village was historically occupied by Aleuts. When the Russians arrived in the 1700s to hunt for furs, they began trade with the natives. During World War II the U.S. military took over and restricted access to the island when it was a factor for American defense. The island later became a Naval Air Station used for submarine surveillance during the Cold War.

AKIAK (309) This Yup'ik village was called Ackiagmute in 1880, then changed to Akiak, Yup'ik for "the other side," or "crossing over," because Akiak was a crossing to the Yukon River during the winter. Reverend John Kilbuck, a Delaware Indian from Kansas and a co-founder of the Moravian Mission at Bethel, established the first school at Akiak in 1911.

AKULURAK (0) Located southeast of Alakanuk near the Yukon River, Akulurak is an Inuit (Eskimo) word for "in between." A mission was established in 1894 by the Sisters of St. Ann's from British Columbia. The gold rush in the Klondike brought massive numbers of prospectors to Dawson, resulting in a typhoid epidemic, so the Sisters closed the mission in 1898 and went to Dawson to help. The mission reopened in 1905, but the permafrost undermined the buildings and they were finally torn down in 1949.

AKUTAN (713) This village is on Akutan Island, about 35 miles east of Unalaska. The name is Aleut, and interpreted as "I made a mistake," or "behind the salmonberry bushes." Nearly treeless, the island does have willows and berry bushes in certain areas. During the 1900s, the Alaska Whaling Company was established, then sold to North Pacific Sea Products in 1913. It operated until 1939, when it was leased to the U.S. Navy as a refueling station.

ALAKANUK (652) Situated on a maze of waterways, Alakanuk is a Yup'ik word that means "wrong way" or "mistaken village." Natives often missed their summer camp and ended up in one of a multitude of sloughs by mistake. The village is about fifteen miles from the Bering Sea and part of the Yukon Delta National Wildlife Refuge. It was called Alerneq by an Eskimo shaman named Anguksuar. In 1899, the name was reported by the U.S. Geodetic Survey. The post office opened in 1947 as Alakanuk, the English spelling of Alerneq.

ALATNA (35) A "twin" village with Allakaket on the Koyukuk River, this site was selected for a mission by Rev. Hudson Stuck. He was also the leader of the first party that successfully scaled the south peak of Mount McKinley. Alatna may be a derivation of a Koyukuk word for the Allakaket River meaning "river mouth." Allakaket became part of Alatna about 1851 and developed as a traditional trading center. The post office was established in 1925.

ALEKNAGIK (221) Known as "the Gateway to Wood-Tikchik State Park," this village is located where the Wood River flows out of Lake Aleknagik, about 300 miles west of Anchorage. Aleknagik is interpreted as "wrong way home." Returning home in their canoes from fishing trips, the natives often encountered fog, losing their way on the Nushagak River. The 1918 flu epidemic wiped out many of the villages in the area and the people who survived at Aleknagik moved away. They returned in the 1950s.

ANAKTUVUK PASS (282) Situated on the divide between the Anaktuvuk and John rivers, this was the last remaining settlement of the semi-nomadic Nunamiuts (inland northern Inupiat Eskimos). The natives moved to Anaktuvuk Pass in the 1940s which was a caribou crossing, derived from an Eskimo expression meaning "the place of caribou droppings." The post office was established in 1950.

ANGOON (572) Predominately a Tlingit native community, Angoon is located on the southwest side of Admiralty Island, the only permanent village on the island. The Tlingits called the island Kootznahoo, meaning "fortress of the bears," and Angoon was interpreted as "right behind the town." The Tlingits settled here in the late 1700s and established two villages: Angoon and Killisnoo. About 1894, the village experienced a bad fishing season at Killisnoo and the natives returned permanently to Angoon.

ANIAK (572) Aniak was established as a trading post in 1914. It is a Yup'ik word for "place where it comes out," designating the mouth of the Aniak River. In 1914, Tom Johnson homesteaded the village, started a general store and opened the post office. An airfield was built in 1939, followed by the White Alice Radar-Relay Station in 1956, creating jobs for villagers until it closed in 1978. Located 92 air miles northeast of Bethel on the south bank of the Kuskokwim River, Aniak is the largest town in the region.

ANVIK (104) Anvik is a small Athabascan village along the Yukon River, just below the mouth of the Anvik River. Reverends Octavious Parker and John Chapman started a mission in 1887 under commission of the American Episcopal Church. The post office was established in 1898 (John Chapman, postmaster). The natives called the site gitr'ingithchagg, meaning "at the mouth of the long, skinny river." Anvik could be a Siberian Yup'ik word for "that place where we come out." Some interpreted it from ingalik, meaning "louse eggs" or "lousy." This definition is incorrect; ingalik was a derogatory term used by the Eskimos for the upriver natives.[1]

ATKA (92) Located on Atka Island in the Aleutian Chain, Atka was inhabited by the Aleuts who survived by hunting sea otters until the late 1800s, when the otter population was almost wiped out by the Russians. The origin of the name is unknown, but it may have been derived from the Aleut words atchu or atghka. During World War II, the U.S. government evacuated Atka, relocating the residents to Ketchikan. Villagers returned in 1944 and the U.S. Navy rebuilt the town for them.

ATQASUK (228) This community is situated next to the Meade River, approximately 60 miles southwest of Barrow on the North Slope. Atqasuk is an Eskimos word that means "the place to dig the rock that burns," descriptive of the coal in the area. After World War II, the name was changed to Meade River, but reverted to Atqasuk in the 1970s. Bituminous coal was mined during the war by residents and the U.S. government. After natural gas was developed in the Barrow region, the demand for coal diminished, and was exploited by the natives for their personal use.

ATTU (20) In 1741, Attu Island was officially discovered by Russian Lieutenant Alexei Chirikov who named the site Saint Theodore. Attu is encompassed by the Bering Sea and the Pacific Ocean. It is an Aleut word (origin unknown). The village was sheltered by Chichagof Harbor, used by whalers and traders as a storm refuge. The island saw bitter fighting during World War II, and more than 500 Americans died. The Japanese lost more than 2,300 men.

CHALKYITSIK (83) This village is situated on the Black River, 50 miles east of Fort Yukon, in the Yukon National Wildlife Refuge. Chalkyitsik is an Athabascan word that means "to fish with a hook at the mouth of the creek" or "fish hooking place." Archdeacon MacDonald met and traded with the Black River Gwich'in natives between 1863 and 1868. When a school was built at Chalkyitsik in the 1960s, the native people created their settlement around the structure.

CHENEGA BAY (86) Chenega is an Alutiiq (Aleut) village and means "along the side." It was occupied for hundreds of years until the 1964 earthquake completely destroyed the village. A third of the people died when a tsunami wave 35 feet high descended on them. The remaining population scattered to different villages. The community was reestablished in 1984 at Crab Bay on Evans Island. After the Exxon Valdez oil spill, Chenega Bay became one of the headquarters for cleanup crews.

CHICKALOON (213) Chickaloon is situated in the Talkeetna Mountains. The village was called Nay'Dini'aa Na by the Ahtna Athabascans, which means "log that crosses over the flowing water." Chickaloon is derived from an Athabascan named Chiklu (origin unknown), and was established in 1916 when the Alaska Railroad made the village its terminus of the Matanuska Branch. Discovery of coal ultimately brought in an influx of miners and settlers, causing disease and alcoholism, impacting the population and killing many of the natives.

CHIGNIK (79) This site was originally a Kaniagmuit village called Kaluak that was destroyed when the Russians arrived during the fur trade in the late 1700s. Chignik was established in the late 1800s as a fishing village, and is a Sugpiaq word that means "wind" or "big wind." The community is located on the south shore of the Alaska Peninsula. Fishermen's Packing Company from Oregon came to Chignik Bay for salmon in 1888, and established a cannery, which drew in people from the peninsula, and as a result the village survived when others were abandoned.

CHITINA (123) The community is on the outside boundary of Wrangell-St. Elias National Park, surrounded by mountains on all sides, except for a gap on the southwest end where Spirit Mountain can be seen. The natives believed the mountain held a great spirit. Chitina comes from the Athabascan words chiti and na, meaning "copper river." With copper easily available, the natives became experts at tempering the ore and hammered copper nuggets into plates, then used them for trade with the Tlingits. When high-grade copper was discovered in the Wrangell Range, Chitina became a supply center.

CHUATHBALUK (119) Chauthbaluk is on the north bank of the Kuskokwin River, 100 miles east of Bethel and has been inhabited by natives since 1833. The name is derived from the Yup'ik Eskimo word curapalek, which means "big blueberries," or "the hills where the big blueberries grow." When the Russian Orthodox Church was built in the 1890s, it was called the St. Sergius Mission. During a flu epidemic many of the residents died, and by 1929 the village was deserted. In 1954, some of the natives returned and resettled the mission.

EEK (280) The first village was located on the Apokok River, but due to constant flooding it was relocated in the 1930s to its present site along the Eek River, about 40 miles south of Bethel. A school was moved to Eek from the village of Tuntutuliak. The Moravian Church was constructed and the post office was established in 1949. Eek is derived from the Eskimo word eet, which means "two eyes." This is a traditional Yup'ik Eskimo village that subsists on commercial fishing.

EGEGIK (116) Egegik is located on the Alaska Peninsula, about 300 miles southwest of Anchorage. The Yup'ik Eskimos and Athabascan Indians were here more than 6,000 years ago; first contact with the natives was about 1818 when the Russians arrived. Egegik began as a fishing camp in the 1870s that was centered around a cannery and a Russian Orthodox church. Egegik means "neck" (derived from the Yup'ik word, igagik), pertaining to the location of the village on the Egegik River. Another interpretation was "swift river," designating river water that flowed into Bristol Bay.

EKLUTNA (*434*) The region was originally home to the Athabascan Indians. This community is situated at the head of Knik Arm in the Cook Inlet, about 25 miles northeast of Anchorage. Eklutna is derived from eydlytnu, and may be a Tanaina word for "by several objects river." During the Russian fur-trading days, Eklutna natives were used as go-betweens with the hostile Ahtna Indians. Eklutna is known for its vibrantly colored spirit houses behind the old St. Nicholas Church. When the deceased was buried, a spirit house was painted bright colors and placed over the grave.

EKUK (3) The farthest community south on Nushagak Bay, Ekuk is an Eskimo word for "the last village down." Located about 17 miles south of Dillingham, Ekuk was visited by the Russians between 1824 and 1828. Erosion and flooding caused the natives to move to a Moravian mission. After the North Alaska Salmon Company established a cannery 1903, the people returned only during fishing seasons. Not much is left in the village; there are no stores, health services or schools, and therefore it has no economic base. About three people live year-round at Ekuk, and the only buildings are bunkhouses for cannery workers.

EKWOK (130) Ekwok is the oldest, continuously occupied village on the Nushagak River, and was used in the 1890s as a fish camp. In Yup'ik Eskimo, the name is translated as "end of the bluff." The settlement grew rapidly, and in 1930 the Bureau of Indian Affairs built a school, followed by a post office in 1941. Since Ekwok was situated in a flat area near the river, it was subject to severe flooding and natives had to build their homes on higher ground. The school was named the William "Sonny" Nelson School, in memory of a village leader who died in a plane crash en route to Anchorage while competing in the Iditarod Sled Dog Race.

EMMONAK (767) Emmonak was moved from its original site to the present location. The first settlement was called Kwiguk, meaning "big stream." When flooding and erosion caused the village to be moved to this site, it was renamed Emmonak, a Yup'ik Eskimo word derived from kuigpagmuit (or imangarmiut), for "black fish." The post office was established in 1920. Emmonak is located in the Yukon Delta National Wildlife Refuge, about 10 miles from the Bering Sea.

GAKONA (215) An Athabascan word for "rabbit" or "rabbit river," Gakona lies at the junction of the Gakona and Copper rivers. The Ahtna Indians lived in this region for more than 5,000 years. Gakona began as a wood and fish camp before it was a permanent village. It was also an important stop for travelers in the early 1900s. At one time there was a post office, blacksmith and stagecoach station. Today, Gakona has a motel, restaurant, sawmill and a dog-sled manufacturer.

HOONAH (860) Hoonah is located on Chichagof Island, 40 miles west of Juneau, and is the largest Tlingit settlement in the Southeast. The first village was called Huna, Tlingit for "place where the north wind does not blow." Legend says when a glacier moved in on them, the natives left and reestablished their village at Brown

Bear Bay. The site was also known as Gaud'ah'kan, Hoonyah, and Kantukan. When the post office was established in 1901 it took the name Hoonah, which means "village by the cliff." Another translation is from hooniah, for "cold lake."

IGIUGIG (53) Igiugig is about 350 miles southwest of Anchorage on the banks of the Kvichak River. The name means "like a throat that swallows the lake water." Another interpretation is from kigusig, a Yup'ik word for "volcano," for the volcanoes in Katmai National Park. The Kiatagmuit Eskimos who lived in at the village of Kaskanak used this site as a summer fishing camp, then settled permanently in the early 1900s. The post office was established in 1934.

ILIAMNA (102) Founded in 1800 by Athabascan Indians who came from the Cook Inlet area, old Iliamna was located near the mouth of the Iliamna River. It was relocated about 40 miles from the first site and retained its original name, an Athabascan word meaning "big ice" or "big lake." The village was an early Russian settlement. In the early 1900s, the post office was established (Fred J. Roehl, Sr., postmaster). Lake Iliamna was one of the most significant places for salmon spawning in the world, and the largest contributor to the Bristol Bay fishery.

KAKE (710) The early Kake Tribe of Tlingits, known as some of the most aggressive and fiercest natives, lived at this place they called Klu-ou-klukwan ("the ancient village that never sleeps") from where Kake is derived. The village is situated along the Keku Strait on the northwest coast of Kupreanof Island. The important trade routes between the Kuiu and Kupreanof Islands were dictated by the Kakes. A cannery was built nearby in 1912 and the village purchased it in the late 1940s. Timber harvesting and processing also began during this time period. Kake's economy today is the seafood industry.

KALTAG (230) Originally used as a cemetery, Kaltag became a fish camp before permanent settlement. It is located along the Yukon River near the Innoko National Wildlife Refuge. Russians named the village for Kaltaga, a Yukon native, whose name was interpreted as a type of salmon. The site was once an important trade center for prospectors during the late 1800s.

KANATAK (0) This former village is situated at the head of Portage Bay on the south coast of the Alaska Peninsula. Kanatak is an Aleut word meaning "snowy." The post office was established in 1922 and discontinued in 1943. Fishing and trapping were the principle sources of subsistence until oil was found in the 1930s. Drilling operations ceased in 1954 and the village was abandoned.

KARLUK (27) Karluk is on the west coast of Kodiak Island. The Russians arrived in 1786 to establish a trading post, and an Orthodox chapel was built in 1888. The name may be from the Aleut word, kunakakhvak, but its meaning is obscure. There were two parts to the village because of a sandbar and spit that separated the town. In 1892, the post office opened and the Alaska Packers Association was established in the early 1900s. After a devastating storm in 1978, the community moved to another site upstream and retained the name.

KASAAN (39) Kasaan was once the territory of the Tlingits until the Haida Indians migrated here from Queen Charlotte Islands in British Columbia. When they arrived at Prince of Wales Island, tradition says they selected the village of Kasaan because it was the only place that looked good. Kasaan is a Tlingit word that means "pretty town," or "town on the point." About twelve miles from the village, copper was discovered, and in 1892 the Copper Queen Mine opened. Kasaan's site was then abandoned and the people moved closer to the mine, but kept the village's name.

KATALLA (0) Katalla ("bay") is a former community located on Controller Bay, about 50 miles southeast of Cordova. In 1894, oil was discovered and drilling commenced in 1902, making Katalla a supply station for the oil fields. Three railroads were built that connected to the town. The Copper River & Northwestern Railway was extending its line to the Kennecott copper mines and coal fields. When a tremendous storm hit in the fall of 1907, the breakwater was destroyed, so the railroad went to Cordova instead, causing Katalla's demise.

KENAI (6,942) Originally established as Fort Nicholas, Kenai is located on the west coast of Kenai Peninsula. Before Kenai became a Russian settlement, it was a Dena'ina Athabascan village called Skitok ("where we slide down"). The Russian American Company became headquarters for the Cook Inlet Region, conducting fish and fur trading. Kenai was named for the Kenatize Indians who were original inhabitants. Others theorize Kenai comes from knaiakhotana, derived by the Russians for an Athabascan word that means "non–Eskimo people." Another interpretation is from kakny, part of the word meaning "river."

KETCHIKAN (7,922) Sandwiched between the mountains and sea with its unusual geographical character, Ketchikan began as a Tlingit fishing camp. It came into prominence about 1899 when gold was discovered in the region, and developed into a mining and outfitting town. Ketchikan is derived from the Tlingit word kitschk-hin, which depicted a creek with "thundering wings of an eagle." One version ascribes the name to a Tlingit chief named Kats'kan, or "spread wings of a prostrate eagle," descriptive of the rocks that divide the waters of Ketchikan Creek.

KIANA (388) Kiana was once a central village of the Kowagmiut Inupiat Eskimos. It became a supply depot and transfer point in 1909 for placer mining camps on the Squirrel River. Located about 55 miles east of Selewik, Kiana is an Eskimo word for "a place where three rivers meet." When the gold rush began in the Kobuk valley, it also brought traders, who mostly came for fur. The natives traded their pelts for metal knives, axes, and guns. The climate was severe, making transportation difficult, so development of major mining was hindered until advanced mining techniques were established.

KISKA (0) This former community is located on Rat Island in the Aleutian Chain. Kiska is an Aleut word that was corrupted by the Russians and means "gut." During World War II, the Japanese occupied Kiska until August of 1943. American troops stormed the island only to find the Japanese gone. The island was later abandoned.

KLAWOK (854) Located seven miles north of Craig on Prince of Wales Island, this village was a Tlingit summer fishing camp named for a native called Kloo-wah, which eventually evolved as Klawock (meaning unknown). In 1868, a salmon saltery and trading post were established by George Hamilton. A San Francisco company purchased the post and built the first cannery in Alaska; it also packed the first can of salmon in the state. The 1980s saw the demise of the canneries.

KLUKWAN (139) Klukwan was home to the Chilcat natives who conducted trade with the interior villages. The village is located along the Chilcat River, near the Haines Highway. The name was reported as Chilcat of Klukquan, meaning "old town." Chilcat Pass was discovered in 1880, enabling travel across the great divide.

KNIK (582) Knik is situated about 17 miles northeast of Anchorage on Cook Inlet, and is a Tanaina word meaning "fire." Furs and mining operations caused Knik to be founded when Russians began trade. After American occupation, the Alaska Commercial Company bought out some of the Russian posts. During the Klondike gold rush days, Knik was a distribution center for the miners on their way to the gold fields in the Talkeetna Mountains. The town declined in the middle 1900s when the gold gave out and Anchorage came into prominence.

KOBUK (109) This village started out as a trading and supply point for miners headed to the Cosmos Hills. About 130 miles from Kotzebue, the site was founded in 1899 with a trading post and Friends Mission. The community was first called Shungnak. Residents later renamed the site Kobuk, an Eskimo word meaning "big river." Because of huge ice jams on the Kobuk River, the town was constantly threatened by flooding. In 1973, the jams were so bad the village was completely flooded.

KODIAK (6,334) Located on the tip of Kodiak Island, the town was known as Kikhtowik, derived from the Eskimo word for "island." The name was adopted in 1901 by the U.S. Board on Geographic Names. Colonization of Kodiak began in the 1700s, led by Stepan Glotov. He and his men spent the winter here, but the natives were so hostile that on May 24, 1763, the Russians left. Kodiak was moved to its present site about 1872 after an earthquake and tidal wave hit. The opening of a cannery in 1882 sparked the development of commercial fishing.

KOTLIK (591) Situated on the tundra, Kotlik is an Eskimo village along the Yukon-Kuskokwim Delta, about 175 miles northwest of Bethel, and was once a fur-trading station. In the 1960s, the Bureau of Indian Affairs built a school, which brought residents from other villages to take advantage of an education. By the mid–1960s, Kotlik had become one of the leading commercial centers of the region. Kotlik is an Eskimo word derived from kwu-tlek, meaning "pants," or "breeches," descriptive of the way the river split, resembling a pair of pants.

KOYUKUK (101) Koyukuk is situated near the junction of the Koyukuk and Yukon rivers, about 300 miles west of Fairbanks. It was originally a Koyukukhotana village. Koyukuk is Eskimo for "village under meneelghaadze bluff" (meneelghaadze described the clay in the bluff). In 1880, a trading post was opened to serve the surrounding communities. The village later became an outfitting and supply point for miners when the gold rush started. In 1939, the first school was built, bringing natives to live permanently at Koyukuk.

KWETHLUK (713) This Yup'ik village is about 10 miles east of Bethel along the Kwethluk River. The name is derived from kwikli, translated as "river," or "bad river." Residents from other villages moved here in the 1800s, and the Moravian Church was built in 1889. Gold was discovered in the region, bringing an influx of miners, but not much ore was found. Kwethluk residents suffered through a measles epidemic in the 1890s, and then in 1939 many died from tuberculosis.

LITUYA BAY (0) This place is 100 miles west of Juneau and known for its gigantic waves. Lituya is a Tlingit word meaning "lake within the point." The entrance to the bay was very dangerous and the Tlingits left in 1853. Jim Huscroft built a cabin in 1917 and started a fox farm on Cenotaph Island in the bay. On October 27, 1936, Huscroft survived 100-foot waves that crashed in on the island. In 1958, one of the largest waves was recorded after a 7.8 earthquake struck, sending a wave of water more than 1700 feet up the bay's slopes.

MANOKOTAK (399) Manokotak did not become a permanent settlement until the 1940s, when a number of other villages consolidated. This Eskimo community is about 25 miles southwest of Dillingham. Manokotak is a Yup'ik word meaning "on the lap of" because the village sits in the 'lap' of Manokotak Mountain. The majority of natives were pure-blooded Eskimos. They did not own the land and were considered squatters. During the 1990s, the site was expected to be surveyed and individual titles given, making the natives eligible for home-building loans through various federal agencies.

METLAKATLA (1,375) Situated on the west coast of Annette Island, this Tlingit village is 15 miles south of Ketchikan. Metlakatla was established in 1887 when missionary William Duncan brought a group of Canadian Tsimshian Indians here from Queen Charlotte Island. Duncan learned their language and converted many of the natives. He died at Metlakatla in 1918. In recent years, Duncan's church was taken over by a charismatic group. Metlakatla is the only Federal reservation in Alaska for indigenous people. It is a Tsimshian word meaning "saltwater channel passage."

NAKNEK (678) Yup'ik and Athabascan Indians settled here more than 6,000 years ago. Naknek may be a Russian translation of the Eskimo word, naugeik, or from a Yup'ik word that means "muddy." First noted by Capt. Lt. Vasiliev in 1821, the site was known as Kinuyak in 1880, and later changed to Naknek by the Russian Navy. This community began in 1890 with the opening of the first cannery in the district operated by the Arctic Packing Company, and became a hub for commercial fishing and processing. The Naknek River is responsible for some of the largest salmon runs in the world.

NANWALEK (177) Nanwalek is located at the southern end of the Kenai Peninsula. Russian explorer Grigorii Shelikov arrived the late 1700s searching for sea otter hunting grounds and established the Fort Alexander trading post. Shortly after the U.S. took possession of Alaska, the Alaska Commercial Company took over the post. It wasn't until 1991 that the town was renamed Nanwalek, which comes from Yup'ik (Sugtestun dialect), meaning "place with a lagoon," descriptive of the lagoon located near town.

NAPAIMUTE (0) This is an unpopulated place on the Kuskokwim River. Napaimute comes from an Eskimo word for "forest people" (mute is a suffix for "people"). In 1906, an Englishman named George Hoffman established a trading post, which drew Eskimos, miners, and trappers. He also built a territorial school. Most of the residents had moved to other villages by the 1950s, and today Napaimute is only a summer subsistence fish camp.

NAPAKIAK (353) Napakiak was established in 1890 as an Eskimo community 10 miles southwest of Bethel. "Napakiak may be a misspelled word when tried to be written into English from a Yup'ik word, naparryaraq. It refers to a small wooden pole or post stuck in the mouth of Johnson Slough to the Kuskokwim. Someone had placed it for some reason."[2] Napakiak was first reported by E.W. Nelson in 1878 when it was originally situated further downriver at the mouth of Johnson River. A Bureau of Indian Affairs school was built and the post office was established in 1951.

NAPASKIAK (390) This Eskimo village is located on the east bank of the Kuskokwim River, about seven miles southeast of Bethel. Meaning "wood people," Napaskiak is derived from the Yup'ik word napaskiagmute. The name was first reported by the U.S. Geodetic Survey in 1867. A Russian Orthodox Church was established in the 1800s. There is no record of any Russian trading center here, but some of the village Elders recall a post operated by a Russian at one time. In the early 1900s, Oscar Samuelson established a trading post.

NENANA (402) Nenana is an Athabascan village at the base of Toghotthele Hill, along the Nenana and Tanana rivers. It was first known as Tortella, the white man's interpretation of toghotthele, for "mountain that parallels the river." The name was changed to Nenana, derived from nenashna, an Athabascan word meaning "a good place to camp between the rivers." Nenana was a river freighting station, supplying interior areas that did not have access to a railroad or highways. The town grew up around the construction site of the Alaska Railroad, and government surveyors laid out the town in 1916.

NEWHALEN (160) This place was historically home to the Tanaina Indians who often fought with the Yup'ik Eskimos. The community is situated on the north shore of Iliamna Lake, 320 miles southwest of Anchorage. Newhalen was established in the 1800s as a fishing village and takes its name from the Yup'ik word noghelingamuit, meaning "people of Noghelin." In turn, Noghelin translates to "land of prosperity or abundance," describing the wealth of caribou and fish at the lake.

NEW STUYAHOK (471) The community relocated to its present site after three prior moves due to flooding at other sites. Stuyahok is an Eskimo word that means "going downriver place," descriptive of the relocations of the village. Natives made their living herding reindeer for the U.S. government in the 1920s, but by the 1942 the number of animals had declined. The post office was established in 1961.

NINILCHIK (772) Ninilchik means "peaceful settlement by a river." The name may have also originated from the Dena'ina word niqnilchint, interpreted as "lodge is built place," in reference to lodges the natives used while subsistence hunting. The Athabascan Indians have historically conducted fur farming and fishing on the peninsula. Ninilchik was settled between 1830 and 1840 by Russian fur traders who married native women. It is about 40 miles south of Kenai, on the west coast of Cook Inlet.

NOATAK (428) Noatak is a remote village located about 70 miles above the Artic Circle. During the 19th century, it was established as a fish camp that eventually became a permanent settlement. The name was derived from noatagamut, interpreted from an Eskimo word for "inland river people." The post office opened in 1940. At one time there was a fur farm at Noatak owned by non-natives. Travel was by boats in the summer and dogsled in winter.

NOORVIK (634) About 400 miles west of Fairbanks, "the place that is moved to" originated when a group of Kowagmiut Eskimo fisherman and hunters relocated from Deering in 1915. The party was led by Charles Replogle, a missionary teacher. He negotiated with President Woodrow Wilson to acquire a reservation here. Replogle brought his group to Noorvik after the fishing supply had been depleted in the Deering area due to hydraulic mining operations. A church was built in 1915 and the post office was established in 1937.

NULATO (336) This name comes from an Athabascan word for "place where the dog salmon come," descriptive of the Yukon River. Located 220 miles east of Nome, Nulato was a traditional trading site between the Athabascans and Inupiat Eskimos. A Russian explorer named Malakof arrived about 1838, and built a blockhouse and trading post. The next successor was another Russian who was so cruel to the natives they rebelled and murdered everyone at the post. After the massacre, what few natives were left went into the Koyukuk Mountains. Eventually, they returned and reestablished their village about a mile from the original site. The first Catholic church in Alaska was established at Nulato.

NUNAPITCHUK (466) Twenty miles northwest of Bethel on a tributary of the Kuskokwim River on Johnson Slough sits the Yup'ik Eskimo village of Nunapitchuk. It is derived from the Yup'ik word nunapicuaq, meaning "small land." The natives who settled permanently at Nunapitchuk once used the site as a winter camp. Some of the first outside people were the Moravian Missionaries, followed by a Russian Orthodox Church in the 1800s. Nunapitchuk actually began as a town in the 1920s when people from other villages came here to live after they survived the 1918-19 flu epidemic.

NUNIVAK ISLAND & VILLAGE OF MEKORYUK (210) Inhabited for more than 2,000 years by the Nuniwarmiut people (Cup'ik Eskimos), Nunivak means "big land," and is located in the Bering Sea. First outside contact was with a Russian named Vasilief in 1821. Arrival of the white man brought disease, nearly decimating the population by 1900. The Evangelical Covenant Church was established at the village of Mekoryuk in the 1930s by Eskimo missionary Jacob Kenick, followed by a Bureau of Indian Affair's school. Mekoryuk is the only community on the island and its meaning has not been identified.

NUSHAGAK (0) Nushagak Bay is a former Eskimo village established as a trading post in 1819. A year earlier, Russian explorers named the site Redoubt Alexander. The natives called the site Tahlekuk ("elbow") for a bend in the river. It was changed to Nushagak (origin unknown) when the post office was established in 1899. The same year the Pacific Steam Whaling Company built a cannery. The area declined after commercial fisheries moved away, and then the flu epidemic annihilated the population.

OHOGAMIUT (0) The abandoned village is 20 miles from Marshall and located on the Yukon River. Its name is derived from the Eskimo word okhnagamiut, meaning "village on the other side." Most of the inhabitants moved to the town of Marshall and Kalskag. Today, it is used during the summer as a subsistence fish camp.

PAIMIUT (0) This unpopulated village is located along Kokechik Bay on the Bering Sea. By 1951, it only had a few frame houses. An Eskimo name that means "people of the stream's mouth," Paimiut is used mainly as a summer fishing camp. It is only accessible by float plane or boat.

QUINHAGAK (555) Quinhagak is 70 miles southwest of Bethel along Kuskokwim Bay, and one of the largest communities in the area. The Yup'ik name for this village is Kuinerraq, meaning "new river channel." Quinhagak was the first village in the lower Kuskokwim that had sustained contact with the white man. Moravian missionaries came to the region in 1884 and built a mission. In 1905, about 1,600 reindeer were imported from Bethel for summer grazing and soon swelled to 6,000. Years later most of the herds had scattered to other areas. Quinhagak saw an upswing in its economy during the gold rush.

SAVOONGA (643) The "Walrus Capital of the World" on St. Lawrence Island in the Bering Sea was inhabited by Alaskan and Siberian Yup'ik Eskimos. Between 1878 and 1880, the population was severely reduced because of starvation. Natives died after traders gave them liquor in exchange for seal and walrus skins. Instead of hunting and fishing, the natives drank, and by the time winter arrived there was no food left. Seventy head of reindeer were imported to the island in 1891 by the U.S. government, and Savoonga was established as a reindeer herding station in 1916. Its name origin is unknown.

SELEWIK (772) This community sits at the mouth of the Selewik River, 70 miles southeast of Kotzebue. When Lt. Zagosin of the Russian navy visited in the early 1800s, he noted the name as Chilivik. The 1880 Census described the natives as Selawigamutes. Selewik is an Eskimo word that refers to a fish. The town was once the center of fox and mink raising. A federal school and Friends mission were built in 1908. In the spring the villagers headed for the fish camps using log rafts with tents, living on them as they went from camp to camp.

SHAGELUK (129) Shageluk is situated along the banks of the Innoko River, about 20 miles east of Anvik. The village was visited by Russian Lt. Zagosin, who reported it as tie'goshshitno. Residents relocated their community in 1966 because the area was prone to flooding. Shageluk was derived from an Athabascan word for "village of the dog people." There is little employment, and subsistence includes trapping and gardening. Shageluk is a check point for the Iditarod Dog Sled Race on alternate years.

SHUNGNAK (256) Shungnak was founded in 1899 as a supply station for mining activities in the Cosmos Hills. When the Kobuk River eroded the village with annual flooding, it was moved ten miles downstream and called Kochuk before it was changed to Shungnak. Jade was mined and cut at the Shungnak River and Dahl Creek. The name is derived from the Eskimo word isinnag, which means "jade." Shungnak is located 300 miles west of Fairbanks.

SITKA (8,835) The Tlingits, who may have been members of the Kiksadi clan, came here from Kiks Bay. When tribal disputes arose, some members of the clan came to the region to settle, built a fortification, and called it Knootlian. It was named New Archangel by the Russians in 1799, and later changed to Sitka, a Tlingit word meaning "near the sea." During the 1800s, Sitka was a port of call for ships all over the world. Sitka also built one of the first salmon canneries in Alaska. When gold was discovered on Silver Bay just southeast of town, it put Sitka on the map.

SKAGWAY (862) During 1897, Skagway became one of the most famous cities in the world because of the gold fields in the Yukon. Gold seekers used two trails that went to the headwaters of the Yukon: the Chilkoot Trail, 33 miles long, and the 40-mile White Pass Trail. With little knowledge of weather conditions, an avalanche buried more than 100 men and women in 1898 on their way up the summit of Chilkoot Pass. Skagway is a Tlingit word that could mean many things: "place where the north wind blows," "rough water," "cruel wind," "end of salt water." Another is "sound a sled runner makes when it breaks loose from the snow and ice."

SLEETMUTE (100) This village is about 240 miles west of Anchorage on the east bank of the Kuskokwim River. Because of the slate deposits in the area, the village was named Sleetmute, derived from a Yup'ik word meaning "whetstone people." Russians built a trading post about a mile from the village at the junction of the Holitna and Kuskokwim rivers in the early 1830s. Frederick Bishop started another post at Sleetmute in 1906. A school was established in 1921, followed by a post office a few years later. The natives subsisted by traveling to outlying fish camps in the summer months.

TALKEETNA (772) Before development as headquarters for the Alaska Engineering Commission during construction of the Alaska Railroad, Talkeetna was a supply station for gold miners headed for the Susitna River. Talkeetna is located at the confluence of the Susitna, Talkeetna and Chultina rivers, and was once a Tanaina Indian village. It is a Den'ina word for "river of plenty." Today, it is a non-native community and serves as a year-round headquarters for hunters and fishermen.

TANANA (308) Tanana is an Athabascan village that started out as a trading post established by the Alaska Commercial Company. The St. James Mission was built in 1871 about three miles above the village by Reverend J.L. Prevost. Located at the junction of the Tanana and Yukon rivers, the site was originally called Nuchalawoya, an Athabascan word that means "the place where the two rivers meet." It was changed to Tanana, interpreted as "river trail." The village was a placer mining district during the gold rush until the prospectors left about 1906.

TATITLEK (107) This community is located on Prince William Sound, 25 miles southwest of Valdez. According to the U.S. Geological Survey of 1910, it was originally at the head of Gladhaugh Bay, but when the Russians discovered copper, the natives were moved to the present site. Tatitlek sits in the shadow of Cooper Mountain, and is an Eskimo word that means "windy place." When Russian fur traders arrived in the 1700s, they took the Aleuts from Hitchinbrook Island and used them for hunting sea otters. After the animals were depleted, the Russians left the Aleuts to their own devises, who eventually settled at Tatitlek.

TAZLINA (149) Tazlina sits along Richardson Highway south of Glennallen. The Ahtna Indians used this place as a fishing camp. Its name is derived from the Athabascan word taslintna, meaning "swift river." A permanent settlement was established by 1900 along the banks of the Tazlina River. When the pipeline was built, the village was developed near the old Copper Valley School.

TELIDA (2) An Athabascan word for "lake whitefish," Telida is situated on the south side of the Kuskokwim River. Local tradition says village descendants are from two sisters who survived a Yukon Indian attack, then fled to Telida Lake and found whitefish at the outlet. The sisters were discovered by men with a Yukon party, who married the women and settled at the lake. The community was established at three different places, and became a permanent settlement at its present site in 1916. During the 1920s, Telida was a stopping point on the McGrath-Nenana Trail.

TENAKEE SPRINGS (104) Tenakee is derived from the Tlingit word tinaghu, which means "coppery shield bay," in reference to three highly prized copper shields early natives lost in a storm. The community is located on the east side of Chichagof Island, 45 miles southwest of Juneau. Officially founded in 1899, prospectors and fishermen came here to wait out the winters and use the natural hot-sulfur springs. Pictographs in the area depict battles between tribes. The winners soaked in the hot mineral springs while their enemies lay decapitated on the beach.

TOGIAK (809) This Eskimo village was once called Tugiatok. Situated on flat tundra at the head of Togiak Bay about 65 miles west of Dillingham, the village was originally located on the other side of the bay and named Togiagamute. It means Togiaga people, but the root word is not known. When the 1918-1919 flu epidemic broke out, many natives from other communities came here to escape the disease. A saltery was established by the Alaska Packers Association in 1895, but abandoned a year later.

TULUKSAK (428) This community was inhabited by Eskimos. In 1907, gold was discovered on Bear Creek, bringing many people to the village. A Moravian Chapel was built in 1912. Tuluksak was first reported in 1861 as "tul'yagmyut," an Eskimo word for "related to loon," or "raven." Subsistence farming provides most of the food source, and some residents fish for herring roe and salmon. It recently had a village store established.

TUNTUTULIAK (370) Located on the Qinaq River, this traditional Yup'ik Eskimo village is about 40 miles southwest of Bethel. The Bureau of Indian Affairs built a school in 1909, but it was closed eight years later because of the teachers' lack of confidence. The building was later moved to the village of Eek. In 1923, a Moravian chapel was established, followed by a trading post and store. The village was called Qinaq, and changed in 1945 to Tuntutuliak, a Yup'ik word for "place of many reindeer."

TYONEK (193) Forty-three miles southwest of Anchorage lies the Tanaina Athabascan village of Tyonek. In 1880, the name was reported as Toyonok, a Tanaina word for "little chief." The Russian American Company had its trading post here until the late 1800s, when the Alaska Commercial Company took it over. Tyonek became a supply and disembarkation point when gold was discovered at Resurrection Creek in the 1880s. The region was flooded about 1930, which precipitated the village's move on top of a bluff a few years later.

UGASHIK (11) Once one of the largest villages in the region, Ugashik is situated on the Alaska Peninsula. Ivan Petroff recorded the name as Oogashik in 1880. It was also called Ougatik. An Aleut word, its meaning has not been determined. C.A. Johnson started a saltery in 1889 on the Ugashik River, which serpentines itself past the community. Ugashik was one of the communities established when the Red Salmon Company built its cannery in the 1890s. Alaska Packers Association established a cannery in 1895 that operated until 1907.

UMNAK ISLAND (0) Umnak Island is part of the Fox Islands. In the 1750s, Russian explorers claimed the territory, and while here they mistreated the natives. But a Russian named Stepan Glotov nurtured a good relationship with them, and today some of the natives still carry his name. An Aleut word, Umnak was defined as "fish line." The early natives called the area Agunalaksh, which meant "the shores where the sea breaks its neck." During World War II, the U.S. established a tactical air base that would be deployed to protect Dutch Harbor.

UNALAKLEET (747) Unalakleet is situated on Norton Sound at the mouth of Unalakleet River, 148 miles southeast of Nome. The name comes means "place where the east wind blows," or "south side," derived from the Eskimo word ungalaklik. Natives moved from the original village across the river when an epidemic almost wiped them out. The Russian American Company built a trading post in the 1830s. Reindeer herds were later imported from Lapland.

UNALASKA (4,283) Founded by a Russian named Solovief, who established a fur trading post in the 1760s, the village was called Iliuliuk, meaning "harmony" or "good understanding." Unalaska may be an Aleut word for "great land." In 1919, the killer Spanish influenza almost decimated the residents. Coast Guard personnel provided medical assistance, and volunteers helped bury the dead and feed the people. Had it not been for the Coast Guard, everyone in the village may have died. During World War II, Unalaska was attacked by the Japanese and the native population was sent to southeast Alaska.

UNGA (0) Located on Unga Island, which is part of the Shumagin Islands of the Aleutian Chain, the village ceased to exist in 1925 after the school closed. Unga was interpreted from an Aleut word meaning "south." During the 1830s, the village was a Russian sea otter station called Delarov until 1836 when it was renamed Ougnagok. When the post office was established, the name was changed to Unga. Prospectors arrived in 1891 after a vein of gold-bearing quartz was discovered at the Apollo Mine which operated until 1912. Unga is occupied only for subsistence purposes.

WASILLA (5,469) Located about 50 miles north of Anchorage, Wasilla was established in 1917 during construction of the Alaska Railroad, and became a supply center for prospectors searching for gold during the 1940s. Wasilla is an Athabascan word meaning "breath of air." The town came into existence after the U.S. government offered lots for sale. Wasilla experienced tremendous growth in the 1970s when the trans-Alaska pipeline was being constructed.

YAKUTAT (680) This community is located at the mouth of Yakutat Bay, about 215 miles northwest of Juneau. It was originally inhabited by Eyak-speaking people from the Copper River area, who were later conquered by the Tlingits. Yakutat means "the place where the canoes rest." It was also interpreted as an Athabascan word for "great river." This is the place where the earth shook for seven days, beginning September 3, 1899. When the earthquake was over, the land had risen almost 47 feet. The magnitude of the quake was estimated to be about 8.6, based on assessing damage from the epicenter.

ARIZONA

AJO (Pima/3,705) Fleeing the warring Apaches who were destroying their homes along the Gila River, the Papago Indians wandered until they found refuge and sufficient water here. They used the red oxide and green carbonate copper ore for paint, which they called au'auho. Tom Childs worked an open-pit copper mine in 1847, which was purchased in 1909 by A.J. Shotwell, who created the famous Cornelia Copper Company. The post office was established on August 29, 1900 (John Hoover, postmaster). Au'auho, meaning "paint," was later Hispanicized to Ajo.

APACHE JUNCTION (Pinal/31,541) During the 1840s, the Peralta family came to the region and developed a gold mine in the Superstition Mountains just west of town. A Dutchman named Jacob Waltz discovered the mine in the 1870s, which went on to become the famous Lost Dutchman Mine. Apache Junction was founded about 1922 when George Curtis filed his claim and built the Apache Junction Inn. The name may be derived from a Zuni word, apachu, meaning "enemy," or from a Yuman word for "fighting men." The Apaches call themselves Tinde ("the people").

ARIVACA (Pima/*100*) This region was originally settled by the Pima and Papago Indians until the Piman Revolt in 1751. Arivaca is a Pima word for "small springs." Part of a land grant purchased by Agustin Ortiz in 1812, Charles Poston bought the ranch in 1846. When silver was discovered in the Cerro Colorado Mountains near Arivaca, Poston and Herman Ehrenberg built a reduction plant for the mines. The post office was established on April 10, 1878. Arivaca is home to the oldest adobe schoolhouse still intact in the state of Arizona.

BAPCHULE (Pinal) Bapchule is a very small community that was once a stagecoach stop. Located on the Gila River Reservation, the site is still occupied by the Pima Indians. The name means "where the river bends," in the Pima language. Today, Bapchule is a small area of private homes and only one church. The Hayes family moved here in 1932. Their son, Ira Hayes, was one of the men that raised the flag at Iwo Jima. Unable to adapt to civilian life or forget the war years and deaths of his friends, Hayes began to drink heavily. He was found frozen to death outside his home on January 24, 1955.

BYLAS (Graham/*1,284*) The Coronado Expedition passed this site in 1540 looking for the famed El Dorado treasure and Seven Cities of Cibola. In 1875, Indian Agent John Clum brought the White Mountain Apaches here because the U.S. government wanted them confined to a reservation. The community took its name from By-Las, an Apache leader, who warned people at the San Carlos Agency in 1882 that Geronimo was on the warpath. No one believed him because they thought he was drunk; as a result a major outbreak occurred. His name was interpreted as "one who does all the talking."

CHINLE & CANYON DE CHELLY (Apache/5,366) Located at the mouth of Canyon de Chelly, Chinle is derived from ch'ínílí, a Navajo word for "water outlet."

Chelly is defined as "where the water comes out of the rock," "the place where it flows from the canyon," or "rock canyon." The Navajo Indians came to the region in the 1750s after they were forced to leave their homes in northern New Mexico by the Ute and Comanche Indians. In 1864, Kit Carson removed 8,000 Navajos to the Bosque Redondo Reservation in New Mexico. They were permitted to return home in 1868.

CIBEQUE (Navajo/1,331) Situated on the White Mountain Apache Indian Reservation, Cibeque may come from the Apache word she-be-ku, designating "my house." In 1881, an Apache named Noch-ay-del-klinne taught a religion that predicted the white man would be thrown out of Indian land. Army troops from Fort Apache captured the medicine man. As a result, a number of Apache scouts turned against the Army and attacked. Noch-ay-del-klinne was killed while trying to escape during the ensuing fight. The scouts were captured near Payson and hanged in 1882.

COCHISE (Cochise/*30*) Cochise had its beginnings along the Butterfield Stage route about 1886. On August 28 of the same year, the post office opened (Silas H. Gould, postmaster). Cochise was made a fuel stop when the Southern Pacific Railway was established in 1887. The community was named for chief of the Apache Indians. His real name may have been Cheis, which means "wood." Cochise was accused of raiding a ranch and kidnapping a young boy. He was taken prisoner, but escaped. Cochise died in 1874, and his body was secretly buried at his stronghold in the Dragoon Mountains. His grave has never been found.

DENNEHOTSO (Apache/*616*) Once a summer camp for the Navajo Indians, farmers from Tsé 'Awe' ("baby rocks") were forced to leave their homes because of floods. They settled at Dennehotso in 1912 where a shallow channel and natural dam permitted them to continue farming. The post office opened on April 18, 1977. Dennehotso is a Navajo word meaning "upper ending of the meadow." It has mistakenly been translated as "peoples' farms," with the assumption it is derived from the root word diné, the Navajos' word for themselves ("the people").

HUACHUCA (Cochise/1,751) About 60 miles from Tucson, Huachuca began as a Southern Pacific Railroad stop, and its history is closely tied to Fort Huachuca a few miles away. First called Campstone Station, then Sunset City, the name was changed to Huachuca, an Apache word for "thunder," referring to the monsoon seasons. The Apaches (Chiricahuas) claimed this region as their ancestral lands. Fort Huachuca was founded in 1877 as an Army outpost to protect the settlers. After the Civil War, an influx of settlers caused some of the tribes to be removed to reservations.

KAYENTA (Navajo/4,922) Kayenta may be derived from the Navajo word teehnideeh, which translates to "boghole," descriptive of a spring where livestock got stuck in its clayey soil. Another interpretation was from ty-ende, meaning "at the pits where animals fall in." It was also defined as "a natural game pit," or "spraying water." The first trading post was established in 1910 by John and Louisa Wetherill, who also opened the post office on March 21, 1911. Kayenta was home to the Navajo Indian code talkers who fought in the Pacific islands and used their unwritten language that encoded, transmitted and decoded messages faster than American mechanical decoders.

NAVAJO (Apache) "The Navajo Indians ... were Athabascans, a hunter-gatherer people from Alaska and northern

Canada... Those Athabascans who adopted Pueblo ways became the Navajo; those who did not became the Apache."[3] Navajo was originally called Navajo Springs, but shortened to Navajo on June 3, 1883, when the post office opened. Lewis and Hugh Lynch also established a trading post here. The word is steeped in mystery and many interpretations have been attributed to the name: "a place of large plantings," "a somewhat worthless field," or a Tewa word, nanahu, designating an Apache Indian band. Some think it is a Tewa word, na-ba-hu-u, for "arroyo of cultivated fields." The name may also signify "great planted fields."

PIMA (Graham/1,989) Situated along the Gila River, Pima was founded by Mormon settlers in 1879 who named the site Smithville in honor of Mormon leader, Jesse N. Smith. The post office was established on August 23, 1880. A request was made to change the office's name to Pima, which occurred on November 25, 1894. The Pima (part of the Piman branch of the Shoshonean stock) Indians were an important tribe in southern Arizona. Pima means "no," which missionaries mistakenly thought was the Indians' proper name. The Pimas call themselves 'Aàtam ("people").

QUIJOTOA (Pima/0) This community developed with the discovery of silver and copper at nearby Ben Nevis Mountain. Four camps were established, and Quijotoa became a town with the merger of these camps. The post office was established on December 11, 1883 (Ransome Gibson, postmaster). James Flood and John Mackey (the Comstock Kings) promoted the region and brought in investors. A tunnel was bored through Nevis Mountain, but within a few years the ore was gone. About all that is left is the hole in the mountain. Quijotoa is derived from the Papago words qui-ho and toa, for "carrying basket mountain," descriptive of the shape of the mountain.

SACATON (Pinal/1,584) Sacaton is located on the Gila River Indian Reservation. Derived from a Pima word, its name could mean "tall, rank herbage, unfit for forage," or "broad, flat land." It has also been suggested that Sacaton is a misspelling of a Spanish word, zacoton, which was a type of fodder grass. This was home to the Pima Indians who subsisted by farming. Also known as the River People, they were descendants of the ancient Hohokam Indians who farmed along the Gila River Basin. The post office was established on January 10, 1871 (Peter Forbach, postmaster). War hero Ira Hayes was born in Sacaton in 1923, and later moved to Bapchule.

SHONTO (Navajo/568) Shonto is a Navajo word that means "sunlight water," descriptive of a pool of water in the area. Located at the base of a headland and in a canyon, the Navajo Indians brought their horses here for water. Another interpretation is from sháá'tóhí for "spring on the sunny side." The first trading post was run by the Babbitt brothers. This region was known as the last stronghold of the "long hairs," Navajo Indians who refused to cut their hair and kept to the old tradition. They were the people who eluded Kit Carson while he was removing the Indians to New Mexico in 1864.

SONOITA (Santa Cruz/826) In 1700, Father Kino made the first written record of Sonoita, a Papago word for "place where corn will grow." The Sobaipuri Indians moved here after fights with the Apaches and named the site. In 1701, the San Gabriel de Guevavi Mission was built by Jesuits. This settlement came into existence in 1882 when the Benson to Nogales Railway was built, making the town a shipping hub for cattle ranchers. Sonoita's growth was impeded by the Apaches until the establishment of Forts Buchanan and Crittenden in 1857 and 1867, respectively.

SUPAI (Coconino/*433*) The Indians who live at the bottom of the Grand Canyon are called the Havasupai, a band who speak the Yuman language. Havasupai means "blue or green water people." The people call themselves ha vasua baaja ("the blue creek people"). Early inhabitants lived in different parts of the region, depending on the seasons. When the plateau would not support agriculture from lack of water, the people moved further down the canyon. In 1863, gold was discovered in the region, bringing thousands of miners, threatening the Indians' way of life. As a result, their farmlands were designated a reservation. When the post office was established (Rufus C. Bauer, postmaster), it was named Supai. Today, mail is still delivered by mules, used since September 5, 1896.

TEEC NOS POS (Apache/799) The first permanent trading post was established by Hamblin B. Noel in 1905. Although other posts failed because the Navajo Indians didn't want them, Noel succeeded after he showed the Indians how skillful he was with a rifle, and the council allowed him to stay. During the 1930s, dams were constructed, which produced enough water for the Navajo Indians to conduct farming. The village is located at the junction of Highways 160 and 64. Teec Nos Pos is taken from the Navajo word t'iis názbas, for "cottonwoods in a circle."

TOPAWA (Pima) Topawa is a Papago community located near Father Kino's route of 1699. The traditional name for the town was Goksamuk ("burnt dog"). Folklore says that during a Papago ceremony one of the dogs was burned. The young Indian boys used to play a game using a red bean they called mawi. Topawa is a derived from mawi and means "it is a bean." The post office opened on June 14, 1917 (Thomas Throssell, postmaster), and a Catholic mission was established on the reservation. The village gained some prominence because of Fr. Bonaventura Oblasser and the church's activities in the 1920s.

TOPOCK (Mohave) Situated near the Colorado River, Topock is a Mohave word that means "water crossing," or "bridge," derived from tohopau-wave. Originally called Acme, the post office opened in 1883 as Needles (closed in 1886). When Needles, California, came into existence, this community changed its name to Red Rock about 1890. It was renamed Mellon when the post office reopened in 1903 (closed six years later). In 1915, the office was once again opened under the name Topock. At one time Union Oil had its distribution center here.

TSAILE (Apache/1,078) Tsaile is located on the Navajo reservation about 72 miles north of Window Rock. It is home to the Diné Community College, established in 1969. A trading post was established by Stephen Aldrich in 1885 and operated until 1892 when it was abandoned because it was too isolated. The community was named after Tsaile Creek, and is derived from the Navajo word, tséhílí, meaning "where the water enters a box canyon," or "flows into the rocks." Tsaile Peak is a few miles from town. It is considered sacred by the Navajo Indians, and used only by the medicine men.

TUBAC (Santa Cruz/949) This region was originally home to the Hohokam Indians. During the 1500s, the Pima and Papago Indians took up residence. Tubac was a Spanish presidio and mission in 1752, and interpreted as a Pima word for "where the water comes out," or "black water." But Pima linguist Dave Shaul said there are no such words as tubac or bac in the Pima language. The Pima words tu and ba'a mean "pool of water" and may be more accurate.[4] Some authorities believe Tubac is derived from tchoowaka, a Pima word for "rotten." Legend says the Pima Indians killed a number of their enemies and left their bodies to rot, and designated "place where some enemies rot."

TUBA CITY (Coconino/8,225) Located on the Navajo Reservation, the site was called Tuba after a Hopi chief from Oraibi. Tuba means "zig-zagging water," because of the many springs in the area. The Navajos called the site tqonah-nesdisi, which means "tangled waters," and the water does flow in many different directions. The town was established by the Mormons in 1878. Because they could not get title to the land, it was taken over by the U.S. Indian Agency in 1903. When the Babbitt Brothers Trading Company of Flagstaff arrived, they opened the largest permanent trading post on the Western Navajo Reservation.

TUCSON (Pima/486,699) Tucson had its beginning when Father Kino established the Mission San Cosme de Tucson about 1694. The ensuing years brought Apache Indian attacks against the settlers, causing the presidio from Tubac to move to Tucson. Southern Pacific Railroad came through in 1881, and Tucson functioned as a major supply center for the territory. Tucson's economy was further spurred by the discovery of silver and copper near Tombstone and Bisbee. The name could be derived from schookson, a Pima word for "black at the foot of," "at the foot of a black hill," or stjukshon for "dark spring." An archaeological discovery in 2002 showed that Tucson may have actually been settled more than 4,000 years ago, making it the oldest continuously inhabited place in the U.S.

TUMACACORI (Santa Cruz/569) Tumacacori was established about 1701 and became part of visitas (frequently visited places). When Father Kino arrived in 1691, he found the Pima Indians very docile and industrious. The year 1801 brought on an attack by the Apaches and the mission Indians fled. Tumacacori was interpreted as a word for a curved peak. But "As near as linguists can tell the name means 'a rocky flat place.' Unfortunately, it comes from ancient O'odham, and since the language has changed radically over the last 300 years, no one knows for sure what the original meaning was, but 'a rocky flat place' is probably pretty close."[5]

WIKIEUP (Mojave) Wikieup was established in the late 1800s. One of the first white men to the region was P.H. Tompkins who had a cabin at Wikieup Wash. Local residents called the site Owens and Neal. The post office was established as Owens, but closed down because there was no salary for a postmaster. Another was opened in 1922 by William Buchanan, and renamed Wikieup, a Paiute word for "lodge," or "dwelling." Miners helped Wikieup's economy when gold was discovered in the region.

YUMA (Yuma/77,515) Some authorities believe Yuma comes from yahmayo, for "son of the captain (or leader)," designating the son of a hereditary chief. It may be a Spanish word, fumar, which means "to smoke," or from the Yuman word uma, meaning "fire." This site was once known as Colorado City and Arizona City. The U.S. purchased the area in 1848 by the Treaty of Guadalupe Hidalgo. Yuma was surveyed about 1857, and the post office opened on October 1, 1866 (Francis Hinton, postmaster). Yuma became a supply point with the discovery of placer deposits in 1858.

Hopi Villages

The designation Hopi is abbreviated from *Hopituh Shi-n-mu*, which means "the peaceful people." For the most part, their villages are perched atop three high, barren mesas located northwestward from Keams Canyon... The federal government established offices there in 1887... From there, the mesas were called "First Mesa," "Second Mesa," and "Third Mesa," going east to west. This was just opposite to the order in which the Hopi themselves regarded their highland sites.— The Pueblos, *Bertha P. Dutton, 1976*

BACAVI (Third Mesa) "Place where the reeds grow." Bacavi was founded in the early 1900s when problems arose between the Indians at Old Oraibi. Dissident groups split from the village and formed Bacavi. A traditional village, Bacavi has a number of good springs which are used for agriculture.

HANO (First Mesa) "Place of the eastern people." After the Pueblo Revolt of 1680, this village was formed by the Tewas from the Rio Grande who fled from the Spanish. The Tewa people are a branch of the Tanoan linguistic stock and are known for their beautiful pottery.

HOTEVILLE (Third Mesa) "A scraped (skinned) back." Designated the mesa's ceilings where the Indians scratched their backs. A group of hostile Indians left Old Oraibi and formed Hoteville in 1906. Federal authorities tried to force the natives to return to Oraibi, but they refused. The post office was established on July 24, 1916.

KYKOTSMOVI (Third Mesa) "Mound of ruined houses." Located near a spring at the base of the mesa, the village was founded in 1910. Also known as New Oraibi, the Hopi Tribal Office is located here. The post office opened on February 19, 1982.

MISHONGNOVI (Second Mesa) "Place of the dark man." Originally settled in 1200 A.D., the village was moved to a mesa top after the Pueblo Revolt in 1620.

MOENKOPI (Third Mesa) "The place of running water." Moenkopi is one of the largest Hopi villages near Black Mesa. This farming settlement was established in the 1870s by Chief Tuba who moved his people here to get away from the overcrowded conditions at Oraibi. At one time the Mormons attempted to operate a woolen mill, but the Indians refused to work and the project failed.

ORAIBI (Third Mesa) "Place of ourai," which was a rock (also defined as "eagle traps"). Situated atop the mesa, Oraibi has been occupied since about 1100 A.D. It may be the oldest, and was once the largest, of the Hopi villages until the Indians moved away because of dissension and formed their own villages. On August 11, 1900, the post office opened (Herman Kampmeier, postmaster). The following year a Mennonite church was built near the mesa without the Indians' consent, who were delighted when lightening struck the church twice and a fire later destroyed it.

POLACCA (Below First Mesa) "Butterfly." Polacca was founded by Thomas Polacca, a Hano resident. It was settled in the early 1900s, and is a long village that stretches about a mile. The post office opened on February 16, 1901. In 1956, a new school was built.

SHONGOPOVI (Second Mesa) "Water place where the reeds grow." Established as Meseeba during the 1100s, the village was moved to the mesa top after the Pueblo

Revolt and renamed Shongopovi. It was home to Tewanima, who was called the "happy Hopi from Shongopovi," one of our greatest distance runners. He died at the age of 92 in 1969 after he fell to his death over Second Mesa. Shongopovi is considered the "Vatican" of the Hopi Indians because it is situated in the center of their Sacred Circle.

SICHOMOVI (First Mesa) "Hill place where flowers grow," or "place of the wild currant." The village was established sometime after 1700, and was formed as a "suburb" of Walpi.

WALPI (First Mesa) "Place of the gap." Walpi sits on the very tip of the mesa above the Colorado Plateau and was established in 1417. Spanish missionaries arrived about 1629 and built a church. The priests told the people they had to conform to the church's religion; part of their meager crops also had to be given as a tithe. During the Pueblo Revolt in 1680, the church was destroyed. In recent years, the village had to undergo reconstruction because the stone- and mud-plastered buildings were beginning to deteriorate.

ARKANSAS

CADDO GAP (Montgomery) This region was home to the war-like Tula Indians, who fought and defeated DeSoto in the 1500s. Caddo Gap evolved when Drue Wallace and his family settled here in the early 1800s, in addition to military officers who were given land grants. The first business established was a grist mill owned by Ballam Strawn. The town was named Centerville, then changed to Caddo Gap, a Caddo word for "real chiefs." Today, the community has a few residents with a small general store and post office.

OSCEOLA (Mississippi/8,875) Osceola is located adjacent to the Mississippi River. William Edmington bartered for the site in 1830, which at that time was occupied by an Indian village. Osceola was a busy trading port, and since it was so small had no military importance during the Civil War. It is still an important port city with the Osceola Port Terminal. First called Plum Point, the name was changed to Osceola in 1875, which means "bread." Osceola was thought by many to be a Seminole Indian, but his father was actually a Creek Indian and his mother was born in Scotland.

SOLGOHACHIA (Conway) Solgohachia was established about 1870, and its name was born from an Indian legend. Before white settlement, Chief Ponti lived here with his tribe until they were forced to leave. It was thought he buried his wealth in the hills (or mounds). Every so often the Indians would return to search for his treasures, digging around the hills. Solgohachia was interpreted from a Cherokee word for "hole in the mountain," and may refer to these mounds and hills.

CALIFORNIA

AGUANGA (Riverside/*600*) The Indians who lived here spoke the Uto-Aztecan language, which included the Aztec and Shoshone dialects. The -nga suffix was used for "place of" or "home of." Aguanga means "home of the Awa [dog] people." Since the name was translated into Spanish, it may have been corrupted and interpreted as "place of the coyote," or "place of falling water." A wagon road was opened by the Mormon Battalion in 1846, and became part of the Butterfield Stage Line's route in 1857. Aguanga borders the Cahuilla Indian Reservation.

AHWAHNEE (Madera/*1,432*) This area was once occupied by one of the largest Awani (also spelled Awalche and Awallache) villages near Yosemite Park. Ahwahnee began as a stage road that went from Raymond to Yosemite during 1870. William Sell opened the Ahwahnee Tavern in the late 1800s, creating a stop for the stages headed into the Yosemite valley. He and his family asked the Indians what the word was for "deep, green valley," and they told him it was Ahwahnee.

APTOS (Santa Cruz/9,396) A tribe of the Oholne Indians were original inhabitants who gave the site its name, meaning "meeting of the waters." In 1794, Mission Santa Cruz was built which brought the Indians under Spanish control. The Mexican government gave Rafael Castro a land grant to the Aptos Rancho in 1833. Sugar magnate Claus Spreckles later purchased it as a summer home. Between 1850 and the early 1900s, the town's economy was tied to the timber industry, later supplanted by apple orchards.

ARCATA (Humboldt/16,651) Founded as Union in 1850 by L.K. Wood, the name was later changed to Arcata, a Wiyot word meaning "union," or "sunny spot." The Wiyot Indians were native inhabitants, but when Arcata became a supply station for packers and miners at the Klamath-Trinity mining camps, they were forced to move elsewhere. After the gold ran out, timber came into prominence. Arcata is located near Humboldt Bay, a deep-water harbor that encouraged a number of companies to start shipbuilding. Bret Harte got his start writing while living at Arcata.

AZUSA (Los Angeles/44,172) A band of Shoshonean Indians known as the Gabrielinos lived at their village of Asuksa-gna, from which Azusa was derived, meaning "skunk hill (or place)." Another theorized it was the name of an Indian woman with healing powers, so the chief gave her a name that signified "blessed miracle." It may have been a derivation of asaksagua, for "lodge." Azusa was originally a land grant given to Luis Arenas in 1841, later sold to Henry Dalton who experimented with orange trees that would become a big industry in the area.

CALPELLA (Mendicino) Situated just north of Ukiah, this former town saw its first settler when C.H. Veeder arrived in 1857 and laid out the site. Settlers found the rich sandy loam and semi-tropic weather perfect for fruit orchards and hops. During 1859, Calpella and Ukiah were on the list of towns to become county seat, and Ukiah was selected. As a result, Calpella began to decline and much of its trade was diverted to Ukiah. Calpella was named for Chief Kalpela of a Northern Pomo village. His name was interpreted as "shell (or mussel) bearer."

CASTAIC (Los Angeles/12,349) Although Castaic didn't emerge as a town until about 1915, the Southern Pacific Railroad constructed a spur line to the site as early as 1887. Early settlers were the Cordova family in 1835 who influenced much of Castaic's development. The post office was established on September 15, 1894, but closed its doors a year later; it reopened in 1917. Castaic was more favorable for settlement when the Ridge Route was opened. The name is derived from the Chumash word kashtük, which means "eyes," perhaps in reference to the view.

CHOWCHILLA (Madera/11,127) This region was home to the war-like Chauchila tribe of the Yokut Indians. Chowchilla was believed to mean "killers," because the Chauchilas (or Chauciles) were an aggressive tribe. Other translations were "dry river," "hot dish," and "horse thief." The last definition was written in the Pico documents of 1834 that mentioned the Rancheria de los Chauciles and made special note of horse thefts by the Indians. Orlando Robertson purchased the site in 1912, the formal founding of Chowchilla.

COLOMA (El Dorado) Coloma has the distinction of being the site that sparked the California gold rush of 1848. Before that time, it was home to the peaceful Maidu Indians, who called it Cullomah ("beautiful valley"). The name was spelled Coloma when the post office was established on January 13, 1851. John Sutter hired James Marshall to build and operate a sawmill at Coloma. During construction Marshall noticed something shiny in the water, and the rest is history. Sutter died a broken man in a Washington hotel room on June 18, 1880. Marshall also died a poor man five years later.

COLUSA (Colusa/5,402) The Colusa (also Ko-ru-sai) Indians first occupied this area and called themselves Coru. The name means "scratch," thought to come from squaws' odd practice of scratching their new husbands' faces. In 1849, Charles Semple purchased a former land grant, and the town had its formation the following year. The fight for county seat began between Colusa and the town of Monroeville in 1853. U.P. Monroe, inspector of elections in the new county, was determined Monroeville be county seat, but Colusa was voted county seat after the general election.

COTATI (Sonoma/6,471) Juan Castenada received a Mexican land grant in 1844 for 17,000 acres of Rancho Cotate. Thomas Page later purchased the property and some of the land was sold to poultry farmers. In 1870, a railroad line was completed between Petaluma and Santa Rosa, and provided freight service for Page's ranch. When the ranch was subdivided in 1888, David Batchelor was hired by the family to sell lots. He assisted those unable to afford the land by setting them up raising poultry and allowing them to pay for the land from proceeds. The town was named for Chief Cotati (or Kotati, meaning unknown), a Miwok Indian.

GUALALA (Mendocino) The Pomo Indians, specifically a tribe called the Bokeya, were the original inhabitants, and eventually consigned to reservations or Spanish missions. Gualala is derived from the Pomo word walali, meaning "water coming down place," because the river went through the woods and down to the sea. Gualala was originally a land grant given to General Rafael Garcia. The town was established after his grant was made invalid by the court. Gualala was a commercial center for all the outlying regions, then came into prominence as a timber town during the 1860s.

HOOPA (Humboldt/*2,500*) This was home to the Naitinixwe (or Hupa, origin unknown) people who were given their name by the Yurok Indians. The Indians called themselves natinook-wa ("people of the place where the trails return"), and were noted for their exquisite basketry. White settlers began encroaching because of the timber resources, resulting in retaliation by the Indians. In 1855, Fort Gaston was established, and 10 years later the Hoopa Valley was designated an Indian reservation, which continues today.

JACUMBA (San Diego/*660*) Known for its hot springs, the town was established as a mail station in 1857 by James McCoy. Jacumba may be a Diegueno word meaning "hut by the water," "dangerous water," or "magic springs." During the 1900s, Vaughn & Weggenman developed the town as a resort promoting the hot springs. The San Diego/Arizona Eastern Railway was completed in 1919, making Jacumba one of its passenger stations, which became very popular because of the springs. By the 1950s, freight was more profitable and Jacumba lost the station.

LOMPOC (Santa Barbara/41,103) This region was the land of the Chumash Indians who may have given the site its name, calling the lake LumPoc, meaning "little lake" or "lagoon." When the Spanish took possession of the land in 1837 they named it Lumpoco. W. Broughton was a temperance man who brought more than 100 farmers here from Santa Cruz because that town allowed alcohol. One of Lompoc's biggest industries was flowers after sweet pea seeds were grown for export to England. Today, Lompoc is known as the "Flower Seed Capital of the World," and grows more than 500 varieties of flowers.

MALIBU (Los Angeles/12,575) Historically occupied by the Chumash Indians, Malibu may be derived from umalibo or humaliwo, for "surf sounds loudly." Jose Tapia had the first legal claim to the land until Frederick Rindge purchased the site in 1891. Rindge's widow had a standard gauge railroad built to keep Southern Pacific from building its line (ICC law banned two railroads on the same track). She eventually sold her property in the 1930s, and Malibu went on to become famous for homes owned by cinema stars. It was also known for its Malibu pottery, using materials and methods applied in Medieval and Renaissance times.

MOJAVE (Kern/3,836) Mojave got its start in 1876 when the Central Pacific Railroad (now Southern Pacific) made the site one of its stations. Before the railroad was established, Mojave was an old stagecoach stop called Cactus Castle. Borax brought from Death Valley was hauled by 20-mule team to Mojave, as was the ore from mines in the region. The Yuman tribe once made their home in this region. The word hamok avi, from which Mojave is derived, means "three mountains." Another ascribes the name from aha and makhave, for "people who live along the river."

MOKELUMNE HILL (Calaveras/774) When gold was discovered in 1848, prospectors flooded to town, creating a population of about 15,000. After the gold was gone, miners deserted the region and Mokelumne was consigned as a bedroom community. The name came from the Miwok Indian tribe living along the Mokelumne River. It may describe the people of "mokol," but the meaning is obscure. It may have been distorted from wakalumitoh, meaning "people of the village of muk-kel." The town is home to the oldest Congregational Church building in the state, which was constructed in 1856.

NAPA (Napa/72,585) The Napa Indians occupied the region until 1838 when they all died from smallpox. Nathan Coombs purchased part of Salvador Vallejo's land grant in 1843 and laid out the town. The Napa region is known for its excellent vineyards begun after early settlers acquired mission cuttings. Riesling cuttings were introduced in 1861, and Napa went on to become the center of the American table wine industry. The name has numerous meanings, depending on interpretation. The Pomo Indians used hoo-la-nap-po, for "lily village," or ha-be-nap-po, meaning "rock village." Other definitions were "wooden village," "fish," and a Patwin word for "grizzly bear."

NIPOMO (San Luis Obispo/12,626) This region was home to the Chumash Indians until the Spanish arrived in the 1700s. Captain William Dana was granted 38,000 acres to Rancho Nipomo in 1837, which became an important stop along the El Camino Real. In 1882, members of the Dana family donated land for right of way to the Pacific Coast Railway. Nipomo is a Chumash word meaning "at the foot of the hills." It may also be derived from nipumu, meaning "house place," or "village."

OJAI (Ventura/7,862) The first people in this valley may have been primitives called Oak Grove People more than 7,000 years ago. They were followed 3,000 years ago by the Chumash Indians. Ojai began as a Spanish land grant obtained by Fernando Tico about 1837. Edward Libbey was a moving force in transposing Ojai from a dusty little town when he had the business district rebuilt, duplicating Spanish architecture from Havana. First called Nordhoff, the name was changed in 1917 to Ojai, from the Chumash word, a'hwai, meaning "moon."

OLANCHA (Inyo/134) Olancha may have been a Shoshonean village. Of unknown definition, Olancha was taken from the Yokuts Tribe who called themselves Yaudanchi. In 1863, Minnard Farley built a sawmill, stamp mill and amalgamating pans. When nearby Cerro Gordo began to develop with the discovery of silver, Olancha was relegated to a stagecoach stop. After the mines played out, Olancha turned to agricultural and ranching. Southern Pacific Railroad laid its tracks through town in 1910, supplying materials for construction of the Los Angeles Aqueduct.

PALA (San Diego/*860*) Pala is home to the Pala Indians (a mix of the Cupa and Luisenos). Fr. Antonio Peyri established the La Asistencia de San Antonio Pala for the Mission San Luis Rey in 1816. By 1829, the priests were gone and the mission in ruins. The Indians once lived at a place called Warner Springs. When the land was surveyed in the 1800s, Juan Jose Warner claimed the Indian land. As a result, President Hayes declared it off limits to the Indians and they were removed to Pala. Today, the Pala Tribe still lives here. Their name means "water."

PASADENA (Los Angeles/133,936) Pasadena was once occupied by the Hahamogna Indians. In the 1800s, the California Colony of Indiana promoted the community for purposes of ranching only. Pasadena's name origin is controversial. It was thought to come from the Chippewa word weoquan pa sa de na ("crown of the valley"), but Kroeber wrote, "No unsophisticated and very few civilized Indians would think of calling any place the 'crown of the valley.' The phrase has all the appearance of having been coined by an American out of Indian or imaginary Indian terms."[6] Another theory is from a Chippewa word that means simply "valley," which makes more sense, since the town is surrounded by a range of hills.

PASKENTA (Tehama) Paskenta is located on a route to the gold mines at Harrison Gulch, and began as a supply station for pack trains and freighters. Before settlement, the region was home of the Nome Lacke (or Nomlaki) Indian Reservation. Samuel Jenison started the town of Paskenta just below the foothills of the Yolla Bolla Mountains about 1856. The name was interpreted as a Nome Lacke word for "under a hill," "pass under a butte," or "under the bank."

PETALUMA (Sonoma/54,548) The peaceful Petalumas were a tribe of the Coast Miwok Indians. Commandante Mariano Vallejo built the Petaluma Adobe, his headquarters and a prosperous livestock ranch. After the Bear Flag Rebellion, the ranch went into decline and squatters took up part of Vallejo's land, which he later sold to them. Lyman Byce invented the egg incubator in 1879 and introduced it to Petaluma, and by 1917 it was a world leader in the egg industry. The name is taken from the Miwok words Pe'ta and luma, meaning "flatback," descriptive of the Indian village situated on a low hill.

PIRU (Ventura/1,196) The Piru Indians who lived here were members of the Haminot Tribe. Pi'dhuky, from which Piru is derived, was their word for the grass (possibly sedge) that grew along Piru Creek and was used for basket-making. In 1877, publisher David Cook moved to the region for his health and purchased the site which was originally the Temescal land grant of Piru Fruit Rancho. Through his efforts, Piru became a great fruit producer. Today, the town retains the largest citrus packing house in the region.

PISMO (San Luis Obispo/8,551) Pismo came into existence because of its beach and went on to become famous for its Pismo clams. In 1840, Jose Ortega was granted land by Manuel Goriod of the Mexican government, and called it Rancho Pismo, taken from the Chumash word pismu, which means "tar" (used by the Indians to seal canoes). In 1887, John Price built the Pismo Beach Hotel, recognizing the weather and beach would bring in the tourists. The last link of the southern Pacific Coast Highway was constructed through Pismo in 1891.

PORT HUENEME (Ventura/21,845) The Chumash Indians established their villages and campgrounds along this section of the Pacific Coast. It was named Hueneme by James Alden with the Coast and Geodetic Survey, derived from the Chumash word wene'mu, meaning "resting place," or "halfway." Port Hueneme grew up with the arrival of Thomas Bard, land and oil developer, and later the first president of Union Oil Company. He built a wharf in 1871 which would become the only deep-water harbor between Los Angeles and San Francisco for commercial oil tankers and the U.S. Navy.

POWAY (San Diego/48,044) Poway was cattle range during the 1820s and used by the Mission San Diego de Alcala; its documents showed the name Paguay. Earlier, the region was home to the peaceful Dieguено and Luiseno Indians. The Spaniards labeled the Indians Dieguenos, but they called themselves Kumeyaay ("the people"). Poway became a stagecoach stop in 1868, and the post office was established two years later by Castonas Paine. He submitted the name Paine's Ranch, but postal officials crossed it out and added Poway, interpreted as "the meeting place of the valley."

RANCHO CUCAMONGA (San Bernardino/127,743) Indians who resided here were called Kucamongas, part of the Gabrielino stock of the Shoshone Indians. Kucamonga means "sandy place." In 1839, Tiburcio Tapia was granted 13,000 acres of land where he raised cattle and also established a successful winery. American settlement of the area began when the rancho period ended. John Rains took possession of Tapai's rancho in 1858. Early settlers cultivated orchards, but vineyards and wine-making became the main industries.

REQUA (Del Norte) This site was originally an Indian village called Rech-wa (or Re'kwoi), from a Yurok word meaning "creek mouth." Because of its location on the Klamath River and proximity to the Pacific Ocean, Requa's industries were salmon fishing and shipping. In 1876, the first salt fishery was built. A boat landing was constructed on the Klamath Slough and canneries established. Requa's source of income (salmon) came to a halt in 1934 when commercial fishing was outlawed, forcing the canneries to close their doors. Today, Requa is a quiet bedroom community.

SHASTA (Shasta/0) In 1814, Alexander Henry and David Thompson came through the region and met Indians who were of the Walla Walla, Shatasla, and Halthwypum nations. The Shastas called themselves weohaw, meaning "stone house," and designated a cave in the region. When Major Pierson Reading found about 50 ounces of gold at Clear Creek Canyon in 1848, Shasta became a gateway to the gold fields. First known as Reading's Springs, the name was changed to Shasta when the post office opened in 1851. When the gold ran out, everyone left and Shasta ceased to exist (this should not be confused with Mount Shasta, a thriving town).

SIMI VALLEY (Ventura/111,351) Spaniards established El Rancho Simi in the 1700s. It wasn't until the late 1800s that Americans claimed the land for farming and ranching. The post office was known as Simiopolis, and later changed to Simi Valley. The name was defined from a Pomo or Miwok word for "valley of the winds," and "village." The most popular interpretation is "cloud." John Harrington, with the American Bureau of Ethnology, recorded the proper Chumash word, simijash, which refers to thread-like cirrus clouds that normally appear in November.

SONOMA (Sonoma/9,128) Numerous Indian tribes made their homes in the region: Wintun, Miwok, Wapo, Patwin, Pomo and Miyakamah. San Francisco Solano de Sonoma Mission was founded in 1823 by Father Altamira, and later secularized by the Mexican government. General Vallejo ran an outpost here until the Bear Flag Revolt in 1846, opening the way for American settlement. Sonoma is derived from tso-noma for "earth village," or the Miyakamah word, noma, for "town." Another interpretation is a Wintun word for "nose," for a chief who had a very large nose.

SUISUN CITY (Solano/26,118) Chief Sem Yeto was head of the Soscol and Suisun Indians in addition to other Indian rancherias in the region. He was baptized Solano by the Franciscan friars. By 1839, most of the Indians died from some epidemic brought by the Russians. First named Embarcadero, the city was renamed for the Suisun Tribe, meaning "west winds," or "big expanse." The site was originally discovered in 1850 by sailors Curtis Wilson and John Baker.

TAHOE CITY (Placer/1,668) The Washoe Indians used this site as a summer camp until white encroachment. The town was named Lake Bigler for a governor of California, and later changed to Tahoe. Starting out as a lumber town, Tahoe City would later become a huge tourist attraction after A.J. Bayley established the Grand Central Hotel. The name comes from a Washoe word, da-a-wa-ga, which means "edge of lake." Others believe it is derived from Da-o, meaning "deep" and "blue," or tah-oo-ee, for "a great deal of water."

TECOPA (Inyo/99) Located in the desert just east of Death Valley National Park, Tecopa began as a gold and silver mining camp before 1872. J.B. Osbourne named the site for Paiute Chief Tecopet, which means "wildcat," although he was a pleasant person and got along well with the whites. He was leader of the Southern Paiute Tribe. Tecopet owned a lead-silver mine that he later sold for a silk top hat. The post office was established on May 24, 1877. The Tonopah and Tidewater Railroad didn't make it to Tecopa until 1907 because of the grading difficulties over the Amargosa River Canyon. Gold mining was later supplanted when gypsum and talc were discovered.

TEHACHAPI (Kern/10,957) The Kawaiisu Indians (Shoshonean lineage) were the first to occupy the territory. In the 1860s, the town was called Williamsburg. Tehachapi was interpreted as "windy place," referring to the desert passes where the wind blows. When surveyor Lt. Robert Williamson came through in 1853, he wrote in his field notes, "...we learned that their name for the creek was Tah-ee-chay-pah,"[7] and described a creek frozen over. Other translations were "sweet water," and "many acorns."

TEHAMA (Tehama/432) An early settler was Robert Thomas who received a land grant from the Mexican government in 1844. The town was a center of transportation after a ferry service was established in 1846. Tehama has been defined by historians as "high water," "low land," "shallow," and "salmon." Doug Kyle wrote, "...The meaning of the word is not clear, but most authorities agree it was probably "low land" or "high water... However, an intriguing complication has arisen with the discovery that the Indians of the Sacramento area called that area Tehama, and that the first use of the name by whites was apparently in Sacramento... A possible explanation is that both the Tehama (Nomlaki) Indians and the Sacramento (Nisenan) Indians had the same word, Tehama, which seems possible because of its simplicity and melodious sound."[8]

TEMECULA (Riverside/57,716) Temecula's foothills were home to the Pechanga Indians until they were removed to the Pechanga Reservation in 1885. Temecula was part of a land grant given to Felix Valdez in 1845. A general store was opened by John Magee in 1849, which was also a stopping place for gold seekers and settlers. The post office was established in the store on April 22, 1859, and was the second post office in the state, behind San Francisco. In 1873, Simon Levi was postmaster until 1876, when he left Temecula and later founded the Simon Levi Company. Temecula is a Luiseno word meaning "sun shining through fine mist."

TOPANGA (Los Angeles/*1,200*) Juan Rodriguez Cabrillo arrived in 1542, claiming the land for Spain, and settlement of the area forced the resident Gabrielino Indians to move away. In the 1890s, Judge Oscar Trippet purchased the property and used it as a weekend getaway. Located near the Santa Monica Mountains, Topanga means "above place," signifying a Chumash Indian village that was located above Topanga Creek. It was also interpreted as "where the mountains meet the sea," and "place of green water."

TRUCKEE (Nevada/13,864) Located near Donner Pass, Truckee became an important town when the Central Pacific Railroad came through in the 1868, followed by the Truckee Lumber Company established by W.H. Kruger. First called Gray's Station, then Coburn's Station, it was changed to Truckee in 1868. Chief Truckee was a Paiute Chief who met explorers while scouting for water. They thought his name was tro-kay ("all right").

UKIAH (Mendocino/15,497) In 1844, Duflot de Mofra wrote on his map the name Jukiusme for the Indians who lived in the region. Cayetano Juarez was granted land by the Mexican government about 1845, and the area was renamed Yokaya ("deep valley"). The name was corrupted to Ukiah. On December 31, 1858, the post office was established. In 1898, the International Latitude Observatory was built at Ukiah, and is one of only four established by the International Geodetic Association.

WAWONA (Mariposa/0) About 1851, captains John Bowling and William Dill and Major Savage were ordered to find the valley where a renegade band of Indian were hiding. They camped near Wawona, and the following morning began their trek that would one day become the old stagecoach route from Wawona to Yosemite. Wawona was interpreted as a Miwok word for "big tree," or may have represented the hoot of an owl that was a guardian spirit. The Washburn brothers built the Wawona Hotel about 1867 in addition to a road that went into Yosemite Valley. In 1932, Wawona was included in all the land declared Yosemite National Park.

YOLO (Yolo) The town of Washington was selected as county seat in 1851 and retained its status until 1857, when it was moved to Cacheville. A few years later, James Hutton moved to Cacheville and built a hotel. Because of his generous hospitality, residents renamed the town Hutton's Ranch. On February 3, 1853, the Yolo Post office opened, but the town retained the name Cacheville. It was changed to Yolo in 1892, derived from the Patwin word, yoloy, for "a place abounding with rushes," or "possession of royal blood."

YREKA (Siskiyou/7,290) Discovery of gold caused Yreka to be formed in 1851 when Abraham Thompson found ore at Black Gulch. First called Thompson's Dry Diggings, then Shasta, and then Butte City, it was changed to Yreka in 1852, which was probably corrupted from its original word, wai-ri-ka, meaning "north place," or "north mountain." Others believe it is a derivation of a Shasta word, I-e-k, which means "the white," descriptive of the snow on Mount Shasta.

YUBA CITY (Sutter/36,758) Yuba was thought to be derived from Uva, the Spanish word for "grape." Others suggest it is from a branch of the Maidu Indian Tribe, the Yu-ba (origin unknown). When John Sutter moved here, he named the river Yuba for the Indian village. This site was deeded by Sutter in 1849 to Samuel Brannan, Pierson Redding and Henry Cheever, who had the town surveyed and platted the same year. After the gold rush days were over, the town became an agricultural community. Just outside Yuba City were found the bodies of 25 migrant farm workers, killed by Juan Corona in 1971.

YUCAIPA (San Bernardino/41,207) A band of Indians known as the Wanakik Cahuillas often traveled through this region using it as their hunting ground, and called it Yuk-ca-pa, which means "big head," descriptive of a large rock. Some authorities believe it means "lush meadows" or "green valley," or from yucaipat, for "wet lands." The site was occupied by Antonio Maria Lugo in 1842 who received it as a land grant. The 1860s brought water via the lower Yukipe ditch, and the town became known as the bread basket to southern California.

COLORADO

CHEYENNE WELLS (Cheyenne/1,010) This town dates back to the 1860s when it was a stop for the Butterfield Stage's Kansas City to Denver route. It was named for the Cheyenne Indians and their water wells. The Kansas Pacific Railroad extended its line to town, making Cheyenne Wells a division point. Railroad worker Louis McLane purchased the site and laid out the town in 1887. The Cheyenne Indians were given their name by the Sioux, who called them sha-hiyena, meaning "those who speak a strange language." In 1894, an experimental farm was established near town, where the now widely practiced contour farming technique was developed.

KIOWA (Elbert/581) Henry Wendling operated a stagecoach station established in 1859, its main purpose to carry supplies to mining camps. He called the site Wendling, which was later changed to Kiowa, for the Kiowa Indians ("principal people") Indian uprisings during the 1860s prevented much development. The Kiowas retaliated because the whites had taken away their land.

MANITOU SPRINGS (El Paso/4,980) The springs in the region were created by a geological uplift, much the same as when Pike's Peak was formed. Cheyenne, Kiowa, Arapaho and Ute Indians were frequent visitors at the springs, which were considered neutral grounds. In the foothills below Pike's Peak, Manitou Springs was founded in 1872 by Dr. William and General William Palmer, and became known for its healing springs. Manitou was forced to close its spas and hotels during the financial panic of 1873. The Mineral Springs Foundation resurrected the springs in 1987. Manitou means "great spirit."

NIWOT (Boulder/4,160) Niwot was created as a section house for rail workers while the Colorado Central & Pacific Railroad was being built. In 1873, two settlers donated 20 acres of land for a townsite, which was platted the same year. The name was spelled Ni Wot until the post office was established. Niwot was an Arapaho chief who was very friendly to the whites. His name means "left hand."

OURAY (Ouray/813) A.J. Staley and Logan Whitlock were early discoverers of silver in the region. W. Begole and Jack Eckles later opened the Mineral Farm Mine, so called because the silver was simply dug up like potatoes. The town was founded in 1875 and became a supply center for the mines. Named Uncompahgre City ("hot water spring," or "red water canyon"), it was later changed to Ouray for a highly respected Ute Chief, whose name means "arrow." Ouray was instrumental in preventing bloodshed between the whites and Utes when the Indians were trying to claim Western Colorado. After the Meeker Massacre in 1879, Ouray was distraught because all his efforts towards peacemaking came to naught. He died near Ignacio, a broken man.

PAGOSA SPRINGS (Archuleta/1,591) In the Ute language, Pagosa means "healing springs," descriptive of the hot mineral springs the Indians used as their winter camp. Because of the medicinal value of the springs, possession of the land was long disputed by the Ute and Navajo Indians. Located near vast timberlands, Pagosa Springs was supported by the lumber mills. Once all the timber land was gone, the springs took over as the town's main source of revenue.

SAGUACHE (Saguache/578) Situated in San Luis valley between the Continental Divide and the Sangre de Cristo Range, Saguache was founded in 1874. Prior to settlement the valley was used by the Ute Indians to round up horses that had wondered away from camp during the winters. They called the area Sa-qua-qua-chi-pa, which means "blue earth" or "water at the blue earth." The community anticipated a railroad, but when it did not occur Saguache became a ranching community, as it is today.

SAPINERO (Gunnison) Soap Creek was laid out by the Denver and Rio Grande Railroad in 1881 as its end-of-track, and served as a supply and freighting center. The name was changed to Sapinero (from sabinero, "small cedar trees"), the name of a Ute Indian subchief who was the brother-in-law of Chief Ouray. Sapinero was sent underwater when the Blue Mesa Reservoir was built. The post office that was established in 1882 was moved to a rural branch in Gunnison on August 11, 1967. The remainder of the community is on the south side of the reservoir, and today has only a gas station and a store.

TABERNASH (Grand/165) John Q. Rollins built a road over Boulder Pass (later named Rollins Pass) in 1873, and the Berthoud Pass stage road was finished in 1874. These two roads merged at the site and called Junction Ranch which served as a staging facility. The town developed when the Moffat roundhouse was built to service the Mallet (helper) engines used to pull trains over the pass. The name was changed to Tabernash (from Tab-we-ap), a Ute Indian chief who was suspected of murder and theft. His name origin is unknown.

TIMPAS (Otero) This town began its formation when railroads came through in the 1870s. The first station on the Santa Fe Trail was located at Timpas, with George Rounds as station master who also laid out the town in 1887. The post office was established in 1891 and closed its doors on October 23, 1970. Since there was very little water near Timpas, residents conducted dry-land farming. Unable to create a successful irrigation system, most of the people eventually left. The town took its name from Timpas Creek, and may come from the Paiute word tump, for "stone," or "iron."

TOPONAS (Routt) Toponas was established in the 1880s as a ranching community. The post office opened on July 25, 1888. Originally known as Upper Egeria Park (Egeria was a mythical water nymph), the name was changed to Toponas, a Ute word interpreted as "sleeping lion," designating a rock formation that looks like a sleeping lion. In addition to cattle ranches, the community was a timber and lettuce shipping point. During World War I, an irrigation dam was constructed, bringing in homesteaders. But in 1922, the dam washed out and the farms lay fallow. Much of the land was purchased by the U.S. and is now part of the Comanche National Grasslands.

TOWOAC (Montezuma/1,097) This community is located on the Ute Mountain Indian Reservation. Towoac (also spelled Towe'yak and Towe'Yak) is a Ute word that means "thank you" or "all right." The Ute Mountain Utes call themselves the Weeminuche. When white men discovered minerals in the San Juan Mountains, the Indians were forced to live on the reservation. The post office opened on April 1, 1915. Today, Towoac is home to the Ute Mountain Ute Tribal Headquarters.

CONNECTICUT

ASPETUCK (Fairfield) This hamlet is located in a corner section of Easton. In 1671, an Indian named John Wampus tried to claim part of Aspetuck. The courts turned down his allegation and ruled in favor of the proprietors. James Sanford built a foundry in 1842 that manufactured agricultural tools. Button factories were another major source of income. Aspetuck is derived from a Paugussett Indian phrase meaning "height" or "high place," and may have referred to the surrounding hills. It has also been translated as "fish net place."

ATTAWAUGAN (Windham) A village in the town of Killingly, Attawaugan may be a Nipmuc ("freshwater people") word that means "knoll," or "hill," although Trumball wrote it was not an Indian name. Another theory was an Algonquin word meaning "small pond place." The Nipmucs were a peaceful tribe who conducted agriculture, and hunted and fished in the region. In addition to a mill established by the Whearhead Company, Attawaugan's economy was tied to orchards and farming.

COS COB (Fairfield) Cos Cob is one of several villages in the town of Greenwich, and was mainly farmland during the 1600s. Local Indians died after English settlement, either from smallpox or massacres. During the 1800s, there was some small-scale fishing conducted. Some believed Cos Cob was named for Chief Koska Koba, but there is no evidence to substantiate the theory. A more likely interpretation is from cassacubque, a Siwanoy word meaning "high rock," descriptive of the Indian village situated on a high, rocky ledge.

EKONK (Windham) Resident Indian tribes were the Pequots, Wampanoags, Nipmucks, and Narragansetts. Ekonk is derived from a Mohegan word, egunk, for "long hill" or "ridge." Another theory is "bend," or a Nipmuk word for "turn." The village is located on the Voluntown-Sterling town boundaries. A group of petroglyphs were found at Ekonk Hill in the 1990s. Archaeologists surmise the rocks represent a corn-planting calendar. Some of them may depict the lunar cycles.

HIGGANUM (Middlesex/1,671) Early records show a general store opened here in 1752. About ten years later James Child established a shipbuilding business which lasted until 1854. At one time there was a witch-hazel distillery near Higganum, where the local shrub was converted into lotion. This product was a source of income for farmers with submarginal fields. Higganum is a village in the town of Haddam, and its name is derived from higganumpus, which means "fishing place." Another interpretation was Mohegan for "quarry where we get stone for axes," taken from tomheganompsk.

MIANUS (Fairfield) During the early 1600s, the Siwanoy tribe of Indians called themselves Myanos after their leader, Chief Mayn Myanos ("he who gathers together"). Daniel Patrick named the site Mianus for the chief. Myanos shot and killed a white man in 1644, surprising since the Indian was known to be peaceful. Patrick killed the Chief and the altercation brought in Captain Underhill and his troops who wiped out the tribe. Mianus is a village in the town of Greenwich.

MOMAUGUIN (New Haven) Momauguin was a Quinnipiac sachem who sold this site in 1638. His name was interpreted as "black feather." This beach community was used mainly by the Indians for their pow wows. It would be the 1890s before any development commenced with the first hotel, followed by a trolley car that took people back and forth from the beach. After World War II, Momauguin went into decline until the 1960s when an exclusive gated community was built.

MOODUS (Middlesex/1,263) This Connecticut River village is located within the town of Haddam. Moodus may be a corruption of machimoodus, a Wangunk word meaning "place of noises," or "there is bad noise," referring to the rumbling of water down the Moodus River. The village was known for its manufacture of cotton twine that was sold as cord or made into fish nets. Out of more than a dozen mills, only three are left.

MOOSUP (Windham/*1,323*) The Nipmuc, Narragansett and Mohegan/Pequot Tribes were resident in the region. Moosup came into existence about 1700. Since the town was located along the Moosup River, its economy was tied to wool carding mills. David Aldrich and Edwin Milner came to the region in the 1870s and built one of the early textile mills. The town took its name from Narragansett Chief Mausup (origin unknown). Moosup is a village in the town of Plainsfield.

MYSTIC (New London/4,001) The first European to see the Mystic River was Dutch explorer Captain Adraien Block, who recorded the name as Sickenames (or Siccanemos) for a Pequot sachem. Mystic comes from missi-tuk, which means "great tidal river." Shipbuilding was Mystic's claim to fame until the War of 1812. Sealing and whaling later came into prominence. In 1929, Dr. Charles K. Stillman, Edward E. Bradley, and Carl C. Culter conceived the brilliant idea of turning Mystic into a maritime museum to preserve its seafaring traditions, which continue today.

NAUGATUCK (New Haven/30,989) Taking its name from the river, Naugatuck was interpreted from a Quinnipiac word meaning "one large tree," "lone tree by the fishing place," or "far distant." Naugatuck's economy was based on the manufacture of notions (needles, buttons, pots and pans). Charles and Henry Goodyear established Goodyear's Metallic Rubber Shoe Company in 1843. During the Civil War, the company made raincoats, blankets and rubber footwear for the Union Army.

NOANK (New London/1,830) This was home to the Pequot Indians, and because they were a warlike people, many years would pass before it became a permanent settlement. In 1712, the new town voted to apportion lots on Noank peninsula to be offered at a lottery. Noank is a village in the town of Groton and grew up around shipbuilding. Today the old shipyards have been replaced by modern marinas. Noank is derived from the Pequot word nawyanque, interpreted as "a point," or "neck of land."

NORWALK (Fairfield/82,951) Roger Ludlow received a deed from the Norwalk Indians, who may have been of the Mohegan tribe. He was given the land on February 26, 1640: "An agreement made between the Indians of Norwalke and Roger Ludlowe ... have granted all the lands ... the one called Norwalke...."[9] The name means "at the point of land." In 1651, the legislature at Hartford approved the establishment of Norwalk as a town. Norwalk's major industry in the 1870s was oyster culturing, and later became known for its stoneware pottery.

ONECO (Windham) After the Indian wars during King Philip's reign, Mohegan Chief Uncas claimed part of the land and split it between his sons, Owaneco and Attanawahood. This site was established in 1830 and named after Owaneco (origin unknown). Discovery of granite brought in the Sprague Company which established the Baltic Mills. Owaneco was friendly to the white men, but had a thirst for the white man's fire water. The English took advantage by unfairly taking his land. He was forgotten by the colonists and died a poor man at the age of 70 in 1715.

PAWCATUCK (New London/5,474) Founded in 1649, Pawcatuck is a village in the town of Stonington. Part of it is located in Rhode Island because of the way King Charles II set the boundaries in 1662. Thomas Stanton established the first business in 1661. Pawcatuck may be derived from a Pequot or Niantic word for "clear divided tidal stream," or "open divided stream."

PEQUABUCK (Litchfield) Pequabuck began as a manufacturing town when W.H. Scott established a mercantile and sawmill. In 1850, the Hartford, Providence and Fishkill Railroad built its line through Pequabuck. The post office was established in 1857 (Theodore Terry, postmaster). Pequabuck is a Wangunk name interpreted as "clear, open pond."

POQUETANUCK (New London) This little two-lane village is part of the town of Preston. At one time it was home to a thriving mercantile center and many sea captains. In 1754, Captain Grant built a hotel that was used to house soldiers during the Revolution, which later became a safe haven for runaway slaves. Pequetanuck was derived from a Mohegan word meaning "lands broken up."

POQUONNOCK BRIDGE (New London/1,592) Derived from an Algonquin word, Pequonnock means "cleared land." Once part of New London, Poquonnock Bridge is a village in Groton. The Pequonnock Bridge was built in 1739 after Benjamin Avery deeded a strip of his land. Because there were a number of places with the same name, the "Bridge" was added in 1845 to avoid confusion.

QUADDICK (Windham) Henry Green built a sawmill in 1719, taking advantage of a dam beavers had built on the Assawaga River. In 1864, the Quaddick Dam was built by a group of men who wanted to bring water power to the town of Killingly. They also purchased six acres of Quaddick. The post office was established in 1882 as Quadic, but closed after one year of operation. Quaddick was derived from pattaquottuck, interpreted as "round hill," or "falls hill." It may be a Narragansett word for "miry place," or Nipmuc for "bend in river."

QUINNIPIAC (New Haven) Once considered a village outside the borough of Wallingford, the site was purchased by Rev. John Davenport, an ordained priest in the Church of England in 1638. The water power from the river brought industry to the region and Quinnipiac became a small manufacturing village. The name was derived from the Quinnipiac word, quinni-pe-auke, meaning "long water land (or country)," or quinnuppinuk, for "where we change our route." Other interpretations were "on great trail," and "turning point."

SCITICO (Hartford) This settlement was established about 1717 when Nathanial Gray built a grain mill, and Israel Meacham began to smelt bog iron at a place called Powder Hollow. The town was named for the chief of the Scantic Indians, Scitico, meaning "the red river place." Other translations were "branched," "forked," and Nipmuc for "land at the river branch." In 1835, the Loomis, Denslow & Company established the gunpowder industry at nearby Powder Hollow.

TACONIC (Litchfield) A grist mill and forge were built at Taconic by Jacob Bacon and Daniel Parke. Called Deacon Camp, the site was renamed Camp's Forge. In 1825, it was changed to Chapinville by Phineas Chapinin. Because there were too many "villes," it was renamed Tatonic in 1920. The root word may have been taughkanghnick or tocconuc, Algonquin for "uncertain and in dispute." The root word, tugh, is also described "tree," "wood," or "forest." Other interpretations were "small field in the forest," and "steep ascent." Tatonic is a village within the town of Salisbury.

TITICUS (Fairfield) Titicus was once part of the town of Ridgefield. The Titicus Store was established in the early 1800s, and the post office opened on February 12, 1885 (Hiram Nash, postmaster). During the early 19th century, tanning was an important business, as was a flour and cider mill built by the Gilbert brothers. In 1868, the great Titicus Flood occurred. A dam the Gilbert brothers had built burst and the tannery was destroyed. Titicus is derived from mutighticoos, a Mohegan word for "place without trees." Another interpretation was "buffalo creek."

WEQUETEQUOCK (New London) Located in the town of Stonington, this hamlet was founded by William Chesebrough in 1649. Wequetequock is a Mohegan expression for "resting place of ducks," "land at the end of tidewater," "head of a tidal river," or "wigwam place." Fergus Macdowel was recorded in 1697 as owning a warehouse at Wequetequock, the only mercantile in the region.

WILLIMANTIC (Windham/15,823) The Nipmuc Indians used this region as their fishing and hunting grounds. Willimantic means "land of the swift running waters," descriptive of the Willimantic River which drops more than 95 feet through a series of falls. It was also interpreted as a Mohegan word meaning "good cedar swamp." Arrival of the New London Northern Railroad in 1849 brought Willimantic into the industrial era. The Willimantic Linen Company was formed in 1854 by amalgamation of several mills, and as a result the town became known as "Thread City," producing some of the finest silk thread and cloth in the world.

DELAWARE

HOCKESSIN (New Castle/12,902) Hockessin saw its first settler about 1688. The land was originally owned by William Penn who gave it to his daughter, Letitia. Known as Letitia Manor, it encompassed more than 15,000 acres. The property was broken up and sold to the settlers. John Houghton purchased one of the parcels in 1715 and the town developed around his land. Quakers were encouraged to move here and they built a Friends Meeting House in 1738. The Baltimore & Ohio Railroad came through in 1872. Mushroom cultivation and the mining of kaolin (a clay) were prosperous industries during the late 1800s. The clay was shipped to pottery makers. Hockessin may be an Algonquin word for "good bark hill," or "place of many foxes." During a cultural survey conducted in the last few years, numerous artifacts were discovered which dated back to the 1800s. An 1864 copper Indian head penny and a hand-blown lightbulb, along with abalone shells used for making buttons were among a few of the relics.

FLORIDA

ALACHUA (Alachua/6,098) The region was once forest land and home to the Seminole Indians until about 1818 when Newmansville was established. A commercial center for the citrus industry, the community disappeared when the railroad bypassed it. As a result, Alachua was formed in the early 1900s. The name was translated from luchuwa, a Creek word for "jug," designating a large chasm. It was also thought to be the Seminole word lachua, for "big jug," descriptive of a marshy area that was fed by an underground water flow.

ALLAPATTAH (Dade) This diverse, ethnic community is situated between Miami and Little Havana, and is close enough to have witnessed first-hand the Elian Gonzalez incident. Allapattah is a Seminole word for "alligator." William P. Wagner started the settlement in 1856. Known as the "Breadbasket of Miami," truck farms and dairies were prevalent until the 1920s when the land boom began. A devastating hurricane caused major damage to Allapattah in the 1964, and numerous homeowners sold their properties to land developers.

APALACHICOLA (Franklin/2,334) After settlement in 1821, the town was named West Point, but changed to Apalachicola in 1831, a Hichiti word for "land beyond," or "those people residing on the other side." Other definitions are from the Choctaw word apelachi, for "ally," or apelichi, meaning "ruling place." During the Civil War, Apalachicola was of strategic military importance because the river provided the military easy access. Apalachicola was home to John Gorrie, early pioneer in the invention of refrigeration and air conditioning.

APOPKA (Orange/26,642) Settled about 1856, the site was called "The Lodge," for a Masonic order formed before the Civil War. In 1887, the name was changed to Apopka, which may be from the Creek words aha and papka, for "potato-eating place." Other theories suggest the name was derived from tsala apopka ("trout-eating place") and tsalopopkohatchee, for "catfish-eating creek."

ARIPEKA (Pasco) Aripeka is a small fishing village on the Gulf Coast built on a sand spit and surrounded by mangrove swamps. Established in the early 1800s, it was named for Aripeka, a Miccosukee Indian chief, one of the signers of the Treaty of Payne's Landing. Aripeka's economy stemmed from logging cedar trees, in addition to fishing. Logging is no more, but the village still gets cash income from fishing. The name may be derived from the Creek word abihka, meaning "pile" or "root," descriptive of a pile of scalps.

BITHLO (Orange/4,626) This community was founded in 1912 when Henry Flagler built the Florida East Coast Railway and made Bithlo one of its stations. His wife, Mary, may have given the town a Seminole word meaning "canoe." After disintegration of the Florida land boom and then the Depression, the community was unable to attract any new residents. Today, with Orlando showing rapid development, people are looking at Bithlo with renewed interest.

CHATTAHOOCHEE (Gadsen/3,287) In 1681, Mission Santa Cruz de Sabacola was established. Because of its proximity to the Chattahoochee River and busy river traffic, a settlement was established as Mt. Vernon. In the early 1900s, the name was changed to River Junction. It was renamed Chattahoochee in 1938, and may come from the Muskogee words huchi and chato, for "marked rock," descriptive of the multicolored rocks found in the river bed.

CHOKOLOSKEE ISLAND (Collier/404) Part of the 10,000 Islands, Chokoloskee was once home to the Colusa Indians; fur trappers later hunted here before white settlement. The post office opened in 1891. Ted Smallwood came to the island in 1906 and established a trading post that served the more remote areas. In 1974, the Smallwood Trading Post (which is still in business) was placed on the National Register of Historic Places. Chokoloskee comes from the Seminole words chukka and liski, for "old house," descriptive of the old Indian houses built on stilts.

HIALEAH (Miami-Dade/226,419) Renown for its racetrack built in 1925, Hialeah was settled about 1910 with the arrival of James Bright, formerly a Missouri rancher, who claimed part of a large prairie area to raise dairy cows. The town had its formation when aviator Glenn Curtiss collaborated with Bright and had structures erected about 1917. The name comes from the Seminole-Creek words haiyakpo and hili, for "pretty prairie."

HOMOSSASA (Citrus/2,294) This name is derived from homo and sasi, Seminole for "pepper is there," or "place where wild peppers grow." The town was supported by sugar manufacturing when David Yulee built a sugar mill in the early 1800s. After the Civil War the sugar mill ceased to operate. The town continued to function in the timber industry, and was also a busy commerce center since it was located along the Homossasa River, a natural port for steamships.

HYPOLUXO (Palm Beach/2,015) Founded about 1873, Hypoluxo is one of the oldest settlements on Lake Worth. It is a Seminole word that could signify "water all around," describing the land-locked Lake Worth, or "round mound" for the Indian shell mounds. In 1886, the post office was established (Andrew Garnett, postmaster).

IMMOKALEE (Collier/19,763) Situated about 36 feet above sea level on a high sandy ridge, this place was first named Gopher Ridge, for the thousands of gophers prevalent in the area. The first recorded people to live here were the Colusa Tribe, followed by Miccosukke Indians. The post office was established in 1897 (Alice Platt, postmaster). Historians disagree on Immokalee's origin. Some think it is a Miccosukee-Seminole word that means "his home," or "his people." Others suggest it is a Cherokee word for "tumbling."

ISTACHATTA (Hernando/65) This site started out as a small landing and logging area along the Withlacoochee River. Growth of the community was slow and consisted of only a church, packing house and a few stores. When a railroad came through and built a depot in 1800, it prospered somewhat, in addition to the discovery of phosphate. Istachatta is derived from the Seminole words iste and chatta, interpreted as "red man."

KISSIMMEE (Osceola/47,814) Once home to the Caloosa, Creek and Seminole Indians, the site was called Allendale when it started out as a trading post. Kissimmee was founded when Hamilton Disston purchased four million acres of swampland. He changed the name to Kissimmee, a Caloosa word for "heaven's place." Disston had the Kissimmee River dredged to make it deeper, connecting the town to the outside world of commerce. In 1883, the South Florida Railroad built the Tropical Hotel for visitors, and Kissimmee was on its way to becoming a resort.

LAKE PANASOFFKEE (Sumpter/3,413) The region was a sanctuary to a Seminole chief named Halleck-Tustenugee. The town of Panasoffkee was founded in 1882. Establishment of the Tropical Florida Railroad brought loggers for the cypress and hardwood trees. By 1904, all the lumber mills closed down after the trees were depleted. During the 1800s, orange and lemon groves were planted among the oak and cypress trees. Panasoffkee is derived from Pvne Sufke (pronounced "pummy soofe"), a Creek word meaning "deep ravine."

MICANOPY (Alachua/653) Originally an ancient village called Cuscowilla, Micanopy was settled in 1821 when Edward Wanton established a trading post, and may be the oldest inland town in the state. The post office was established in 1828 as Wanton, and changed to Micanopy in 1834, which means simply "chief." Micanopy was a friendly Seminole Indian until settlers took over more and more of the Seminole land. After the second Seminole War, his tribe was removed to Oklahoma.

OCALA (Marion/45,943) Ocala was claimed for the King of Spain by Ponce de Leon, traded to Britain in 1763, then returned to Spain 20 years later. The U.S. acquired the region in 1821. An Indian trading post was established near town four years later. County commissioners declared that the "county site of this county shall be known as Ocala,"[10] on February 19, 1846. The name may have been derived from a Timucuan Indian word for "fair land" or "big hammock," although other interpretations have been suggested: "water's edge," "heavily clouded," and "fertile soil."

OCHOPEE (Collier/10) The rich soil drew farmers to Ochopee which created the center of a tomato-growing industry. Located on the Tamiami Trail, Ochopee was home to Capt. J.F. Jaudon, who established a sugar cane mill. Ochopee is a Seminole word for "hickory tree." Eventually, the National Park Service purchased all the land that encompassed Ochopee. It is now part of the 729,000-acre Big Cypress National Preserve, set up because of its importance as a watershed to the Everglades National Park.

OCOEE (Orange/24,391) This community was formed when Dr. J.D. Starke and a group of slaves moved to the region about 1857. Captain Bluford Sims purchased about 50 acres from Starke in 1863, then founded the town and named it Ocoee, a Cherokee word for "no cold." Crops such as corn and cotton were first grown, but were later abandoned after Starke developed the first citrus nursery in the United States. Today, Ocoee is still a center for the citrus industry.

OJUS (Miami-Dade/16,642) Ojus was originally an Indian trading post and today is considered more of a neighborhood than a town. Located in the Snake Creek region, Ojus developed when Henry Flagler built a railroad to Miami about 1896. Albert Fitch named the site Ojus in 1897, a Seminole word for "plentiful," and may have described the lush vegetation in the region. Because the town fathers failed to collect taxes, the state legislature took away Ojus' incorporation papers in 1936.

OKAHUMPKA (Lake/251) Okahumpka was founded about 1885 by Rev. Edmund Snyder. It was once the village of Chief Micanopy. The name may come from the Muskogean words oki and hamken, meaning "one water," or "lonely waters." Another theorizes it was derived from okeehumpkee, for "deep waters," descriptive of a nearby deep spring. The town's economy was tied to the turpentine and timber industries.

OPA-LOCKA (Miami-Dade/14,951) Developer Glenn Curtiss (aviation industry pioneer) and James Bright created the town of Opa-Locka in the 1920s. They also developed Hialeah. The town was designed with an Arabian Nights theme. Most of the buildings were compete with minarets and elaborate domes that were painted bright colors. The streets were named from places in *A Thousand and One Arabian Nights*. Curtiss selected the name Opa-Locka, which is derived from the Seminole words opilwa and lako, for "swamp big."

PAHOKEE (Palm Beach/5,985) Pahokee is situated along Lake Okeechobee, and was settled in 1914 as East Beach. It was changed to Ridgeway Beach, then renamed Pahokee, from the Seminole word pah hay okee, meaning "grassy waters." The Pahokee Reality Company was formed by B.A. Howard, a celery grower, and a group of men who staked out the townsite and had the land surveyed. Farmers had a windfall in 1917 when a severe freeze hit the region. None of the crops froze at Pahokee, and as a result vegetable prices skyrocketed, bringing added wealth to many of the growers.

PALATKA (Putnam/10,033) This site is located on a bluff overlooking the St. Johns River and was used as a gathering place for the Seminole Indians, who called the site pilotaikita, meaning "cow's crossing," or "crossing over." In 1820, James Marver built a trading post along the riverfront. The post was burned down by Chief Halleck-Tustenugee during the early days of the Seminole War. Since the town was along the river, it was commissioned as a port of entry and became a center of commerce for schooners and stern-wheelers.

PENSACOLA (Escambia/56,255) Pensacola was first occupied in 1559 when Don Tristan de Luna built a settlement called Ochuse. In 1719, France captured the town, and in 1722 the land was given back to Spain. King Ferdinand VI named the site Panzacola for the Panzacola Indians who may have been part of the Choctaw Tribe. A treaty was signed in 1763, bringing the region under British control until it was regained by the U.S. in 1821. Pensacola is interpreted from the Choctaw words panshi and okla, for "hair of the head," or pasca and okla, for "bread people."

SOPCHOPPY (Wakulla/*367*) Located along the Sopchoppy River, the village saw its first settlers when the Roddenberry family arrived in the 1850s. The site was platted by the CT&G Railroad in 1894. Sopchoppy comes from the Creek sokhe chapke, meaning "twisted long," descriptive of the river. It was also interpreted from the Seminole-Creek work lokchapi, meaning "red oak acorn stem." The community is surrounded by St. Mark's Wildlife Refuge and the Apalachicola National Forest.

STEINHATCHEE (Taylor/*1,300*) Steinhatchee is a small fishing village first known as Deadman's Bay. The site was a strategic spot during the Second Seminole War in the 1830s. The timber industry came into prominence in the 1870s begun by James Stephens. The post office was established in 1876 as Stephensville. In 1938, the name was changed to Steinhatchee, a Creek word that means "dead man's creek."

TALLAHASSEE (Leon/150,624) This town was founded when it was made the capitol by the legislative Council in 1824. Tallahassee comes from an Apalachee word meaning "abandoned villages," "old fields," or a Creek word for "old town." During the 1830s, the town was linked to the outside by the Tallahassee-St. Marks Railroad driven by mule power. Cotton and corn were important commodities until the farm lands were slowly bought up for residential use.

TAMPA (Hillsborough/303,447) First called Fort Brooke in 1824 for Col. George Brooke, the town began as a small fishing village. Residents wanted the name changed when the post office was established in 1831. It was renamed Tampa Bay, defined as "split wood for quick fires," descriptive of the abundant driftwood in the region, or "close to it," referring to the nearby Indian village. Tampa became known as a world leader in the manufacture of handmade Havana cigars.

THONOTOSASSA (Hillsborough/6,091) Lake Thonotosassa was a camping place for the Seminole Indians who called the lake Tenotosassa, which means "lake flints," or "flint is here." This region became known for its orange orchards. While Major Dade and his men were on their way to Fort King in 1835, they stopped here to rest. They were eating oranges which came from Cuba and spit the seeds on the ground. William Miley later found the seedlings and transplanted them on his property. His son went on to help General Hazen, who was a pioneer in growing oranges on a commercial level.

WAUCHULA (Hardee/4,386) During the Seminole War, Fort Hartsuff was built at this site to protect the settlers. The name was later changed to Wauchula, derived from the Creek words wakka and hute, for "cow house." It may have been taken from watula for "sand hill crane." Another interpretation was from wewa and hute, meaning "water house." At one time Wauchula was known for its frog-leg industry.

WEEKI WACHEE (Hernando/12) The Seminole Indians used an underground spring they called weekiwachee, which means "little spring," or "winding river." Weeki Wachee today is a recreation area. The spring the Indians used is the surfacing point of an underground river. It is about 100 feet in diameter, but no one knows its depth. Newton Perry, a former Navy frogman, conceived the idea of breathing underwater using an air compressor and hose, and in 1947, perfected his apparatus at Weeki Wachee.

WELAKA (Putnam/586) Situated on a bluff, Welaka came into existence about 1768 when it was known as Mount Tucker, named by Dr. William Stork. Settlement didn't begin in earnest until about 1853 when Colonel James Bryant purchased 500 acres of land. During the Civil War Welaka was all but destroyed by the Union Army. The name has been defined as a Seminole word for "river of lakes," "intermittent springs," and "tide." The Indians called the site ylacco.

WEWAHITCHKA (Gulf/1,722) This town was founded about 1875 by Confederate veterans. The community's economy was based on the citrus industry, and later for its famous Tupelo honey. This product did not turn to sugar or crystallize and was used in the pharmaceutical industry. The tupelo wood was used for bowling alleys and regular hard-wood flooring. Wewahitchka was named by the Creek Indians and was their word for "water eyes," descriptive of the twin lakes along the edge of town.

YALAHA (Lake/1,175) Captain W.J. McEaddy relocated from South Carolina in 1869 and became Yalaha's first permanent settler. He established the first orange grove after acquiring sour stock. Ebenezer Harris introduced grapefruit to the Northern markets, and also helped develop interest in phosphate. McEaddy and a group of men named the town Yalaha, a Seminole word meaning "yellow orange." A postal error recorded the name as Yalahar, which took many months to correct. Although oranges were a cash crop, Yalaha's main industry was growing Asparagus ferns, introduced by John James.

GEORGIA

ARMUCHEE (Floyd) This was home to the Cherokee Indians until the Trail of Tears to Arkansas and Oklahoma in 1838. The early 1900s brought the establishment of grist mills and cotton gins that took advantage of the water power of Armuchee Creek. The Rome & Northern Railroad was completed, spearheaded by industrialist R.G. Peters. Armuchee is a Cherokee word that means "land of beautiful flowers," "much water," or "much fish." It has also been translated from the Choctaw word alamushi, meaning "hiding place."

ATTAPULGUS (Decatur/492) The town was settled in 1818 as Borough of Pleasant Grove, and changed to Attapulgus about 1839. The post office was established in 1838. Fuller's earth was a big industry, used for removing grease from woolen goods. Attapulgus is derived from a Creek word that means "dogwood grove." Another theory suggested "boring holes in wood to make a fire," taken from itu-pulga.

CHICKAMAUGA (Walker/2,245) One of the bloodiest battles of the Civil War was fought here on September 19–20, 1863, with more than 34,000 casualties. James Gordon built his home at a place called Crawfish Springs, which General Rosecran used as his headquarters before the famous battle. It was later occupied by the Union Army and served as a hospital. The town took its name from the Chickamauga River in 1891, a corruption of tsikamagi, a Cherokee word meaning "bloody run," or "bloody river," describing the malaria and death the Indians suffered. It has also been translated as "good place," and "to become filled with snags (or roots)."

DAHLONEGA (Lumpkin/3,638) During the 1820s, the Cherokee Indians dominated the region they called ta-lo-ne-ga, their word for the color of gold, "yellow." The white man pronounced it Dahlonega. In 1828, gold was found in the county and the first gold rush in America began. Since the Cherokee Indians controlled the gold, the Georgia legislature had them removed to Oklahoma in 1838. The Dahlonega mint was constructed the same year. Between 1828 and 1848, the region produced more than $35 million in gold.

ELLIJAY (Gilmer/1,584) Called "the Apple Capital of the World," Ellijay was a trading center from its earliest days to the white man's arrival about 1832. The Cherokee Indians who once lived here were harvesters of the wild apples that grew in the region. Settlers brought with them root stock from superior apple trees, and experiments in the 1840s led to successful crops by the 1860s. Interpretations to the name were "many waters, "new ground," or" from elatsay yi, meaning "earth green there," or "place of green things."

EUHARLEE (Bartow/3,208) Originally Creek Indian territory before 1755, the Cherokee Indians moved in and called the site Eufaula. White settlement began during the 1840s as Burge's Mill. In 1852, the town was incorporated as Euharleeville, but the "ville" was dropped. Derived from Eufaula, the name means "she laughs as she runs," or "she laughs." The Euharlee Creek Covered Bridge was built in 1886, spanning 138 feet. One of the oldest covered bridges in the state, it is listed on the National Register of Historic Places.

HIAWASSE (Towns/808) The community was named for the river, which is a Catawba word for "pretty fawn," or the Cherokee a-yu-wa-se, for "meadow." In 1832, a land lottery was held in what was Cherokee County. Hiawasse was selected as county seat in 1856 when Towns County was created. The following year the Hiawassee Railroad Company applied for a charter, but it never occurred due to the onset of the Civil War. Hiawasse was a popular summer retreat for the wealthy during the 1800s.

NAHUNTA (Brantley/930) Nahunta became home to the Quakers when Matthew Pike gave them land in 1866 so they could build a meeting house. They also established the Nahunta Friends First

Day School. In the early 1900s, the Nahunta Methodist Church was built and called the "Hatchery" because neophyte ministers got their start there. Known as Victoria, the named was changed to Nahunta, an Iroquoian word for "tall trees."

OCHLOCKNEE (Thomas/605) Ochlocknee was established as a protective enclave against Indian uprisings. During the Battle of Brushy Creek in 1863, there were reports of Creek Indians in the region, who were chased off by volunteers headed by Col. T.E. Blackshear. It wasn't until 1911 that the town was surveyed and platted. Ochlocknee comes from the Hichiti words oki and lakni, for "yellow water." Much of the town's economy centered around agriculture.

SUWANEE (Gwinnet/8,725) Suwanee was created when the Southern Railroad laid its tracks in 1871 and built a depot at the site. The same year a narrow-gauge railroad was constructed that connected with Southern, making Suwanee a changing station. The town was named in recognition of an old Indian settlement located along the Chattahoochee River. It may be a Muskogean word for "echo," or a Creek word, skw'ni, the Indians' attempt to pronounce Savannah. The post office was established in 1837 (James Brown, postmaster).

TALLAPOOSA (Haralson/2,789) Called Possum Snout in the 1830s, this was Creek Indian country until they ceded their land in 1825. The Southern Railroad came through about a mile from town in 1884 and ended as a terminus. The name was changed to Tallapoosa, a Creek word which means "golden water," "stranger," or "swift current." The only industry in town was the Dixie Glass works, which manufactured chimney lamps and tableware.

TOCCOA (Stephens/9,323) Known as Dry Pond, the name was changed to Toccoa (Cherokee for "beautiful") in 1873 after the site was surveyed. Toccoa didn't see much growth until the 1800s. Resident Mary Jarrett White was the only woman in Georgia to vote before the 19th Amendment was adopted. She complied with the law and registered at Toccoa six months before election time. There was no explanation as to how Mrs. White managed to get her name registered before the amendment.

TYBEE ISLAND (Chatham/3,392) This island was originally home to the Euchee Indians. The 1500s brought the Spaniards who claimed the island and called it Los Bajos. John Wesley, founder of the Methodist Church, settled on Tybee and was the first person to say a prayer on American soil. The Tybee lighthouse was constructed under the direction of James Oglethorpe and completed in 1736. After the Civil War the island became a summer resort. Tybee is a Euchee word which means "salt," or may be for Choctaw Chief Itu Ubi, meaning "wood killer."

TY TY (Tift/716) Ty Ty grew up around the tracks built by the Brunswick and Albany Railroad in 1871. The I.L. Ford Company built a cotton gin in 1900, but when the bank closed in 1926, so did the cotton company and other industries. Most of the people then survived by farming; pecan and peach groves were also cultivated. The town was originally named Ti Ti, a word the Indians gave to an evergreen bush that grew in the area, but the postmaster spelled it Ty Ty.

WILLACOOCHEE (Atkinson/1,434). Named Danielsville for one of the settlers, this site was chartered on November 12, 1889. It was changed to Willacoochee, a Creek word that means "home of the wildcat." Its economy was tied to agriculture and the mining of sand from the banks of the Alapaha River, used for construction purposes throughout the state. By the end of the 20th century, Willacoochee had gone from agriculture into industry when a major connecting highway was built.

IDAHO

AHSAHKA (Clearwater) Located about three miles southwest of Orofino, Ahsahka is a Nez Perce word that could mean "the spot where the two rivers meet," "forks of a river," or a Salish word for "brushy country." It was also interpreted as "box canyon." The community owes its existence to the Northern Pacific Railroad which was built in 1899. The post office was established a year earlier. Dworshak Dam, the largest concrete dam ever built by the U.S. Army Corps of Engineers, was constructed in the 1960s.

ARIMO (Bannock/348) This town was originally called Oneida. An early settler's residence served as a stagecoach stop called Ruddy's Station. In 1878, the Utah Northern Railroad built a narrow-gauge track through Oneida, which became a freighting point until the railroad was completed to Montana. The post office was established the same year, and the name was changed in 1912. An engineer suggested Arimo for a Shoshone chief, interpreted as "the uncle bawls like a cow."

BLACKFOOT (Bingham/10,419) This name was applied to an Indian tribe after they traveled through a burnt prairie, coating their moccasins with ashes. A band of Crow Indians who saw the travelers called them siksika, meaning "black foot." About 1880, the Utah and Northern Railroad built its line through Blackfoot, which served as an outfitting center for the gold mines in the county. American Falls Canal Company built a ditch for irrigation in 1879, enabling farmers to grow sugar beets, and the first sugar mill was established, one of the best industrial resources for the region.

COCOLALLA (Bonner) Cocolalla was derived from a Coeur d'Alene word meaning "very cold." The Northern Pacific Railway extended its line through the Cocolalla Valley in 1881. The region is probably best known for its ice harvesting. During the early 1900s, Cocolalla Lake had an ice house big enough to hold ten railroad cars. Teams of horses were used to pull out the cut blocks of ice; spiked shoes were made for the animals so they wouldn't slip. Railroad cars were loaded daily and shipped to Northern Pacific's ice stations in the Northwest.

INKOM (Bannock/738) Inkom is located about 12 miles southeast of Pocatello, and began with the land rush of 1902. The name may be derived from the Shoshone word eggakabni, for "red structure," or ingacom, meaning "red rabbit," descriptive of a red rock formation shaped like a rabbit. It was also interpreted as "come ahead," derived from ink-um. The 1920s brought in a Portland cement factory, one of the largest producing cement companies in the state.

KAMIAH (Lewis/1,160) Situated on the banks of the Clearwater River, Kamiah is the birthplace of the Nez Perce Indians who called themselves Nee-mee-poo ("the chosen ones"). During the winter they stayed in long houses and braided ropes from the Cannabis hemp and made baskets. Kamiah could mean "tattered ends of hemp," or "the place of many rope litters." Asa B. Smith and his wife came to Kamiah in 1838 to establish a mission under the auspices of Presbyterian missionary Henry Spalding. The post office was established in 1870, but closed in 1877 due to the Indian war. It reopened in 1894.

KOOSKIA (Idaho/675) This region was Nez Perce land until it opened for settlement in 1895. Kooskia started out as a trading center when the Northern Pacific Railroad was completed in 1899. Originally called Stuart, it was renamed Kooskia by the railroad in 1909, thought to be a contraction of a Nez Perce word for the Clearwater River. Frank T. Gilbert wrote in 1882: "...Koos-koos-kee erroneously supposed to be a Nez Perce word meaning Clearwater... The Nez Perces probably, in trying to explain to Lewis and Clark that there were two large streams running through their country ... repeated the words "Koots-koots-kee" and pointed to the visible stream, meaning "this is the smaller," ... whites inferred that this was its Indian name. Kaih-kaih-koosh is the Nez Perce word signifying clear water."[11] Literally translated, the word meant "water see."

KUNA (Ada/5,382) Kuna means "the end," a Shoshonean word descriptive of the end of the railroad line. It was also translated as "snow" or "good to smoke." Kuna was situated near a freight road that went to Silver City along the Oregon Short Line Railroad. F.H. Teed filed a claim for the site in November 1904, and became the first postmaster in 1907. He was also manager of the Coast Lumber Company. In 1905, the Arrowrock dam was begun and canals dug that would bring water for agricultural use. The Teed homesite became the town of Kuna after a lottery sale.

LAPWAI (Nez Perce/1,134) Presbyterian missionary Henry Spalding moved here in 1836 and built a mission he named Lapwai. It is a Nez Perce word that means "butterfly," and referred to the butterflies that gathered at a nearby millpond. Mrs. Spalding published the first book printed in the Pacific Northwest, a children's book in the Nez Perce language. Just south of town, Fort Lapwai was established in 1862 to keep the white man from encroaching on the Nez Perce Reservation.

MENAN (Jefferson/787) Menan is about 18 miles north of Idaho Falls, on an island 20 miles long and four miles wide. The geography was created by the Snake and Dry Bed rivers. While building the Utah and Northern Railroad in 1878, a contractor named John R. Poole settled here. Through his efforts and influence, an entire section on the island was reserved for a townsite. First called Island, then Heald's Island and then Poole's Island, it was renamed Cedar Buttes. When the post office was established in 1885, it was changed to Menan, a Shoshone word for "island," "surrounded by water," or "many waters."

MINIDOKA (Minidoka/129) The Oregon Short Line Railroad laid a siding in 1884 and began the formation of Minidoka. In 1902, President Teddy Roosevelt signed the New Reclamation Act which enabled Minidoka to benefit from irrigation by construction of the Minidoka Dam. E.P. Vining selected the name Minidoka, meaning "fountain" or "spring of water." It was also thought to be a Shoshone word for "broad expanse." But Professor Shomer, a Dakota language instructor, stated the "mini" sound in Minnesota is the same word as in Minidoka, and that "doka" sounded like the Dakotas word "dokahum," meaning "without any," "gone," or "not there."[12] So Minidoka could be interpreted as "place with little or no water," an appropriate phrase, since the region was once nothing but sagebrush.

NAMPA (Canyon/51,867) Nampa started out as a section house for the Oregon Short Line in 1883. The Boise and Nampa Canal Company was established in 1887 for the purpose of bringing water to the region. Nampa saw rapid growth when Col. W.H. Dewey purchased part of the townsite and built the Dewey Palace Hotel in 1902, which became a major focal point. The town was named for a Shoshone Indian called Nampuh, whose name means "big foot," or "moccasin print." This story originated because the Shoshones stuffed extra-large moccasins and made huge footprints to scare off the settlers.

NOTUS (Canyon/458) Located on the Boise River a few miles from Parma, the site was first known as Lower Boise until the Oregon Short Line laid its tracks in the 1870s. It was one of three towns in Idaho located on the Oregon Trail. The post office was established in 1874 as Lower Boise. It was renamed Notus on April 14, 1904, and may have been the name of a railroad official's daughter, or an Indian word that means "it is all right." The Sebree Ditch Company was built in 1902, bringing much-needed irrigation to Notus.

ONAWAY (Latah/230) This town began as a stage stop that went to the Hoodoo mines. It was named Bull Town in 1905 for founder John Bull, who anticipated growth because Potlatch was in the process of building a lumber mill. The name was changed to Onaway (perhaps after Onaway, MI, meaning "awake"). The town's growth was stifled because the neighboring town of Potlatch was a company town and allowed no liquor. Potlatch officials tried to stop Onaway from being granted a liquor license, and as a result it thwarted more building and Onaway declined.

PICABO (Camas) The Kilpatrick brothers were roadbed graders and built the railroad for the Oregon Shortline in 1883. They homesteaded at Picabo, established a ranch, and platted the town about 1900. Today, the ranch is comprised of about 12,000 acres that surround the town. Concerned with the environment, the Purdys, who own the ranch around Picabo, built dams to prevent overflow from Copper Creek in 1982. The dams failed, so numerous beavers were brought in, and by 1985 the animals had built more than 50 permanent dams. Picabo could mean "come in," "shining water," or, from a Shoshone word, "friend."

POCATELLO (Bannock/51,466) Pocatello's history is centered around the Utah & Northern and Oregon Short Line Railroads, organized by the Union Pacific. The Shoshone Bannock Indians gave settlers access to their lands. A freight depot was built and in 1883 the railroad established the Pacific Hotel. White encroachment on Indian land caused the Indians to be removed onto a smaller reservation. Pocatello was a shifty fellow who hated the settlers, probably because he saw his father hanged by them. His name may be an obscure Shoshone word, Paughatello, interpreted as "he does not follow the road."

POTLATCH (Latah/791) This site was

a campground for the Nez Perce Indians, who foraged for camas roots and berries, and also held potlatches, ceremonial gatherings held in the spring. Potlatch is a word similar to "convention." In 1906, the Potlatch Lumber Company was established, which provided employees and their families with a company store, church, and school. Potlatch lasted almost 50 years as a company town, and its railroad opened up more remote areas for settlement.

SHOSHONE (Lincoln/1,398) Shoshone was organized in 1882 when it was anticipated the Union Pacific Railroad would build its short line. In October 1882, the post office was established as Naples, and later changed to Shoshone, interpreted as "abundance of grass," or "grass lodge people." Since the town was located at the confluence of the Big and Little Wood rivers, it flourished as a transportation center. Water was diverted from the Snake River, and the Milner and Magic Dams were completed for irrigation purposes about 1910.

TENDOY (Lemhi/*208*) This small community is located just north of Lemhi, the birthplace of Sacajewea. Tendoy is the point where Lewis and Clark crossed the Continental Divide. When the post office was established in 1911, it was named Tendoy for the chief of the Lemhi Indians. His name was derived from Un-ten-doip, meaning "he likes broth," referring to the Indian's excessive fondness for the coagulated blood of meat. Tendoy died of overexposure in 1907.

WEIPPE (Clearwater/416) Lewis and Clark stopped here in 1805 and were given food and shelter by the Nez Perce Indians. The site began as a trading outpost and stopping place for miners on their way to the gold fields at Pierce in the 1860s. Wellington Landon laid out the town about 1874. During the Nez Perce War of 1877, all the buildings were destroyed and the settlers took refuge at Fort Pierce. Weippe is located near Lewiston, and was once one of the largest producers of lumber in the state. The name was derived from oyipe, meaning "a very old place, "beautiful place," or "gathering place," descriptive of the Nez Perce who got together at certain times of the year.

ILLINOIS

ANNAWAN (Henry/868) This name may have been taken from Wampanoag Chief Annawon from Massachusetts (origin unknown) who was captured during King Phillip's War in 1675. When the Chicago, Rock Island and Pacific Railroad was building its line in 1850, a survey for right of way was made. As a result, Charles Atkinson and James Grant platted a new town. A prominent resident was I.G. Heaps, breeder of Clydsdale horses.

CAHOKIA (St. Clair/16,391) Cahokia is oldest town in Illinois and was once a summer camp for the Tamoroa Indians. Missionaries arrived in 1698, led by Father

Joliet de Montigny with the Seminary of Foreign Missions. Then the Jesuits appeared and erected their mission. Problems arose between the two orders and Father Montigny went to France to resolve the matter. The Jesuits ended up having no jurisdiction over Cahokia. Actual settlement did not begin until 1700 when fur traders established a trading post. Cahokia is an Illini (Illinois) word meaning "wild goose."

CHENOA (McLean/1,845) The Kickapoo and Potawatomi Indians roamed the region to fish and hunt, and remained until 1823, when they were removed to Kansas. When the Chicago and Alton Railroad was established in 1854, Matthew Scott founded the town. The railroad station was known as Peoria Junction. After Scott platted the town, he renamed it Chenowa. Postal officials spelled it as Chenoa, and it was never corrected. The name was interpreted as a Cherokee word for "dark and bloody ground," or "white dove."

CHICAGO (Cook/2,896,016) Father Jacques Marquette and Louis Joliet were the first Europeans to see what would someday become Chicago. Jean Baptiste Point du Sable built the settlement in 1779. Chicago didn't come into prominence until the Industrial Revolution, and eventually became the rail center of the nation and the largest grain market in the world. It was also known for its slaughterhouses and stockyards, and of course, the Great Chicago Fire in 1871. Chicago is Algonquin for "place of the skunk," or "wild onion." Some historians believe it means something "strong" or "great."

ITASCA (EuPage/8,302) Founder of Itasca in 1841 was Dr. Elijah Smith. The post office opened in 1843 (Augustus Eddy, postmaster). It was renamed Pierce in 1850, then Sagone in 1864. When the Chicago and Pacific Railroad came through, Smith donated part of his land for right of way. The name was changed to Ithica, but a misspelling caused it to end up Itasca. There is confusion as to its origin. Some believe it comes from the Latin words veritas caput, meaning "true head." But others say it is a Chippewa word for "fount of water."

KANKAKEE (Kankakee/27,491) Kankakee was home to the Potawatomi Indians until they ceded their land in 1832 at the Treaty of Camp Tippecanoe. A trading store was established by Noel LaVasseur and his Potawatomi wife, Watchekee, at a place called Bourbonnais. (Kankakee later split from Bourbonnais and was incorporated as a separate town.) Kankakee is derived from a Potawatomi word, theatiki, and means "wonderful land (or home)," although it has also been interpreted as "wolf," "swampy place," and "returning track."

KEWANEE (Henry/12,944) Captain Sullivan Howard was a driving force in the development of Kewanee. In 1852, work began on the Central Military Tract Railroad, and the town was laid two years later as Berrien, for a railroad engineer. He refused the honor and suggested Kewanee, a Winnebago word for "prairie chicken (or hen)." The post office was established in 1854 (Colonel Bliss, postmaster). Kewanee came into prominence with the discovery of coal, and later became a manufacturing and hog producing center.

MACKINAW (Tazewell/1,452) Located along the Mackinaw River, this region was home to the Kickapoo Indians, who were removed in 1832 after the Blackhawk War. An inn was built along the stage coach line in 1827. This same year the town was laid out by surveyor William H. Hodges, who also established the first mercantile, and the post office opened (Mordecai Mobley, postmaster). Mackinaw was thought to mean "little chief," but some believe it is an Ojibway word for "turtle."

MANTENO (Kankakee/6,414) During the 1840s, Canadian French migrated to Manteno. The Potawatomi Indians who lived here were removed to Iowa after the Camp Tippecanoe Treaty of 1852. The Illinois Central Railroad came through in 1853, and Manteno would be the only station between Kankakee and Chicago for many years. Manteno was the daughter of Francois Bourbonnais, Jr. Her name may have originally been spelled Manito or Manitou, which means "spirit."

MAQUON (Knox/318) The Potawatomi Indians who lived in the region used the shells along the river as spoons. They called the river amaquonsippi, amaquon for "mussel," or "mussel shell," and sippi for "river." Residents translated Maquon as "spoon." Not much settlement occurred until after the Blackhawk War of 1832. The post office was opened in 1847 (William McGowan, postmaster).

MASCOUTAH (St. Clair/5,659) Located along the St. Louis-Shawneetown mail route, the site was called Mechanicsburg, and later platted as Enterprise, but the plat was never filed. In 1836, the town was officially established, and its economy was tied to saw and grist mills. When the post office opened, officials changed the name because of duplication. A county clerk suggested Mascoutah, for the Mascouten tribe of Indians. Their name origin described "fire people (or nation)," or may have been derived from mush-ko-doin-sug, for "people of the little prairie."

MENDOTA (LaSalle/7,272) Railroads played a key role in the establishment of Mendota. In 1852, the Illinois Central Railroad was being built at the same time the Chicago and Aurora was laying its line. The following year, both lines converged and a station was established as Mendota, and may be derived from a Sioux word meaning "where two trails meet." The town was an important agricultural community, with its main supporting industry a canning center, which shipped out millions of cans of corn each year.

MINONK (Woodford/2,168) Minonk was located on the Pekin branch of the Atchison, Topeka and Santa Fe Railroad built in 1872, and was terminus of the Illinois Central Railroad. The site was selected by David A. Neal, and surveyed in 1854 by Peter Folsom, deputy surveyor of the county. The post office was established the same year (Charles Dobson, postmaster). Coal mining was a prosperous industry until the 1950s. Minonk may be an Ojibway word that means "good place." A Potawatomi named Smokey noted that the words onk and min meant "blueberry flower star."

MINOOKA (Grundy/3,971) This region was used as a game reserve by the Potawatomi Indians until they were forced to leave in the 1830s. George Comerford was an Irish immigrant and surveyor for the Rock Island Railroad, and may have been responsible for the railroad extending its line to Minooka in 1853. Railroad workers named the site Summit because it was the highest point in the state on the Rock Island line. Dolly Ann Smith renamed the site Minooka, Algonquin for "contentment," "high place," "place of the maple trees," or a Delaware word for "good land."

MOKENA (Will/14,583) A band of Algonquin Indians moved from New York to the region in 1670. Their trail was known as Wolf Road and used by Jesuits and fur traders in the early 1800s. A trading post was built in 1832 and the site was laid out the same year by Allen Denny. In 1883, the Rock Island and Pacific Railway came through and built its depot. Mokena's economy depended to a great extent on the dairy industry. It is an Algonquin word for "turtle."

MOWEAQUA (Shelby/1,923) Indian tribes prevalent in the region were the Kaskaskia, Peoria, Miami, Plankashaw and Shawnees, who were eventually forced out by white settlers. Mattie Wells named the site Moweaqua, a Potawatomi word meaning "weeping woman," or "wolf woman." Moweaqua's source of income in the 1890s was from coal mining. On December 24, 1932, more than 50 men were killed by a mine explosion caused by methane gas.

NACHUSA (Lee/613) John Dixon came to the region in the 1830s. He was known by the Winnebago Indians as Nadah-chu-rah-sah, which means "head hair white," from where Nachusa was derived. He went on to found the town of Dixon, of which Nachusa was once a part. The community grew slowly because of its proximity to the towns of Dixon, Ashton, and Franklin Grove, which had already been established. Nachusa never grew substantially and remained a bedroom community.

NOKOMIS (Montgomery/2,389) The Kickapoo Indians were early inhabitants of the region. The Alton and Terre Haute Railroad extended its line through town in 1855 which was the beginning of Nokomis, and the following year the post office was established (Oliver Boutwell, postmaster). P.C. Huggins and Captain Samuel Ryder surveyed and platted the site in 1856. Nokomis was taken from the book, "Hiawatha," and may be an Iroquois word meaning "daughter of the moon."

OQUAWKA (Henderson/1,539) In 1828, Stephen Phelps had the site laid out after he established a trading post. Oquawka had expectations of becoming a center of commerce with an extension of a railroad through town. But when the panic of 1837 occurred, the tracks went only as far as the Mississippi River and it went to Burlington instead of Oquawka. The name is derived from the Sauk word oquawkiek, which means "yellow banks," descriptive of the sand bluffs dotting the Mississippi River.

PECATONICA (Winnebago/1,997) In 1835, Ephraim Sumner and his family built a tavern that was a stopping place for travelers and stagecoaches. Pecatonica was one of the precincts established when the county was organized. Daniel Reed, Sr., purchased the land that would become the townsite in 1846. A branch line of the Galena and Chicago Union Railroad was constructed in 1852. Starting out as Lysander, the railroad changed the name to Pecatonica, taken from peeketolika, Algonquin for "crooked river."

PEOTONE (Will/3,385) Peotone became a permanent settlement in 1856 when the Illinois Central railroad purchased the land and built a station. The name may have been for an Algonquin Indian chief, but the most popular theory is that it means "a good place to live." H.A. Rathje established a grain mill in 1872 to serve the rye and wheat growers. By the 1880s, the mill had extended its service to wheat farmers from Kansas to Minnesota.

PONTOOSUC (Hancock/171) Located along the Mississippi River, this town was founded by Hezekiah Spillman, who called it Spillman's Landing about 1825. He supplied the river boats with fuel from his wood yard. A blockhouse was built for settlers' protection with the onset of the Black Hawk War. Pontoosuc is an Algonquin word that may signify "small waterfalls," designating the spot where Snake Hollow Stream empties into the Pontoosuc River. The name may have been taken from Pontoosuc, Massachusetts.

SHABBONA (DeKalb/929) This site was selected in the 1870s as a train depot and called Shabbona Grove. When the railroad bypassed the town, it literally moved and the name changed to just Shabbona, for a friendly Ottawa chief, whose name meant "strong built like a bear." Shabonna was one of Tecumseh's aides and witnessed a man named Johnson kill Tecumseh in 1812.

SKOKIE (Cook/63,348) In 1673, French explorers and Father Marquette came across a band of Potawatomi Indians who lived near a large swamp. They ceded their lands in 1821 which opened the region for settlement. Henry Harms founded the site as Niles Center. The name was changed in 1940 to Skokie, Potawatomi for "great swamp," descriptive of the region. Skokie's growth was stimulated when the Northwestern Railroad came through in 1903, enabling travel to Chicago.

SOMONAUK (Dekalb/1,295) The Chicago-Dixon mail route was established in 1834. Removal of the Indians the following year encouraged Eastern settlers. When gold was discovered in California in 1849, some of the residents left their homesteads to seek their fortunes. They returned with enough money to invest in businesses and build schools. Somonauk was interpreted as a Potawatomi word for "paw paw grove."

TISKILWA (Bureau/787) Chief Wappe brought his tribe from Wabash in 1789, and his village was the most important Indian center in the U.S. during the 1830s. The Indians were removed to Kansas about 1836. The Chicago, Rock Island & Pacific Railroad came through, and the Mississippi Canal was built near town. Folklore says Tiskilwa came about when two Indians named Tis and Wa had an argument regarding a young Indian maiden. Tis killed Wa, which ended up Tis-Kil-Wa, but it was an Algonquin word for "gem of the valley."

WATSEKA (Iroquois/5,760) First known as South Middleport, the site started out as a trading post, and was surveyed by Moses H. Messer in 1859. The name was changed to Watseka in 1863, derived from Watch-e-kee, a Potawatomi woman, whose name is interpreted as "pretty woman." Gurdon Hubbard was employed by the American Fur Company assigned to the region in 1818, and married Watch-e-kee. A.B. Roff was postmaster when the office was established in 1862.

WAUCONDA (Lake/9,448) Once home to the Potawatomi and Winnebago Indians, Justus Bangs and his family moved to Rice's Prairie in 1836. They were followed by pioneers attracted to the rich soil and cheap land. The post office was established in 1842. Settlers believed Chief Wauconda was buried along Bangs Lake, and changed Rice's Prairie to Wauconda which means "spirit water," in his honor. Wauconda became a resort area because of the lake, and today depends on retail and industry for its economy.

WAUKEGAN (Lake/87,901) Starting out as a trading post in 1695, the site was called Little Fort. The Potawatomi Indians had their village here until 1836 when treaty forced them to remove. The name was changed to Waukegan about 1846, Algonquin for "fort," "trading post," or "house." Since the town was located near a deep-water port, it experienced rapid growth and became a trans-shipment point for furs and grain. Its economy was later tied to industry.

WAUPONSEE STATION (Grundy) This former community was born when A.P. Hill donated a right of way to the Chicago, Cincinnati, Cleveland and St. Louis railroads to build a branch line in 1881. Wauponsee began to decline with the advent of automobiles. The railroads eventually closed and the right of way was deeded back to the original owners. Roy Johnson was the last owner and sold the property in 1995. The site was named for a Potawatomi Chief named Wabansi, defined as "day break."

WINNETKA (Cook/12,419) Charles Peck was considered the founder of this town, and along with Walter Gurnee, laid out the town in 1854. Gurnee was president of the Chicago and Milwaukee Railroad, which extended its line through town. Peck established the Academy of Design, the forerunner of the Art Institute of Chicago. When deciding on a name for the town, a resident suggested Pecktown, but Peck's wife disagreed and named it Winnetka, an Algonquin word that means "beautiful place (or spot)."

INDIANA

ASHKUM (Iroquois/724) When the Illinois Central Railroad was establishing its line during the 1850s, one of its stations was at Ashkum, a Potawatomi word that means "more and more," signifying something that would increase, e.g., sickness, wealth, or the area. Ashkum was one of the Indians who signed the "Treaty with the Potawatomi" with the U.S. government on February 11, 1837. He died in 1856, soon after the town was founded.

KEWANNA (Fulton/614) Kewanna was founded in 1845 as Pleasant Grove until the post office was established on February 18, 1847. To avoid duplication, the town was renamed for Potawatomi Chief Keewaunay who lived in the region until 1838. His name was interpreted as "prairie chicken." The Terre Haute and Logansport Railroad came through in 1883, and brought in numerous industries, including the Heinz Pickle Company.

KOKOMO (Howard/46,113) David Foster moved to Kokomo in 1842. Commissioners selected Kokomo as county seat in 1844, and Foster donated 40 acres of his land and built a courthouse. The commissioners asked Foster to name the town. He said that "since it was the worst town in the state,"[13] he would name it Kokomo, for an ornery Indian (Miami) named Ko-ka-ma, meaning "the diver." Another interpretation was "a young grandmother." Natural gas discovered in 1887 caused Kokomo to go from agriculture into industry.

MAJENICA (Huntington) A plank road that was built in 1856 was significant to the development of Majenica. James Crosby had Frank Calvert survey the land the same year and named the site Kelso. When the post office was established, it was changed to Majenica, derived from Manjinikia ("big frame), a Miami chief who lived in the region. Although the plank road made transportation possible, it did not attract settlers because of the poor soil. As a result, the Majenica Tile Plant was established to manufacture tile for soil reclamation.

MAXINKUCKEE (Marshall) The Potawatomi Indians were residents along the lake shore until Chief Neeswaugee ceded the land in 1836 and moved west of the Missouri River. In 1875, a clubhouse was built in anticipation that Maxinkuckee Lake would become a summer resort. By 1890, the Vandalia Railroad Company had purchased the property. Maxinkuckee was thought to mean "moccasin." Simon Pokagon, last of the Potawatomi Indians, said the name was an Algonquin word that meant "there is grass." Another version was from mogsinkeeki, for "big stone country."

MISHAWAKA (St. Joseph/46,557) M'shehwahkeek was once a camping spot along the St. Joseph River used by travelers. The discovery of bog iron ore deposits precipitated settlement in 1831. Its growth encouraged Alanson Hurd to purchase land in 1833 and build St. Joseph's Iron Works. Mishawaka's economy was also tied to river trade and boatbuilding. Completion of the Michigan and Central Railroad signed the death warrant for the river traffic in the 1850s. When the post office was established about 1833, Henry Yerrington suggested Mishawaka, for an Indian princess. Another interpretation was "country of dead trees," from the Potawatomi word m'sehwahkeek.

MONGO (LaGrange) French fur traders established a trading post in the early 1830s to trade with the Potawatomi Indians. The dense forest of black walnut, oak and hickory drew men who established sawmills and formed logging companies. First known as Union, Judge Seeley renamed the town Mongoquinong in honor of a Potawatomi Chief (later shortened to Mongo). The name was interpreted as "man and woman." Others have suggested it means "white squaw," or "big squaw prairie."

MUNCIE (Delaware/64,430) Named for the Munsee (Wolf) Tribe of the Delaware Indians, the region was open for settlement after the tribe ceded its land in 1818. The post office was established in 1828 (Dickinson Burt, postmaster). Discovery of gas in 1876 brought new industries to Muncie. The Ball bothers moved here from New York in 1887 because of the inexpensive gas and established a glass manufacturing plant, famous for its canning jars. Munsi was derived from Minsi or Minthiu, meaning "people of the stony country."

NAPPANEE (Elkhart/6,710) In 1874, a group of men platted the town when they thought the Baltimore & Ohio Railroad was coming through. The village was named Nappanee, and may have been taken from Napanee, Canada, originally spelled Appanee. The Canadian Indians are not sure what the true meaning is, but they do agree that it has a secondary meaning, which is "much flour."

OTISCO (Clark) Samuel Crowley inherited the property from his father and had it surveyed and platted in 1854, the same year a branch of the Ohio & Mississippi Railroad came through. A railroad official named the station Otisco, an Iroquois expression that means "waters much dried away," probably descriptive of the surrounding land. The post office was established on April 21, 1870 (Hiram Nevill, postmaster).

PATOKA (Gibson/749) The 1780s brought people who lost their homes during the Revolution. The town was platted in 1813 and named Smithfield (later changed to Columbia). Patoka is a Miami word for "log on the bottom," descriptive of the logs bogged down in the Patoka River's bed. It was also interpreted as a Miami word for "Comanche." The town was once a commercial center for grist and sawmills, and the river was a shipping point for grain and fruit. Today, there are only a few businesses left.

SHIPSHEWANA (LaGrange/536) This town was established near an old Potawatomi village. Amish and Mennonites were early settlers. It was founded in 1889 by Hezekiah Davis. The name was taken from Chief Shipshewana whose tribe was removed to Kansas in 1838. His name was interpreted as "vision of a lion," and may come from folklore that says Shipshewana saw a lion (or cougar) in his dreams.

WABASH (Wabash/11,743) Colonel Hugh Hanna and David Burr platted the site in 1834, and the Wabash and Erie Canal was opened to town three years later. Wabash is derived from the Miami word wah-bah-shik-ki, signifying something white or bright, perhaps the light limestone bed on the river. Another interpretation was from ouabache, for "water over white stones." Wabash has the distinction of being the first town in the world to be wholly lighted by electricity when four 3,000 candle-power lamps were lit on March 31, 1880.

WAKARUSA (Elkhart/1,618) Early settlers were here about 1834 and called the site Salem. When the post office was established, it was renamed Mt. Olive. After the town was surveyed and platted in 1852, settlers elected to rename the village Wakarusa. According to tradition, while the town was being surveyed, an Indian girl was holding the survey chain. She fell down in the wet earth and shouted, "Wakarusa!" which meant "knee deep in mud."

WANATAH (LaPorte/1,013) Wanatah came into existence about 1857 when Joseph Unruh built a flour mill on land once occupied by an Indian village, led by Potawatomi Chief Wanatah. The town became a junction point when two railroads built their line through the site (Pittsburg, Ft. Wayne, and Chicago & Monon), and depended on these railroads for its economy. The post office was established in 1867 (G.P. Long, postmaster). Wanatah was interpreted as "lazy Indian," or "he who charges his enemies."

WAUPECONG (Miami) Much of this community's early records were destroyed when court records were transferred from Cass County (of which Waupecong was once a part). Established as White Hall, the name was changed to Waupecong, translated as "white bones," or "black dirt." No railroads ever came through, so Waupecong did not expand or bring in industries. There are only a few businesses still operating.

WINAMAC (Pulaski/2,418) Located along the Pennsylvania Railroad, Winamac was settled in 1837 with the arrival of Joseph Wason and the Hackett family. It was platted by Jesse Jackson, John Niles and John Brown in 1839. Winamac was a Miami Indian, who may have been called Wee-ned, interpreted as "mudfish" or "catfish." Winamac's economy was slow and only grew as other towns were established in the county.

WIWAKA (Noble) This hamlet came into existence when the New York Central

Railroad was built during the 1850s, giving farmers outlet for their produce, their main product being onions. The land was owned by Isaac Tibbot who had the site platted in 1857. The year 1874 brought in the majority of businesses, which included two churches, general mercantiles, and the flour and sawmills. Wiwaka means "big heron."

IOWA

ALGONA (Kossuth/5,741) Judge Asa Call was instrumental in the development of Kossuth County, and a co-founder of Algona. Establishment of the Milwaukee and the Northwestern railroads in the 1870s made great contributions to growth of the town. Algona is derived from Algonquin, interpreted as "at the place of spearing fish and eels."

ANAMOSA (Jones/5,494) Colonel Thomas Cox laid out the town on June 28, 1838, named the site Dartmouth, and established the post office two years later. Anamosa became a trade center when three railroads were established: Chicago, Milwaukee & St. Paul; Chicago & Northwestern; and Chicago, Anamosa & Northern railways. The name was changed to Anamosa ("white fawn"), daughter of an Indian named Nasinus. But the *History of Jones County* refers to Anamosa as a large-sized man.[14]

KEOKUK (Lee/11,427) An Algonquin tribe called the Illini (Illinois) were the original inhabitants in this region. The site was once called "foot of the lower rapids," and puck-e-she-tuck ("where the water run shallow"), descriptive of the rapids on the Mississippi River. Fur traders later suggested changing the name to Keokuk, chief of the Fox and Sac Indians whose name means "the watchful fox." Keokuk was embarkation point for soldiers during the Civil War. The post office was established in 1841.

KEOSAUQUA (Van Buren/1,066) Located in the middle of Horse Shoe Bend, Indians used the region as a lookout and called the site kat-ua-na, a Sac or Fox word meaning "beautiful valley." The townsite was named Keosauque, translated as "river of the monks," because French monks lived here for a short period of time. The name was also defined as "big bend." Keosauque became a trade center after numerous mills were established.

KEOTA (Keokuk/1,025) First known as Dutch Creek, Keota was settled about 1858 by Hanno Newton. Growth began in 1762 when the Rock Island Railroad built a branch line, replacing the old stagecoach route. Keota was laid out the same year by J.P. Yerger and C.H. Achard. The post office was established in June of 1872. First named Keoton, it was changed to Keota, a Sioux word that means "gone to visit," or "fire has gone out." It also means "shining star" in the Cherokee language.

MAQUOKETA (Jackson/6,112) John E. Goodenow and Lyman Bates came to

Maquoketa in 1838 from Moriah, New York. Starting out as a rest stop for travelers, the town's economy was later tied to farming and cattle ranching. Goodenow was postmaster when the post office was established in 1840 as Springfield. The name was changed to Maquoketa in 1843, derived from the Iowa word mauanteutan, meaning "bear river," or makwok-eteg, for "there are bears."

MUSCATINE (Muscatine/22,697) Colonel John Vanater, founder of the town, had earlier visited the site when it was called Grindstone Bluffs. A fur trading post was established in 1833. The site was named Bloomington for Vanater's hometown in Indiana. In 1849, it was renamed Muscatine, from the Mascouten Indians, whose name stands for "fiery nation (or people)." Muscatine was once the largest freshwater pearl button manufacturing center in the world.

NODAWAY (Adams/132) James Harlow purchased the site from the U.S. government in 1854. In 1869, the Burlington Railroad extended its line to the region and the townsite was created when train crews set up a permanent camp. Nodaway's growth was later stimulated by the cattle industry. The name was interpreted as "deep channel." It may also be an Ojibway word for "snake," a name they gave to their enemies.

OCHEYEDAN (Osceola/536) This town was born when the Burlington, Cedar Rapids and Northern Railroad built its tracks in 1884. D.H. Boyd and L.B. Boyd laid out part of the town, while the Iowa Land Company platted the remainder. Mennonites were among the early arrivals, as were veterans from the Civil War. Ocheyedan means "spot where they weep." It may have been derived from the Sioux words acheya and akicheya, which symbolized mourning for two young boys who were killed here by an enemy tribe.

ONAWA (Monona/3,091) Members of the Lewis and Clark expedition were probably the first white men to see this site in 1804. The Monona Land Company was organized in 1857 for the purpose of establishing the town, which was surveyed by B.D. and C.H. Holbrook. It was named Onawa by T. Elliott from the poem "Hiawatha," derived from onaiweh, which means "wide awake." Lumber played an important part in Onawa's economy with the abundance of cottonwood trees. Christian K. Nelson worked in a confectionary store at Onawa and went on to create the famous ice cream dessert, Eskimo Pie.

OSKALOOSA (Mahaska/10,938) Captain Nathan Boone (Daniel Boone's nephew) and his U.S. Dragoons were given orders to select a site for a fort. On June 11, 1835, a high ridge called "The Narrows" between the Des Moines and Chiquaqua rivers was selected for the fort. It was later selected as a townsite and called Oskaloosa. The name was derived from Ouscaloosa, a Creek princess, whose name signified "last of the beautiful." The Des Moines Valley Railroad reached Oskaloosa in 1864. Coal mining was an important industry during the 1870s.

QUASQUETON (Buchanan/574) Located along the Wapsipinicon River, Quasqueton is the oldest town in the county, and was an occasional camping site for Indians. They called the area Quasqueton, Algonquin for "swift running waters." The first pioneer was William Bennett who arrived about 1842 and built a dam and mill. The post office was established in 1844 (Joseph A. Raynolds, postmaster). The following year, D.S. Davis purchased the townsite, which he laid out and platted. By 1912, the Chicago, Anamosa and Northern

Railroad had been completed through Quasqueton.

SAC CITY (Sac/2,368) This region was a favorite camping ground of the Sac and Fox Indians. The town was surveyed by John F. Duncome and platted in 1855. The majority of businesses were built along the Coon River, and the post office began operating in 1857, followed by the Milwaukee Railroad in 1899. The words Sauk and Sac were used interchangeably. Derived from osakwugi, Sac means "people of the yellow earth."

SIOUX CITY (Woodbury/85,013) Sioux City is situated on bluffs along the Big Sioux River and at the head of navigation on the Missouri River. This old buffalo trail site was founded in 1855 by Dr. John Cook, who purchased land from Theophile Bruguier, a French-Canadian who married a Sioux woman. Bruguier's influence with Chief War Eagle discouraged Indian problems with the white settlers. Sioux City became an important shipping point with establishment of the Pacific and the Illinois Central railroads during the 1870s. The Livestock Exchange was formed here in 1887. Sioux means "the snake-like one," or "enemies."

TAMA (Tama/2,731) This town began its life when the Chicago and Northwestern Railway was built in 1862. The site was platted and the post office established as Iuka (J.H. Beaumont, postmaster), but changed to Tama City by postal officials in 1866. It was later shortened to Tama. Chief Tama was a Fox Indian, but some believed Tama was the wife of Chief Poweshiek, a chief of the Fox Indians. The name was interpreted as "beautiful," or "lovely." Manufacturing began when the Iowa River was dammed and a reservoir built in the 1870s.

TITONKA (Kossuth/584) Anticipation of the Cedar Rapids, Garner and Northwestern Railway determined the site of Titonka. George Dieckman donated forty acres of his property for the townsite and the land was surveyed in 1898. The same year the post office opened (Ella Graham, postmaster). Originally called Ripley, the name was changed because of duplication. Early settler W.H. Ingham suggested Titonka, a Sioux word for "big black," derived from ti tanka ("black buffalo"). It was also defined as "big house."

WASHTA (Cherokee/282) Andrew Whisman was the first settler in 1867 and established the post office along a stage road the next year. He also suggested the name Washta, a Sioux word meaning "good." The town moved to a new site in 1887 when the Illinois Central Railroad built a branch line and Washta became one of its stations. This town holds the record of the coldest temperature in Iowa. On January 12, 1912, the temperature extreme was minus 47 degrees Fahrenheit, and the record still stands.

WAUBEEK (Pepin) Waubeek is a former town that was located along the Wapsipinicon River and settled in 1855. Its most prominent citizen was Cadwallader Washburn who purchased more than 10,000 acres of timber land and established a sawmill. He left during the Civil War, and had to sell his property to clear his debts when he returned. Knapp, Stout and Company purchased his land, but instead of receiving cash, Cadwallader made a deal to get lumber at a future date. He became a millionaire after waiting for timber prices to rise, then sold the lumber at three times the original price. In 1870, the mill burned down and took the town with it. Waubeek was thought to have been named for an Indian princess, but it was also interpreted as "metal."

WAUCOMA (Fayette/299) Situated along the Little Turkey River, Waucoma was settled in 1855. The same year a grist mill (The Old Red Mill) and log dam were built, and the post office opened (Milo Goodell, postmaster). Goodell also owned the first hotel. The Chicago, Milwaukee and St. Paul Railway built its branch line to Waucoma in 1879, which operated until 1972. Waucoma was the wife of Chief Decorah. Her name means "snow comes" in the Winnebago language. It was also interpreted as a Winnebago word for "bad fish" and Ojibway for "the water is clean, clear."

WAUKON (Allamakee/4,131) In 1849 numerous springs attracted G.C. Shattuck, who agree to donate 40 acres if the town would be made county seat. Allamakee College was built in 1859 under the supervision of the Presbyterian Church. The Huffman family opened a photographic studio in 1865, and their son, Laton, went on to become a famous Plains frontier photographer. Waukon was named for Winnebago Chief Waukon (or Wawkon) Decorah, translated as "snake skin." In the Sioux language it means "spirit," designating something powerful or supernatural.

KANSAS

CHAUTAUQUA (Chautauqua/113) Mineral springs attracted settlers in 1881 who founded the town on the site of an old Indian trading post. The recreational and healing potential of the springs caused hotels to be built, and promoters celebrated the power of its curative water. When it was discovered that the springs held no medicinal value, the town went into a decline, losing much of its population. Chautauqua may be an Iroquois word meaning "foggy place," "one has taken fish here," or "bag tied in middle," descriptive of the lake's shape.

CHEROKEE (Crawford/722) When the Kansas City, Fort Scott & Gulf Railroad began construction, Cherokee was one of its stations. John Hoke and John Knox were the original property owners who donated their land to the railroad company. The town was platted in 1870 and named for the Cherokee Indians, derived from chelokee, which means "people of a different speech." It was also suggested the Choctaws gave the Cherokees the name chiluk-ki, meaning "cave people."

CHETOPA (Labette/1,281) Dr. George Lisle was the founder of Chetopa in 1857. This site was once an Osage village named for Chief Chetopa, meaning "houses four," designating a house for each of the chief's four wives. Chetopa continued to increase in population until the Civil War, when state rights and slavery issues came into play. The community was burned to the ground by William Quantrill the day Lincoln gave his Gettysburg Address.

ERIE (Neosho/1,211) This town was established in 1866 when the Erie Town Company was founded and its members donated 40 acres of their land for a townsite. The post office opened on April 6, 1866. The name comes from the Eriez Indians of the East, translated as "at the place of the panther (or cat)." In 1872, a fire destroyed most of the businesses, and a year later, a devastating cyclone came through. Erie suffered another blow when the railroad bypassed the town.

IUKA (Pratt/185) A group of men organized a wagon train that took them from the crowded cities of the East and brought them here. The post office was established on December 6, 1877 (Andrew Axine, postmaster). When the town company was formed in 1878, the site was called Ninnescah. Because of duplication, it was changed to Iuka, for an Indian Chief in Mississippi. His name was interpreted as "place of bathing," "place by the water," or from the Choctaw word iyukhana, meaning "where two roads cross."

KECHI (Sedgwick/1,038) Kechi is located about six miles north of Wichita. Jesse Chisolm mapped out the trail from Texas to Kansas in 1862, making Kechi a stopover point for cattlemen driving their herds to Abilene. Charles Sullivan organized Kechi township in 1870, and the Rock Island Railroad completed its line through town in 1888. The post office also opened the same year on May 29 (John F. Neher, postmaster). This community was originally a campground for the Kichai Indians, whose name means "walking in wet sand." The Pawnee Indians translated the word as "water turtle," and the white man's definition became "turtle in wet sand."

KIOWA (Barber/1,055) This settlement was established along the banks of the Medicine Lodge River in 1872. A town company was formed which purchased the site and named it for the Kiowa Indians ("principal people"). Another suggested the name came from kwuda, meaning "going out." The Southern Kansas Railroad extended its line in 1885, making Kiowa a major shipping point for livestock coming through the Cherokee Outlet. It lasted until President Harrison ordered all livestock removed from the Outlet.

LEOTI (Wichita/1,598) A group of men from Garden City conceived the idea of starting a town that would rival Chicago and named the site Leoti, meaning "prairie flower." On January 1, 1886, western Kansas experienced a terrible blizzard. Many settlers died because of the cold, and it was estimated more than eighty percent of the livestock perished. Still a tent town when the Denver, Memphis and Atlantic Railroad came through in 1887, Leoti went on to become county seat. Willard Meyer was the first postmaster on February 19, 1887.

MAHASKA (Washington/107) Mahaska was laid out in 1887 after a railroad was built, and the station called Bonham for a family who donated part of their land for a townsite. When the post office was established, the name had to be changed because of another community called Bonham. One of the settlers saw a coffee can that said "Mahaska Coffee," and decided to call the town Mahaska, an Iowa word that means "white swan," or "white cloud." The post office opened on December 22, 1887 (George M. Cook, postmaster).

MANHATTAN (Riley/44,831) The site was originally a Kaw Indian village. In 1854, two settlements were established, Canton (founded by a group of men from the east) and Poleska (created by Col. George S. Park), which were consolidated as Boston. The Cincinnati Company actually founded the town in 1855, selected by Professor Issac Goodnow, who changed the name to Manhattan, a Lenape word derived from menating, meaning "place that is an island." In 1863, the Kansas State

University was established here. The city is affectionately called "the Little Apple."

MUSCOTAH (Atchison/200) Muscotah is a Kickapoo or Potawatomi word that means "prairie on fire." It was also interpreted as "beautiful prairie." Another theory is a derivation of ma-shi-o-shkooteha, meaning "big fires," descriptive of the great prairie fires that swept through the region. Pioneers moved in and settled along the Little Grasshopper River after the Kickapoo Indians ceded a portion of their lands in 1854. The site was surveyed in 1856 by Dr. William Badger and Major C.B. Keith, and the post office was established on December 12, 1861 (Horace C. Pursel, postmaster).

NATOMA (Osborne/367) The first settler may have been Oscar Harkness, who filed a claim in 1874, borrowed money from a Colonel Stowe using his land for security, then went on a buffalo hunt. He never returned, and Stowe was given a deed to the property. When the Salina, Lincoln and Western Railway laid its tracks in 1888, the station was called Natoma for an Indian railroad worker, an Algonquin word for "new (or newly) born." This same year Stowe deeded his land to the Union Town Company, which surveyed the townsite.

NEKOMA (Rush) Early settlement began with the Walnut Valley and Colorado Railroad in 1887. The post office was established on June 23, 1890 (John W. Felch, postmaster), and a general merchandise and lumber company opened by Elmer Miller in 1893. In 1957, Nekoma experienced a terrible flood which brought in almost 12 inches of water that covered the town, and residents were unable to return for many weeks. Nekoma is a Chippewa word for "grandmother."

NEODESHA (Wilson/2,484) The township of Neodesha was created in 1869. It may be a corruption of an Osage word for "meeting of the waters," but it may be a coined word. A more accurate translation could be from Nioshode, meaning "the water is smoky with mud," describing the Verdigris and Fall rivers that were "slow running mud-cutters." The post office opened on June 13, 1870 (A.K. Phelon, postmaster). Establishment of the Missouri Pacific Railroad occurred in 1886. Neodesha experienced growth in the 1890s with the development of oil and gas in the region.

NEOSHO FALLS (Woodson/179) Nathanial Goss and I.W. Dow were the first settlers on April 6, 1857, and constructed a dam and sawmill on the Neosho River, calling the site Neosho Rapids. Goss established the post office the same year. Because there was another town by that name, it was changed to Neosho Falls, possibly derived from an Osage word for "clear or abundant water." A more accurate definition may be taken from necoitsahha, meaning "dead man's creek," a name the Indians gave the area because of a battle between the Kansas and Plains Indians.

NINNESCAH (Cowley) This town took its name from an Osage word translated as "abundant water," "white spring," "salt water," or "running white water." The original form of the word is Ninneskua (skua means "salt"). "Salt water" is the accepted name origin since the Indians used the salt springs in the area. Richard Freeman was postmaster in 1871.

NIOTAZE (Chautauqua/122) A community with many names, it was first called Jay Hawk in 1870 because the postal officials could not read the name on the application, then changed to Matanzas.

The Santa Fe and the Denver, Memphis and Atlanta Railroads bypassed the town in 1886, so residents moved closer to the tracks and renamed that site Niota. Because of confusion with the town of Neola, it was renamed Niota in 1887 with a "ze" added. It may be a coined Siouan word translated as "water river." A post office and volunteer fire department are all that remain today.

OKETO (Marshall/87) Located along the California Trial, Oketo was a frontier trading post. It bordered the Big Blue River, a favorite rendezvous for trappers and Indians. Ben Holliday operated the Overland Stageline and established the "Oketo Cutoff." The stage followed the cutoff but bypassed Oketo, so the town was rebuilt across the river. The name was derived from an Oto Chief named Arkaketah, which means "stands by it." On a treaty, he spelled his name Arkekeetah ("stay by it"). His name was shortened to Oketa because settlers could not pronounce Arkaketah.

OLATHE (Johnson/92,962) Olathe was established in 1857 after the Shawnee Indians ceded their tribal lands. John Barton was appointed physician to the Indians during the 1850s and asked Chief Joseph Parks what "beautiful" meant in the Shawnee language. Parks stated it was olathe. The post office opened on May 4, 1857 (John T. Barton, postmaster). By 1863, Olathe was a major jumping-off place for stages and wagon trains headed for the Santa Fe or Oregon-California trails. Olathe Naval Air Base is located here, which is an important training center in aircraft maneuvers.

ONAGA (Potawatomi/704) Onaga is situated in the northeast part of the county. Paul E. Havens, President of the Kansas Central Railroad, founded and platted the town in 1877. He wanted to give the site an Indian name and asked an Indian agent if Onaga was the name of a Potawatomi chief. The agent replied that Onaha (or Onaje) was just an Indian, but the origin was never translated.

OZAWKIE (Jefferson/552) In 1854, the Delaware Indians ceded their land to the U.S., which opened the area for land sales. When the L&T Railroad was built, Ozawkie was one of its stations. The post office was established on March 15, 1855 (George Dyer, postmaster). The town had to relocate when the U.S. Army Corps of Engineers built a dam and lake across the Delaware River in the 1960s. Ozawkie was derived from a Delaware or Sac word that means "yellow earth."

PENOKEE (Graham) Ben Chadsen was instrumental in the founding of this town when he procured the services of the Union Land Company to plat the site in 1884. Four years later the Lincoln & Colorado Railroad laid its tracks. The site was named Reford, but caused confusion with mail delivery to the town of Rexford. Railroad officials selected Penokee for the Penokee Mountains located in Wisconsin. The name may be a corruption of the Chippewa word pewabic, which means "iron."

QUENEMO (Osage/468) Quenemo was once the original site of an Indian agency. Disease and settlers' efforts to take over the land led to a reduction in tribe sizes, and the Indians were removed to reservations in 1870. This site was named for Sauk chief Quenemo, which means "I am lonely." Other sources believe it meant something like "Oh my God," or a cry of despair. Quenemo had a number of railroads come through: the Santa Fe in 1885; the Pea Vine in 1885; the Missouri Pacific in 1886; and the same year the Kansas, Nebraska & Dakota line was built. By the 1970s, the population had dwindled due to floods that put most of the town under water.

SATANTA (Haskell/1,239) Once just cattle range, it was 1912 when the town was established by the Santa Fe Railroad which named it Satanta, for chief of the Kiowa Indians. It was derived from Set-t'ainte, meaning "white bear." Although Satanta was known as a brutal man, he was also called the "Orator of the Plains" because of his eloquence and directness. The settlers were mainly farmers, as are many today. In addition, oil and natural gas production are part of the town's economic stability.

SENECA (Nemaha/2,122) In 1857, J.B. Ingersoll staked off a portion of land he called Castle Rock, but the town company changed it to Seneca, for the Seneca Indians ("people of the stone"). The post office opened on November 5, 1858 (John E. Smith, postmaster). In 1870, O.C. Bruner surveyed the site and the St. Joseph & Grand Island Railroad arrived the same year. One of Seneca's big industries during the 1870s was a barb wire works.

SHAWNEE (Johnson/47,996) The town took its name from the Shawnee Indians, from shawun, meaning "southerner." The site was chosen in 1828 as Indian headquarters for the newly created Shawnee Reservation. It was also the first stopping point in Kansas along the Santa Fe Trail. The post office was established in July 1858 (M.P. Randall, postmaster). During the Civil War the town was pillaged and almost destroyed by guerillas led by William Quantrill.

TONGANOXIE (Leavenworth/2,728) This was a stop on a stage line that went from Fort Leavenworth to Fort Scott in the 1840s. The U.S. government built Delaware chief Tonganoxie a cabin and tavern which also served as a stagecoach stop. Tonganoxie means "little man," because the chief was a short and stocky person. He was recognized by the U.S. government as a great leader of his tribe and lived to be 70 years of age. Mrs. Magdalena Berry purchased the site from the Union Pacific Railroad and had it platted in 1866. The post office had already been established on March 16, 1863 (William English postmaster).

TOPEKA (Shawnee/122,377) Three French-Canadian brothers were among the first permanent settlers who established a ferry service in 1842. Anti-slavery settlers drew up an agreement in 1854 which began the Topeka Association and the city's growth. Topeka developed slowly because of a drought in 1860, followed by the Civil War. The name may be a Kaw word meaning "a good place to dig potatoes," descriptive of the rich bottom land where wild potatoes grew. But Rydjord cuts holes in this theory with citations of numerous interpretations.[15]

TOWANDA (Butler/1,338) C.L. Chandler was an early settler in 1860 after giving up his search for gold. The post office was established on December 13 the same year (Albert S. Blackstone, postmaster). James R. Mead purchased land, built a trading post, and Towanda served as a commerce center for the region. In 1870, Reverend Isaac Mooney purchased the Mead property and founded the town. The name may be an Osage word that means "many waters," or "rushing waters," descriptive of a gushing spring near town.

WABAUNSEE (Wabaunsee/646) Reverend Henry W. Beecher persuaded his congregation to make the westward movement and find a place where they could live in an anti-slavery state. The Brooklyn

Church supplied money for rifles for protection which enabled the Beecher Bible and Rifle Colony to found Wabaunsee in 1856. The post office was established on December 29, 1855 (John H. Nesbitt as postmaster). Wabaunsee was named for a Potawatomi chief. His name meant "dawn of day," from wabonishi, or "causer of paleness." Wabaunsee signed a peace treaty in 1835 which gave away the remainder of Potawatomi ancestral lands in exchange for land to the west.

WAMEGO (Potawatomi/4,246) A child of the Kansas Pacific Railroad, the site was surveyed by railroad engineers in 1866. Since Chief Wamego was friends with the surveyors, they named the town for him. The post office opened on October 11, 1866 (Leonard Prunty, postmaster). The community served as a port of entry for Louisville. Wamego may have been derived from wah-me-go, meaning "passing away," or a Cheyenne word that means "clear springs." It was also interpreted as "running water."

WATHENA (Doniphan/1,348) Peter Cadue, an Indian trader and interpreter for the Kickapoo Indians, was an early resident. After he left, no permanent settlement occurred until 1852, when Kickapoo Chief Wathenah settled here (origin unknown). Settlers later used his wigwam as a church. He later sold his land to Milton Bryan, who became postmaster. A railroad was supposed to be built, but Congress failed to vote bonds for continued construction when it discovered some of the backers were for the Confederacy.

WICHITA (Sedgewick/344,284) J.R. Mead built a trading post on the banks of the Arkansas River in 1868 and the site was named for the Wichita Indians, meaning "scattered lodges," "painted faces," or from wechate, meaning "red river people." The post office was established on February 17, 1869 (Milo B. Kellogg, postmaster). Wichita went on to become the "Cow Capital of the West," where hundreds of thousands of cattle came via the Santa Fe and Chisholm Trails to Wichita to be sold. By 1880, farmers had put up fences across the trails, forcing cattlemen to drive their livestock west to Dodge City. Wichita regained its economy with its wealth of wheat crops and the discovery of oil.

KENTUCKY

ELKATAWA (Jackson) Located southeast of Jackson, Elkatawa was established in 1891, the same year the post office opened (Eli Jones, postmaster). Settlers named the town after a Shawnee shaman named Tenskwautawa who was the brother of Chief Tecumseh. The name signified a prophet. The Kentucky Union Railway was built through town in 1890. Coal mining began in earnest when the Hurst Coal Company was established in 1917.

KINNICONICK (Lewis) This little

village is located along Kinniconick Creek, and is a Shawnee word for "willow bark," descriptive of the willows prevalent in the region. It may also be a name that meant a substitute for tobacco, or the plant producing it. A post office served the area off and on from 1820 until the 1950s. Thomas Harrison built the Kinniconick Hotel in the early 1800s, which is still in existence.

KUTTAWA (Lyon/596) William and John Kelley purchased property to start an iron forge in the 1830s. Charles Anderson, Lieutenant Governor of Ohio in 1836, retired here and bought the Kelley property in 1866. His influence brought in more settlers to start their businesses. As a result, the town progressed rapidly in industry and commercial ventures. The post office was established in 1872 (Andrew P. Comant, postmaster). Kuttawa may have been a Delaware or Shawnee word for "great wilderness," or may have been the name of an old Cherokee village. It was also suggested the name meant "beautiful," or "city in the woods."

PADUCAH (McCracken/26,307) This town is situated along the Tennessee River and was once home to the Chickasaw Indians. Although George R. Clark claimed the site in 1795, settlement did not occur until the Chickasaws signed a treaty in 1818. Lumber became a thriving industry at Paducah. Because of its proximity to the Tennessee and Ohio rivers, the town became an important junction point, followed by establishment of locomotive repair shops. Paducah was a Chickasaw chief whose name was derived from pakutukah or po'ki tukali, meaning "a place where the grapes hang down." Another definition was "tall chestnut tree."

LOUISIANA

AMITE (Tangipahoa/4,110) Before 1827, this region was home to the Choctaw Indians. Surveyor Major S.M. Wentz laid out the town in 1860 and named it Amite, of which there are many interpretations. Some believe it is a Choctaw word that means "red ant," supposedly to signify thrift. Others think it is a French word for "friendship" or derived from the Choctaw word himmita (corrupted by the French), meaning "young." Industry began in 1869 when the Gullett Gin Company moved its business from Mississippi. The post office opened in 1872 (C.S. Stewart, postmaster).

ANACOCO (Vernon/866) In 1835, Reverend Luke Conerly was instrumental in the establishment of the Holly Grove Methodist Church at Anacoco, believed to be the oldest Methodist church west of the Mississippi. In 1875, J. Kirk became the first postmaster. In addition to cotton, timber stimulated the town's economy, but by 1928 logging companies had depleted the forests. Anacoco may be derived from a Caddo word that means "muddy sands," descriptive of a local creek.

BAYOU GOULA (Iberville) This is the

oldest settlement in the Parish and home to the Bayougoula Indians (a Muskhogean tribe) who were discovered by Frenchman Iberville about 1699. During the same time frame, the first Catholic church was established by Father Du Ru, a Jesuit who worked among the Bayougoula Indians. The name is derived from the Choctaw words bayuk and okla, interpreted as "river people." The smallest church in America is nearby. Only the Celebrant and Acolyte will fit inside, and all who attend church must listen to services outside.

BOGALUSA (Washington/13,365) Taking its name from the creek, Bogalusa comes from the Choctaw words bok and lusa, meaning "creek black." Located in a heavily wooded pine belt, a laboratory and forest school were established to experiment with different species of trees. The town grew up around the Great Southern Lumber Mill founded in the early 1900s by Charles and Frank Goodyear. When the Pennsylvania hemlock was depleted, other timber sources had to be found, so Charles Goodyear III established the Bogalusa Tung Oil Company in 1906. William Sullivan, general manager of the lumber mill, had a railhead built from Pearl River to Bogue Lusa Creek, and was considered the town's founder.

CARENCRO (Lafayette/6,120) Originally home to the Attakapas Indians, very few white men ventured into the area during the first half of the 18th century. Exiled Acadians from Nova Scotia migrated to Carencro, raising cattle and engaging in agriculture. Carencro has been interpreted from the Spanish word carnero, which means "bone pile," to carencro, a French word for "buzzard (or carrion crow)." Others believe the name came from the Karankawa or Karaulcrow Indians, or a Choctaw word meaning "maneaters."

CHACAHOULA (Terrebonne) When the Opelousas and New Orleans Railroad came through this swampland in 1852, it brought an influx of Catholic settlers. Armogene Aycock donated land for a church, and the St. Lawrence Church Parish was completed in 1858. Cypress trees brought in the timber men until the trees were depleted, forcing residents to seek work elsewhere. When oil was discovered in the 1940s, supporting industries were established. Chacahoula (also spelled Chuckahoola) was translated from Choctaw as "beloved home," derived from chuka ("home") and hullo ("beloved").

COUSHATTA (Red River/2,299) A band of Indians known as Koasati were part of the Muskhogean tribe who moved here from Alabama about 1793. Coushatta, derived from Koasati, means "white reed brake," for the canes that grew around the Indian settlement. The Coushatta Riot occurred in 1874 when members of the White League quelled an uprising of Negroes led by carpetbaggers who were threatening to wipe out the white men. When the Louisiana Railway & Navigation Company was built in 1898, the town moved its businesses closer to the train depot.

HOUMA (Terrebone/32,393) The Houma Indians may have actually come from Natchez, Mississippi, since LaSalle mentioned that he found a number of Oumas there. After the Tunica tribe massacred the Houmas in 1706, they moved to this area. Hubert Belanger and Richard Grinage donated part of their property in 1834 for a townsite. Houma is derived from the Choctaw words humma (or homma), meaning "red," signifying the Indians' practice of painting their bodies red. Some believe it means "red crawfish," the tribe's war emblem.

KEATCHIE (DeSoto/323) Keatchie

started out as a trading post in the mid–1800s, and was located along the Houston and Shreveport Railroad. The name may have originated from kichai, a Caddo word that means "panther." A women's college was built about 1852, followed by a railroad established by the Houston East and West Transportation Company.

MANCHAC (Tangipahoa) This little fishing settlement is located just south of Ponchatoula along the Illinois-Central Railroad line. The post office was established in 1894 as Akers (William Akers, postmaster). Manchac sustained itself as a lumber town, in addition to truck farming. The town is located at Pass Manchac, which is a channel that connects Lakes Pontchartrain and Maurepas. Manchac was derived from imashaka, a Choctaw word for "rear entrance."

MARINGOUIN (Iberville/1,262) Early explorers came through in the late 1600s and experienced fierce flying insects they called marigoui, a word found in the Indian dialects of Brazil. Surveyors were mapping the area in 1831 when they were attacked by a swarm of huge black mosquitoes, so they called the site Maringouin, theorized to be a Choctaw word for "mosquito." When the Texas and Pacific Railroad was built in 1882, the town became one of its stations. The post office opened in 1897.

MERMENTAU (Acadia/721) Once a haven for pirates and smugglers and a crossing along the Old Spanish Trail, settlement began about 1802 a little south of the present site. Jean Gastex (or Castex) was one of the earliest residents who established a sawmill and grist mill. Most of the prairie settlers built their home with wood from his mill. He also built the first cotton gin in the county about 1860. William Cottrell became postmaster when the post office opened in 1857, and the Louisiana Western Railroad reached town in 1880. Mermentau was derived from an Attakapas Indian named Nementou. Although its significance has been lost, some interpreted his name as "sea cow."

NATALBANY (Tangipahoa/1,739) Natalbany is a Choctaw word that could mean "lone bear," or "bear camp," as written, "...Nita Albany, or Bean-Camp, at Lake Maurepas ... someone almost assuredly dealt in the curing of bear meat along the Natalbany River."[16] The town's main industry was timber. After the New Orleans, Natalbany and Natchez Railway was chartered in 1902, it began operating between Natalbany and Grangeville hauling timber to the mill. During the late 1930s, the lumber company closed its doors, relegating Natalbany to a bedroom community.

NATCHITOCHES (Natchitoches/17,865) The oldest town in the state, Natchitoches began as a French trading/military post in 1714, and was named for a Caddo Chief's son, interpreted as "paw-paw eaters," or "chestnut eaters." Others believe it comes from nacicit, meaning "a place where the soil is the color of red ochre," descriptive of a creek that ran through red soil. It was predicted that Natchitoches would become as large New Orleans and gain importance as a place of riverboat commerce. But it never occurred, because the "great raft" was removed from Red River, causing it to cut a new course away from the town, leaving Natchitoches without its means of transportation.

OPELOUSAS (Opelousas/22,860) The French were the first white men to settle in this region (1690) until the Spanish took over and built a post in 1765. The site was home to the friendly Opelousas Indians, although they were thought to be an offshoot of the cannibalistic Attakapa tribe. The name has been deciphered as "man with black leg," descriptive of the Indians' legs that were darker than the rest of their bodies. It was also interpreted from aba lusa, meaning "black headed" or "black haired." During the 1700s, the Acadians from Canada were expelled and migrated to the Opelousas region. They later became known as the Cajuns.

PLAQUEMINE (Iberville/7,064) The town took its name from the bayou. Early explorers discovered the banks of a stream lined with persimmon trees. Plaquemine is a French-Creole word derived from the Illinois Indian word, plakimin, for "persimmon." The fruit was used by the Indians to make a type of bread they called plakmine ("dried persimmons"). This community was founded in 1755 on Bayou Plaquemine. The first railroad in the parish was completed in 1859, used mainly for transporting troops during the Civil War.

PONCHATOULA (Tangipahoa/5,180) Ponchatoula was founded by William Akers in 1832 when he purchased more than 1,000 acres from the U.S. government. Previous to his arrival, the area was a logging camp. Akers named the place Ponchatoula, in honor of a friendly Choctaw chief. The name signified "falling (or flowing) hair," descriptive of the Spanish moss growing on the trees. Another translation was from ponchatalawa, translated as "singing hair." This was in error, and should actually be defined as "singing cattails." An important industry for Ponchatoula was strawberries, after Robert Cloud introduced his famous Klondike stock.

SHONGALOO (Webster/162) The Caddo Indians occupied what became one of the oldest settlements in Webster Parish. They fished and hunted the region until the white man intruded on their territory and they were forced to move on. The Caddo Indians called this place Shakalo (or Shakato), from which Shongaloo is derived. The meaning is uncertain, but some authorities believe it is for "running water," or from the Choctaw word shakolo, for "cypress tree."

TANGIPAHOA (Tangipahoa/747) Rhoda Singleton, known as "Granny" Mixon, was considered the founder of Tangipahoa. She accumulated considerable land and had the first house built in town. When the Illinois Central Railroad went through in 1854, the site was divided into lots and platted. Between 1866 and 1870, Tangipahoa grew into a prosperous cotton shipping center. The name was interpreted from the Choctaw word, tanchapi, meaning "cornstalk gatherers."

TICKFAW (Tangiphahoa/617) During this town's early settlement, the area served as a turnaround station for the Illinois Central Railroad. Tickfaw is derived from the Choctaw words tiak and foha, which mean "pine rest," an apt name since Tickfaw was a lumber town. It was also translated as "wild beasts shed their hair," from poa and tikafa, also Choctaw. Many of the people who came to work the timber emigrated from Italy, and today the town's population is mainly Sicilian.

MAINE

ALLAGASH (Aroostook/277) Many of today's residents are descendents of American Loyalists who moved to the region in 1783. Although the Gardner family and William Mullins were here in 1838, establishment of the town did not occur until 1886. Allagash is an Abnaki word for "bark cabin." The town depended on the timber industry, in addition to farming hay and grain. Allagash has a special program called "Precious Memories" for terminally ill children, which hosts numerous events the children will never forget.

ASTICOU (Hancock) Explorer Samuel de Champlain arrived in 1604 and named the island Deseret. Severe fighting broke out when England and France tried to claim the island, followed by the American Revolution. After the war, wealthy settlers used the island as a vacation getaway. Augustus Savage and his family moved to the village of Asticou about 1790, and later built the Asticou Inn. Chief Asticou was a Penobscot Indian whose name means "boiling kettle," or "deep river."

CHEBEAGUE ISLAND (Cumberland) The island was once a summer retreat for the Maine Indians who gave Chebeague its name, an Abnaki word meaning "island of many springs," or "almost separated." George Cleeves held the original grant and gave the island to Walter Merry in 1650. Zachariah Chandler took title in 1746 and cleared the land for settlement, which occurred after the American Revolution. Chebeague depended, for the most part, on the rock slooping industry, which was used to build lighthouses and breakwaters. In the mid–1800s, Chebeague's economy turned to the tourist industry.

DAMARISCOTTA (Lincoln/2,041) John Brown purchased land in 1625 from a Wawenock Indian named Samoset. Settlers arrived about 1730 and made their living in timber and agriculture. Shipbuilding later came into prominence, since the town was at the head of navigation of the Damariscotta River. During the 1940s, clams were an important local industry. Damariscotta was translated in 1798 by an Abnaki Indian named Sabatis, who told a reverend the name meant "many little alewives." It was also interpreted as "the place of abundance of fishes."

KENDUSKEAG (Penobscot/1,171) Samuel de Champlain came up the Kenduskeag Stream in 1605 and found an Indian village he called Kadesquit. This was the place where the French and Indian river trade was conducted. The village was created when the towns of Glenburn and Levant were "cut" and Kenduskeag formed in 1852. The name was taken from the stream, which comes from a Quoddy (or Maliseet) word meaning "eel-weir place." Kenduskeag's economy was based on lumber, which included the manufacture of shingles and barrels.

KENNEBUNK (York/10,476) Situated between the Kennebunk and Mousam rivers, Kennebunk began its development about 1650. It was originally part of the town of Wells until 1820. Because of the site's proximity to the rivers, shipbuilding and trade with the West Indies were important industries. Development of the timber industry also lent to the local economy. Shipbuilding continued until 1918. Kennebunk is an Abnaki word meaning "the long cut bank," or "long sandbar," designating an Indian landmark at the mouth of the Mousam River.

MACHIAS (Washington/2,353) Englishmen established a trading post here after the Plymouth Colony was destroyed in 1633. This coastal town was settled in 1763 by people who fled the great fires in western Maine, and were drawn to the timber and salt marshes. Since Machias was located along the Machias River, it was an important lumber and shipbuilding center. Machias means "bad little falls," or "a bad run of water," an Abnaki word signifying a section of the Machias River that drops down into deep gorge.

MADAWASKA (Aroostook/4,534) Madawaska was founded by the Acadians in 1785, who came from St. Anne Des Pays-Bas, New Brunswick. The name was derived from madoueskak, which may be a Micmac word for "porcupine place." Other definitions were "grass lands extending to the river banks," and "a junction of rivers." Timber was intensely exploited in the 1880s and lasted for about 50 years. Another source of revenue was maple sugar. The trees were tapped around March and processed by hand. Today, the maple sugar industry is totally mechanized.

MATINICUS ISLAND (Knox/51) Located about 20 miles south of Rockland, this small island is only two and a half miles long and one mile wide. The name has been defined as "place of many turkeys." It may have come from manasquesicook, an Abnaki word for "a collection of grassy islands," or "far out island." Cod fishing was an important industry, in addition to ship building and outfitting ships for the West Indies trade during the 1840s.

MATTAWAMKEAG (Penobscot/825) The earliest recorded history of Mattawamkeag was in 1624 when M. Devilliere met with Chief Taxous. While Joseph Chadwick was passing through in 1764 searching for a new route to Quebec, he wrote in his field notes: "Mederwomkeag is an Indine Town & a place of resedence in time of War, but mostly vacated...."[17] The site was a staging area for the army during the Bloodless Aroostook War in 1838. Mattawamkeag is an Abnaki word that means "the river that runs through it," or "a river with many rocks at its mouth." The latter refers to the large gravel bar at the entrance of the Mattawamkeag River. It was also interpreted as a Micmac word for "on a sand bar," and "fishing place beyond gravel bar."

MEDDYBEMPS (Washington/150) The Etchemin ("canoe people") Tribe used this region as a camping place because the lake outlet was an ideal place to catch salmon, shad, and alewives. The population had grown large enough by 1841 that portions of the towns of Charlotte and Baring were separated to form the new community. Residents named it Meddybemps, Abnaki for "plenty of alewives."

MILLINOCKET (Penobscot/5,203) Located in the lakes region of the county, Millinocket was founded in 1829 with the arrival of Thomas Fowler. Bog iron ore was discovered about 1843 but was not profitable because of lack of transportation and inaccessibility. Charles Mullen and Garret Schenck took advantage of the forest resources and established the Great Northern Paper Company (newsprint plant) on the Penobscot River. Millinocket is an Abnaki word for "many islands," or "this place is admirable."

MONHEGAN ISLAND (Lincoln/75) This rocky island is about ten miles off the coast of Maine, and was named by the local Indians (who may have been Micmacs), which means "island of the sea," or "out to sea island." It was a landmark for sailors, headquarters for exploring expeditions, and a place for men to trade furs with the Indians. Early residents made their living fishing for lobsters. Today the small population is still engaged in the industry.

NORRIDGEWOCK (Somerset/3,294) Jesuit Priest Father Biart visited in 1610 to work with the Norridgewock Indians. Father Sebastian Rasle arrived in 1695 and worked with the Indians for more than 30 years. He also wrote the Abnaki dictionary. It was 1772 before permanent settlement. Growing potatoes was a sustaining industry, in addition to raising and selling sheep. Norridgewock refers to the location of the Abnaki Indian village, "smooth water below," or "between the falls." Another definition was "where swift water descends."

OGUNQUIT (York/1,226) In 1641, Edmund Littlefield built a sawmill at the falls of the Webhannet River, bringing a thriving business to the settlement. Ogunquit was translated from a Micmac word, pog-um-ik, meaning "lagoons formed at mouths of rivers by dune beaches driven by the wind," or from obumkegg, for "sand bar." Another interpretation was "place of waves," from antegw-quit. It was also thought Ogunquit was a Natick word meaning "a beautiful place by the sea," but there was no Natick Indian tribe; rather they called themselves Natick because of the part of country in which they lived. They were named the Praying Indians by missionary John Eliot.

ORONO (Penobscot/9,112) Joseph Orono was chief of the Penobscot Tribe and lived at this site before the white settlers arrived, and from whom the town takes its name. He was kind to the new arrivals and always tried to keep the peace. Orono was not a full-blooded Indian; his father was French, and his mother half French and half Indian. The town was initially called Stillwater, and later changed to Orono (origin unknown). Its growth was stifled by the War of 1812 when the British destroyed the coastal trade. After the war, the timber industry came into prominence.

PASSADUMKEAG (Penobscot/441) The Indians who roamed the region were called Red Paint People as evidenced by artifacts found near Passadumkeag. Early inhabitants were Enoch and Joshua Ayers in 1813. The Passadumkeag River provided water power for the manufacture of shingles and staves, shipped out via the European & North American Railroad. The town took its name from the Passadumkeag River (a branch of the Penobscot River), Abnaki for "above the gravel bar," "stream above falls," "falls running over gravelly bed," or "quick water."

PEMAQUID (Lincoln) The Wawenocks were a peaceful tribe who camped along these shores. Pemaquid is an Abnaki word that means "situated far out," or Micmac for "extended land." It is a village within the town of Bristol. Permanent settlement began about 1625 when John Brown purchased Pemaquid for 50 beaver pelts from two Wawenock sachems, Samoset and Unogoit. The village became a port of entry for the British shipping supplies between the St. Croix and Kennebec rivers. During King Philip's War, the people abandoned the site, and it would be almost 20 years before anyone returned.

PENOBSCOT (Hancock/1,344) Situated along the Penobscot River, the site was first known as Majorbagaduce ("big tidal salt bay"). The town was established in 1785 as Penobscot, Abnaki for "where the rocks spread out," or "descending ledge place." Jeremiah Wardwell was a prominent citizen who helped the town's growth by financing construction of a school and church. In 1840, more than 2,000 coins were found, some of which were Spanish pieces of eight. The money may have been hidden by pirates or buried by a family named deCastin. The coins are now in the possession of the Maine Historical Society.

SACO (York/16,822) Although a few people lived here in the 1600s, constant Indian uprisings prevented much settlement until about 1752. William Pepperell was a driving force in the growth of the community when he donated some his land for a townsite and named it Pepperellborough. In 1805, the name was changed to Saco because it was easier to pronounce. It is an Abnaki word for "flowing out," or may be derived from sawacotuck, for "mouth of tidal stream." Cotton mills were the backbone of the town, with the Saco Manufacturing Company the biggest in the world.

SEBAGO (Cumberland/1,433) This region was originally home to the Presumpscots who were a subtribe of the Sokokis ("people of the outlet") Indians. Sebago was founded in 1826, and originally part of Baldwin. Joseph Laken purchased part of the property and the new site was named Flintstown. It was later changed to Sebago (for Lake Sebago which the Indians called sebug), and means "big stretch of water." Today, the town is a popular resort area.

SKOWHEGAN (Somerset/8,824) The Red Paint Indians established settlements along the banks of the Kennebec River thousands of years ago, followed by the Abnaki Indians. Settlers were drawn to the timber and river resources in the 1770s. Abner Coburn was an early settler who went on to become one of Maine's Civil War governors. Senator Margaret Chase Smith was also born here. The town grew to be predominantly a manufacturing center. Skowhegan is an Abnaki word for "a place to watch," and refers to the Kennebec River where the Indians watched for salmon.

WISCASSET (Lincoln/3,603) This site was named Pownalborough for Royal Governor Pownal. George and John Davies purchased land from the Indians about 1600. After the Indian wars began in 1676, the site was abandoned and wasn't resettled until 1729. Wiscasset was one of the largest working eastern waterfronts because of its deep harbor. After the Revolution, growth continued with the sea trade until the Embargo Act went into effect in 1807, crippling the industry. Wiscasset was derived from Wichcasset, an Abnaki word meaning "at the outlet." Others have defined it as "meeting of three tides," and "at the hidden outlet."

MARYLAND

CHAPTICO (St. Marys) Chaptico got its start in 1689 when Lord Baltimore ordered the region surveyed and towns built. One of Maryland's oldest hamlets, Chaptico was derived from the friendly Choptico Indians, which means "big broad river that is." The town was established as a river port of entry for St. Mary's County. In 1814, the British came to Chaptico, ransacking the town. The Alexandria Herald wrote: "...their conduct would have disgraced cannibals;... the sunken graves were converted into barbecue holes."[18] The old Christ Church that was built in 1736 was badly damaged. The church's chalice, which dates back to 1771, is still in use today.

CHATTOLANEE (Baltimore) This hamlet is a historic black community established during slavery years. After the Civil War was over, the white population induced the Blacks to stay here by giving them homes and building them a church. The Green Spring United Methodist Church was established in 1880 and is still supported by members. About 1889, W.L. Stock and a number of prominent businessmen came to Chattolanee because of its pure spring water and built a hotel as a summer resort to draw in wealthy clients (it was torn down in the 1920s). The name comes from a Piscataway word that means "clear water," or may be an imported Muskohegan word for "yellow rock."

CONOWINGO (Cecil) Tradition says the Susquehannock Indians settled here and named the region Conewago, which meant "at the falls (or rapids)." Historians believe that as far back as 1884 the Susquehanna Water, Power and Paper Company was granted a charter by the Maryland legislature to condemn the land and build a dam. But it only built part of the dam; actual completion did not occur until about 1926, and "residents ... watched with mingled emotions as the sites of their homes were slowly but irrevocably submerged beneath the great backflow of the Susquehanna River...."[19] Today, the original Conowingo is under 90 feet of water, and the new village consists of a few small businesses, in addition to local farmlands.

LONACONING (Allegany/1,205) Lonaconing grew up around the coal mines in 1835. John Alexander and Philip Tyson were granted the right to create the George's Creek Coal and Iron Company, and the first iron furnace was completed in 1837. Living out its life as a coal company town directed by investor capital, the people's lives were not their own until the 1850s. Lonaconing may have been for an Indian scout named Nemacolin, or derived from Algonquin words meaning "where many waters meet," "the great right hand pass," or "stream where the going is bad."

MATTAWOMAN (Charles) No longer in existence, Mattawoman was a small village near the headwaters of Mattawoman Creek. Derived from mataughquamend, Mattawoman is a Piscataway word meaning "where one goes pleasantly." In the 1600s, Captain John Smith met the Piscataway Indians during his explorations, which was the Indians' first contact with the whites. The Mattawoman Indians were part of the Piscataways, principal tribe of the Conoy Federation.

NANJEMOY (Charles) Nanjemoy Creek was named for the Indian village of Nushemoick (or Nussame-k), meaning "one goes downward." Others derived it from the Algonquin word nachenumook, for "raccoon," or "haunt of raccoons." One of the first buildings was a grist mill in the 1880s, using the water power from Mill Brook. The mill operated until the late 1940s. Nanjemoy was the first town selected as a major telephone company's testing field for its new system using underground lines.

NANTICOKE (Wicomico) The Nanticokes were an Algonquin tribe who lived along the Nanticoke River, and in 1608 Captain John Smith found their village. When the Maryland Colony was settled, settlers did not get along with the Indians, and as a result reservations were set aside in the late 1600s. Nanticoke prospered with the oyster industry in the late 1800s, and dredging of the harbor brought in a number of seafood companies. The name is derived from nentego, a variant of the Delaware word unalachtgo, which means "tidewater people."

POCOMOKE CITY (Worcester/4,098) The largest town in the county, Pocomoke was established in 1700 as a meeting house called Warehouse Landing, and later changed to New Town. It became Pocomoke City in 1878, translated from Algonquin as "it is pierced," or "broken ground." Located along the Pocomoke River, the city's economy was tied to shipping tobacco and agricultural products. When the New York, Philadelphia and Norfolk Railroad came through, Pocomoke turned to timber, and later to shipbuilding.

POTOMAC (Montgomery/44,822) This site was originally inhabited by the Canaya Tribe, who were part of the Susquehannock Nation, until the site was settled as Offutt's Crossroads in 1724. The name was changed in 1881 because postal officials wanted a shorter name. Major John McDonald is credited with selecting Potomac, an Algonquin word meaning "where something is brought." Located only 15 miles from the Nation's Capitol, the town became home to the wealthy (as it is today).

MASSACHUSSETS

ACUSHNET (Bristol/10,161) Throughout history, Acushnet has been spelled at least 60 different ways on old court and church records, deeds, and wills. Derived from acushena, it is a Wampanoag word for "swimming place," or "wet place." A tribe of Indians from the Wampanoag Federation known as the Cushenas lived in the region until settlement in 1639. Located along the Acushnet River, the town was a port for whalers and shipbuilding. With the demise of the whaling industry, residents went to work at New Bedford in cotton manufacturing plants.

AGAWAM (Hampden/28,144) In 1631, two Indians from the Agawam Tribe went to Boston and asked that people from the

Massachusetts Bay Colony settle their land. They told prospective settlers they would give them a yearly tribute if they would do so. This offer was made so the settlers could protect them from the Mohawk Indians. The site was called Springfield in 1640, and later named after the Agawam River, an Algonquin word for "crooked river," "low land," "place to unload canoes," or "fish curing place."

ANNISQUAM (Essex) Abraham Robinson established fishing stages and flake yards at Annisquam in 1631. Squam is Abnaki for "harbor" or "end of the rock." "Annis" was added and may have been for Queen Anne. The region had a half-dozen shipyards and was one of the first shipbuilding ports on the Atlantic seaboard. Extensive commercial fishing and lobster activity began in the 1700s and continued until about 1870. Annisquam was home to Dr. Isaac Adams, Jr., who invented the nickel-plating process.

AQUINNAH (Dukes/344) This community did not receive its Indian name until 1998. Bartholomew Gosnold was probably the first explorer to see the peninsula in 1602. During the 1660s, the site was named Gay Head, descriptive of the gaily colored cliffs. This was home to the Wampanoag Indians, as it is today. Although the Commonwealth of Massachusetts tried to take control of Gay Head, the Indians were able to maintain their control. During the 17th century, the Wampanoags taught the colonists how to kill whales and plant their corn. Aquinnah is derived from the Wampanoag word acquiadene-auke," meaning "land under the hill," descriptive of the topography.

ASSINIPPI (Plymouth) Assinippi is a part of the town of Norwell. The village was formed in 1766 when members of the Congregational Society asked that the southern section be set off as a separate entity. Many of the colonists engaged in producing salt marsh hay. Others were skilled craftsmen who made shoes, but had to travel to another town to the larger shoe factories. In need of transportation, citizens from the two villages sold stock and were granted a franchise which enabled the Hanover Street Railroad Company to lay its track through Assinippi. The name means "rocky water," and referred to a branch of the Third Herring Brook.

ASSONET (Bristol) A tract of land known as Ye Freemen's Purchase was transacted in 1659. Wamsitti deeded the land, which was broken up into lots and formed into distinct communities, to 26 people, one of which was Assonet. John Barnes' portion became Assonet village. The name signifies a Narragansett Indian song of praise or "at the rock." In 1671, an Indian named Awashonk claimed the Freemen's Purchase was invalid. The Plymouth Colony government stated the land was purchased in good faith, but Awashonk disagreed. He eventually recognized the original purchase.

CATAUMET (Barnstable) Cataumet is a village in the town of Bourne, and named for Wampanoag chief Kitteaumut (or Kataumet), translated as "at the ocean," or "landing place near open sea." About 1665, Robert Lawrence purchased land from an Indian named Pohunna. Plymouth Colony Records show that in June of 1675, "Mr. John Smith, teacher of the Church of Christ at Sandwich," was given right to purchase a tract of Indian land at Pinguin Hole in Cataumet.[20] Early industries were oysters and quahogs. The post office opened as Pocasset until 1899 when it was changed to Cataumet.

CHICOPEE (Hampden/54,653) Indians who lived along the Chicopee River were the Nipmuc ("freshwater") Indians. In 1641, Chief Nippumsuit deeded land to William Pynchon. An iron foundry was established in 1805 after iron ore was discovered. Before the Civil War, Chicopee was part of the Underground Railroad. The name is an Algonquin word, chikee (or chikeyen), meaning "violent water," or "raging, rushing water," descriptive of the Chicopee River.

COCHITUATE (Barnstable/6,768) Cochituate is part of Wayland, and became known for its shoe-making industry, started by the Bent family. The industry was successful until the early 1900s and the factories closed their doors. The economy then turned to farming and agriculture until World War II. The name may be from a Nipmuc word that means "swift water at." The Cochituate Preservation Society is trying to stem development in order to preserve the village.

COHASSET (Norfolk/7,261) Cohasset was once the fishing and hunting ground for the Indians from the south. The first white man was Captain John Smith in 1614 when his two vessels lay off of Monhegan Island. While there, he visited many Indian villages, one them Quonahassit, from where Cohasset is derived. Interpretations of the Algonquin word include "fishing promontory," "long tidal river," "high place," and "long rocky place," which is the accepted version, since the region is very rocky.

COTUIT (Barnstable/*2,364*) In 1658, representatives for the town of Barnstable acquired a deed from Sachem Paupmunnuck for the region that encompassed Cotuit and Cotuit Neck. Cotuit is a Wampanoag word for "long fields," or "planting fields." The post office was established in 1821 (Roland Crocker, postmaster). Cotuit was settled by Samuel Hooper, who was a member of Congress. Industries were farming and packing oysters. Shipbuilding later came into prominence.

CUTTYHUNK ISLAND (Dukes) Cuttyhunk is the outermost of the Elizabeth Islands off Falmouth on Cape Cod. Bartholomew Gosnold made landfall in 1602 and settled here temporarily. In 1688, Peleg Sanford purchased the island, selling half of it to Ralph Earle, who became the first permanent resident. Peleg Slocaum became owner of the island in 1693 and raised sheep. In 1924, the last square-rigged whaler was lost at sea near Cuttyhunk. The name may be derived from a Wampanoag word, poocutohhunkunnoh, meaning "point of departure," or "open, cleared field."

HOUSATONIC (Berkshire/1,335) Housatonic grew up around numerous mills that were established along the Housatonic River. Most of them were part of Monument Mills, a textile company that made cotton warp. The mill era flourished from the 1890s until the 1950s. Equally important were the papers mills that followed Henry Potter's first mill in 1852. A Mohican word, Housatonic means "beyond the mountain," or "at the place."

MANCHAUG (Worcester) In 1826, a group of men from Providence, Rhode Island, came to the region to build a textile mill utilizing the power of the Mumford River. They purchased land owned by Aaron Elliot. Numerous mills were established at Manchaug, one of which was owned by the Knight brothers, who went on to manufacture the now famous brand "Fruit of the Loom." Manchaug was interpreted as a Nipmuc word for "island of rushes."

MANOMET (Plymouth) Manomet is a

village in the town of Plymouth. The Manomet Trading Post was established along the Manomet River and spent many profitable years trading with the New York Dutch. In 1638, John Richards was granted 25 acres of land that was due him by indenture for his services, and the town was established the next year. Manomet has been translated from a Wampanoag word for "a path," "trail of the burden carriers" and "the burden pathway."

MASHPEE (Barnstable/12,946) This site was inhabited by the Wampanoag Indians whose name means "people of the first light." By 1640, settlers had taken over most of the region, and Mashpee became the Indians' only haven. Missionary Richard Bourne helped the Indians register their deeds to protect their lands, which consisted of about 13,000 acres called the Mashpee Plantation, and ratified by the General Court. New legislation in 1693 took away many of the Indians' rights. Mashpee is Wampanoag for "great waters," or "great pool."

MATTAPOISETT (Plymouth/6,268) Mattapoisett Harbor was the site of an Indian village for centuries. Papamo, Achawanamett and Machacam sold the land in 1678, which became the "Plantacion of Matapoyst" when Moses Barlow, Samuel Hammond and William Dexter staked their claims in 1680. Derived from a Wampanoag word, Mattapoisett means "a place of resting," or "edge of a cove." The town was a busy coastal trading port, and between the American Revolution and the War of 1812 more than a dozen shipyards were established. Discovery of petroleum in 1856 brought about the demise of the shipyards.

MENEMSHA (Dukes) This small fishing village is located in the town of Chilmark. The region was granted by patent in 1671 to Thomas Mayhew, Sr. New residents were considered tenants. Whaling was a source of income from the 1500 through 1600s. First known as Creekville, it was changed to Menemsha, a Wampanoag word for "place of observation." This described a marker pole on a hill that was raised when a whale was sighted. During the American Revolution Major Basset organized his troops for defense of the seacoast, and ordered that "Each party to keep suitable Guard... Lieut. Bassett to Intrench at Manamsha as soon as he can procure Tools."[21] Today, the main industry is fishing and a Coast Guard Station is located on a bluff above Menemsha Harbor.

MONPONSETT (Plymouth) Part of the town of Halifax, this site is located on White's Island and home to the Wampanoag Indians. During King Phillip's War when Phillip's uncle was killed in 1676, Captain Benjamin Church rounded up the Indians from Monponsett pond and imprisoned them on Clark's Island. Monponsett was translated as an Algonquin word for "at the deep clear place." But the Wampanoag Tribal historian noted the name was pronounced munponsett and meant "island crossing place."[22]

NAHANT (Essex/3,632) Nahant was once a high, rocky place covered with trees and used during colonial days for grazing cattle and sheep. The Indians who lived here were ruled by Sachem Nanapashemet. Nahant may have been derived from Chief Nahanton, or nahanteau, which means "twins," referring to the two islands that form the town. Other interpretations are from the Natick words describing "two things surrounded," and "the point." The land was sold by Chief Poquanum in 1630 to Thomas Dexter. Nahant became a maritime community and today is a resort area.

NANTUCKET (Nantucket/9,520) Nantucket Island is about 14 miles long with its widest point at 3.5 miles. Nanticut is a Wampanoag word meaning "the far away land." In 1621, the island was included in the royal grant to the Plymouth Colony. Colonists came here during the 1660s because of religious intolerance in other towns. When the soil would no longer produce crops, whalers were recruited to teach the local men how to whale. Nantucket was known as the "Whaling Capital of the World" until the industry declined when other petroleum products replaced whale oil, and tourism took over as its economy.

NATICK (Middlesex/32,170) Puritan missionary John Eliot established the town in 1651 when he brought a group of Praying Indians to Natick. In 1675, they were sent to Deer Island against Eliot's protest. Natick was a farming community until industry developed. One of the largest industries was shoe-making. By 1880, there were about 25 shoe factories, which flourished until the last one closed its doors in 1971. Natick has been defined as "a place of hills," "my home," and "a clearing."

PONKAPOAG (Norfolk) Part of the town of Canton, Ponkapoag was home to the Nesponset Indians. At a place called Vose's Grove, John Eliot preached his gospel to the Indians in 1646. After they sold their land, Eliot established a town for them and named it Ponkapoag, a Natick word that means "sweet water." Most of the settlers were farmers, but modern times have transformed Ponkapoag in to a recreational area.

QUINAPOXET (Worcester) Purchased in 1827 by Samuel Damon and a Mr. Thaxter, Quinapoxet is a village in the town of Holden. In 1831, Damon built a cotton sheeting mill, using the water power of the Quinapoxet River. The mill contained 1,400 spindles and 40 looms, which manufactured more than 250,000 yards of sheeting. The Quinapoxet Mill continued operations until 1929 when the Metropolitan Water Commission took it over. The post office opened as Woodville in 1882. It was later changed to Quinapoxet, a Nipmuc word for "at the place of the little long pond (or swamp)."

SAUGUS (Essex/26,078) This site was once part of the town of Lynn. In 1851, the people split from Lynn and created the community of Saugus, a Natick word for "great," or "extended." Thomas Dexter established the earliest industry when he opened the first iron forge. Benjamin Sweetser purchased the property in 1794 and turned it into a chocolate factory. Other than these industries, the area was largely agricultural.

SCITUATE (Plymouth/5,069) Located between Plymouth and Boston, Scituate was settled about 1630. Chief Wampatuck of the Mattakeesett Tribe sold the land to white settlers about 1653. Scituate's early industries were shipbuilding and brickmaking. The *Columbia* built here was the first American ship to circumnavigate the globe. The 1930s brought the Irish moss industry, a marine alga used for brewing and dyeing. Scituate may be derived from satuit, a Wampanoag word for "cold brook," descriptive of a brook that runs into the harbor.

SEEKONK (Bristol/13,425) This site was originally home to the Wampanoag Indians. Roger Williams purchased land from Chief Osamequin. Unfortunately, the pilgrims also brought their diseases with them, which killed many of the Indians. The town once had a factory that manufactured tennis racquets and croquet sets. Seekonk is derived from a Wampanoag expression meaning "black goose," because of the abundance of birds. Another translation was "pouring out place."

SIASCONSET (Nantucket) Siasconset is located on Nantucket Island. The name was interpreted from the Narragansett words for "at the elbow," and "near the great bone," referring to the shape of the shoreline. Siasconset was originally established as a fishing village. Because fisherman living in Nantucket had to use bad roads to reach the village, they built small shacks rather than travel back and forth during the fishing seasons. Eventually, more permanent buildings were established.

SWAMPSCOTT (Essex/14,412) Once home to Sachem Poquanum and his people, Francis Ingalls came to Swampscott in 1629 and established a tannery. The town's economic stability was based on the fishing industry. In 1856, the Egg Rock Lighthouse was built because of the many shipwrecks that occurred off the coast. This as also the place where the famous Swampscott dory was built in 1841 by Theophilus Brackett. Swampscott is a Natick word meaning "at red rock," or "at the place of red rocks." Mary Baker Eddy, founder of Christian Science, was born here.

MICHIGAN

AHMEEK (Keweenaw/157) Ahmeek owes its growth to copper mines. Located on the Keweenaw Peninsula, the town was founded about 1904 by John Bosch who named it Ahmeek, a Chippewa word meaning "beavers." The post office was established in 1909 (James Hamilton, postmaster). The Eagle River Lighthouse filled with sand and failed to perform. After an ore carrier became stranded on the shoals and broke up, the Sand Hills Lighthouse was built in 1919.

ALPENA (Alpena/11,304) Located on Thunder Bay, Alpena was inhabited by the Michekewis and Sahgonahkato Tribes. The town was settled about 1856 as Fremont and was a lumber town. A year earlier, George N. Fletcher and James K. Lockwood purchased the site. The post office was established on December 2, 1857 (Daniel Carter, postmaster). The name may be an Ojibway word for "good partridge country," or simply "partridge." Henry Schoolcraft had a reputation for coining Indian names and may have suggested Alpena.

ASSININS (Baraga/9) Assinins was founded on the western shore of Keweenaw Bay by Father Frederic Baraga, who established a mission there about 1843. He devoted years to educating the Ojibway Indians, and went on to write the Ojibway dictionary. In 1881, Father Gerhard Terhost built an orphanage here, the majority American Indian children. Assinins is derived from the Ojibway word, asin-nee meaning "little rock."

CHEBOYGAN (Cheboygan/5,295) This area was the traditional boundary line between the Chippewa and Ottawa Indians. The Ottawas were allotted two townships by a treaty signed in 1855 and the rest was restored to public domain by acts of Congress in 1872 and 1876. Alexander McLeod and his brother moved to Cheboygan, which was platted by Jacob Sammons. Cheboygan was one of the northern Michigan lumber towns in the 1800s, and flourished with the industry, becoming a major port on the Great Lakes. Cheboygan is an Algonquin word for "through passage," or "place of entrance," in reference to the Cheboygan River and the Inland Route.

CHESANING (Saginaw/2,548) Chesening is situated along the Shiawassee River and was claimed by Thomas W. Wright in 1839. Known as Northampton, the town was opened for settlement after the 1847 Treaty of Detroit between the Saginaw Tribe of the Chippewas was signed. In 1853, the name was changed to Chesaning, derived from a Chippewa word, che-as-sin-ing, which means "big rock," or "big rock place," which referred to a huge limestone rock in the river.

COPEMISH (Manistee/232) Copemish was founded in 1886 and became a lumber town. The Buckley/Douglas Lumber Company set up a logging camp about 1883, in addition to a company store. An interesting business was a bowl mill factory that made butter bowls. Railroads came through about 1889. Copemish may be a Chippewa word for "big beech tree," which was descriptive of council meetings held under a beech tree. Today, Copemish is a bedroom community.

DOWAGIAC (Cass/6,147) William Renesten moved here in 1830 and established a carding mill, using the water power of Dowagiac Creek. The village was platted in 1835 by Jacob Beeson and Nicholas Cheesebrough when they found out the Michigan Central Railway was coming through. By 1860, Dowagiac was the largest wheat and cattle-shipping station for the railroad. Dowagiac may come from a Potawatomi word, ndowagayui, meaning "foraging ground."

ESCANABA (Delta/13,140) Escanaba was founded about 1830 when settlers were attracted by the large stands of timber, but it was iron ore that put Escanaba on the map in 1863. It became one of the most important ore-shipping points in the upper peninsula. A dock was built because of the deep port on Lake Michigan, and the following year the first shipment of ore was loaded. Fishing was another important industry. Escanaba means "flat rock," or may have been derived from eshkonabang, an Algonquin word which means "land of the red buck."

ISHPEMING (Marquette/6,686) Folklore says the Ojibwa or Cherokee Indians were terrified of this site because they thought it was bewitched. Settlers moved here in the mid–1800s with the discovery of iron ore. The site was called Lake Superior Location, and changed in 1862 to Ishpeming, an Ojibway word meaning "high place" or "high up." Iron ore proved to be the town's main industry, and numerous mines opened, some of which are still active. The Cleveland Cliffs Iron Company is a major employer.

KALAMAZOO (Kalamazoo/77,145) This site was originally a fur trading post until the Potawatomi Indians gave the land to the U.S. in 1827. Titus Bronson founded the town about 1831 and called it Bronson. It was changed to Kalamazoo in 1837, derived from the Potawatomi word kikalamazoo, which means "the rapids at the river crossing," or "boiling waters," descriptive of a bubbling over at a ford in the river. Another interpretation from an authority on the language (George Fox) was from kuknahmzu, for "he smothered."[23] Kalamazoo's economy was supported by celery after James Taylor experimented with the seeds which proved to be a great success.

KALKASKA (Kalkaska/2,226) The Copelands were the only people here until after the Civil War. Since the Grand Rapids and Indiana Railroad was being built through the region, A.A. Abbott and a partner purchased the land. Some of the first buildings to go up were saloons that served the railroad crews. The town became a logging railroad grading camp and its economy continued to grow with the lumber industry. When the lumber played out, agriculture took over. Kalkaska is a Chippewa word for "burned over land."

KAWKAWLIN (Bay/5,104) Located at the mouth of the Kawkawlin River was the oldest trading post in the region, where traders conducted business with the Chippewa Indians. The wealth of pine and hemlock trees drew Israel Catlin who in 1844 built a sawmill. The river was called oganconning (or uguhkonning) by the Indians, and may be a Chippewa word meaning "the place of the pike," from which the town took its name. The post office was established in 1868 (Dennis Stanton, postmaster). Farming supplanted the lumber industry after the forest was depleted.

MACKINAC ISLAND (Mackinac/523) Jean Nicolet was the first white man to the island while he was searching a route to the Orient in 1634. Father Claude Dablon wintered on the island in 1670, his purpose to do missionary work with the Hurons. With the swelling beaver population, the American Fur Company was established in the early 1800s. Fishing took over when the fur trade declined. Mackinac may be an Ojibway word derived from michinnimakinong, interpreted as "land of the great fault," designating a large crevice on the island. Others have defined it as "great turtle."

MANISTEE (Manistee/6,586) Manistee is situated along the east shore of Lake Michigan. John Stronach and his family moved here in 1841 and built the first steam-powered mill on the banks of Manistee Lake and the town developed around it. At first the Chippewa Indians resented the intrusion, but the Stronachs offered them food in a gesture of friendship, which the Indians accepted. Manistique may be an Ojibway word for "red."

MANISTIQUE (Schoolcraft/3,583) In 1871 explorer Henry Schoolcraft founded Manistique which developed as a lumber transfer town. About ten years later, the Chicago Lumber Company deeded part of the town to the county so a courthouse could be built. When the supply of pine was exhausted, tanneries, lime kilns and iron furnaces replaced them. The post office was established in 1873 as Epsport. In 1879, the name was changed to Manistique, which is derived from the Ojibway word unamanitigong, meaning "red."

MEAUWATAKA (Wexford/*10*) Located in the Manistee National Forest, Meauwataka started out as a stage route, and was settled about 1867. Five years later the first sawmill was built, turning the town into a prosperous lumber community. The post office was established about 1877 (E.C. Dayhuff, postmaster). By 1918, the village had all but disappeared. There are a few houses and a store left. Meauwataka may be Ojibway for "half way."

MECOSTA (Mecosta/2,435) The enormous stands of white pine in the region caused Mecosta to be founded. Its growth as a lumber town began in 1879 when the Detroit, Lansing and Northern Railroad established its line. Mecosta was known as Little River when the train depot was built, and was platted in the 1880s by timber magnate Giles Gilbert. Mecosta was a

Potawatomi Chief, whose name means "bear cub."

MUNISING (Alger/2,539) The Munising Company was created in 1850 by a group of Philadelphia men to build a resort community, but the Civil War thwarted attempts to sell the idea. Timothy Nester was the town founder in 1895, and the Munising Railway was built, which connected with the Chicago and North Western. Saw mills were established to harvest the forests, bringing in supporting businesses. The post office was established in 1868 (William Cox, postmaster). Munising was interpreted from a Ojibway expression for "island in a lake," or "near the island," descriptive of an island in Munising Bay.

MUSKEGON (Muskegon/40,105) Muskegon was established in 1812 when John Baptiste Recollect built a trading post, but permanent settlement did not occur until about 1837, when Theodore Newell platted part of the town. Transportation consisted of a stage line until the Muskegon and Ferrysburg Railroad Company was formed in 1869 and built a narrow-gauge railroad for the timber. Muskegon began its life as a logging town until the trees were depleted and industry took over. Muskegon is derived from an Ottawa word, masquigon, meaning "marshy river," or "swamp."

NEGAUNEE (Marquette/4,567) The first mining city on the Marquette Range was Negaunee. In 1844, iron ore was discovered while William Burt was running a survey line. The Jackson Iron Company began small-scale mining in 1846, and later expanded to open-pit mining. Negaunee's growth soared with an influx of miners when the Soo Canal opened in 1857. The town was platted in 1865 and named Negaunee, Ojibway for "pioneer," or "he goes before."

NEWAYGO (Newaygo/1,670) Located in a valley near the Muskegon River, Newaygo is one of the oldest towns in northern Michigan. It was platted in 1854 by John Brooks and Sarrell Wood who came to harvest timber. The post office opened in 1852 (J.A. Knapp, postmaster). Newaygo has various interpretations: "we go no farther," "land of many waters," or "land of blue sky." A full-blood Ottawa woman stated the name was derived from kenewaygoing, meaning "place where boy have fish bone in throat."[24]

OKEMOS (Ingham/22,805) This site was established as Hamilton, named by a Mr. Bray in 1841. The first settler was Sanford Marsh in 1839 who was a justice of the peace. The post office opened in 1840 as Sanford (Joseph Kilbourne, postmaster). Ebenezer Walker settled here about 1854 and purchased a mill. The Detroit, Lansing and Northern Railway laid its tracks through town in 1871. The name was changed to Okemos in 1857 for Chippewa chief Okemos, nephew of Chief Pontiac. His name means "chief little," descriptive of the chief's stature. Okemos died in 1858.

ONAWAY (Presque Isle/993) The Swamp Land Board of Control used its allotted lands in the 1870s to encourage development of transportation in northern Michigan. It authorized a survey for a road, which was completed about 1875. The site was settled by Thomas Shaw and Marritt Chandler in 1888. When the post office opened in 1883, it was named Shaw (Thomas Shaw, postmaster). Chandler platted the land and named it Onaway, which means "awake," taken from the poem, "Hiawatha." The Huron Handle and Manufacturing Company was the town's main source of revenue.

ONEKAMA (Manistee/647) Although

people settled here as early as 1856, the settlement didn't take form until a sawmill was built. The Manistee and Northwestern Railroad laid its tracks in 1888 and Onekama was one of its stations. The name was derived from onekamaengh, meaning "portage." Another translation was the Chippewa word meaning "arm," taken from Father Frederick Baraga's Chippewa dictionary. It was also defined as "place of contentment." The Smithsonian Institute translated it as being derived from onigana, a Chippewa word meaning "to carry on the shoulder."

OSSINEKE (Alpena/1,059) Chippewa, Ottawa and Potawatomi Indians used the region during the summers for fishing and hunting. The first permanent settlers in the region were Jonathan Burtch and David Oliver in 1844 who built sawmills. Oliver named the town Ossineke, derived from the Ojibway word wawsineke, meaning "image stones," descriptive of a pair of stones the Indians worshipped. Legend says Shingawba was a divine chief who told his people that after he died, he would return to the stones as a spirit. These stones were later used by a fisherman for an anchor and are now at the bottom of Lake Huron.

OWOSSO (Shiawassee/15,713) A French trapper named Henri Bolieu may have been the first white man to enter the region in 1820. Benjamin Williams founded the town, which was situated near the Shiawassee River, enabling sawmills and grist mills to use its water power. First called Big Rapids, the name was changed to Owosso in 1839, in honor of a Chippewa chief named Wasso, translated as "one bright spot," or "he is far off." The Detroit, Grand haven and Milwaukee Railroad extended its line to Owosso in 1856, bringing in a new era of industry, resulting in a decline of river traffic.

PEQUAMING (Baraga) This little town almost went out of existence, but is in the process of being revived as people slowly move back in. In 1879, Charles Hebard laid out the village and built a sawmill. Henry Ford purchased the peninsula in 1924 and continued mill operations using the wood for his Ford station wagons and wood-sided cars, which continued until World War II. The mills were dismantled in the 1960s. Pequaming may have been derived from a Chippewa word meaning "wooded peninsula (or point)."

PETOSKEY (Emmet/6,080) Located on Traverse Bay, the town emerged as Bear River in 1855. It was renamed Petoskey, for Chippewa Chief Petosega, which means "sun shining through," or "rising sun." The Grand Rapids & Indiana Railroad was brought to the area in the 1870s, bringing more income to the town. Logging was Petoskey's support in the late 1800s. Freighters ferried lumber from Lake Michigan to various ports, and some of it was used to help rebuild Chicago after its disastrous fire.

PEWAMO (Ionia/560) Pewamo was created when the Detroit & Milwaukee Railroad extended its line through the region in 1857. Robert G. Higham had a depot built and was considered founder of the town. W.C. and J.C. Blanchard purchased the tract and had it surveyed in 1857. From its earliest days, Pewamo was a farming community and continues today. The name was taken from Ojibway Chief Pewamo, who name was defined as "one who scattered in many parts a thing he struck." It was also interpreted as "trail diverges," descriptive of a trail that split.

PINCONNING (Bay/1,386) The stands of white pine and the Pinconning River brought George VanEtten and Henry Kaiser to create the town in 1872. Pinconning is derived from opinakonning, Algonquin for "a place to get wild potatoes." An increase in population occurred with the advent of railroads. By the early 1900s, unscrupulous timber companies destroyed the forests, and Pinconning turned to manufacturing for its economic stability.

QUANICASSE (Tuscola/0) This was once a small settlement on Saginaw Bay. The region was used as an Indian trail where hunting and fishing were ideal. The name means "long tree." Because the settlement was located in swampy ground, there was no farming until canals were dredged.

SAGINAW (Saginaw/61,799) Established as a fur trading post in 1816 by Louis Campau, Saginaw was founded when Normal Little purchased the land in 1836. Large tracts of timber drew in the lumber companies. When the timber declined, the town's economy was tied to the development of coal, discovered while prospectors were drilling for salt. In 1906, the Jackson, Church, and Wilcox Company was established for the purpose of machining automobile parts. Buick Motor Company became one of its largest customers. Saginaw is derived from an Ottawa word, sak (or sag), interpreted as "go outward," or "to flow out," descriptive of rivers that flowed into other rivers or lakes.

SAUGATUCK (Allegan/1,065) Located near the shores of Lake Michigan, Saugatuck was settled in the mid–1800s, most of the residents in the timber trade. After the great Chicago fire in 1871, Saugatuck contributed lumber to help the city rebuild. By the early 1900s, the town was looking for other avenues of income, and found it in the tourist trade and as an artist's retreat when the Summer School of Painting moved here from Chicago. Saugatuck is Algonquin for "river's mouth."

SEBEWAING (Huron/2,944) Looking for a place for his followers to live, Lutheran minister John Auch found the site in 1845. He planned on doing missionary work among the Indians, which he conducted for more than five years. He met Charles Rodd, a half-breed, and with his aid built a log house. Until other means of transportation were built, the settlers had to get their supplies by boats to Saginaw. In 1862, Richard Winsor received a grant to set aside land for a channel to keep the waters from overflowing the farmlands. Sebewaing is a Chippewa word for "river nearby," "river little at," or "crooked creek."

TEKONSHA (Calhoun/1,734) The first permanent settler was Timothy Kimball in 1833. Harris Goodrich, Charles Smith, and Cornelius Wendell laid out the town in 1836. The post office was established the same year (Harris Goodrich, postmaster). First named Wirt, the name was changed to Tekonsha, for Potawatomi Chief Tekonquasha, translated as "caribou little."

TOPINBEE (Cheboygan) Topinbee is located on a steep hillside, and was founded by railroad officials in 1881, who believed it would make an excellent place for a resort because of a nearby lake. H.H. Pike named it Topinbee for a Potawatomi chief, meaning "great bear heart." Topinbee signed a treaty ceding his land that is now the city of Chicago. Today, Topinbee is still a small resort area with a post office and small store.

MINNESOTA

AH-GWAH-CHING (Cass) This site is a state facility within the boundaries of the Chippewa National Forest. It was founded in 1906 as a treatment center for patients with tuberculosis. Although it is not a town in the true sense of the word, it does have its own post office (established on July 14, 1908). During its early days, any mail sent here was addressed "State Sanatorium." Employees and patients did not like the name and changed it to Ah-Gwah-Ching, a Chippewa expression for "out of doors." In 1958, the sanatorium was converted into a nursing home by the Minnesota Department of Welfare.

ANOKA (Anoka/18,076) The county was neutral territory for the Dakota Sioux and Ojibway (or Chippewa) Indians. Anoka was founded by Orrin W. Rice and Neal D. Shaw in 1853, and the post office was established in 1853–54 (George W. Branch, postmaster). In the Dakota Sioux language, Anoka is derived from A-No-Ka-Tan-Han, meaning "on both sides," descriptive of the site's location at the confluence of the Rum and Mississippi rivers. At one time, it was thought Anoka would be bigger than Minneapolis because of its location at the rivers. In the Ojibway/Chippewa language, An-O-Kay means "working the waters."

BEMIDJI (Beltrami/11,917) One of the last regions open for settlement along the Mississippi River between Lake Itasca and the Gulf, Bemidji is the first city on the Mississippi where it starts as a stream. An Indian named Shaynowishkung and his people lived here during the early 1800s. George and Merian Carson established a trading post in 1888, and Carson named the site Bemidji when the post office opened in 1894. This Ojibway name was derived from bemidgegumaug, meaning "the lake where the current flows directly across the water," or "river flowing crosswise." Another interpretation was "cross lake."

BIWABIK (St. Louis/954) Originally an old Indian camp, Biwabik had its beginnings in 1891 when someone discovered iron ore on the roots of an upturned tree. The product was a high-grade blue iron ore, and in 1891 the Biwabik Mine began mining operations. Biwabik became the first of what were called Mesabi Range towns. In addition to mining, part of the town's economy was tied to the Hill Lumbering Company. Biwabik is a most appropriate name for the town, a Chippewa word for "iron."

CHASKA (Carver/17,449) Thomas Holmes acquired a license to trade with the Indians in the area of his choice along the Mississippi River in 1851. He selected Chaska (in addition to Shakopee) and the following year he purchased the townsite from David Fuller. Chaska is interpreted from a Sioux word that means "one" or "first," as the first-born male Indian children were named. Brick manufacturing was a large industry, as was the cultivation of sugar beets.

COKATO (Wright/2,727) The year 1856 was the beginning of the town's settlement. The St. Paul & Pacific Railway laid tracks to Howard Lake in 1858, and extended its line to Cokato the following year. The post office was established in 1857 at Sucker Creek, but moved to Cokato two years later. In 1904, the second canning factory in the state was established (later bought out by Green Giant). Government surveyors renamed the lake Cokato, from which the town took its name. It is a Lakota Sioux word that means "in the midst (or middle) of."

EYOTA (Olmsted/1,644) This site was surveyed in 1875 and named Springfield. It was later changed to Eyota, from the Dakota word, iyotay, meaning something "great," or "superior." The name designated the townsite's location on the highest point of land between the Mississippi River and Sioux Falls, Idaho. Agriculture was the town's economic base, in addition to stock raising. In the early 1900s, the Chicago and North Western Railway built its roundhouse, depot, and stockyards at Eyota.

HOKAH (Houston/457) The village of Hokah was settled in the 1850s by Edward Thompson, and platted in 1855. The site was once home to Dakota Chief Hokah, which means "root." Establishment of the Southern Minnesota Railroad in the 1860s brought an influx of settlers. At one time there was a lake dotted with summer cottages for tourists, and a dam was constructed to keep up the water level. During the 1930s, the lake became muddied and the dam started leaking. The lake was later drained and turned into farmlands.

KANARANZI (Rock/286) Named for Kanaranzi Creek, the town was founded when the Burlington Railroad was built in 1884. During initial grading of the line, representatives of farmers and landowners of the area negotiated with railroad authorities on where to locate Kanaranzi. It would be a year before an agreement was reached. Originally the property of Charles Thompson, the site was surveyed by Leroy Grant in August of 1885. On January 28, 1887, the post office was opened (G.T. Bandy, postmaster). Kanaranzi was interpreted as "crazy woman."

KASOTA (LeSueur/680) Kasota saw its first settlers in 1851, and the site was platted four years later. The post office opened in 1854 (Joseph W. Babcock, postmaster). This same year the Chicago and North Western Railway made Kasota one of its stations. Kasota is a Dakota word that means "clear," or "cleared off," and may be descriptive of a treeless ridge. An early settler built a sawmill and started quarrying a particular limestone unique to this region. Because of its geology, the limestone recrystallized so that it could take on a high polish. Until concrete replaced the stone, it was used for building bridges and roadbeds.

KEEWATIN (Itasca/1,164) As the Great Northern Railroad extended its line it opened up the surrounding country for settlement. After large amounts of iron ore were discovered and the St. Paul and Minnesota Mines began operating, the Pillsbury Estate platted the village, which was surveyed by W.B. Patton. Usually the first business in the early settlements was the general store, but at Keewatin it was a tent put up by a Mr. Logan who sold whiskey. Keewatin is an Ojibway word designating "northwest wind."

MENDOTA (Dakota/197) In 1820, Mendota became the first permanent white settlement in Minnesota. Its position on Mississippi River and the mouth of the Minnesota River made it an ideal meeting place for trappers and traders. In 1834, Henry Sibley was factor for the American Fur Company. As governor of the state, he became a moving forces in the development of Mendota. First called St. Peters, the name was changed to Mendota in 1837, a Sioux word for "meeting of the waters," or "mouth of the river."

MINNIESKA (Winona/*127*) This site became an export trade center sometime after 1850, shipping tons of wheat via the Mississippi River. With the advent of railroads, the town decreased in importance as a river port. The post office opened in 1856 as Mount Vernon, but reverted to Minneiska. The Sioux Indians gave the site its name which means "water white," descriptive of the water turbulence caused by the Whitewater and Zumero rivers that joined at the Mississippi River.

MINNETONKA (Hennepin/51,301) Part of Spanish territory in 1803 that was included in the Louisiana Purchase, Minnetonka was home to the Dakota and Ojibway Indians. Immigrants from Czechoslovakia moved here about 1822 and brought with them their expertise of growing raspberries. The town eventually became the "Raspberry Capital of the World." Minnetonka grew up around the sawmill that was built in 1852, the first privately run mill in the state west of the Mississippi. Wood from the mill was used to build the first suspension bridge across the Mississippi at St. Anthony in 1853. Minnetonka is from the Dakota Sioux expression, minne and tonka for big water."

NASHWAUK (Itasca/35) This was home to the Sioux Indians until they were run out by the Chippewas. Site of the first mine in the county, Nashwauk was platted in 1902. It may have been named for a river in New Brunswick, Canada, which in the Algonquin language means "land between." The post office opened in 1902 (Paul Tweed, postmaster). Iron ore was discovered in 1900 by the Itasca Mining Company on land owned by Deering-Harvester Company (now International Harvester). As other mines were developed, Nashwauk became one of the more important mining communities in the Mesabi Range.

NAYTAHWAUSH (Mahnomen/583) Located on the White Earth Indian Reservation, the site was named by Ah-bid-way-we-dung who called it Gah-nee-shoo-cum-mon ("Twin Lakes"). The community was built along North Twin Lake and saw its first white settlers in 1869 with the arrival of Henry Beaulieu and his family. Part of the town's economy was tied to the timber industry. When the post office was established in 1906, Star Bad Boy was the postmaster, and named the community for Chief Nay-tah-waush, a Chippewa word for "smooth sailing."

OKABENA (Jackson/185) This little village was established along the Milwaukee Railroad in 1879 as one of its depots. Okabena is a Sioux word for "nesting place of the heron," descriptive of nearby Lake Heron. The same year a warehouse was built, followed by the post office in February, 1880 (K.C. Jackson, postmaster). The site was surveyed by J.L. Holst in 1892 and platted by Henry J. Schumacher. A major industry in the early 1900s was the Okabena Clay Works, makers of brick and tile that operated until 1931.

OSAKIS (Douglas/1,567) The Ihankton band of Dakota Indians lived near a lake they called O-Za-Te, fishing and hunting and harvesting the wild rice beds. Sauk Indians ventured here in the 1720s, followed by the Ojibwa Indians during the 1750s who took over the Dakota rice beds. When the fur trappers arrived, they called the site O-Zah-kees. Osakis went on to become a trade center that served rural farm communities. Through the years the meaning has become clouded, but some believe Osakis is an Ojibway word for "yellow earth," or "danger," referring to the many fights that took place between the Indians.

OSSEO (Hennepin/2,434) Pierre Bottineau and his traveling companions named the area Bottineau Prairie in 1852. Two years later, Warren Sampson built the general store and the post office was established as Palestine. The area was so rich in timber that Sampson established a wood market in 1855. The town was platted two years later by Sampson and Isaac LaBissonniere who renamed it Osseo, taken from the poem, "Hiawatha," and derived from waseia, meaning "there is light."

OWATONNA (Steele/22,434) A.B. Cornell and an engineer named John H. Abbot purchased the land and each donated 60 acres for a townsite. Edward Doud was employed to conduct the survey. In 1855, the post office was established as Owatonna, derived from the Sioux word, ouitunya, which means "straight." The town prospered because of the rich prairie land, and the trail that went past town used as a stopping place for settlers making their way west.

PUPOSKY (Beltrami) Puposky was established by the Minneapolis, Red Lake and Manitoba Railway in 1905. The town of Buena Vista thought the railroad would come through at that point, but an owner of the railroad decided otherwise. As a result, many of the residents from Buena Vista moved to Puposky, which became a lumber town. Eventually the timber played out and by 1939 the railroad ceased to exist. Today, Puposky has only a few buildings. The name may be an Ojibway word for "end of shaking lands," descriptive of the marshes or bogs common in the region.

QUAMBA (Kanabec/98) Although a sidetrack of a railroad was built in 1882, there was no settlement at what was called Mud Creek until the late 1890s. One of the early residents was Abraham Selander in 1895, followed a few years later by logging companies and sawmills. Oric Whited platted the town in 1901 and renamed it Quamba, which means "mudhole." The post office opened the same year (Andrew J. Edstrom, postmaster).

SEBEKA (Wadena/710) This town was formed in 1891 by Col. William Crooks, an engineer with the Manitoba Railway. It was platted the same year, and the post office opened (John Anderson, postmaster). Sebeka's economy was tied, in part, to the timber industry. Because the town was located in a heavily wooded area, it almost burned to the ground in 1894. The largest influx of settlers was in 1892 when the Great Northern Railway came through town. Sebeka is an Ojibway word for "by the river," or a modification of Sebekaun, meaning "by the made channel."

SHAKOPEE (Scott/20,568) Located along the Minnesota River, this site was once an Indian village of the Dakota Sioux. Townsite promoter Thomas A. Holmes was the first permanent settler who conducted trade with the Indians. He had it surveyed in 1852 and called it Shakopee, taken from Dakota Sioux Chief Shak-pa, meaning "six," a hereditary name. The Chicago, St. Paul, Minneapolis & Omaha Railroad built its repair shops at Shakopee in 1866. Five years later the Hastings and Dakota Railroad was completed, making Shakopee a junction with the Chicago rail lines.

TAOPI (Mower/93) This town was platted in 1875 by the Taopi Farming Company and became a station on the Chicago, Milwaukee & St. Paul Railroad. Later, the Chicago Great Western came through and the two lines crossed at this point. The Company established the first steam flour mill, the largest in the southern part of the state. The post office was established in 1875 (W.P. Brainard, postmaster). Taopi was named for a Sioux Indian chief who befriended the white people during the New Ulm Massacre. His name was interpreted as "wounded."

WABASHA (Wabasha/2,599) Once a trading post along the Mississippi River, the town has been occupied continuously since 1826. Wabasha's economy was tied to factories that made buttons after it was discovered that local clam shells could be utilized for that purpose. The post office was established about 1841 (Francois La Bathe, postmaster). Wabasha was named for a great Dakota Chief, translated as "red leaf," or "red hat." Another suggestion was a derivation of an Algonquin word meaning "a cloud blown forward by an equinoctial wind." This seems highly unlikely, since the Indians probably had no knowledge of the word 'equinoctial.'

WABASSO (Redwood/643) In 1899, the Minnesota & Iowa Railway built its tracks and named stations along the route. This site was purchased by the Chicago & Northeastern Railway Company, which platted and laid out the town. The origin of the name was written by land commissioner Howard Larimer: "I happen to remember hearing the engineer who laid out this plat tell why this named was used. He was a great admirer of Indian Lore and particularly of Longfellow's 'Hiawatha' … 'Wabasso' occurs in this poem, the reference being to a white rabbit … He said that when they were up there the plains were so full of rabbits…."[25] Wabos may also be the Ojibway word for "rabbit."

WADENA (Wadena/4,294) Wadena was originally located on the Red River Ox Cart Trail, which was a major trade route during the mid-1800s. The town flourished as a trading post until it was moved to be near the tracks of the newly established Northern Pacific Railroad in 1872. With rail service, Wadena then became a distribution center for the outlying regions. The name comes from an Ojibway word that means "little round hill," and may have described the original town's location near the river bluffs.

WASEKA (Waseca/8,493) Settlement was encouraged in the 1850s because of the fertile area. Land speculators planned the village of Waseca in 1856, which is a Dakota word that means "rich in provisions." When the Winona and St. Peter Railroad was being built, Ira Trowbridge purchased more land north of the railroad tracks and actually founded the town in 1867. It is home to the University of Minnesota Southern Experiment Station, located in a prime corn and soybean producing region. Its purpose is to provide site-specific, research-based agricultural information to clients.

WAYZATA (Hennepin/4,113) The Dakotas spent part of the their time here, and when a treaty was signed in 1851 they asked that some of the land be reserved for them, but it was denied. Civil Engineer Oscar Garrison came from St. Anthony in the 1850s and hacked out a road to plat the town. In 1862, he sold all his holdings to Lucius Walker, Ojibway Indian agent. Wayzata may be derived from the Dakota Sioux word, waziya, referring to the Indians' god of the north, or "at the mouth."

WINONA (Winona/27,069) Before 1851, there was not much interest in this site because it was low-lying and often submerged by the Mississippi River. Captain Orren Smith was the founder and named the site Sand Prairie. After settlement in 1852, the name was changed to Winona, a Dakota word meaning "eldest daughter." In 1862, the Winona and St. Peter Railroad was built from town, and by virtue of good transportation Winona became the fourth largest grain market in the country until the industry peaked about 1877.

MISSISSIPPI

BOGUE CHITTO (Lincoln/533) Located about 65 miles south of Jackson, Bogue Chitto was earlier named Big Bow, then Lick Skillet. The name was changed about the time the New Orleans and Northern Railroad was built in the early 1800s. Bogue Chitto took its name from the river, which is a Choctaw word for "big creek." The post office opened in January 1870 (Celia Smith, postmaster). The town's economy centered on shingle and saw mills.

BUCATUNNA (Wayne) Bucatunna is situated near the Chickasawhay River and was established in the early 1800s when William Powe was given permission by the Army to cross the Creek Nation to settle here. After the Mobile & Ohio Railroad was built, the site was called Shiloh. When the railroad moved its tracks because of high water, it renamed the station Bucatunna, a Choctaw word for "bend of the creek," or "collected together."

BYHALIA (Marshall/706) Resident Chickasaw Indians gave up their homelands after the Treaty of Pontotoc in 1832. Settlers were attracted to the region because of its productive land, and built a plank road to Memphis to facilitate travel. First named Farmington, the town was a busy center of commerce in the 1850s. During the War between the States, Byhalia was a recruiting and training center for the Confederate Army until the capture of Memphis. When the post office was established, postal officials denied Farmington, and Byhalia was suggested, which may be Choctaw for "great oaks."

CHATAWA (Pike) Isaac Carter moved into this area after the Revolutionary War, and his son homesteaded on land he named Carter's Hill. When the post office was established in 1860, the name was changed to Chatawa, a Choctaw word for "the land of sparkling waters." Ken York, who was a language teacher on the Choctaw Reservation, stated it was probably a contraction of Chahta oka, meaning "Choctaw water."[26] Chatawa was supported by timber, but once the stands of longleaf pine disappeared, the sawmills closed down and Chatawa was relegated to a sleepy little village.

CHUNKY (Newton/344) This community was originally a Choctaw village named Chanki Chitto, which means "big chunky." It was descriptive of a ball game the Indians played near the river. Chief Tecumseh visited the village in 1811 in an attempt to unite all the tribes against the white men. Founding of the town brought in the A & V Railroad, and Chunky became a prosperous sawmill town during the 1890s.

COAHOMA (Coahoma/325) In 1851, Dr. Issac Hull purchased this site from an early settler. When the railroad came through in the 1880s, its tracks went through Hull's property, and as a result a town was formed. The Montroy brothers built a school for the community and the post office was established in 1885 (Issac Hull, postmaster). Residents suggested the name Florence, but there was already a town by that name, and Coahoma was chosen, which is Choctaw for "red panther."

CONEHATTA (Newton/997) This town was established as Centerville in 1867 by J.L Carver. Conehatta suffered many fires during its early life. In 1883, the entire business district went up in flames. Then in 1893 the majority of town was destroyed. Most of the businesses did not rebuild and the town went into decline for some time. Conehatta is Choctaw for "white skunk," and may refer to the albino skunks noticed by the Indians from time to time. Descendants of the Choctaw Indians who signed the Dancing Rabbit Treaty in 1830 made Conehatta their home.

HOULKA (Chickasaw) Andrew Jackson cut the Natchez Trace through Houlka in 1812. An Indian Agency was established in 1835 and became an important trading center. The Chickasaw and Choctaw Indians owned much of the land until 1837 when they moved westward. They called the creek Houlka, from which the town took its name, and means "low water," or "low land," descriptive of the topography. Another definition was "sacred place."

ITTA BENA (LeFlore/2,208) Benjamin G. Humphreys, along with a group of men, came up the Yazoo River in search of rich farmland. Humphrey named his tract Itta Bena, a Choctaw word meaning "home in the woods." His descendants converted part of their property into the townsite, located in one of the richest agricultural sections in the Yazoo and Mississippi Delta. J.L. Haley was a pioneer in the development of Itta Bena and by 1912 was one of the largest planters in the region. Once a segregated city, residents voted in the first African-American female mayor in 1996.

IUKA (Tishomingo/3,059) Iuka grew up around the Memphis and Charleston Railroad in 1857 (it was home to the Chickasaw Indians until about 1790). The town was situated on property owned by David Hubbard, who donated part of his land containing mineral springs for a townsite. These springs caused Iuka to became a popular resort until the Civil War. Iuka was named for a Chickasaw subordinate chief who came here to drink the mineral water for his health. Iuka was originally spelled Ai Yu Pi, meaning "a place of bathing," "place by the water," or from I-yak-hana, for "where two roads cross."

MASHULAVILLE (Noxubee) Located about 10 miles southwest of Macon, this little village was originally a Choctaw Indian town. Its name was derived from Chief Mashulatubbe, which means "one who perseveres and kills." Nearby was the site of the Treaty of Dancing Rabbit Creek, where the Choctaw Indians ceded about one-third of their lands and received annuities, plus land further west. There were more than 20,000 Indians in attendance at the treaty site. In the 1930s, Mashulaville had one store, a school, church and a few scattered homes.

NATCHEZ (Adams/18,464) Natchez was built on the site of an ancient Indian village, and visited by DeSoto as early as 1541. When French settlers tried to take the Indian land, the Natchez Indians retaliated, but were driven out of their homelands. The tribe eventually disappeared. Located along the Mississippi River, Natchez prospered with the flatboat trade, and became a trade and supply center. It went on to become one of the largest cotton ports in the world. The name may have been taken from naksh'asi, for "hurrying man," or nawadishe, interpreted as "salt."

NESHOBA (Neshoba) Establishment of the GM&N Railroad in 1905 brought Neshoba into existence. It is situated at the headwaters of the Kentawka drainage canel. Residents tried to get the railroad to built a depot, but it refused, until the State Railroad Commission later mandated one. The post office was established in the 1890s as Centralia. In 1905, postal officials changed the name to Neshoba, interpreted as a Choctaw word for "wolf" or "gray wolf," or taken from Chief Neshoba-Homo, meaning "Red Wolf."

NITTA YUMA (Sharkey) The Phelps family were early residents about 1768, followed by Henry Vick who built a plantation. In 1890, George Brown acquired about 100 acres and established a distillery. The Nitta Yuma Company was formed which called for owners to pay a pro-rated share for upkeep and other expenses for the exclusive community. The name was taken from a Choctaw word meaning "high land," designating the high banks along Deer Creek.

OKOLONA (Chickasaw/3,056) Littlebury Gilliam settled a few miles from the future townsite in 1836, naming it Prairie Mount, and opened his home as an inn for travelers. A post office opened in 1846 at the present site of Okolona. Establishment of the Mobile and Ohio Railroad brought settlers here, and rivaled Prairie Mount, which Okolona eventually absorbed. The postmaster at Aberdeen named the site Okolona, derived from Chickasaw Chief Oklalokonlih, whose name means "people gathered together." Others ascribe it to "clear, calm water."

PASCAGOULA (Jackson/26,200) The only natural seaport in the state, Pascagoula flew under numerous flags until the U.S. took possession in 1811. The Port of Pascagoula began in the 1830s when the east branch of the Pascagoula River was dredged, precipitating commerce along the river. Pascagoula was derived from the Choctaw expression, paska and okla, and means "bread people" (okla evolved to goula). The Pascagoula River is called "The Singing River." The sound is similar to a swarm of bees, but there is no explanation of its origin. Folklore says it is somehow connected to the extinction of the Pascagoula Indians.

PELAHATCHIE (Rankin/1,461) The town was named for the creek it borders, and is Choctaw for "hurricane creek," or "crooked creek," because the creek twists and turns. A half-breed Indian named Billy Goforth once owned the site. The early 1900s brought the lumber industry until the 1940s. With the timber gone, the poultry industry came into prominence. The last poultry plant burned down in 1997, destroying more than 1,000,000 pounds of processed chicken, and the whole town had to be evacuated. New high-tech industries have moved in.

PONTOTOC (Pontotoc/5,253) This site was an allotment given to a Chickasaw Indian named Lawach, who sold it to General Thomas McMackin in 1836. The land was surveyed by John Bell, Surveyor General of the Chickasaw Lands, and the post office was opened in 1837 (William Leland, postmaster). In 1836, the Pontotoc Female Academy was established, later converted to the Chickasaw College in 1852. Pontotoc was derived from the Chickasaw expression paki-takali, translated as "hanging grapes;" or ponti-tokali, meaning "upper end of the cattail." It has also been defined as "battle where the cat-tail stood."

SCOOBA (Kemper/632) Scooba was founded in 1832. When the Mobile and Ohio Railroad expressed interest at the current site, the town moved closer to the tracks that were completed in 1848. Mr. Sanders was the landowner and donated half interest to railroad as an enticement. Once known as Hell's Acre and a Half, Scooba was originally spelled Scoober, a

Choctaw word defined as "reed brake," for the reeds along the Little, Big, and Flat Scooba Creeks. Another interpretation was "muddy water."

SHUBUTA (Clarke/651) Shubuta started out as a trading post in the 1830s. Homesteads were taken up after the Treaty of Dancing Rabbit Creek the same year. It wasn't until about 1850 that the town showed much growth when the Mobile and Ohio Railroad selected this site for its shops and roundhouse. Shubuta was derived from a Choctaw word, shoboti, for "smoky waters." Warm water from a creek entering the Chickasawhay River created fog, which to the Indians looked like smoke.

SHUQUALAK (Noxubee/562) James Slaughter and Stanton Field erected the first buildings at Shuqualak about 1849. A year earlier, Samuel McNees had donated part of his land for a townsite and gave the Mobile & Ohio Railroad right of way. Completion of the railroad in 1857 made Shuqualak an important railroad point when it enabled farmers to ship their cotton out of the county. The name may be derived from shu-wa-lah, Choctaw for "hog wallow." Other theories were from the Choctaw language for "many branches," and "many headed waters."

TALOWAH (Lamar) Two Choctaw Indian families were living at the townsite when Napoleon Davis moved in with his family. The wealth of hardwood enabled Davis to start the business of manufacturing charcoal. He named the site Talowah, Choctaw for "catfish." Talowah's early life was as a First Adventist community after a book published by Brother J.L. Waller was sold and passed on to new families who took up the faith.

TOCCOPOLA (Pontotoc/189) This was once a Chickasaw Indian village where Allison and Tobias Furr built a watermill and general store in 1840. Toccopola is derived from tokapula (or toka-lapulli), a Chickasaw word for "crossing of the roads." Susan Allen was a Chickasaw who went through litigation over a slave given to her by her father and claimed by her husband's creditors in 1829. The slave had been given to her under Chickasaw law. She went to court in 1837, which resulted in establishment of women's rights to own property and not liable for the debts of their husbands. It was the first decision in the U.S. to give property rights to a woman.

TUPELO (Lee/34,211) The Chickasaw Indians ceded the site by the Treaty of Pontotoc in 1852. Called Gum Pond for the Tupelo gum trees, it was changed to Tupelo, which may be a Chickasaw word meaning "lodging place." It has also been interpreted from tuhpulah, which signified a scream or something making a noise. The Mobile & Ohio Railroad came through in 1859, followed a few years later by the Memphis & Birmingham Railroad, giving Tupelo excellent rail transportation, and enabled the town to quickly develop. Tupelo came into prominence with the cotton industry. It is also credited with establishment of the first fish hatchery in the United States.

WAHALAK (Kemper) Wahalak is the oldest town in the county, situated near Wahalak Creek. The Baptist Church was built in 1833 and a year later the post office was established. When the Mobile and Ohio Railroad came through in 1855 the town moved to be closer to the tracks. Not much is left of Wahalak but a church and restaurant, with a few scattered cottages. The name was derived from wawhallock, a Choctaw word that may have signified a low hill.

YAZOO CITY (Yazoo/14,550) As part of the Treaty of Doak's Stand, Chief Greenwood Leflore received a plot of land in 1826, and later sold it to developers. The town was named Manchester until 1839, when residents change it to Yazoo City. The name may have come from the Choctaw word, yazoo-ok-hinnah, "Yazoo, river of ancient ruins." It has also been defined as "home of the people who are gone." Some historians believe Yazoo refers to blowing on an instrument.

MISSOURI

KAHOKA (Clark/2,241) The last tribes in this area were the Sauk and Fox Indians. They ceded their lands to the U.S. in 1804, but Chief Black Hawk refused to go to a reservation and started the Black Hawk War. He and his band were eventually captured and sent to a reservation near Fort St. Louis. William Muldrow purchased 25,000 acres of land in 1856, part of which included Kahoka. William H. Huyck was appointed postmaster on October 25, 1858. The name was first spelled Cahoka, presumably taken for the Cahoka Indians, and was changed to Kahoka in June, 1874. The name was derived from gawakie, interpreted as "the lean ones."

KENOMA (Barton) This community is located near Pettis Creek, and was a railroad construction camp in the 1870s. When the Fort Scott, Southwestern and Memphis Railroad was built, engineers created a lake east of town. Barnabus Boggess laid out the town and had it platted in 1880. Kenoma is thought to be an Indian name, but its meaning is unknown. Kanomi in the Choctaw language means "all are relatives," and may possibly be its origin.

KOSHKONONG (Oregon/205) Sereno Standley acquired the homestead of Hardy Shurron for $10, a ham and side of bacon in 1880. The cabin Standley and his wife built served as their home, store and post office. Koshkonong's economy was based on peaches. Fruit growers planted peach orchards in the 1890s, and by 1901 the first load of peaches was headed for New York. The post office was opened in 1893. Then, in 1939, a cheese factory was established by the Cudahy Packing company which operated only a few years. Koshkonong means "wild rice." Another theory was from an Ojibway word for "shut in with fog." R.R. Hammond, supervisor for the Kansas City, Fort Scott, and Memphis Railroads named the town after a lake in Wisconsin.

MONEGAW SPRINGS (St. Clair) This site was originally occupied by the Osage, Shawnee and Sac Indians. They drank from what they believed were healing waters from over 100 springs in the region that were full of sulfur and other minerals. One of the early businessmen bottled the water and promoted the product. The U.S. Congress heard about it and sent medical experts to test the water, who found it did indeed have healing properties. Monegaw was an Osage chief who received his name after he helped an injured Spaniard, who told him of buried silver.

Monegaw used it to purchase horses and food for his people. His name means "owner of much money."

NEOSHO (Newton/10,505) John W. McCord acquired the site by right of preemption. On August 16, 1839, he deeded the land to the U.S. In 1870, the Atlantic and Pacific Railroad reached town, followed in 1887 by the Kansas City-Fort Smith and Southern Railroad. Neosho became a large trade center of agricultural products. The name was derived from neozho ("big springs"), an Osage word descriptive of nine springs within the city limits. It was also interpreted as "clear, cold water," "many waters," "meeting of the waters," and "dead man's creek."

NIANGUA (Webster/445) First known as Miteomah, the town was surveyed in March of 1870 for the South Pacific Railroad Company. The name was later changed to Niangua, an Osage word that means "bear." John J. Redmond was an early settler who built the first general store and was also postmaster when the office opened about 1870. The first hotel was built about 1860 by Christian Mikkelson, and used mainly by railroad men while they were laying the tracks. The depot and express office were opened at Niangua about 1870.

SARCOXIE (Jasper/*1,400*) First named Centerville because it was the geographical center of old Barry County, the town was settled as Vivion in the 1831, for settler Thackery Vivion. When application was made for a post office, the name had to be changed because of duplication. A Shawnee Indian named Chief Sarcoxie lived at the a spring for numerous years. Since it was called Sarcoxie Springs, Vivion thought it appropriate to rename the town after the Indian, translated as "rising sun."

TARKIO (Acthison/1,935) Tarkio was founded about 1880 and is a Sac or Fox word for "walnut" or "place where walnuts grow." It was once known as the center of the corn belt because one of the farms comprised over 30,000 acres and was the largest corn farm in the world. Out of a total of 4,300,000 bushels of corn taken out of the county, this farm raised more than 1,500,000 bushels of the product. In anticipation of becoming the county seat, residents had a courthouse built. It never occurred, so the building was converted into the Tarkio Valley College.

WAPPAPELLO (Wayne) Before settlement, the region was a camping and hunting ground for the Cherokee, Shawnee and other nomadic Indian tribes. Louis Houck made this site a station on the Cape Girardeau Southwestern Railway in September of 1884. William S. Allison became postmaster on October 21 the same year. The town's founder, Samuel R. Kelly, served in the 12th Calvary Missouri State Militia. Tradition says he was given a horse and told he could have all the land he could circle in the Wappapello area in one day. It was named for Shawnee Chief Wappepello (or Wapelillese), thought to mean "white bird."

MONTANA

ABSAROKEE (Stillwater/1,234) The community bears the name of the Crow Indians, interpreted as "large-beaked bird," perhaps referring to the crow bird. Another definition was ab-sar-o-ka, which means "forked tail bird," for the blue jays that inhabited the area. Absarokee was once surrounded by the Crow Reservation and opened for settlement in 1892. Although the town was not near a railroad, it continued to flourish with development of the Midget Marvel Flour Mill.

BANNACK (Beaverhead/0). Named for the Bannack Indians, this former community was the site of the first major gold discovery in Montana Territory. In 1858, James and Granville Stuart discovered gold near the Clark Fork River. Starting out as a crude mining camp, Bannack went on to become the territorial capital, then county seat. By 1864, the town declined after a richer goldfield was found at nearby Alder Gulch. The ghost town is under the direction of the Montana Fish Wildlife & Parks. Bannack was derived from penointikara and shortened to panak, for "honey eaters."

CHARLO (Lake/439) In 1855, Isaac Stevens negotiated a treaty with the Salish Indians, promising they could stay in the Bitterroot Valley. But in 1872 President Grant rescinded that promise and ordered the Indians removed to the Flathead Reservation. Chief Charlo pleaded with U.S. officials to stay in the Bitteroot, but he and his people were removed to the Jocko Reservation. Charlo was well regarded by other chiefs of the Flathead Nation. He died on January 10, 1910. This site was called Tabor for a reclamation engineer until the post office was established in 1918 (Pontus Haegg, postmaster). It was renamed Charlo, but the origin is unknown.

CHINOOK (Blaine/1,386) This town started out as Fort Belknap. After the fort moved, settlers relocated across the Milk River to be closer to the railroad tracks. It became known as Dawes, but the name was changed to the Chinook word which means "warm winds." These winds blow off the eastern slopes of the Rocky Mountains during the winter months, causing temperatures to rise up to 70 degrees in a few hours. Coal brought prosperity to some of the settlers in the 1890s when outcroppings were found on the bluffs along the rivers and creeks.

EKALAKA (Carter/410) A buffalo hunter named Claude Carter may have been the founder of this town. It was nicknamed Puptown because the region was full of prairie dogs. Carter built a saloon called the Old Stand, which served the cowboys for more than 50 years. Ijalaka was a Sioux woman whose great uncle was Sitting Bull. The site was given her name about 1881, translated as "swift one," but spelled Ekalaka. She acquired her name because she could break camp faster than the other Indian women. David Harrison married Ijkalaka in 1875 and was the first homesteader here.

KALISPELL (Flathead/14,223) Because of the rough terrain over the old Tobacco Plains Trail, there was no permanent settlement until about 1883. This was once home to the Blackfoot and Blood Indians, who called it Kalispel, meaning "prairie above the lake." The post office was established in 1890 by Angus McDonald for the Hudson's Bay Company, and the name was changed to Harrigan. It was later renamed Kalispell. During 1891, the townsite was a division point for the Great Northern Railroad.

LOLO (Missoula/3,388) This town took its name from Lolo Creek. Nez Perce Indians came from Washington and Idaho through the pass to hunt buffalo, and named the creek tum-sum-lech, which meant "without salmon." Father Desmet visited this valley in 1841 and was so impressed by its beauty, he called the creek "River of St. Francis Borgia." Then in 1854 Governor Stevens of the Washington territory designated the creek as "Lou Lou Creek." Eventually Lou Lou was changed to Lo Lo. Postal authorities closed the word up and it became Lolo. Of doubtful origin, it was interpreted from a Chinook word meaning "to carry."

MISSOULA (Missoula/57,053) Although Lewis and Clark came through in 1805, no settlement occurred until 1860, when C.P. Higgins and F.L. Worden took advantage of the Mullan Military Road. They built a trading post and called it Hellgate Village. After a sawmill and flour mill were established, it was changed to Missoula Mills. The name is a corruption of nemissoolatakoo, a Salish word for "near the cold, chilling waters." Others believe it comes from lmisuletiku, a Salish word meaning "at the stream or water of surprise," which describes Hellgate Canyon. During the 1880s, Missoula was the hub of Montana's timber industry.

SACO (Phillips/224) Tradition says an employee of the St. Paul Minneapolis and Manitoba Railway was blindfolded when naming the town in 1889. A globe was spun and he set his finger down on a place called Saco. There is a Saco in Maine, which is an Abnaki word for "flowing out," or "outlet." The post office was established in April, 1892 (Helen Parker, postmaster).

NEBRASKA

ARAPAHOE (Furnas/1,028) In 1871, a company was organized for the purpose of establishing a town on the Republican River. Named for the Arapaho Indians, the community was a principal grain market and shipping point for Furnas County. The name was derived from tirapihu, for "trader." The post office was established on August 11, 1873. Arapaho prospered until 1874 when grasshoppers destroyed all the crops. Growth was spurred when the Burlington & Missouri River Railroad laid its tracks about 1880.

DAKOTA CITY (Dakota/1,821) This site was platted about 1855 and designated county seat on January 23, 1856. The post office opened on January 28 the same year. Speculators thought the city had a prosperous future, but when Nebraska became a state the U.S. Court ceased holding its annual meetings here. Dakota City became a debarkation point for trade and travel along the Missouri River. Dakota was named for the Dakota (Sioux) Indians, and means "friend" or "ally."

MINATARE (Scotts Bluff/810) The region was originally home to the Minnataree, a branch of the Sioux Tribe, until they ceded their lands between 1833 and 1876. Otto Juergens brought in a herd of Shorthorn cattle, which was the beginning of a great cattle industry. When the town of Tabor was bypassed by the Burlington Northern Railroad in 1900, the community was moved to its present location and renamed Minatare, taken from Minnataree, which means "clear water." The post office was established in 1887 (W.H. Rockford, postmaster).

MONOWI (Boyd/2) Emil Schindler was the first settler at this tiny village, which was formed in 1902 when the Fremont, Elkhorn Missouri Valley Railroad came through. Its post office opened on July 3 the same year (closed in 1971). Monowi means "snow on the mountain," referring to a wildflower that grows in abundance in the area. The train depot was no longer used by 1960, and one of the residents moved it to his farm where it became a cattle shed. Over the years, fires took their toll on the business district, and today there is only one business, the Monowi Tavern, which is owned and run by Rudy and Elsie Eiler, the town's only residents. Monowi is the smallest incorporated city in the state.

NEHAWKA (Cass/232) Samuel Kirkpatrick claimed land along Weeping Water Creek in 1855 which became the center of town. When a post office was established in 1875, the postmaster wanted an Indian name that was easy to pronounce and selected Newhawka, derived from an Omaha or Otoe word meaning "rustling (or murmuring) water." It wasn't until the Missouri Pacific Railroad came through that the town saw any growth. Limestone quarrying was a profitable industry until about 1914, when more modern methods of dredging gravel from the Platte River were put in use.

NEMEHA (Nemaha/178) This townsite was founded by Dr. Jerome Hoover. Nemeha took its name from the river in 1854, which is defined as "miry (or swampy) waters," a Sioux expression descriptive of the bottom land. River boats boosted the economy by hauling grain during the 1860s. Nemeha became a station for the underground railroad during the Civil War, helping slaves work their way north.

NIOBRARA (Knox/379) Dr. Benneville Shelly and a group of men from Council Bluffs arrived in 1856 and formed a company called L'eau Qui Court. The Ponca Indians were also living here until about 1877 when the government forcibly removed them to Oklahoma. When the post office was established in 1859, it was named Niobrara, a Ponca or Omaha word meaning "spreading (or running) water," for the river that enters the Missouri River at this point. The town grew up on the river, but after the 1881 flooding from the spring thaws Niobrara was moved uphill from the river.

OCONTO (Custer/141) Located on the Kearney & Black Hills branch of the Union Pacific Railroad, Oconto began in 1887 when the Lincoln Townsite Company purchased 160 acres of land. The company wanted to name the town Olax, but another place in Nebraska was called Lomax. Since they were similar, Oconto was selected, a Menominee word for "place of the pickerel."

OGALLALA (Keith/4,930) Once a vigorous cow town, Ogallala was the place where the Oregon Trail, Mormon Trail, Pony Express, Union Pacific Railroad and Texas Trail all converged. The post office was established on July 11, 1873. Between

1875 and 1885, Ogallala was known as the "Gomorrah of the Cattle Trail," because of gunmen, gamblers, robberies, and Indian uprisings. Ogallala is a Sioux word that means "to scatter one's own." The Indians spelled it Ogala, but pronounced the word as Oklada.

OMAHA (Douglas/390,007) Omaha means "upstream," or "above all others upon a stream." The city got its start when fur traders established a trading post. Omaha benefited after gold was discovered in Colorado in 1859, bringing an influx of miners on their way to the goldfields. When Abraham Lincoln signed the Pacific Railway Act in 1862, the Union Pacific began to lay its tracks west and made Omaha its headquarters. It also became a town of stockyards, handling millions of head of livestock shipped via the Union Pacific. Today, most of the stockyards are gone.

PAWNEE (Pawnee/1,033) The name comes from the Pawnee Indians, which means "horn people," because of their distinctive hair style. Some of the earliest settlers arrived about 1856. The Burlington Railroad was built through Pawnee in 1881, the same year a terrible fire destroyed more than 20 business structures. Stagecoach service provided transportation until the railroad arrived.

TEKAMAH (Burt/1,892) This site was originally an Indian camp ground and village. New Yorkers founded the town in 1855, as Niles Folsom wrote "...Each member of the company wrote a name on a ballot and "Tekamah" the name which Wm. N. Byers wrote, was drawn;... In April 1855 we made permanent settlement at Tekamah—Col. John B. Folsom, Z.B. Wilder, Wm. F. Goodwill, N.R. Folsom and Miles Hopkins..."[27] Tekamah means "big cottonwood," and was descriptive of the cotton trees abundant along a creek. After settlement, the residents experienced trouble with the Indians so the military came in 1855 to protect them by building a blockhouse. This same year a terrible drought occurred that was so bad it left three-foot fissures in the ground.

UNADILLA (Otoe/342) Families from Upper New York were early residents about 1869 and named their new town for a place in New York. Unadilla is an Iroquois word for "a place of meeting." An influx of settlers occurred after the Civil War and when the Homestead Act went into effect. The Midland Pacific Railroad reached Unadilla about 1871, precipitating the establishment of a stockyard from where the largest shipments of cattle were made out of the county. The post office was established on April 4, 1872 (John Abbott, postmaster).

WAHOO (Saunders/3,942) An early resident in 1865 was Moses Stocking. When the post office was established in 1868, the community was named Leesville for James Lee. It was later changed to Wahoo. This area was a favorite camping ground of the Otoe Indians. Wahoo was thought to be an Otoe word meaning "burning bush," descriptive of a bush used for medicinal purposes by the local medicine man. Another definition is from Pawhoo, Pawnee for "round bluffs." Wahoo was the home of George Beadle, Nobel Prize winner in 1958 for his pioneering work in genetics.

WINNETOON (Knox/70) Defined as "dividing of the waters," or "big water," Winnetoon's post office was established about 1890 (John Culberton, postmaster). A year later Seth Jones founded the town when he learned that a railroad was going to be built. Farmers prospered raising livestock and crops until the Great Depression and a drought. Many of the people were unable to support themselves and were forced to move on.

YUTAN (Saunders/1,216) In the 1830s, missionary Moses Merrill built a mission east of Yutan. First called Clear Creek, the town was renamed for Otoe Chief L'etan (pronounced Yutan, origin unknown). His given name was Shaumonekusse (or Shon-mon-i-case), the "prairie wolf." This was the site where the Pawnee, Delaware and Oto Indians signed a treaty, and by 1853 the village had been abandoned. The town came into existence about 1876 after the Omaha & Republican Valley Railroad extended its line from Valley to Wahoo and on to Lincoln. When passenger traffic dwindled, the service was discontinued, and today only freight trains are in operation.

NEVADA

BEOWAWE (Eureka/*60*) Beowawe was established about 1850 when a trading post was built, and grew up around the Central Pacific Railroad. The post office was established in 1870 and closed its doors in 1995. Beowawe may be a Shoshone expression for "gate." Because of the conformation of the hills on either side of the valley, the community looks like it stands in an open gateway. In addition to serving as an ore shipping point for the Cortez Mining District, Beowawe profited from stock raising. When the town of Buckhorn was established, it greatly affected growth of Beowawe.

HIKO (Lincoln/0) Hiko began its life in 1866 as a mining camp after the Indians told the white men about silver in the region. After purchasing some of the miners' claims, William Raymond laid out the site. Hiko became county seat the following year, but lost it to the town of Pioche in 1871. Transport of machinery and the stamp mill proved costly, and there were not enough workers for the mines. As a result, Hiko lost most of its residents and the town declined. Hiko is Shoshone for "white man," or "white man's town."

JARBIDGE (Elko/*15*) Jarbidge was founded as a gold camp in 1909, and is situated 2,000 feet down along the steep confines of Jarbidge Canyon. In 1890, John Ross found a float (pieces of gold washed out from a gold vein), but was driven out by a snowstorm. The strike was later discovered by Russ Ishman. The post office opened on March 5, 1910. Jarbidge is from the Shoshone word, jahabich, which means "devil." It came from Indian legend about a man-eating giant called Tswhawbitts who lived in a crater. He captured Indians, put them into a basket he had strapped on his back, took them home and ate them.

PAHRUMP (Nye/24,631) Chief Tecopa was a Southern Paiute born near Las Vegas about 1815, and became leader of the Ash Meadows and Pahrump region. Although his name means "wildcat," he was actually a very peaceful Indian. Lt. Daniel Lockwood was sent by the Army Corp of Engineers to explore the region in 1871. The Paiutes were eventually displaced when the white men came and developed trails and miners came to seek gold. The post office was established on July 27, 1891. Pahrump is a Paiute word interpreted as "water stone," "great spring," "water mouth," or "big flow of water."

PANACA (Lincoln/*800*) During the winter of 1863, missionary William Hamlin was shown a rich ore deposit, and prospectors rushed to the site when the word spread. The place became known as Panaca Ledge. Settlers arrived the following year led by Francis Lee, a Mormon missionary. Ditches and canals were built to bring water to their land for agriculture. Panaca has been defined as "warm water," and there was a warm spring near the town. Another interpretation is "metal," derived from the Paiute word, panukker, descriptive of gold ore in the region.

TOANO (Elko/0) This site was created in 1868 when the Central Pacific Railroad made it a division point and eating station. It also built its train repair shops and a roundhouse. The community evolved as a supply center for the eastern Nevada mining camps. When the railroad ceased repair operations here and moved them to the town of Cobre, many of the buildings were also moved Toano became deserted. Toano is a Goshute word meaning "black coated," descriptive of the Toana Range topography, or "pipe-camping place."

TONOPAH (Nye/2,627) Tonopah owes its existence to Jim Butler who discovered silver in the region which would eventually net millions. A school superintendent named Walter Gayhart platted the town. Mining companies were formed and regular freight routes established. The Tonopah & Goldfield Railroad further lent to Tonopah's growth. The post office opened as Butler on March 3, 1905, until it was changed to Tonopah. Eventually, many of the mines closed down and the 1940s brought them all under leases. Tonopah comes from a Shoshone or Paiute word for "small spring," describing the spring used by the Indians on their wanderings from the Cowich Mountains.

TUSCARORA (Elko/*20*) Tuscarora had its beginnings in 1864 near Beard Mountain with the discovery of gold. The year 1869 brought the Central Pacific Railroad which employed more than 2000 Chinese who stayed near Beard Mountain after the tracks were completed and gleaned what was left out of the abandoned mines. Miners moved their camp here in 1871 when silver was discovered, and the post office opened on July 18 the same year. It was named for the Tuscarora Indians, interpreted as "hemp gatherers."

WABUSKA (Lyon) This community is situated on a branch line of the Southern Pacific Railroad. It was once served by the Carson and Colorado Railroad when the site was one of its stations in 1881. The post office was established as Wabuxka on September 18, 1874. It is a Paiute word meaning "white grass," or "vegetation." Wabuska was a supply center for mining operations in the surrounding area in the early 1900s. During World War I, Wabuska saw some growth when the region experienced a copper boom. By 1919, the gas engine replaced the railroad and Wabuska lost much of its business industry.

WINNEMUCCA (Humboldt/7,174) Established in the early 1850s, Winnemucca was formerly a hay ranch. A hotel and trading post were built to serve settlers going to California and Oregon, and the post office was established on February 1, 1866. Arrival of the Central Pacific Railroad in 1868 transformed the town to a stage and mining outfitting center. Once known as French Ford and Centerville, the name was later changed to Winnemucca by C. Bannon who wanted to named it after Chief Wan-ne-muc-cha as the white man called him. It is a Paiute/English word that means "one moccasin" (muc-cha is Paiute for moccasin, and the "wan-ne" was added by white men). He received this name as a boy when he was found wearing only one moccasin while playing by the river.

NEW HAMPSHIRE

ASHUELOT (Cheshsire) Squakheag Indians occupied the territory until 1720, when they may have disbanded and gone north to join the St. Francis tribe in Canada. Ashuelot is a village in the town of Winchester, and was established about 1733. The post office opened in 1833 as West Winchester, and changed to Ashuelot in 1854. This village became a manufacturing center, which brought Irish and French immigrants to work. Ashuelot is derived from nashue (or nashueut), a Narragansett word meaning "in the midst," designating a point or angular piece of land lying between two branches of a stream.

CHOCORUA (Carroll) Chocorua is a small village in the town of Tamworth. An iron forge was established along the Chocorua River during the 1700s. The post office was established in 1847 (Samuel Merrill, postmaster). The site was originally called Tamworth Iron Works until nature writer Frank Bolles headed a drive to have it changed to Chocorua in 1890. Chief Chocurua was a member of the Pequawket Indian tribe, and his name was translated as "frog," "fox," or "a sharp knife."

CONTOOCOOK (Merrimack/1,444) A village in the town of Hopkinton, Contoocook took its name from one of the tribes of Penacook Indians, meaning "nut trees river," "small plantation at river," or "crow river." People were attracted to water power of the Contoocook River and built numerous mills. The Concord and Claremont Railroad was built in 1849 that ran from Concord to Bradford, and construction of the Contoocook Bridge began the same year. In 1856, the Contooccook Academy was opened. By 1880, the village had become the business center of Hopkinton.

GONIC (Strafford) Gonic was derived from squamanagonic, Abnaki for "water from the clay-hill place." Other interpretations were "salmon-spearing place," and "day and water." Gonic is part of the town of Rochester and was settled during the late 1600s. Mills were established about 1785, the most prominent being the Gonic Manufacturing Company, producer of woolen goods for the general market and the backbone of Gonic's economy. The post office opened on January 28, 1851 (Charles Whitehouse, postmaster).

MERRIMACK (Hillsborough/25,119) Indians of the Penacook Tribe were early inhabitants with whom John Cromwell conducted trade in 1656. Because he cheated the Indians, they set out to kill him, but Cromwell fled and never returned. Merrimack was once part of Massachusetts until boundaries were established in 1746. John Chamberlain claimed 300 acres of land and established the first grist mill and saw mill. He later became a selectman and member of the general assembly. Merrimack was derived from monnomoke or merramake, an Abnaki word interpreted as "sturgeon," or "at the deep place."

NASHUA (Hillsborough/86,605) This region was home to the Nashaway Indians who were part of the Penacook Tribe. Nashua started out as a trading post in the 1600s, but Indian attacks deterred permanent settlement until the late 1700s. The site was named Nashua, a Penacook word interpreted as "land between two rivers," or "between streams." Textile mills established along the Nashua and Merrimack rivers were the focus of activity during the early 1800s. Most of the mills had closed by the 1950s. Today, Nashua's economy is supported by high-tech corporations.

OSSIPEE (Carroll/4,211) Attention was focused on this area about 1600, which was visited by both English and French explorers. British settlers built a fort near Lake Ossipee in 1650 in order to help the Ossipee Indians fight of off the Mohawks. The fort was rebuilt in the 1700s when skirmishes occurred between Americans and British. The town took its name from the lake, named for the Ossipee Indians, interpreted as "water on other side," or "beyond the water." Historically, Ossipee has been a manufacturing town.

PASSACONAWAY (Carroll) This former hamlet was once a section of Albany. The name is derived from Penacook Chief Papisseconwa, meaning "papoose bear," or "bear cub." His tribe lived along the Merrimack River. The chief was regarded as a magician, and was thought to have lived to be about 120. Today Passaconaway is located entirely within the White Mountain National Forest, and the Forest Service maintains a historic museum.

SUNAPEE (Sullivan/3,055) This section of land was granted by colonial authorities in 1768 to John Sprague under the name of Saville. The community was settled in 1772 by emigrants who came from Rhode Island, and the name was changed to Wendell in 1781 for one of the original settlers, John Wendell. By an act of Legislature in 1850, it was renamed Sunapee, an Penacook word meaning "wild goose water," or "rocky pond."

WINNISQUAM (Belknap) This hamlet is situated in sections of the towns of Sanbornton, Tilton and Belmont. It was named for the lake that borders the site, an Abnaki word that means "pleasant water," or "salmon fishing at lake outlet." The earliest date of settlement was about 1748. It still has its own post office, and today the lake's 25-mile shoreline is dotted with summer cottages. Water for the lake comes from the Winnipesaukee River.

WONALANCET (Carroll) Wonalancet is a village in the town of Tamworth. First called Birth Intervale, it had to be changed when the post office opened in 1893 because of confusion with the summer resort of Intervale. Kate Walden was postmaster at the time and suggested Wonalancet, the son of Penacook Chief Passaconaway. Wonalancet means "breathing pleasantly," or "governor." The town was known for its Chinook Kennel, owned by Kate's husband, Arthur. He and his dogs accompanied Admiral Byrd's first expedition to the Antarctic. Chinook was Arthur's favorite dog, and sadly died during the polar expedition, possibly caused by old age (he was 12).

NEW JERSEY

ABSECON (Atlantic/7,638) The site was called Absegami by Indians who held their summer feasts here. In 1695, Thomas Budd purchased a tract of land that would later become Atlantic City. He sold some of his property to John Reading who called his place Mount Eagle. The town became a port of call for sailing ships in the 1700s. In addition, a staple industry was the harvesting of oysters and clams. Joseph Sharp became postmaster when the office was established on April 1, 1808. The name was changed to Absecon in 1900, an Algonquin word for as "little [sea] water," or "place of the swans."

CHEESEQUAKE (Middlesex) This region was inhabited by the Lenape Indians more than 6,000 years ago. The name may have been taken from Cheesequake Creek, so called because of the "quaking bogs" or marsh land. There was once an Indian village nearby called Chaquasitt, derived from chese-hoh-ke, a word for "upland." Indian derivations of chessak (fur) or chasquem (maize) was thought to have generated this name. But it comes from the Lenape word, chickhake, meaning "land that has been cleared." The site is now part of Old Bridge Township and a state park.

CINNAMINSON (Burlington/14,595) Settlement began in the 1860s, but growth didn't increase until 1876 when the Exposition in Philadelphia premiered. One of the biggest industries was a nursery, established by William Parry. His property and mansion were purchased in the early 1900s by the Campbell Soup Company, where the method of condensing soups was developed by Dr. John Dorrance. Cinnaminson has been interpreted as "stone tree," "sweet water," and "place of tangled roots." But Herbert Craft, an authority on the Lenape language, wrote that it was derived from ahsenamensing, meaning "rocky place of fish."[28] Cinnaminson was the place where the first Japanese Beetle in the U.S. made its presence known (1916).

CROSSWICKS (Burlington) The Lenape Indians named the site Crossweeksung, which means "separation." designating separation of boys from girls during certain periods. Others believed it referred to a separation of Crosswicks Creek. Quakers established the town about 1677 and lived peacefully with the Indians. In 1733, they built the Chesterfield Friends Meeting House. During a battle in 1778 between Hessian soldiers and Colonial troops, the building served as a hospital. Since Crosswicks never had benefit of a railroad or canal, it became a sleepy rural town.

HACKENSACK (Bergen/42,677) Hackensack was settled by the Dutch in 1647 who started the first trading post, calling the site New Barbadoes. During the Revolution, the town was a strategic point with its proximity to the Passaic River and Fort Lee. The post office was established in 1797. Hackensack experienced growth when the Hackensack and New York Railroad made it the northern terminus. It wasn't until 1921 that the name was changed to Hackensack, derived from the Lenape word, ahkinkeshaki, for "place of sharp ground."

HOBOKEN (Hudson/38,577) Home to the Lenape Indians, the region was settled by the Dutch in 1640. Aert vanPutten established the first brewery in the United States at Hoboken. The land was owned by Peter Stuyvesant, purchased by Colonel John Stevens in 1874 who laid out the site. He named it Hoboken, derived from hupoken, a Lenape word for "tobacco pipe." During the 1900s, Hoboken gained importance as a transportation center when the Delaware, Lackawanna and Western Railroad made the town its terminus. The first ice cream cone was invented and patented at Hoboken

HO-HO-KUS (Bergen/4,060) Albert Zaborowsky came from Poland in 1662 and became the town's first settler. His descendents built an inn and stagecoach stop in 1790. During the Revolution, the town found itself embroiled in conflict because it was situated on a route that was used by both British and the Americans. Ho-Ho-Kus is derived from a Lenape word, but its meaning is disputed. It has been defined as "hollow rock," running water," "red cedar," "cracking of a tree," and "cleft in the rock." The hyphens were added when mail for Hohocus was going to Hoboken.

HOPATCONG (Sussex/15,888) Originally home to the Munsi Indians, the site was claimed by James Logan in 1715. Others who moved here came for the furs they could use for trade, and later the iron industry came into prominence. During the Revolution the iron forges were vital to Continental Army. First named Brooklyn, the name was changed to Hopatcong, derived from the Lenape word, hapakonoesson, meaning "pipestone," and may have described the soapstone to make the Indians' pipes. It was also interpreted as "body of still water," and "stone over water."

MAHWAH (Bergen/24,062) The Lenape Indians used the flat plain for their pow wows and council meetings. This land was deeded to Blandina Bayard in 1700, who established a trading post. Since she knew the Lenape language, Blandina got along well with the Indians. During the Revolution, Colonial troops established a camp to protect the road near Mahwah to keep the British from coming through. Mahwah may be derived from Lenape, mawewi, interpreted as "a meeting place where roads and streams come together," or "beautiful."

MANAHAWKIN (Ocean/2,004) First seen by Henry Hudson during his explorations in 1609, Manahawkin was settled in the mid-1700s by a group of men from Staffordshire, England. Early industries were whaling, oyster harvesting, and farming. The Manahawkin Militia was formed during the Revolution to guard the beaches against Loyalists. After the war, principal occupations consisted of cranberry cultivation and the manufacture of iron ingots. Manahawkin is derived from the Lenape word, menanhoking, meaning "where the land slopes."

MANALAPAN (Monmouth/33,423) A Scot named John Anderson and his wife, Anna, were given a tract of land known as Manalapan by Anna's father in 1701. Tradition says that George Washington stayed with the Anderson family the eve before the Battle of Monmouth. Manalapan was once the home of the Unami (Turtle clan) of the Lenape Indians. The name has been interpreted as "land that produces good bread," "good cultivation," and "covered swamp with edible roots."

MANASQUAN (Monmouth/6,310) Originally settled as part of Shrewsbury in the late 1600s, Manasquan later became part of Wall Township. The year 1665 brought in the first English settlers who named the town after the river. Manasquan suffered through the Revolution and War of 1812 when the British attacked American ships sailing the Manasquan River. The Lenape Indians called the site menaskung, for "place to gather grass."

MATAWAN (Monmouth/8,910) Situated at the crossing of two Indian trails, Matawan was a bartering site for the Indians. Dutch traders referred to the place as Muttovang, and the English called it Mittevang. In 1686, Stephen Warne purchased 400 acres and named it Warne's Neck. Matawan has been defined as "enchanted skin" (referring to animal pelts) or "where two rivers come together." Donald Becker wrote, "Matawan is said to be found in its pure form in the Abnaki tongue… Also intriguing is the speculation in the similarity of the designation Matawan to Mattawang. This last term has been translated to mean "bad to travel…"[29]

METUCHEN (Middlesex/12,840) Metuchen was settled during the 1680s with the arrival of Dutch and English Settlers. But it would be the early 1800s before the town saw much growth. This was a result of the New Jersey Railroad being built in 1836. Named for Chief Matouchin (or Metochshaning), whose name was interpreted as "rolling land," descriptive of the regional topography.

NETCONG (Morris/2,580) As South Stanhope, the town developed when the Morris Canal opened in 1831, but the Civil War thwarted much growth. Workers on the Delaware, Lackawanna and Western Railroad were early settlers. South Stanhope severed its ties with the township in 1894 and became the borough of Netcong. The name is derived from musconetcong, meaning "grass creek," or "swamp stream." Another definition was "place of stream."

PARAMUS (Bergen/25,737) Paramus was previously part of New Barbadoes and Midland Township. An unrecorded indenture showed a transfer of land at Parames between Alert Zabriskie and Albert A. Terhune in 1708. A year later the Indians sold more then 40,000 acres to French Huguenots, part of which would become Paramus. Explorers came to the region for furs, and a trading post was established. The Lenape Indians gave the region its name, which designated "a fertile land where corn was grown attracting wild turkeys," or "place of wild turkeys."

PARSIPPANY (Morris/50,649) This township was originally granted to Lord John Berkely and Sir George Carteret by King Charles II in 1644. People were attracted to the region because of the gently rolling plains that provided them with good farm land, where extensive apple orchards were also cultivated. Parsippany is derived from paceponong, a Lenape word that means "the place where the rivers run together," signifying the convergence of the Parsippany, Rockaway and Whippany rivers.

PASSAIC (Passaic/67,861) Hartman Michaelse (or Vreeland) purchased Dundee Island from the Indians for a bottle of rum and set up a trading post in 1678. First known as Acquackanonk Landing, the name was changed to Passaic in 1854, derived from the Lenape word, pahsaek, for "valley." The first factory was established by Stephen Basset in 1735 when he opened a tannery, and was the only industry for more than a hundred years. After the Revolution, Passaic enjoyed its growth as a river port and agricultural center.

PENNSAUKEN (Camden/35,737) This region was home to the Lenape Indians whose chief was Eriwonek. In 1698, Samuel Burrough, Jr. established a grist mill using water power of the Delaware

River. As the population increased, sawmills and forges were established. Following the Revolution, the fishing industry came into prominence. Pennsauken was served by a post office established at the town of Merchantville in 1865. Pennsauken is a Lenape word that means "tobacco pouch," derived from pindasenaken.

PEQUANNOCK (Morris/13,888) The rich soil in this township attracted Aarent Schuyler who purchased a tract of land in 1695. Settlers who followed were mainly those from Holland and members of the Dutch Reformed Church. They purchased the land by acquiring the Indians' rights, then applied for the land through the Proprietors. Pequannock has been defined as Lenape for "small field," "land naturally clear and open," and "water that flows clean," and may have designated the Pompton River.

PISCATAWAY (Middlesex/50,482) Piscataway was founded in 1666 by Charles Gilman, John Martin, Hugh Dunn and Hopewell Hull. Dunn was a moving force in the organization of the Baptist Church in 1689. Many of the settlers were Quakers and Baptists fleeing religious persecution from England. Piscataway is a Lenape word interpreted as "great deer river," or "dark," which may have described the soil.

PLUCKEMIN (Somerset) The region was settled in the 1700s. A Lutheran church known as Church on the Raritan held the first Lutheran Synod in America in 1735. During 1776, the British Cavalry raided the town and used it as an access to the Continental Army's artillery encampment behind a settler's property. Pluckemin's name is in dispute. Some believed it was not an Indian word, but came from a local innkeeper who was so anxious for customers, he would "pluck 'em in." Others interpreted the name as "persimmon."

RAHWAY (Union/26,500) The early 1600s brought Europeans and Quakers who pushed the Lenape Indians out of their land. The Merchants and Drovers Tavern was established in 1750, serving as a stagecoach stop. Rahway's stability was tied to carriage factories, which numbered more than 30, and earned Rahway its nickname as "Carriage City of the World." In 1903, Merck and Company made its headquarters here, one of the largest manufacturers of drugs and chemicals in the world. Rahway was derived from the Lenape word, nawak-wa, for "in the middle of the forest."

ROCKAWAY (Morris/22,930) Rockaway Township was formed in 1844. Early settlers were the Dutch who named the site in 1715. Rockaway was derived from a Lenape word, rechouwakie, which means "place of sands." During the 1730s, the region was the center of a thriving iron-mining district. During the Civil War, the Hibernia Railroad extended its line which linked Rockaway to the Hibernia Mines. When surface ore was discovered in the Mesabi region at the Great Lakes in 1876, the iron industry declined at Rockaway. Its stability was insured when the Navy built the Picatinny Arsenal in 1879.

SECAUCUS (Hudson/15,931) The Indians who resided in the region were the Hackensack, a subtribe of the Lenape Indians. In 1658, Peter Stuyvesant purchased the land, which included Island Siskakes (Secaucus). Stuyvesant granted a patent of 2,000 acres to Nicholas Bayard and Nicholas Varlet in 1663. The Lenape Indians contested the patent, but the Indians ceded the land when they were offered ten gallons of rum. Secaucus is derived from sukachgook, meaning "snake hill," or from sikkakaskeg, for "salt sedge marsh."

SHAMONG (Burlington/6,462) In 1710, this region was identified as Edgepilleck. It later earned the name Indian Mills because of the grist mill and saw mill run by the Indians in 1742. Missionary John Brainerd arrived ten years later and built a school and church for the Indians. Governor Bernard called the site Brotherton, then set it aside for an Indian reservation in 1758. The township of Shamong may be Lenape for "place of the horn," and probably referred to the wealth of deer in the region.

TEANECK (Bergen/39,260) Although the town was not established until 1895, the name Teaneck was known in the late 1600s. It name may have come from a Dutch word. Some historians translated it as a Hackensack (tribe of the Lenape) word for "place where there are woods." Dutch farmers settled at Teaneck in the early 1700s and lived a peaceful existence until the uproar at Fort Lee. Teaneck was the first town in the United States to vote for integrated schools in the 1960s.

TOTOWA (Passaic/9,892) The Minsi, a subtribe of the Lenape Indians, lived in the region until smallpox, measles, and alcohol decimated them. The Totowa Patent was owned by the Van Houten family, and by 1750 the region had become a thriving Dutch farming community. Joshua Hott lived at Totowa and was involved in Benedict Arnold's plot. He received a summary court martial, but there was not enough evidence to confine him. Totowa was translated as "where you begin," because the town was situated on the edge of a wilderness. Other interpretations were from the Lenape word, totauwei, for "to dive and reappear," and tetauwi, meaning "it is between."

WANAMASSA (Monmouth/4,551) Part of the Township of Ocean, this site was purchased from the Lenape Indians in 1687 by Gawen (or Gavin) Drummond, a Scotsman and surveyor. The deed was signed by the chief sachems, Wanamassa, Wallammassekaman and Waywinotunce. The town experienced slow development until the early 1900s when a YMCA organization purchased the land to use for camp meetings and revivals. The project was later abandoned. Wanamassa's name origin is unknown.

WATCHUNG (Somerset/5,613) Watchung was originally part of Bernards and Bedminster Township, and called Washingtonville. In 1897, the name was changed to Watchung, which is derived from ohchung, a Lenape word meaning "hilly place." During the 18th Century, copper mining was a thriving industry, in addition to hat-making and rock quarrying. Dr. Charles Eaton was a prominent citizen, who had a hand in formation of the United Nations.

NEW MEXICO

ABIQUIU (Rio Arriba) Located along the Chama River, this former Tewa pueblo was settled by the Spaniards in 1747. Utes also lived in the region and conducted trade with the settlers. Later, the Penitentes arrived to tend to the needy and sick of Abiquiu. They were a confraternity of the Catholic Church, called the Brotherhood, who believed in performing flagellation on themselves, depicting Christ's suffering. Abiquiu may be derived from the Tewa word, abay, which means "chokecherry." Or it may be a Spanish corruption of another Tewa word, pay shoo boo-oo, meaning "timber end town."

ACOMA PUEBLO (Valencia) Four hundred feet on top of a mesa sits Acoma Pueblo, which archaeologists have shown to be inhabited since 1075 A.D. The first European visitor was Captain Hernando de Alvarado in 1540. Don Juan de Onate came to Acoma in 1598, followed by Captain Gaspar de Villagra, who was received by Chief Zutucapan. He left because of the Indians' hostility. In 1629, the mission San Esteban del Ray was built, and is now listed as a National Historic Landmark. According to some historians, Acoma comes from the Indians' name for themselves, Akomi, for "people of the white rock." But the Acoma people say Acoma is derived from the Keresan word, hak'u, which means to prepare or plan for something.

CHAMA (Rio Arriba/1,199) Chama is situated at the foot of Cumbres Pass in the Chama River Valley, and may bear the Tewa name, tama, for "here they have wrestled." Another interpretation is a descriptive word for the color of a river, "red." The town saw more residents during the early 1800s with increased wagon traffic from Santa Fe to Colorado. Chama became an outfitting center when the Denver & Rio Grand Railroad was built in 1880, and the post office opened on December 28 the same year. The town's economy was dependent on logging, mining and ranching.

CHIMAYO (Rio Arriba/2,924) Chimayo was established about 1692. The name comes from tsimayo, a Tewa word meaning "good flaking (or striking) stone," referring to the obsidian in the area. Sanctuario de Nuestro Senor de Esquipulas was sacred ground to the Tewa Indians. The sanctuary was built by Don Bernardo Abeyta, a Penitente, between 1813 and 1816. Chimayo is best known for its exquisite weavers, brought to Santa Fe from Spain in 1805 to develop their craft. Juan and Ignacio Balzan were two weavers who didn't like Santa Fe and moved to Chimayo, where they taught the craft. Their fine weaving has been passed down through the generations.

COCHITI (Sandoval/507) This pueblo is 30 miles southwest of Santa Fe and has been at the same site since about 1250 A.D. Fray Agustin Rodriguez was the first European visitor in 1581. The Mission of San Buenaventura was established about 1630, but destroyed during the Pueblo Revolt in 1680. Residents hastily abandoned Cochiti but returned after the rebellion. The Indians had to flee again to a mountain stronghold called Cieneguilla in 1692 when Diego de Vargas began his reconquest of New Mexico. The post office was established on October 24, 1907, and discontinued on

September 30, 1980. Cochiti was taken from kotyete (or kao tay-ay), a Keresan word meaning "stone kiva."

NAMBE (Santa Fe/*1,246*) The first recorded visit to Nambe was in 1591 when explorer Gaspar Castano de Sosa and his men erected a wooden cross. The Indians were told they were part of the Spanish province of New Mexico and required to pay tribute to the king. Tradition says that as soon as Gaspar left, the Indians tore down the cross. Friar Cristobal de Salazar founded a mission that was occupied for more than 700 years. During the Pueblo Revolt of 1680, the mission was destroyed. Nambe is derived from the Tewa word, nambay-ongwhee, meaning "mound of earth in the corner," or "people of the roundish earth," descriptive of the topography of a more ancient pueblo nearby.

NASCHITTI (San Juan/360) This village is part of the Fort Defiance Agency located on the Navajo Reservation. Here was situated the oldest trading post on the east side of the Chuska Mountains, established in 1880 by Charlie Verden and Thomas Bryan. They operated the post until 1902 when it was sold to C.C. Manning. This community was founded in 1893 as Naschitti, derived from the Navajo word, nahashch'idí, meaning "badger." Residents discovered a badger digging for food, but found water instead. Tradition says the people later tapped an artesian well at the spot. The Christian Reform Church was given permission by the Navajo Tribe to build its church here in 1922.

PICURIS (Taos/86) Priests came to Picuris about 1620 and forced the Indians to build the San Lorenzo Mission. Fray Martin de Arvide taxed them so heavily that the people almost starved. As a result, Pueblo Governor Luis Tupato had enough and led the Pueblo Revolt, completely destroying the mission. Reconquering of New Mexico in 1692 brought the Picuris Indians under submission a second time, until they revolted again in 1696. Picuris may be a Spanish corruption of pay kwee lay ta (or piwwe-tha), which means "at mountain gap" or "pass in the mountains." Another translation is from a Keresan word, pee-koo-ree-a, for "those who paint."

POJOAQUE (Santa Fe/1,261) Mission San Francisco de Pojoaque was established in the early 1600s. It was abandoned after the Pueblo Revolt and partially resettled in 1706. The 1800s brought non-white encroachment on the Indian land, followed by a smallpox epidemic. By 1900, most of the people left for other villages. The Commissioner of Indian Affairs persuaded the Indians to return in 1934 under the Indian Reorganization Act. Pojoaque is derived from the Tewa word, po-suwae-geh (or posoong wa ghay), defined as "water drinking (or gathering) place." It may be a corruption of povi age, meaning "place where the flowers grow along the stream."

SANOSTEE (San Juan/429) This Navajo community sits on the eastern side of the Chuska Mountains on the Navajo Reservation. It was once home to Chief Narbona, a great leader and man of influence who promoted peace with the whites. In 1849, he was killed in a fray when an army officer thought one of the Indians had stolen a horse. This village became known for its Two Gray Hills rug patterns in the late 19th century when weavers discarded the red pattern designed by J.B. Moore and began using the natural colors produced by the sheep. Today, these rugs are coveted world-wide. Sanostee is derived from the Navajo word, tsé alnáozt'i'i, meaning "crisscrossing rocks."

TAIBAN (DeBaca) This ranching community took its name from Taiben Creek.

A Portuguese immigrant took up a settlement near Taiban which was first called Brazil Springs and later changed to Taiban Springs. The town was named by the Atcheson, Topeka and Santa Fe Railroad in 1906. The same year the site was laid out by Judge McGill, J.B. Sledge and a Mr. Lindsay. Taiban had its 15 minutes of fame when Pat Garrett captured Billy the Kid up an arroyo near town in 1880. Today, it is a ranching community. Taiban is a Navajo or Comanche word for "horsetail," possibly referring to all the tributaries on the Taiban Arroyo that all come from the same direction. Another meaning is "three creeks."

TAOS (Taos/4,700) Taos was a trading site for the Ute, Apache and Comanche Indians in the 1700s, followed by mountain men who arrived in the 1750s and used the site as their headquarters. The post office was established on March 9, 1885. The late 1800s brought artists to Taos. While two men were studying painting in Paris, they were told to paint the west before it was gone. As a result, Taos has continued to flourish as an art colony. The town was officially named Don Fernando de Taos, but the post office shortened it to Taos, which is a Tewa word, tu-o-ta, meaning "red willow," or derived from tua-tah, for "down at the village."

TESUQUE (Santa Fe/ 909) Hernando de Alvarado, with the Coronado expedition, was the first European at this pueblo in the 1700s. Founded about 1300, the people believed their ancestors originated in an underworld north of the community. It was from this place that the Pueblo Revolt started. Residents fled and did not return for fourteen years. The village was originally called Taytsoongay, but was corrupted to Tesuque. The original spelling means "cottonwood tree place," or may be a Tewa term, tat' unge' onwi, for "spotted dry place," referring to the way the river comes and goes under the sand.

TOHATCHI (McKinley/1,037) Built on a site of ancient ruins, the community was first called Little Water by white settlers. The United States Indian Service School was established in 1896. Four years later, missionary L.P. Brink arrived and was one of the first to print the tonal language of the Navajos. The post office was established in 1898. Tohatchi is derived from the Navajo word, tqohachee, meaning "scratch for water," designating the way water was obtained; that is, the people scraped the top soil in the arroyos to get their water. It may have come from tqo qachi, for "water dug out," or "water in rock ledge."

TUCUMCARI (Quay/5,989) Tucumcari grew up as a railroad town about 1901 with construction of the Rock Island Railroad, followed by the Southern Pacific. The post office opened on January 27, 1902. Tucumcari had earlier nicknames: Ragtown, because of the winds that blew, scattering the residents' belongings that looked like rags in the wind; and Six-Shooter Siding, (an engineer thought he heard gunshots when considering a name). Tucumcari is a Jemez word that means "place of buffalo hunt." Other translations were "squatty mountain," and "mother's breast." This was Comanche territory, and the word may have come from, cuchtonaro and uah, translated as "two fires" or "burn, make a fire," for the Indian smoke signals. Others believe it was derived from tukamukaru, meaning "to lie in wait for someone," descriptive of an Indian lookout.

NEW YORK

AMAGANSETT (Suffolk/1,067) Although this hamlet (located in the town of East Hampton) had no natural harbor, it has historically been a fishing village since the 1690s. It was founded in 1680 by the Schellinger family. The name was taken from a Natick word for "place of good water." It was also interpreted as "well at," for an ancient Indian well. Amagansett was home to many whaling captains, and by 1907 the last whale was killed. During World War II, four Germans landed at Amagansett in an inflatable boat with the intent of sabotage, but all were caught before any damage occurred.

AQUEBOGUE (Suffolk/2,254) Once part of Southold, Aquebogue was settled in 1758. Today, it is a hamlet in the town of Riverhead. Aquebogue was defined as "cove place," or "head of the bay." Another suggestion was it might be a Chippewa word for "shore," and referred to a place where water and land met. Aquebogue became known for its excellent vineyards and wineries.

ARMONK (Westchester/3,461) Part of the town of New Castle, Armonk was settled in the early 17th century by Quakers looking for a place to practice their religion, free from persecution. Armonk comes from a Siwanoy word that means "beaver," or "fishing place." These Indians were slaughtered by the whites in 1644. The name was also interpreted from the Mohican word, cohamoog, meaning "wide, flat place where the water runs."

CANAJOHARIE (Montgomery/3,797) Dutch and German immigrants arrived about 1730. A grist mill was established by Goshen Gose Van Alstine in 1760, followed by John Roof in 1777 who opened a tavern. Mohawk Chief Brant defined Canajoharie as "the pot that washes itself," descriptive of a large pothole created by the constant action of water and pebbles on the limestone rocks in a gorge. It was also translated as "the boiling pot." Just east of town one of many Mohawk castles was built in 1634.

CANANDAIGUA (Ontario/11,264) This site was once the Seneca village of Ganadarque that was destroyed by General Sullivan in 1779. William Walker was an agent for the owner of the property and opened the first office in the U.S. for land sales here. The site was occupied by settlers in 1789 and may have originally been named Canandarguay. This was home to the Lisk Manufacturing Company, which revolutionized the cooking industry when it developed rustproof pots and pans. Canandaigua is a Seneca word that means "chosen spot," or "town set off."

CANASTOTA (Madison/4,425) The village of Canastota was created when construction began on the Erie Canal in the early 1800s. The name was derived from the Oneida words, kinste and stoat, for "pine tree standing alone, "or silent cluster of pines." It was also interpreted as an Onondaga word for "frame of house." Canastota's industry increased with completion of the canal and the establishment of the Syracuse and Utica Railroad in 1839. The town was once a major onion-growing center. Nathan Roberts was a resident who was largely responsible for the design and building of a section of the Erie Canal.

CANEADEA (Allegany/*2,000*) Caneadea was one of the first towns established in the county, founded in 1808. An earlier settler was a Mr. Schoonmaker, who established the first apple nursery in the region. Caneadea was located on the site of an old Seneca village that Joel Seaton purchased in 1830. The name was derived from the Iroquois word, gah-yah-o-de-o, interpreted as "where the heavens rest upon the earth."

CANISTEO (Steuben/3,583) The people who survived the Wyoming Massacre in Pennsylvania came here to settle in 1788, and the town was formed in 1796. The name was derived from te-car-nase-teo, an Iroquois word for "board on the water," referring to the town's location at the head of navigation of the Canisteo River. A major industry was the Canisteo Silk Company, established in the early 1900s. When the government took silk off the market in the 1930s, with the exception of manufacturing silk parachutes, the company went into synthetic fabrics.

CASSADAGA (Chautaqua/676) Cassadaga was part of the Holland Land survey, and settled in 1809 by Abel Beebe, Joel Fisher and Othello Church, who saw the potential of industry because of the timber resources. Cassadaga was derived from gusdago, a Seneca word for "water under the rocks." One of the main industries was the manufacture of grape baskets.

CHAPPAQUA (Westchester/9,468) Chappaqua is an Algonquin word derived from shapequa, for "place of separation," or "running water." During the Revolution, the town was a battleground for both sides. Chappaqua entered the industrial age by the advent of numerous factories in the 19th century. Horace Greeley came here during the summers during the 1850s. His residence gave rise to the term "Chappaquacks," when he ran for President in 1872.

CHEEKTOWAGA (Erie/94,019) The first permanent resident arrived in 1809 after purchasing land from the Holland Company. He built a gristmill and distillery, and also became Indian Agent for the Buffalo Creek Indian Reservation. The largest influx of settlers occurred in 1826 with the immigration of Germanic people. When railroad lines bisected the town, it opened up other parts of the region for settlement and helped development of Cheektowaga. Derived from ji-ik-do-wah-gah, Cheektowaga is an Iroquois word translated as "land (or place) of the crabapple," a native plant.

CHITTENANGO (Madison/4,855) This name may be an Oneida word for "where the waters divide and run north," because Chittenango Creek enters from the south, forming a western boundary on Oneida Lake, with Canasaraga Creek flowing in a northerly direction. Early settlers were here as early as 1790, attracted by the water power of the creek. The first gypsum in the state was found in the nearby hills and used in construction of the Erie Canal. L. Frank Baum, author of the *Wizard of Oz*, was born at Chittenango.

COHOES (Albany/15,521) In 1630, Kiliaen Van Rensselaer of the Dutch West Indies Company purchased the site located at the mouth of the Mohawk River where textile mills were developed. Just before the Battle of Saragota, Cohoes became a camp for the Continental Army led by General Gates. It was named for Cohoes Falls, and its meaning comes from legend. A tired maiden got into a canoe and fell asleep. The canoe got loose, carried the maiden over the falls and she was never seen again. The Indians (Mohawks or Iroquois) called the falls Cohoes, which means "the place of the falling canoe."

COMMACK (Suffolk/36,367) Straddling the towns of Smithtown and Huntington, Commack began in 1689 when the Governor of New York granted the Winnecomac Patent to two settlers. Commack may be derived from the Secatogue Tribe's word for "pleasant field," derived from winnecomac, descriptive of the rolling hills. During World War I, the Army trained pilots at Brindley Field near town. The Commack Methodist Church is the oldest Methodist church still continuously operating in the state.

COPAKE (Columbia/3,278) This site was originally home to the Mohican Indians. Settled by the Dutch and Germans, it began as the Town of Granger, until the community was split from Taghkanic in 1824. The first people to settle at Copake were the Dutch in 1753. Copake Falls is located within the town. It was known for its iron forge which operated intermittently until World War I. In Algonquin, Copake means "snake pond," taken from achkookpaug.

COPIAGE (Suffolk/21,922) Early inhabitants were Indians of the Massapequa Tribe. The site was named Huntington and settled by the English and Dutch in the early 1600s. The townsite was purchased from Chief Wyandanch in the form of coats, powder, hatchets, and knives. Copiage's economy was supported by paper and straw mills. The name was changed to Great Neck in the mid-1800s, then renamed East Amityville. In 1895, it became Copiage, which means "sheltered harbor (or place)."

COXSACKIE (Greene/8,884) Coxsackie was predominantly a Dutch settlement in the late 1600s. The first grantee of the land was Pieter Bronck. When English settlers arrived, the Dutch wrote up their own Declaration of Independence in defiance of what they believed to be England's suppression and control of their community. Located next to the Hudson River, Coxsackie experienced growth when industries sprang up in the early 1800s. The Delaware Indians called the site Caniseek, interpreted as "place of the owl," or "place where the owl hoots." Another translation was from kuk and auke, for "cut earth," and may have described water from the Hudson River that eroded, creating ledges.

CUTCHOGUE (Suffolk/2,849) Once inhabited by the Corchaug Indians, white settlement began in the 1660s because its rich farmlands were conducive to agriculture. Seaweed was also harvested for home insulation. Today, award-winning vineyards have replaced the farmlands. The name may come from Corchaug, meaning "the principal place," possible describing a place of refuge.

GENESEO (Livingston/9,654) This region was once an important Seneca settlement until Sullivan and his troops destroyed it in 1779. Settled by L.B. Jenkins and Captain Noble in 1788, Geneseo was developed by the Wadsworth brothers ten years later. As the business and cultural center of the region, the town was called Big Tree. Geneseo might have been anglicized from chinisee or gen-nis-he-yo, Iroquois for as "valley beautiful," or "there it has fine banks."

GOWANDA (Cattaraugus/2,842) Gowanda is situated on both sides of Cattaraugus Creek. First called Aldrich's Mills, it was changed to Lodi in 1823. Confusion with another town named Lodi caused the post office to be changed to Persia, but the town itself was still called Lodi. It was later named Gowanda, a Seneca word meaning "valley among the hills," or "almost surrounded by hills," derived from djo-gowandeh or ogowanda. When the Buffalo and Southwestern division of the Erie Railroad laid its tracks, Gowanda became one of its stations.

HAUPPAUGE (Suffolk/20,100) Hauppauge began as a crossroads community for travelers going from Smith Town and Islip. Thomas Wheeler was the first resident in the 1700s. During the Revolution the site was known as Wheeler's Farm. It was changed to Hauppauge which could be derived from winganhauppage, Algonquin for "a place of springs," or "overflowed land."

HONEOYE (Ontario) Originally called Hannayaye by the Seneca Indians who had a small village near the lake, the name is defined as "quiet water" and peaceful waters." Another interpretation was "finger lying," derived from hahnyah and gayah. Apparently, an Indian cut off his finger after he was bitten by a snake. Early settler Gideon Pitts was a known abolitionist who used his home as one of the Underground Railways. His daughter married Black statesman, Frederick Douglass, in 1884. Principal industries were hops, barrelmaking and raising sheep.

IRONDEQUOIT (Monroe/52,354) The Seneca Indians probably did not have villages here, but there were many trails through the area they used for travel. The site was called Gerundegut (or Irondequat) Landing. Its location at the head of Irondequoit Bay made the town a shipping point for schooners. The name has been interpreted as a Seneca word for "bay," Other theories were "opening into the lake," and "where the waters gasp and die," or a Huron word, qua-or quoi, meaning "toward the sunrise."

JAMAICA (Queens) Jamaica was first inhabited by the Canarsee and Rockaway Indians. It is not known when the settlers arrived, but proprietors were here in 1644. The first written document was a deed from the Indians to the whites dated September 13, 1655. Residents established mills, and a dam was built in 1670. Jamaica means "wood and water," or "beaver," in the Mohegan language

KATONAH (Westchester) Katonah is part of Bedford Township, founded as Bedford in 1680. John Whitlock and Squire Wood established a store and tavern after the Revolution. The year 1847 brought in numerous settlers when the New York and Harlem Railroad was built. The town had to move its more than 50 buildings to another site over the Cross River when the New Croton Dam was constructed in 1897. Katonah was derived from Chief Catoonah who sold the townsite to the colonists in 1680. He was chief of the Confederation of Ramapoo Indians (Mohegan branch). His name was translated as "great mountain."

MACHIAS (Cattaraugus/2,482) Located in the northern part of the county, Machias was settled by Major Timothy Butler In 1813. He established a maple sugar business and employed settlers to tap and manufacture the product. Cheese factories were also important industries. Originally known as Machias Five Corners, the town took its name from Machias, Maine, where many of the settlers originated. It means "bad run of water," or "bad little falls," derived from the Algonquin word, machisses.

MAMARONECK (Westchester/18,752) This site was originally owned by Indians from the Wickquaskeck Tribe, who sold it to John Richbell in 1661. Mamaroneck may be a Mohegan word for "the place where the fresh water falls into the salt." This described the action of fresh water falling directly into salt water where a ledge of rocks prevented the tide from coming in. Others interpreted it as "he assembles the people." The New York, New Haven & Hartford Railroad was built in 1848, bringing European immigrants who went into the rubber business and established the Macintosh Coat Factory.

MASSAPEQUA (Nassau/22,652) The Marsapeague Indians were resident at this site located on the south shore of Long Island. The first settlers were Major Thomas Jones and his wife, Freelove, in 1696 after they were given the land by John Townsend, Freelove's father. He had originally purchased the land from Sachem Tackapousha. During the 1700s, farming was the way of life. Establishment of the Long Island Railroad in 1841 turned the town into a resort area. Massapequa is derived from Marsapeague, meaning "great water land," descriptive of its location along the shore and the many lakes in the region.

MATTITUCK (Suffolk/4,198) The Corchaug Indians sold this land to Theophilus Eaton, who was governor of the jurisdiction of New Haven. Founded in 1641, the base of the village's economy was growing salt hay. Matticuck was taken from matta and tuck, meaning "great creek." Except for the oyster business, Mattituck did not show much growth until the Long Island Railroad came through in 1844.

NANUET (Rockland/16,707) This land was purchased from the Indians in 1686, and ten years later King William III granted the Kakiat Patent to early settlers. The name comes from Chief Nanewit, which James DeClark suggested in 1856 (origin unknown). Nanuet's economy was spurred when the Erie Railroad built its line in 1841. The post office opened in 1846 (George Edsall, postmaster).

NAPANOCH (Ulster/1,168) Abraham and Jean Bevier purchased a considerable amount of land in the early 1700s. Benjamin Bevier constructed a grist mill in 1754 and harnessed the water power from the Rondout River. The first road built near Napanoch was about 1730 after a lead mine was found in the Shawangunk Mountains. Napanoch means "land overflowed by water," a Lenape word that refers to the Rondout River. At one time, Napanoch was home to a boys school called Napanoch State Institute for Male Defective Delinquents.

NESCONSET (Suffolk/11,992) One of the last pieces of land to be settled between Smithtown and Lake Ronkonkoma was the village of Nesconset. The post office was established in 1910, as was the general store. Mayor Gaynor may have suggested the name when the post office was dedicated. Nesconset could mean "at or near the second going over" (to wade across a river), derived from Nassaconseke, an Indian Sachem of the Nissequogue Tribe in 1650.

NISKAYUNA (Schenectady/20,295) Taken from the Connestigiune Tribe's word, nis-ti-go-wo-ne, signifying "extensive corn flats," the town was established in 1809. Although the Indians were generally on good terms with the residents, Chief Ren-warrigh-who-go-wa ("fault finder" or "grumbler") was known to have said, "after the whites had taken possession of our lands, they will make Kaut-sore (spoon-food or soup) of our bodies."[30] He made sure a covenant was added to all deeds that the Indians' fishing and hunting rights be preserved.

NISSEQUOGUE (Suffolk/1,543) The last full-blood Nissequogue Indian was a sachem named Jeremiah Cuffee, who was born in 1824 and died at Setauket in 1909. Derived from n'issaqu-ack, Nissequogue means "clay or mud country," indicative of clay deposits the Indians used to make pottery. Part of the land in the area has been reserved as a "forever wild" status with its wildlife preserve. After World War II, numerous estates that had been established were subdivided because they became too expensive.

NUNDA (Livingston/3,017) Once the heart of the Six Nations Indian Confederacy of the Iroquois, Nunda was created in 1808 when it was cut off from the town of Angelica. A Mr. Lovell built a sawmill in 1818, followed by a gristmill. There was not much development until about 1823. The site was named Hubbell's Corners, for Alanson Hubbell who opened a tavern in 1824, and later changed to Nunda, taken from nundao, an Onondaga word that means "hilly." Another version was from a Seneca word for "potato ground."

ONEIDA (Madison/10,987) Sands Higinbotham purchased the site in 1829 and gave the New York Central Railway right of way, which completed its line about 1839. The town was named for the Oneida Indians, who were friendly to the settlers. Their name means "people of the living stone," and designated a large boulder the Indians revered. It is home to the Oneida Community, founded by John Humphrey Noyes in 1848. Beginning with the manufacture of animal traps, chains and utensils, it became famous for its Oneida stainless-steel flatware.

ORISKANY (Oneida/1,459) The Oneida Indians, members of the Iroquois Confederation, were resident in the early 1600s. They called the site Oriska, which meant "place of nettles." Settlement began in the mid-1700s, bringing those attracted by the creek that would power their mills. The post office was established in 1820 (Gerrit Lansing, postmaster). One of the biggest industries was the Oriskany Manufacturing Company, the first woolen mill in the U.S. Financial problems caused the company to close its doors in 1857.

OSSINING (Westchester/36,534) During the 17th Century, this region was home to the Sint Sincks, a tribe of the Wappinger Confederation. Located on the east bank of the Hudson River, Ossining became famous for Sing Sing Prison, which was established with the idea of using prisoners to work the local marble quarries. The Chippewa Indians called the site Sinsing, interpreted as "stone upon stone," descriptive of the hillsides. The post office was established in 1797 as Mount Pleasant, changed to Sing Sing in 1813, and later named Ossining.

OTEGO (Otsego/3,183) Otego was home to the Susquehanna Indians until they were driven away by the Iroquois in 1675. Richard Smith and Richard Wells surveyed Otego in 1779. Since the Susquehanna River was recognized as an important waterway, there was some timber industry. Otego has many definitions, taken from wauteghe, atega, aiga, odego, and others. Some early authorities believed Otego was derived from one of these Iroquois words, and meant "place of the butternut," or "place of the sugar maples." Another could be from atigen, meaning "to have a fire there," or from ots-ka-wa for "big or tall hemp."

OWEGO (Tioga/20,365) Before settlement, this was an Indian community called Ahwaga, and home to the Onondaga and Cayuga tribes of the Iroquois Confederacy. They were defeated when General Sullivan came through during the Revolution. Situated on the bank of the Susquehanna River, Owego was settled in 1787 and means "where the valley widens." Development of the town depended on river traffic. Because of the massive amount of merchandise plying the river, the Ithaca and Owego Railroad was built in 1828, and made the town a commercial trading center.

PATCHOGUE (Suffolk/*1,100*) Known as Winthrop's Patent, Patchogue was settled about 1758 with a land lottery. An early business started by Jonas Wicks was a paper mill that made strawboard and wrapping paper. The post office opened in 1802 (Nathan Mulford, postmaster). Patchogue was thought to mean "turning place," or "place of many streams," from the Pachaug Tribe's word that designated where two rivers separated. The Union Twine Mill established in the early 1800s was the first in the U.S. to manufacture cotton carpet warp.

PECONIC (Suffolk/1,081) This site was called Hermitage because of a recluse who lived here. Peconic was formed during the 1860s, and is an Algonquin word for "nut trees." Another interpretation was "little plantation," derived from pehikkonuk. During the 1840s, the town began attracting artists, and by the early 1900s the Peconic Art School was formed. This is the site where Albert Einstein visited in 1939 and got his conception for the atomic bomb. He wrote a letter to Franklin Roosevelt and tried to convince the President to look into the possibility of nuclear fission.

POUGHKEEPSIE (Dutchess/42,777) Robert Sanders and Myndert Harmense established Poughkeepsie in 1687 when they received a land patent. The name is derived from uppuquiipising, a Wappinger expression for "reed covered lodge by the little water place," descriptive of a small spring in town. It was also interpreted from the Lenape word, apokeepsingk, meaning "safe harbor," or "shallow inlet." The post office was opened in 1792 (Nicholas Power, postmaster). In 1847, Samuel Morse purchased land in the area, and went on to invent the telegraph and Morse Code. Poughkeepsie's growth was spurred with the establishment of the IBM Corporation in the 1940s.

QUOGUE (Suffolk/1,018) John Ogden purchased this site from the Shinnecock Indians in 1659. Quogue is derived from quaquanantuck, a Shinnecock word interpreted as "the land that trembles under foot," or "creek flowing through shaking marsh," signifying movement of water in a cove. Industry in the 1680s was offshore whaling and shipment of whale blubber. By the 1800s, Quogue residents turned to farming; the town also became a summer resort. Before the post office was established in 1828, mail was delivered to the 'Old Box Tree,' an oak tree with a hole in it.

SAGAPONACK (Suffolk/582) This village is located south of Bridgehampton. Early records show that Josiah Stanborough came here in 1656 when it was called Sagg. Most of the settlers were farmers, although a few became whalers. When the post office was established in 1889, it was named Sagaponack, possibly Chippewa for as "a place where big ground nuts grow," but may also describe a potato.

SARANAC LAKE (Essex/5,041) Jacob Moody arrived about 1819 and purchased land. About eight years later, Captain Pliny Miller built a sawmill which began Saranac's development as a lumber town. In 1894, the Saranac Laboratory for Tuberculosis was established in 1894, its purpose to develop bacteriological techniques to help tubercular patients. Saranac is an Iroquois word interpreted as "river that flows under rock," or "to ascend," and may have referred to a gradual rise of land.

SCHODACK (Rensselaer/12,536) Located along the Hudson River, Schodack had its beginnings in 1795 and became a station on the Hudson River Railroad. Agriculture was the main industry, in addition a brick factory. Before the appearance of the white men, this region was home to the Mohegan Indians. Schodack is derived from ischoda, which means "a meadow," or fire plain." the latter possibly referring to the seat of the council fire of the Mohegans.

SCHOHARIE (Schoharie/3,299) The first resident was Karighondontee, a French-Indian prisoner from Canada whose father-in-law gave him land to protect him from the Mohawk Indians. The village was first called Brunnes Dorf (German for "spring"), then Fountain Town. It was later renamed Sommersville, and finally in 1795 to Schoharie, derived from the Iroquois word, to-wos-scho-hor, which means "driftwood," pertaining to the buildup of driftwood on Schoharie Creek during the spring.

SETAUKET (Suffolk/15,931) This site was purchased from the Delaware Indians by a group of men and their agents in 1655. These lands were conveyed for "inhabitants of Setauket," and designated the Indians' camp site, meaning "land on the mouth of the creek," derived from setalcott, a Secatogue word. Another theory was from seauhteau, meaning "to scatter anything." The town was named Cromwell Bay until John Scott renamed it Ashford for his hometown in England. Shortly thereafter it reverted to Setauket. During the Revolution, Setauket was headquarters for Washington's spy ring. The 1840s were the era of shipbuilding; today, it is mainly residential.

SHANDAKEN (Ulster/3,235) Conrad Meisner may have been the first person to take up residence in the early 1800s. Frank Chichester arrived about 1863 and built a sawmill and chair factory, which became quite successful after the Chichesters invented the rocking cradle. The majority of town is now part of the New York State Forest Preserve. An Algonquin word, Shandaken was thought to mean "land of rapid waters," or "creek that runs through bluffs."

SKANEATELES (Onondaga/7,323) This town was once part of the Great Military Tract given to Revolutionary soldiers in lieu of pay. The name was taken from the lake, which may be a Mohawk expression for "long waters," or "long lake." An important industry was teasel, a thistle-like plant with a burr head of natural hooks used in the woolen industry to raise the material's nap. Other profitable industries were sleigh-making and boat-building in the early 1800s.

SYOSSET (Nassau/18,544) Syosset is an unincorporated area within the town of Oyster Bay. Robert Williams purchased land from Chief Pugnipan of the Matineock Indians in 1648 for an unspecified amount of cloth. The town was first called East Woods, until Syosset was officially adopted in 1855, taken from suwasset, Algonquin for "place in the pines." Syosset's growth was slow until the Long Island Railroad came through in 1854, and the post office was established the following year.

TUCKAHOE (Westchester/*6,302*) Part of Eastchester, this village began as Bompo's Bridge. With the opening of marble quarries in 1825, the town's population increased. Some of the marble was used to rebuild the Capitol building in Washington, D.C. after it was destroyed in the War of 1812. The name was changed to Tuckahoe, which has been defined as an Algonquin word for "the bread." Another version ascribes it from ptuckweoo, for "it is round." Both referred to bulbous roots such as mushrooms or truffles used for making bread.

WANTAGH (Nassau/18,971) This village is an unincorporated section of Hempstead. When Captain John Seaman and Robert Jackson come to Wantagh in 1644, the site was occupied by Indians of the Mericoke and Massapequa Tribes. The place was called Jerusalem until the South Side Railroad came through and changed it to Ridgewood. In 1891, it was renamed Wantagh for an Indian Chief who was friends with the white men (origin unknown). The name may be a variation of Wyandanch.

YAPHANK (Suffolk/5,025) The year 1739 brought Captain Robert Robertson who built a mill after obtaining a grant from town trustees. John Homan was also granted permission to establish his mill in 1762. The town became a commercial center after the Long Island railroad was built in 1843. The site was first named Milltown until the post office opened in 1846 when it was changed to Yaphank, derived from the Delaware word, Yamphanke, for "bank of a river."

NORTH CAROLINA

CATAWBA (Catawba/698) Catawba was one of the earliest railroad stations established before the War Between the States, and may be the oldest town in the county. The post office was established in 1859 (Gilbert Sherrill, postmaster) as Chestnut Grove, and later changed to Catawba Station, named for the Catawba Indians who roamed the area. Their name was interpreted as "cut off" or "separated."

CHOCOWINITY (Beaufort/733) Located along the Pamlico River, this town was known as Godley's Crossroads. One of the first structures was the Trinity Church which was built in 1773. Some of the families started plantations, with tar as the cash crop taken from the pine trees and manufactured into various products. Chocowinity took its name from the river, derived from choca-wa-na-teth, for "fish from many waters," or chocowinekee, which means "smoking stumps."

COOLEEMEE (Davie/905) This village was named after the Cooleemee Plantation, owned by Col. Jesse Pearson. While in the Army, he went to Alabama just after the Battle of Horseshoe Bend, and accepted the surrender of the Kulami tribe of Creek Indians. When he returned to his plantation, he named it Cooleemee Hill, a derivation of the Creek word, kulami, which means "where the white oaks grow." Cooleemee was one of hundreds of mill villages that dotted the Carolina piedmont.

CULLOWHEE (Jackson/3,579) Adam Corn was an early settler in 1820, and a Baptist preacher, but the majority of people didn't arrive until about 1850. The town owes its growth to the establishment of Western Carolina University, founded in 1889 by Robert L. Madison and was originally a teacher's college. Cullowhee is derived from the Cherokee words, gualiya, or callaugh-ee, defined as "place of the spring salad." It may have just meant "place of the spring," because it is doubtful the Indians had a word for salad.

CURRITUCK (Currituck) Settlement is traced back to Lord Berkeley when he granted John Harvey 600 acres of land in 1663. Once part of Albemarle County in Virginia, a boundary dispute put the town in North Carolina. Timothy Hanson came to Currituck in 1770 and developed Timothy grass. Near town is the Pilmoor Methodist Church where the first Methodist sermon in the state was preached by Rev. Joseph Pilmoor in 1772. Currituck may be a corruption of the Algonquin word, coratank, which means "wild geese." Thousands of geese and ducks winter here, including the Whistling Swan that breeds in Alaska.

HATTERAS (Dare/*700*) Colonists spent time on Hatteras Island trading with the Hatteras Indians, collecting shells, and keeping an eye out for other ships. The village of Hatteras is located on the southwest side of the island. Federal troops stormed the island during the Civil War and set up an encampment just outside the village. The post office opened in 1858 (Robert Styron, postmaster). In 1878, a lifesaving station was built next to the village, as was a weather station in 1880. Hatteras may be a corruption of an Algonquin word that described an area of sparse vegetation.

LAKE TOXAWAY (Transylvania) Home to the Cherokee Indians until settlers pushed them out, Lake Toxaway was created when J.F. Hayes arrived in 1890 for his health and constructed a 540-acre lake and the Toxaway Hotel. He also built exquisite homes and advertised for millionaires to move to the lake. The hotel opened in 1903 and boasted steam heating, elevators, and imported French chefs. In 1916, heavy rains resulted in a huge flood, bursting a dam, and destroying the lake. The hotel was closed in 1916. Toxaway was taken from a Cherokee chief whose name means "red bird."

LAKE WACCAMAW (Columbus/1,411) Land in this region was granted to a Lord Proprietor during the 1700s by Charles the Second, who in turn made individual grants to settlers. This site started out as Flemington in 1852, and the post office was established in 1869. Charles Beers moved to Waccamaw the same year and built a shingle mill along the lake, followed shortly by Henry Short. These two businesses eventually merged and became the North Carolina Lumber Company. In 1890, the name was changed to Lake Waccamaw. It may be connected to Waccanaow, translated as "tobacco."

MANTEO (Dare/*1,576*) Located on Roanoke Island, Manteo was the name of an Indian chief who was taken to England by Philip Amadas and Arthur Barlow in 1584. Queen Elizabeth I gave Manteo the title of "Lord of Roanoke." The Lords Proprietors ordered their representatives to build a main town (Manteo) on the island in 1676, which was called Shallowbag Bay. When the post office was established in 1875, it was renamed Manteo (unknown origin). The town's growth was spurred with the tourist industry.

OCRACOKE (Hyde/769) Wild ponies, thought to be descended from the Barbary ponies, roamed the island before settlement. In 1715, the Colonial Assembly passed an act to establish Ocracoke as a port and to maintain pilots to guide ships safely over the shoals. The site was initially called Pilot Town. When Cockle Creek was dredged and Silver Lake Harbor was constructed in 1931, Ocracoke developed a large fishing industry. The name may be a corruption of an Algonquin word, waxihikami, designating an enclosed place or stockade.

POTECASI (Northampton) This little village was settled in 1723 when Sam Ellson received a land patent. Potecasi may have been derived from pohake, an Algonquin word for "parting of the waters." In 1745, Sam Maggett bought part of Ellson's land. Jordan Beale was a wealthy planter at Potecasi, and also postmaster when the post office opened in December, 1839.

SALUDA (Polk/575) Starting out as a crossroads used by traders, the site was called Pace's Gap for a early resident. Establishment of the Asheville and Spartanburg Railroad caused more than 35 hotels to be built. Because of the terrain, numerous railroad workers were killed building the tracks, and after the trains were in operation, there were accidents because of the widow-making Saluda Grade. It was estimated the grade was anywhere from 5.1% to 5.3% at its steepest point. In 1927, William S. Viner came to Saluda and built an apple mill, serving the apple orchards, which is still in business today. Saluda is derived from the Cherokee word, tsaludiyi, which means "green corn place," or "corn river."

SAXAPAHAW (Alamance/1,418) The Sissipahaw Indians were living in the Carolinas as far back as 1569, and were believed to have been part of the Siouan linguistic family. John Newlin was a town founder in 1844 and named it for the Sissipihaws. He pronounced the name as Saxapahaw, interpreted as "south of the Haw River." During the 1970s, developer John Jordan owned the village and purchased the mill from Dixie Yarns, renovating the structure in the 1990s.

WAXHAW (Union/2,625) The Waxhaw Indians were members of the Siouan language group, who practiced the art of head-flattening. John Lawson made the first written record of these Indians in 1709. Most of them had died off by the early 1700s from smallpox, and rest were wiped out during the Yamassee wars. Those who managed to survive were absorbed into the Catawba tribe. Scotch-Irish and German immigrants were probably the first settlers about 1740. Waxhaw was thought to mean "people of the cane."

NORTH DAKOTA

LAKOTA (Nelson/781) A Chippewa Indian named Joseph Gardepie sold the land that would become Lakota. In 1883, the St. Paul, Minneapolis and Manitoba Railroad extended its line. Lakota comes from the Teton Sioux word for "allies." The first home at the townsite was built in 1882, followed by a general store established by the Holman brothers. The post office opened on July 16, 1883 (Francis Kane, postmaster).

MAKOTI (Ward/145) When the area near the Fort Berthold Indian Reservation was open for homesteading, Edward Kamrud requested that the Soo Line put in a siding. The railroad asked the site be given an Indian name, and Kamrud selected Maakoti, a Mandan word for "earthen lodge." The railroad granted the request, but asked that the extra "a" be left out and spelled Makoti. The town was platted in 1911, and this same year the post office was established (William Nutting, postmaster).

MANDAN (Morton/16,718) The Mandan Indians lived here until a smallpox epidemic nearly destroyed them. The disease began with an ill crewman on the steamer *St. Peter*. "How the disease was passed may never be known, but during the night of June 19, 1837, smallpox invaded its newest host – the Mandans..."[31] The town got its start in 1873 after a railroad survey was made, and Northern Pacific laid its tracks in 1879. The post office opened on March 3 the same year (Arthur Linn, postmaster). This was the point from which General Custer led his men to their slaughter to the Little Big Horn in 1876. Mandan could mean "river dweller," Another interpretation was "people on the bank," derived from the Dakota word Mantani. The Mandans called themselves Nu eta ("we the people").

NECHE (Pembina/1,437) Situated between Walhalla and Pembina, this little town was owned by Catherine Cyr. Her son, Dan Shay, bought her out and formed a contract with the St. Paul, Minneapolis and Manitoba Railroad, which stipulated the railroad lay out the town. Jim Hill, president of the railroad, named the site Neche, which means "friend" in the Chippewa language. Numerous railroads were built in the region and most of the grain coming in from Western Canada came through Neche. The advent of all these railroads spurred the town's growth with access provided for the eastern markets.

PEMBINA (Pembina/642) In 1797, Charles Baptiste Chaboillez was sent by the Northwest Fur Company to establish a temporary trading post here. Not much development occurred until Commodore N.W. Kittson, employed by the American Fur Company, built a more permanent store trading in furs in 1843. Pembina became an important river port when steamboats on the Red River began shipping out the furs. The post office was established in 1843, with Kittson as postmaster. Pembina's origin has been disputed. It was interpreted as "all around a place of meeting," derived from the Ojibway words, pam and bian. Most authorities believe it comes from anepeminian, which means "summer berry," and designated a local flame-red berry that grew in abundance.

TIOGA (Williams/1,125) Nick Comford purchased this site from soldiers who received the land for their services to the government. Located along the Great Northern Railroad, Tioga was once a major grain market in the world. Some oil was discovered in the 1950s, and a gas processing plant was built by Signal Oil and Gas. Although the discovery of oil gained some prominence in Tioga's economy, its mainstay is still in the agricultural and ranching industries. An Iroquois word from the East, Tioga received its name about 1902, and means "peaceful valley."

WAHPETON (Richland/8,586) Wahpeton is located on the banks of the Bois de Sioux River. The first settler was Morgan Rich in 1869 who named the site Richville. Two years later the post office was established as Chahinkapa, which meant "the end of the woods." In 1873, it was renamed Wahpeton, derived from the Sioux word, warpeotonwe, for "leaf village," or "dwellers among leaves." Wahpeton was just a sleepy little town until 1872 when the St. Paul and Pacific Railway built its tracks across the river. Then, in 1880, the St. Paul, Minneapolis and Manitoba Railroad came through and built a depot, which spurred further growth for Wahpeton when it became a branch line.

OHIO

ASHTABULA (Ashtabula/20,962) The first permanent resident was Thomas Hamilton in 1801. During the Civil War, the town held strong abolitionist sentiment and served as a northern terminus of the Underground Railroad. The 1870s brought prosperity to Ashtabula when it became a Great Lakes Port, shipping iron ore and coal. The name was interpreted from an Algonquin phrase meaning "beautiful river," "river of fish," and "many fish."

CHILLICOTHE (Ross/21,796) Nathaniel Massie surveyed the site in 1793 and prepared to build a town, but Indian problems curtailed his plans. It wasn't until after the battle of Fallen Timbers that any settlement could begin. Massie returned in 1796, laid out the town, and donated four acres each to the first 100 people who could build a house the first year. Chillicothe became the state capital in 1803, until it was removed to Zanesville in 1810. Chillicothe is a Shawanese word for "town," or "town at the leaning bank."

COSHOCTON (Coshocton/11,682) Prior to settlement, Colonel Henry Bouquet established a camp in 1764. The town was platted in 1802 as Tuscarawas ("shirt wearers"), and laid out by John Matthews and Ebenezer Buckingham. In 1811, the name was changed to Coshocton, derived from coshogunk, a Delaware word meaning "black bear town." It may have come from an Algonquin word for "river crossing." Opening of the Ohio and Erie Canal in 1830 dramatically increased the town's economy.

CONNEUT (Ashtabula/12,485) This region was home to Chief Macqua Medah and his people who may have been a remnant of the Massasaugua Tribe. They were forced to leave after the chief killed one of the white settlers. During 1830, the Ohio Furnace was established, manufacturing cast-iron stoves and castings. A cheese factory was also built. The importance of Conneaut Harbor caused the town to grow rapidly. It became an important shipping point for boats hauling out grain, as well as distilled whiskey. Conneut may have been derived the Algonquin word, gunniate, meaning "it is a long ime since they have gone." Other interpretations were "fish" and "snow place."

LITTLE HOCKING (Washington) George Washington was one of a number of men granted land by the governor for service to their country. While surveying his section, Washington wrote in his field notes that they came across a small river the Indians called Little Hockhocking. The site was known as Belpre when Nathaniel

Sawyer arrived in the 1780s and built a station along the Ohio River. Growth was slowed somewhat because of problems with the Indians who frequently used the river. Hockhocking is a Delaware word that means "bottle." The river was narrow and straight, like the neck of a bottle and suddenly widened near the falls, which gave the appearance of a bottle.

PATASKALA (Licking/10,249) Richard Conine purchased about 2000 acres but stayed only long enough to plat the site and name it Conine. He sold his land to Jess S. Green, who laid out lots and sold them to the settlers. The post office was established in 1851 as Pataskala, derived from the Delaware word, pt-aaps-'ku-'l'u, meaning "up to a point always a swell exists." This designated a point where floodwaters from the Muskingum River ran into the Licking River, causing it to swell up.

PIQUA (Miami/20,738) Armstrong Brandon established this town in 1807 and named it Washington. In 1816, it was changed to Piqua, which comes from legend about the creation of the first Piqua man who rose out of the smoking embers of a campfire and said "Ohtah-he-waugh-Pe-qua," meaning "out of the ashes." When the Miami-Erie Canal was built in 1837, it began an active period for the town. A branch of the Dayton and Michigan railroad came through in 1854, followed by the Columbus, Piqua and Indiana Railroad in 1858, making Piqua a crossroads for the rail lines.

SANDUSKY (Erie/27,844) Early settler John Garrison founded this town in 1810, which was platted in 1816 by Zalmon Wildman who named it Portland. Prior to establishment, the site was called Ogontz Place, for an Ottawa Indian. Since Wildman was not a permanent settler, others re-platted the site, naming it Sandusky. It was derived from an Iroquois (Wyandot) expression, lacsandouske, for "lake of cold water," or from outsandouke, meaning "pure water here." Blackboard chalk was invented at Sandusky in 1835.

TONTOGANY (Wood/364) An Indian village headed by Ottawa Chief Tondoganie was once located at this site along the Maumee River. Tontogany was derived from his name and means "the dog." Willard Way and Erasmus Peck had the site surveyed in 1855. The Dayton & Michigan Railroad built a spur line to town in 1859, which gave the farmers an outlet for their produce. General George Custer's parents lived here, and were often visited by their son.

WAPAKONETA (AuGlaize/9,474) Located at the headwaters of the Auglaize River, this site was home to the Shawnee Indians until 1831, when they signed a treaty and were removed to Kansas. Peter Hammel built a general store in 1815, followed by George Johnson who established a trading post. The county had four railroads, which made Wapakoneta the ideal shipping and distribution point. Wapakoneta is Shawnee for "daughter of our chief," or "clay river."

WAUSEON (Fulton/7,091) E.L. Barber and J.H. Sargent were railroad surveyors who knew a train station would be built near the site and purchased 160 acres of land. The town was named for Potawatomi Chief Wa-se-on, which means "far away." Wauseon was mainly an agricultural community. Thanks to Jim Brailey, who discovered that Alexander Graham Bell's telephone patents were about to expire, Wauseon became the first town in the U.S. to have an independent phone company.

OKLAHOMA

ACHILLE (Bryan/506) Settlement occurred when a band of Cherokee Indians moved here during the Civil War. The town was formed after the Dawes Act went into effect and the site became an Indian allotment. The post office was established as Achilla on June 30, 1910 (Alford Connelly, postmaster). Two months after the post office opened, the name was changed to Achille, derived from the Cherokee word, atsila, which means "fire." White settlers later made their living growing peanuts and hay. Today, there are only a few businesses in operation.

ANADARKO (Caddo/6,645) An Indian agency was established near Anadarko during the 1870s for the welfare of the Indians. Traditionally hunting grounds for the Wichita, Kiowa and Comanche Indians, the town was founded on August 6, 1901. The site received its name in 1873 when Indian trader William Shirley requested a post office and submitted the name Nadarko, for a band of Caddo Indians. The "A" was accidentally put in front of the name, and it was corrupted to Anadarko. Two meanings of Nadarko were reported: "eaters of bumblebee honey," and "brown water bug."

BOKCHITO (Bryan/564) Once known as the "Biggest Little Town in Oklahoma," this location was moved in 1900 when a railroad came through and a hotel built to accommodate the rail workers. Bokchito was an agriculture community. The post office was established in 1894 (William R. Senter, postmaster). Bokchito is a Choctaw word that means "big creek (or stream)." The Armstrong Academy was built near Bokchito in 1845. It was a boy's school the Baptist Mission Society ran for the Choctaw Nation until destroyed by fire in 1919.

BOKOSHE (LeFlore/450) Bokoshe was platted in 1899, and initially called Shake Town, from the fact the people had to flag down the train in order for it to stop. Some coal towns in the east were named Shake Rag because the women shook their rags to let the men know their dinners were ready. Since Bokoshe was a coal town, this may also be the reason for Shake Town. It was later renamed Bokoshe, derived from the Choctaw words, bok and ishi, for "little creek." Coal was Bokoshe's economic backbone up until the 1970s. Many retired miners still live here.

CADDO (Bryan/944) Before the Choctaws arrived, this was home to the Caddo Indians ("real chiefs"). It later became a station on a trail that went from Fort Smith to Fort Sill, then was established as a Choctaw court town. In 1872, the Katy Railroad laid its tracks, and by 1890 Caddo had become an important cotton market. The Choctaw Code Talkers were instrumental towards the end of World War I during the Meuse-Aegonne campaign. After the Germans broke the American code, the Choctaw code was put in use.

CATOOSA (Rogers/5,449) This town was founded about 1882 and the post office opened the following year. With the St. Louis-San Francisco Railroad in place, Catoosa became the terminus and a stockyard town. After the rails reached Tulsa, there was talk of dredging the Verdigris River to provide navigation to the Mississippi river. When the project was completed, the Port of Catoosa became a reality at the head of the McClellan-Kerr Arkansas River Navigation System. In 1970, President Nixon dedicated the Port. Catoosa is a Cherokee word for "hill," or derived from gatv gitse, meaning "new settlement place." Another interpretation was "duck."

CHECOTAH (McIntosh/3,481) Located on the Creek Indian Nation, this region was used for agriculture and stockraising. When the Katy Railroad laid its tracks in 1872, the site was named Checote's Switch for Chief Samuel Checote, the last full-blood Creek Indian. The name was later spelled Checotah (meaning unknown). Robert Burton was the founder of Checotah in 1888. The town developed when natural gas was discovered in the region. Samuel Checote was an educated man and elected principal chief of the Creek Indians. He brought with him a constitution to his people which he modeled after the white man's.

CHOCTAW (Oklahoma/9,377) Plez Alexander established the first trading post at Choctaw. Jesse Chisholm founded the 7C Ranch about 1865 which was run by his son, William. He later sold the ranch which encompassed part of the town. On April 22, 1889, unassigned lands were officially opened for settlement. The post office opened a year later. The Choctaw, Oklahoma & Gulf Railroad Company purchased almost 80 acres of land from John Muzzy, which then surveyed and platted the town. Choctaw ("red") maintained its small-town status because of competition with the neighboring town of Oklahoma City.

GOTEBO (Kiowa/272) This town came into existence in 1901. When the Chicago, Rock Island and Pacific Railroad extended its line west, it built a depot and named it Gotebo, but the town proper was named Harrison. This caused confusion and mail was sent to Harrison, Arkansas instead of here, so it was renamed Gotebo, who was a Kiowa subchief. His real named was Kau-Tau-Bone (origin undetermined), but the white man pronounced it Gotebo.

HOMINY (Osage/2,584) Hominy is located in the center of a former Osage Reservation, and began as a trading point for the Indians from the southern part of the reservation. Settlers named the place Hominy, derived from Osage Chief Ho Mo I, meaning "night walker," although some do not believe it is an Indian word. The site was established as a sub-agency for the Osage Indians who came from Kansas in 1874. The Hominy Trading Company was constructed in 1905 and conducted trade with the Osage Indians. Establishment of the Missouri-Kansas-Texas Railroad brought economic stability for agriculture and cattle-raising.

INOLA (Rogers/1,589) Inola did not become a permanent settlement until the St. Louis Iron Mountain Southwestern Railroad was built in 1889. The Indians did not settle here, but leased their lands to cattlemen from Texas. Shortly after the railroad was completed, the first general store was opened by W.W. Hubbard. Inola also became a shipping point for cattle. William P. Ross, who was once Chief of the Cherokee Nation, named the town Inola, derived from Enolah, a Cherokee half-breed, meaning "Black Fox."

KAW CITY (Kay/372) Kaw City was founded by a group of settlers in 1902 whose leader was William Jenkins, Governor of the Oklahoma Territory. The Santa Fe Railroad built one of its branch lines in 1903, making Kaw City a shipping point for farmers and ranchers. It further prospered when oil was discovered in the 1920s. Kaw comes from Kanza, which means "the wind people," or "people of the south wind." Lucy Tayiah Eads was born in 1888 near Kaw City. In 1923, She became the only woman chief of the Kaw Indians because of her education. She stressed to her tribe to seek education and progress rather than return to their primitive ways.

KEOTA (Haskell/517) Keota began as a tent town in the early 1900s, founded by Major W.C. Wells when the Midland Valley Railroad was built. William Jennings Bryan promoted the town and encouraged people to move here. The name comes from a Choctaw word that means "fire gone out," indicative of numerous Choctaw Indians newly arrived who died of pneumonia. Keota's rich bottom land was conducive to growing cotton. The industry lasted until the 1950s, when all the bottom lands were covered with lakes.

KINTA (Haskell/243) The last principal chief of the Choctaws, Green McCurtain, had his home at a place called San Bois Town. When the Fort Smith and Western Railroad was building its tracks it missed the site, forcing residents to move their businesses to a new town called Kinta that was located near the railroad. Kinta is a Choctaw word for "beaver." By 1905, the town was pretty well established, but when McCurtain died and Choctaw activities decreased, Kinta went into decline.

KONAWA (Seminole/1,479) Violet Springs was founded in the early 1890s as a saloon town. After fire destroyed the town in 1899, and the railroad refused to lay its tracks here, the business district was moved a distance away and the settlement of Konawa started near the Oklahoma City-Ada-Atoka Railroad. While trying to come up with a name, one of the participants suggested the Seminole word, Kona-wa, which means "bead," and not "string of beads," as commonly believed. Konowa became a prosperous agricultural community.

MINCO (Grady/1,672) Located along the old Chisholm Trail, Minco was a product of the Chicago, Rock Island & Pacific Railway when it extended its line in 1890. The land was occupied by C.B. Campbell who founded the town. Early settlers moved to Minco when they thought the Indian reservations would be open for settlement, but that didn't occur until 1901. The town was surveyed and platted the same year. Minco's economy depended heavily on cattle ranches, which were later supplanted by agriculture. Minco is a Choctaw word for "warrier wise man leader," or "big chief."

MUSCOGEE (Muscogee/38,310) Reverend Robert Loughridge was the first missionary to the Creek Indians of the Muscogee nation. He wrote a dictionary that translated the Creek language into English. Settlement at Muscogee began in 1871 when the Missouri, Kansas & Texas Railway built its station. The name is taken from the Muscogee (or Creek) Indians, and could mean "swamp," or "open marshy land." Muscogee's permanence was assured when the Union Agency for the Five Civilized Tribes was established in 1874. The town gained six railroads in addition to the oil industry in 1903, further insuring its importance.

NINNEKAH (Grady/994) Ninnekah's beginning is credited to George Beeler after the Rock Island Railroad built its line through his property. Assisted by Percey Smith, Beeler surveyed and platted the town, then established a general store. His wife named it Ninnekah, derived from the Choctaw word, ninek, meaning "dark." Beeler was a delegate to the Sequoyah

Convention by virtue that his wife was part Chickasaw. The convention was an attempt to keep Indian territory a separate state. In 1910, Beeler established a car dealership, but it closed down when Detroit stopped building cars during World War II.

NOWATA (Nowata/3,971) This was part of the land that was sold to the Cherokee Indians by the Delawares in 1868. The name was spelled Noweata, but postal authorities wrote on Nowata on the application. It is a Cherokee word for "welcome," or "we welcome you to come." Not long after the land sale, a trading post was established. The St. Louis and Iron Mountain Railroad came through in 1889. Three years later, the town was platted by the Cherokees. Nowata's economy was tied to the development of oil and gas in 1904.

OCHELATA (Washington/494) This community was a quarantine station for cattle drives before it was founded as a town. In 1882, T.J. Ellis, Sr. bought 40 acres of land that was called Otis. When the Santa Fe Railroad came through in 1899, it changed the name to Ochelata. Texas Longhorns were shipped here and quarantined until they were tested safe for shipment to their destination in Osage County. Ochelata was a Cherokee Indian and principal chief of the Cherokees from 1875 to 1879. His name was defined as "at the foot of the hills." Preston McIntosh, a Cherokee, stated there is no word in Cherokee for Ochelata, but there was one in the Creek language, which means "skipping a rock across the water."[32]

OKEMAH (Okfuskee/3,038) Okemah was opened for settlement on April 22, 1902. H.B. Dexter was making a temporary survey for a railroad and had selected the townsite two years earlier. Okemah became a junction point when the Ozark and Cherokee Central and the Fort Smith & Western Railroads were completed. Perry Rodkey was the first postmaster in July, 1902. The town was named for Creek Chief Okemah, which means "big man," or "chief."

OKLAHOMA CITY (Oklahoma/506,132) Before this pioneer town sprang up overnight in the land rush of 1889, the Santa Fe Railway had already built its depot, a boarding house was in operation, and the post office had been built. More than 10,000 anxious settlers camped overnight to await the opening. When Oklahoma City became the capital of the state, it experienced vigorous growth as a trade and milling center, in addition to meat packing enterprises. The city came into the dawn of a new age when oil was discovered in 1928, and the well blew out more than 110 barrels of oil before it could be capped. Oklahoma is derived from the Choctaw words okla and humma ("people red").

OKMULGEE (Okmulgee/13,022) The Creek Indian Tribe established this site as its capital until the end of the 19th century when Indian governments gave way to federal jurisdiction. Originally known as Ocmulgee, the name was spelled Okmulkee when the post office was established in 1869. It was changed to Okmulgee in 1883. The name comes from two Hitchita words, oki and mulgi, for "water it is boiling." The town was the center of activity with discovery of the oil fields in 1904. The 1980s brought the oil bust, creating a mass exodus from town. Citizens then revitalized Okmulgee through historic preservation.

OOLOGAH (Rogers/883) The Attorney General asked William P. Ross, a Cherokee statesman, to name stations along the Iron Mountain Railroad Switch.

This site was named Oologah. The correct spelling, Oo-log-gu-lah means "clouds." Another definition was "cloudy weather." It was also the name of a Cherokee chief, meaning "Dark Cloud." When the lots went up for sale only citizens of the Cherokee Nation were permitted to buy land. The post office was established on May 25, 1891 (Bill Hewitt, postmaster). Oologah emerged as an Indian Territory coal-mining town. Clem Rogers owned and operated a ranch here, where his famous son, Will Rogers, was born.

OWASSO (Tulsa/18,502) When the Atchison, Topeka and Santa Fe Railroad stopped its line short of Tulsa, this parcel was called Owasso, an Osage word for "the end," or "turn around." It was descriptive of the town's terminus of the railroad. After the Cherokee Strip was opened for settlement, this town was established in 1906 as Elm Creek, and later changed to Owasso. It remained a very small community until the 1940s, when veterans from World War II moved here as the aircraft industry began to develop.

PAWHUSKA (Osage/3,629) This is home of the Osage Nation. In 1870, an Act of Congress forced removal of the Indians from Kansas to a reservation, around which Pawhuska developed. Chief Pah Hiu Skah, meaning "hair color white," received his name after an incident involving Major General Arthur St. Clair. During a battle, a young Indian found a soldier with white hair protruding from his hat. The boy prepared to scalp the man, and the man got up to flee. To the boy's shock he was left with a white powdered wig in his hand, and was thereafter called Pah Hiu Skah. The first Boy Scout Troop in America was organized at Pawhuska in May of 1909.

POCOLA (LeFlore/3,994) Pocola is a Choctaw word that means "ten," indicative of its location exactly ten miles from Fort Smith. Before settlement, the site was home to an Indian family named Page. During the Civil War two battles were fought near Pocola at a place called Backbone Mountain: one led by Brig. Gen. W.L. Cabell on September 1, 1863 when they ambushed a Union army troop; and August, 1864, when Captain Jackson McCurtain defeated a Federal cavalry force with his Choctaw battalion.

PONCA CITY (Kay/25,919) Ponca City began with the land rush in 1893 when homesteaders by the thousands lined up at Arkansas City to claim the land. B.S. Barnes formed the Ponca Townsite Company. Ponca comes from a Siouan dialect derived from pa-honga, which means "head leader." E.W. Marland, a wildcat promoter from Pennsylvania, commissioned a 17-foot statue of the well-known Pioneer Woman at Ponca City, a memorial to all women who survived their many hardships.

QUAPAW (Ottawa/984) This town was built on land that once belonged to the Quapaw Indians, and became a hay-shipping point in the early 1900s. The community got its start when the Kansas City, Ft. Scott and Memphis Railroad built its line across the Quapaw Reservation in 1896. The railroad paid the Indians about $365.00 for a right of way, which amounted to little more than a dollar for each Indian, as written in their Council minutes. Isaac Bingham and A.W. Abrams bought some buildings from the old Quapaw boarding school and had them moved to the tracks, which became the town of Quapaw ("down stream people"). The discovery of zinc in 1904 contributed to the town's growth.

SAPULPA (Creek/19,116) Sapulpa was a Creek Indian of the Kashita Tribe who came from Alabama about 1833 and built a store near the present town in 1850. The Atlantic and Pacific Railway came through in 1886 and named the site Sapulpa in the Indian's honor. The post office was established in 1899. Sapulpa was important cattle-shipping center for a while, but the discovery of oil in the 1920s transformed the quiet town into a active community with a population of more than 20,000. Sapulpa was interpreted as "sweet potato."

SASAKWA (Seminole/150) John F. Brown was a wealthy Seminole Chief who lived here, and the town grew up around his two-room home. He opened a general store in 1868 and also established the post office which he named Sasakwa, for "wild goose." Construction of the Frisco Railroad in 1900 added to Sasakwa's growth. The town is best known for its "Green Corn Rebellion." Farmers who were required to register for the draft in 1917 refused after General Spears urged them to rebel. Posses descended at a place called "Roasten' Ear Hill," where the farmers had their encampment and had stolen green corn because of hunger. The men were rounded up and thrown in jail, but most got suspended sentences and were sent home.

SEMINOLE (Seminole/6,899) The Seminole Indians, who were originally part of the Creek Indian Nation, were removed to Oklahoma in 1842. The town was named Tidmore, then changed to Seminole in 1906 when the Rock Island Railroad built its line. The meaning has been interpreted as "runaway," or "those who camp at a distance." Seminole became a trading center for cattlemen and farmers until the early 1920s, when one of the greatest oil pools was discovered and the town exploded with oilmen and more settlers. Today, Seminole's economy lies in manufacturing companies in addition to the oil fields.

SKEDEE (Pawnee/102) E.L. Lemert homesteaded this site along Crystal Creek and named it Lemert. While the Santa Fe Railroad was building its line, it purchased part of Lemert's land and platted a town. When the post office opened about 1903, it was changed to Skedee, derived from skidi, a Pawnee word for "wolf." The town saw growth with the discovery of oil in the region, bringing the Osage Indians who made their fortunes to trade at Skedee. The Osage Indians lost their wealth through unbelievable means. White men married Indian women, killed their families, making the wife inheritor of the oil rights. She was then killed, leaving the white man sole recipient to the oil rights. With the depletion of oil reserves and loss of the railroad, Skedee became a sleepy little town.

SKIATOOK (Osage/5,396) Skiatook emerged as a town in 1882 when W.C. Rogers established the first general store. He was the last hereditary chief of the Cherokees. Colonel Adair, a delegate in Congress for the Indian territory, petitioned for a post office and named it Skiatook. Taken from a Cherokee word, Skiatook was defined as "big injun me," in reference to a very big person or a large piece of land. The town experienced rapid growth when the Midland Valley Railroad laid its tracks in 1905.

TAHLEQUAH (Cherokee/14,458) In 1839, Tahlequah was selected as the permanent capital of the Cherokee Nation, and grew up around the council ground. Tahlequah is a Cherokee word derived from talikwa, meaning "lost." Tradition says Tahlequah meant "two is enough," which came from three men appointed to locate the Cherokee capital. When one did not show up, the other two men decided "tahlequah." During the Civil War, General Stand Watie pillaged and burned the Cherokee National Capitol Building. In

1844, the Cherokee Indians started the Cherokee Advocate, a newspaper that was written in the alphabet that Sequoyah created in 1821. It enabled the Indians who could not read or write English to keep posted on what was going on in their world.

TALALA (Rogers/270) This vast, fertile prairie covered with blue-stem grass was once home to the Plains Indians. Clem Rogers (father of Will Rogers) came to the region in 1856 and located a cow town and trading post. He staked out 60,000 acres on the future townsite. F.M. Connor arrived in 1890 and laid out the town, and the post office opened on June 23 the same year. Talala is a Cherokee word that means "woodpecker." The Indians associated the tapping of a woodpecker's bill with the musical syllable ta-la-la. They also called the Cherokee girls who had red hair ta-la-la.

TALIHINA (Leflore/1,211) In 1888, the Frisco Railway built its tracks across the mountains from Fort Smith Arkansas. As the Choctaw Indians watched the construction, they called the tracks talihina, which means "iron road." They were superstitious and believed that white men would steal their women, lock them up in the houses on wheels and take them away. A small missionary settlement was established after completion of the railroad. Until 1919, there was no access to this region except by rail until convict labor was used to build a road through the mountains.

TALOGA (Dewey/372) Before the area was opened to settlement, Taloga was made county seat after the Cheyenne and Arapaho Reservation was surveyed in 1891, and the post office opened a year later. Taloga may be a Creek word for "rock water." Located at what was called the edge of the Dustbowl, the region had small sheltered valleys where broomcorn was successfully grown. Tradition has it that Carrie Nation made her presence known when she entered Captain McFaddin's saloon and got permission to pray there. When she asked McFaddin if he wanted his children to see the nude pictures on the wall, McFaddin took them down.

TAMAHA (Haskell/198) Starting out as a steamboat landing, Tamaha was originally a Choctaw village called Pleasant Bluff. The site was established as a port and ferry crossing about 1836, then changed to Tamaha which means "town." During the Civil War, Tamaha saw battle when Bridagider General Stand Watie, a Cherokee Indian, captured the Union Army's steamboat, *J.R. Williams*, along with its $120,000 worth of cargo destined for Fort Gibson. Today, Tamaha is a small bedroom community, where the general store is only open seasonally for fisherman.

TECUMSEH (Potawatomi/6,098) Tecumseh was born overnight when the land run began in 1891. The post office was established on September 18 the same year. Residents thought the Choctaw, Oklahoma and Gulf Railroad would come through, but it bypassed the town by three miles. City leaders raised enough money to build a branch line that would connect with the railroad at Shawnee. Tecumseh was a great statesman and warrior who fought with the British and died in the Battle of Thames in 1812. Although he never lived here, part of the Shawnee tribe settled in the county after Tecumseh's death. In the Shawnee language, Tecumseh means "a panther crossing the sky."

TONKAWA (Kay/3,299) When 40,000 parcels in northwestern Oklahoma were opened on September 16, 1893, more than 100,000 homesteaders made a run for the land. Eli Blake and Wiley Gregory claimed a tract, formed the Oklahoma Townsite Company, and donated land for the townsite. Tonkawa was surveyed and platted in 1894. The same year the post office was established. Santa Fe's subsidiary, the Blackwell and Southern Railroad extended its line in 1899, a boon for the wheat farmers. Tonkawa was taken from the Tonkawa Tribe, meaning "they all stay together."

TULSA (Tulsa/393,049) The Creek Indians ceded their land that included this site in 1832, opening the land for white settlers. It was named Tulsey Town, from the Creek word, tallasi, which means "town." When the post office was established in 1879, the name was shortened to Tulsa. In 1882, the Atlantic & Pacific Railroad built its line to Tulsa and established a terminal, loading pens, and a roundhouse. Tulsa experienced extensive growth when the first oil well came in across the river in 1901.

WAPANUCKA (Johnston/445) This name is thought to be a Delaware word that means "eastern people." When the Wapanucka Female Manual Labor School was established in 1852, it was one of the first schools in the Chickasaw Nation. The post office was opened at the school until 1888 when it was moved to the townsite. In 1865, a little-known battle was waged near town when more than 350 Comanche Indians raided the settlers' homes and stole their horses. The Chickasaw Indians went after them, killing many of the raiders and their chief.

WATONGA (Blaine/4,658) Located 70 miles northwest of Oklahoma City, Watonga began in 1892 with the opening of the Cheyenne-Arapaho Reservations. It was named after an Arapaho Indian scout whose name means "black coyote." Another interpretation was from a Cheyenne Indian named Watnooka, but the Cheyennes maintain it was not named for Watonga. Dr. Berthrong, wrote, "I have always understood that Watonga's name came from Black Coyote, an Arapaho... Cheyennes predominate in Blaine County (especially, in the Watonga area) and because of the Cheyenne-Arapaho rivalry, it is natural for Cheyennes to doubt the origin of the town's name."[33]

WAURIKA (Jefferson/1,988) Waurika was once part of the Kiowa-Comanche Reservation. After the town was laid out about 1890, the post office was named Peery. When the Rock Island Railroad came through and built a depot, it changed the name to Moneka. It was later renamed Waurika, which means "good water." Located along the Chisholm Trail, ranchers rested their stock here to fatten them up during cattle drives. The town's economy was based on the railroad's train repairs in addition to agriculture. Eventually, both industries decreased and Waurika turned to another profitable business: raising parakeets. As a result, the state legislature labeled the town "Parakeet Capital of the World."

WAYNOKA (Woods/993) First called Keystone in 1886, the town was an important division point and the second largest railroad yard in Oklahoma. It is located on the Cherokee Outlet that was settled in 1893. Six years later the name was changed to Waynoka, which means "sweet water." Waynoka was the site Charles Lindbergh used for the first transcontinental air transport in 1928, providing coast-to-coast travel across the U.S. in 48 hours. It is also the place where the first published tornado was recorded and the last wild buffalo was killed. The animal was on a wild game preserve in Montana, and because he was so troublesome, it was brought to Waynoka where the Indians slaughtered the animal according to their tradition.

WELEETKA (Okfuskee/1,014) George Clarke and Lake Moore founded the town after a Creek Indian named Martha Lowe signed an agreement allowing a townsite on her property. Civil engineer C.M. Lawrence platted the site at the junction of the Frisco and Fort Smith and Western Railroads. Weleetka is an ancient Creek word that means "running water," and was headquarters of the Crazy Snake Rebellion. Led by Chitto Harjo, hundreds of Indians were against the allotment system of Indian lands. They were arrested and sent to the prison at Leavenworth, Kansas.

WEWOKA (Seminole/3,562) This was the end of the Seminole Indians' Trail of Tears journey from Florida. They named the site We-wo-ka after the falls north of town, a word for "barking waters." In 1866, Wewoka became the capital of the Seminole Nation. Oil was struck at the Greater Seminole Field in 1926, and Wewoka became one of the state's leading oil producers overnight. This led to the phrase, "the Wewoka Switch." With a swell in population, freighting congestion and stocking problems occurred. Local merchants told their customers when they couldn't find the merchandise it had been lost on the Wewoka Switch.

WYANDOTTE (Ottawa/363) Named for the Wyandotte Tribe (for "islander"), the site was founded as Prairie City in 1872. When the Atlantic and Pacific Railroad was laying its tracks, the post office was moved from the Wyandotte Nation to the present site in 1876, and renamed Grand River. Wyandotte received its present name after a city ordinance in 1894 and the official plat for the town was filed in 1896. Wyandotte lost much of its agricultural land when the Pensacola Dam Project was built on the Neosho and Grand rivers in 1940. The highways were rerouted and the town had to move to higher ground.

OREGON

CANEMAH (Clackamas) This former town was founded by Absalom Hedges in the 1840s. First called Falls City, it was renamed Kanim, from a Kalapuyan word for "canoe place," and later anglicized to Canemah. The railroad that came through was known as the richest railroad mile in the Northwest because of the tremendous tonnage that was hauled in a one-day period. When the Willamette Locks were completed in 1873, Canemah's economy dropped from loss of freighting, and it was eventually annexed to Oregon City.

CHAMPOEG (Marion) Champoeg became a major settlement after Hudson's Bay Company retirees moved here. During this time, the site was called "Campment de Sauble." Champoeg was thought to be derived from the Kalapuyan expression interpreted as a type of edible plant or "place of the camp," designating the prairie that extended to the river bank. In 1843, Champoeg was selected as a meeting place to consider the first provisional government in the territory. In 1862, a flood destroyed the entire town, and in 1901 the site was turned into a state park.

CHEMULT (Klamath) A small community located about 70 miles north of Klamath Falls, the town was purchased by Gideon Palmer in 1926, who constructed the first building in town. The Southern Pacific Railroad named its siding Chemult, a Klamath word meaning "wife dies." Palmer later named the town after the siding. Chemult may have been named for an Indian who signed the 1864 treaty at Klamath Falls. A mail stage route was established by the Gilbride brothers during the 1930s.

CHILOQUIN (Klamath/716) Located at the confluence of the Williamson and Sprague rivers, this was a camping ground for the Klamath Indians. Although settlement began in the mid-1800s, it would be the early 1900s before Chiloquin saw any growth. Settlers had to purchase land allotments because the town was on the Klamath Indian Reservation. When the Southern Pacific Railroad was built, Chiloquin became one of the largest livestock shipping points in Oregon. It also benefited when the timber industry came into prominence. Closure of the lumber mills turned Chiloquin into a small bedroom community. It was named for Klamath Chief Chay-lo-quin (origin unknown).

CLATSKANIE (Columbia/1,528) The Klatskani tribe were here as recently as 2,000 years ago, relatively new compared to other tribes in the Northwest. Their name may have referred to a place in the hills where two rivers originated. It was also thought to mean "round head," or "swift running water." The first mention of the Indians was reported by Alexander Kennedy of Hudson's Bay Company in 1825. He noted that the Clatskaneyes lived on the upper part of the Chilwitz River. The majority of Klatskanies died in the 1830s due to malaria or smallpox. Klatskanie Chief Chewaman and what was left of his tribe moved here, with the first white people arriving in 1852. The post office opened in 1871.

KLAMATH FALLS (Klamath/19,462) There was no settlement until 1867 due to hostilities of the Klamath Indians, who were removed to the Klamath Reservation the same year. They were a Lutuamian tribe and called themselves Eukshikni or Auksni ("people of the lake"). George Nurse built a trading post at Link River, established a post office, and named the site Linkville. The town's economy was stimulated by the construction of mills and building of a branch line of the Southern Pacific Railroad. In 1893, the name was changed to Klamath Falls. The name may be derived from a Sahaptin (Nez Perce or Cayuse) word, kalamat, interpreted as "yellow water lily," a major food source for the Indians. It may come from maklaks, a Klamath Indian word meaning "encamped."

MOLALLA (Clackamas/5,647) The Molalla Indians lived off the land, hunting and fishing. They did not grow agricultural products, but foraged for their food. Molalla is derived from mo and alli, for "deer berries." The community was first known as Four Corners, and a stagecoach stop was established midway between here and Oregon City. Molalla was an important trading center when timber companies were established in the early 1900s. Harvey Gorden came to Molalla in 1846 to work as a surveyor. A Constitutional Convention met in 1857 and appointed a committee to come up with a state seal. Gorden submitted his design to the committee, and it was adopted as the Oregon Seal.

NECANICUM (Clatsop) Necanicum was settled about 1886 and is located some ten miles from Seaside. Herman Ahlers was an early resident, for whom the community was named. He established the post office on January 10, 1896. Three years later he renamed the site Push because he thought the place would become an industrious town. In 1906, it was changed to Necanicum, meaning "gap," descriptive of a gap in the mountains, or it may been derived from Ne-hay-ne-hum, for an Indian lodge. When the post office closed in 1916, Necanicum became part of a rural delivery route.

NEHALEM (Tillamook/203) The Nehalem Indians were of the Salish Tribe and their name means "place where people live." The first settlers in the region were John Crawford and Jack Keaton. When railroads made their way to the region, cheese-making and lumber became important industries. Many captains lost their ships near Nehalem because of sandbars and frequent fog. Beeswax in the form of 20-pound blocks was found on Nehalem Beach, and may have come from a wrecked Spanish ship in 1769. The blocks were stamped with I.H.S. and I.H.N., suggesting it was destined for west coast Catholic missions.

NESKOWIN (Tillamook/169) This was home to the Nestucca band of Tillamook Indians. In 1855, the Nestucca country was set aside as an Indian reservation until 1876 when the region opened for homesteading. First known as Slab Creek, the community was settled in the 1880s. Henry Page and his family established the Neskowin Hotel in 1895. The post office was opened on December 4, 1886 (Mrs. Page, postmaster). Observing an Indian pointing to the creek one day, saying, "Neskowin, Neskowin," Mrs. Page asked him what it meant. He said, "plenty fish, plenty fish." In 1925, Slab Creek was officially changed to Neskowin.

NETARTS (Tillamook/744) As early as the 1400s, the Tillamook Indians inhabited the Netarts region. This community once extended from Cape Lookout to Cape Meares. The Indians called the site Ne Ta At, meaning "near the water;" it was later spelled Netarts. The Tillamooks who were still here were removed to the Siletz and Grand Ronde Reservations about 1859. The post office was established in 1871 (Edward Bunnell, postmaster). The local economy was tied to oystering and the timber industry.

SCAPPOOSE (Columbia/4,976) The Scappoose Plains area was once used by the Chinook Indians for their potlatches. In 1828, Boston trader Captain Dominus brought his ship into Scappoose Bay and traded with the Indians. He left them with more than just merchandise, because soon after the Indians got sick and most of them were wiped out (probably from smallpox). S.T. Gosa built a boat dock, store, and post office in 1870, which he called Gosa's Landing. William West offered to donate some acreage to the railroad in 1883 if it would build a depot and switching yard, and requested the name be changed to Scappoose, a Chinook word for "gravelly plains."

SILETZ (Lincoln/1,133) Siletz was developed as an administrative headquarters for the Siletz Indian Reservation established in 1856, composed of 27 bands of Indians who became known as the Confederated Tribes of Siletz. When gold was discovered in Southern Oregon, the Indians were forcibly removed to Siletz in 1856. Siletz may be derived from a Rogue River word, silis, for "black bear." The native interpretation is "crooked rope (or water)," referring to the Siletz River, one of the snakiest rivers in the state. When an agent asked the Indians their name, they said "Se-La-Gees." He could not pronounce the word so called them Siletz. The Indian headquarters is gone and the reservation was dissolved in 1956.

TAKILMA (Josephine) The discovery of copper brought Colonel T. Draper in the early 1900s. Prior to settlement, the region was home to the Takelma and Latgawa Indians, better known as the Rogue River Tribes. They were later removed to a reservation at Table Rock about 1853 because of continued hostilities with the whites. Gold was discovered in the region shortly after the rush began in California. The town was named for Chief Takilma, but its origin has not been identified. Takilma made headlines when one of the residents established the Out n' About, a complex of tree houses that were rented out to vacationers. Citing public safety, the county forced the business to shut down operations about 2001.

TILLAMOOK (Tillamook/4,352) Captain Robert Gray arrived at Tillamook in 1788, the first American to land in Oregon. The site was first called Hoquarten. Thomas Stillwell purchased a 320-acre farm in 1861 and laid out a town he called Lincoln. When the post office was established in 1866 as Lincoln, postal officials discovered a duplication in names, so Tillamook was selected for the resident tribe, meaning "land of many waters." It is descriptive of the more than 70 miles of coastline and numerous bays and rivers in the region. In 1933, the county experienced one of the worst fires of the century. More than 311,000 acres were burned, including the largest remaining stand of Douglas fir in the state.

TUALITIN (Washington/22,791) The region was home to the Atfalatis, who were a tribe of the Kalapuya Indians. An early arrival was Zenas Brown when he claimed land in 1850 through the Donation Land Act, and established the first ferry at Tualitin. In 1853, John Sweek helped to plat the town and named it Tualatin, which comes from Tuality, a Kalapuyan word for "slow and lazy." It described one of the rivers that had limpid pools encompassing about half of its 80 miles. Others believe the word denotes "fork" for the many creeks that converge on the Tualatin River. Tualatin became an important waterway for the transportation of lumber, grains and other produce.

UMATILLA (Umatilla/4,978) The Indians of the Blue Mountains roamed this region more than 300 years before Lewis and Clark came on the scene. Founded as Umatilla Landing in 1863 or 1864, the community sprang up overnight as an important trade and shipping center during the gold rush. The site was surveyed by Timothy K. Davenport in 1863 and known as Columbia. It was later changed for the Umatilla Indians, thought to mean "water rippling over sand." Umatilla landing was a shipping point for the Powder River, Owyhee, and Idaho mines. When construction of Oregon Railway and Navigation Company was completed, it took most of Umatilla's trade.

WALLOWA (Wallowa/869) An early settler from the town of Lostine came to this site about 1886 and decided to found another town. L.J. Cole owned the land, which was purchased by a Mr. Johnson who named it Wallowa, a Nez Perce word designating a willow fish trap. The Indians' name for the region was hi-paah, meaning "bear robbing salmon catch." The post office was established in 1874, and the Mercantile and Milling Company was founded in 1890. Most of the town's economy was dependent on farming, fruit growing and cattle raising.

WAPINITIA (Wasco) Hiram Coram moved to this former town in the 1880s and built the first store. He also donated some of his land for a townsite. A stage service ran between The Dalles in the early

1900s. Until irrigation was installed about 1920, residents had to haul in their water and store it in cisterns. The site was first named Oak Grove, then changed to Wapinitia, derived from the Warm Spring word, wapinita, and referred to a location near the edge of something (perhaps a mountain or desert).

YACHATS (Lincoln/617) Yachats is located along the Pacific Coast. The Alsea Indian Agency was established in 1855 just north of town and was a substation of the Siletz Indian Agency. The government opened the area for homesteading in 1875. When the post office was established in 1877, it was named Ocean View. In 1916, it was changed to Yachats, defined as "at the foot of the mountain," "dark water between timbered hills," "silent waters," "little river with big mouth." The syllable "ya" in the language of the Alsea Indians is "water." The Little Log Church By the Sea was built about 1929. This historic building began to deteriorate by 1986, and was completely refurbished using volunteers, many who were in their 70s and 80s.

YONCALLA (Douglas/1,052) Botanist David Douglas met the Yoncalla Indians and his notes may be the earliest accounts of the tribe, who were a dialectic group of the Kalapuya Indians. Most of the Yoncallas died out because of the epidemics that ravaged the region in the 1830s. Jesse Applegate, famous for blazing the Applegate Trail, came to Yoncalla in 1849 and took up a homestead. In 1872, George Burt offered the O&C Railroad some of his land if it would build a depot on his property. When the post office was established, the name was changed to Yoncalla, derived from yonk and colla for "eagle mountain," or yonc-alla-alla, meaning "eagles nest on top."

PENNSYLVANIA

ALIQUIPPA (Beaver/11,734) Aliquippa became a town with the merger of three small villages. It was named for a Seneca woman, whose name was interpreted as "hat." The Pittsburgh and Lake Erie Railroad came through in 1877 and the post office was established. Within the next ten years, Aliquippa developed into an industrial town.

AQUASHICOLA (Carbon) This town was first called Millport, but when the post office was established in 1862 it was renamed Aquashicola. George Ziegenfuss was the first settler to establish a grist mill in 1806. The Bethlehem Slate Quarry was built in the 1860s and was the only area north of the Blue Mountain in the Lehigh Valley where slate was produced. Aquashicola is an unincorporated village in Lower Towamensing township. It is a Lenape word for "fishing with bull (or bush) nets."

CATASAUQUA (Lehigh/6,588) The "Iron Borough" was established as Chawton. John Page was deeded more than 2,000 acres from William Penn's daughter in 1731. When the Biery brothers moved here 1801, they changed the name to Biery's Port. Discovery of pig iron brought the establishment of the Lehigh Crane Iron Company in 1839, and the town was renamed Craneville. Duplication caused it to be changed to Sideropolis. In 1845, an application was made for a post office, but Sideropolis was turned down. Finally, in 1846 the name was changed to Catasauqua, interpreted as "dry ground" or "earth is thirsty." It was also translated from gottoshacki for "parched land."

CATAWISSA (Columbia/1,589) Originally an Indian village called Lapachpeton's Town for a Delaware Chief, William and Mary Hughes purchased the site in 1786. It was called Hughesville until made part of the county in 1813. The town had grown as large as geographically possible by the 1930s. Because of the lay of the land, it could support only so many people, and remained a bedroom community. Catawissa is Delaware for "pure water." The name may also come from gatawisi, which means "growing fat."

CHICORA (Butler/1,021) While searching for a suitable place to live, James Hemphill and Rudolph Barnart arrived at Chicora in 1794. New businesses were established in the early 1800s. The place was named Barnhart Mills, then changed to Chicora, derived from the Catawba word, yuchikere, meaning "yuchi are there," descriptive of an Indian tribe, but it is not known what yuchi means. It was also suggested the name meant "those far away," or "at a distance."

COCALICO (Lancaster) In 1724, Eberher Ream requested 200 acres of land on an Indian settlement. About ten years later, John Taylor surveyed the site. Distilling was a thriving business which brought income to farmers when their crops did not do well. The 1860s brought the Reading & Columbia Railroad. Cocalico may be derived from koch-hale-kung, a Delaware word that denotes a den of serpents. It was also thought to be a corruption of achgookwalico, which means "where the snakes gather in holes," or just "snake dens."

COCOLAMUS (Juniata) The land was claimed in 1762 by John Gallagher, who sold it to William McAlister four years later. It wasn't until after the Civil War that the first general store was built. The Indians called a species of hawk kakon, from where the town's name may have been derived. The 1800s brought in a creamery, which was later purchased by the well-known Breyer Ice Cream Company.

CONESTOGA (Lancaster/3,749) This region was once home to the Susquehanna Indians. Conestoga may come from the Susquehanna word, kanastoge, meaning "at the place of the immersed pole," or derived from andastoegue, for "people of the cabin pole." Located at the confluence of the Conestoga and Susquehanna rivers, Conestoga saw its first business when a trading post was established by Jacques Le Tore in 1696. During the 1760s, Indian uprisings almost destroyed this settlement. It would be 1797 before the town was laid out and platted. This is where the large, broad-wheeled Conestoga wagons were made during the 1700–1800s.

CONNEUTVILLE (Crawford/848) Conneutville saw its first settler about 1799 when Alexander Power built a grist mill on Conneut Creek. Settlers would subsist on the natural resources until a general store was established in 1815. The town was platted by Alexander Power in 1814, and called Powertown. He later requested the name be changed to Conneutville. Conneut may be an Iroquois phrase meaning "the snow place," or a corruption of gunniati, for "it is a long time since they are gone." The post office was established in 1822 (Alexander Power, postmaster).

CONNOQUENESSING (Butler/564) In 1758, G.F. Post passed through on his way to Kuskuski, and wrote, "We came to the River Conaquanosshan, an old Indian Town; we was then fifteen miles from Chschcushking."[34] Daniel Graham, who was a soldier of the Revolution, convinced a number of Scotch families to resettle here. The name may be derived from gunachquenesink, Delaware for "for a long way straight."

CONSHOHOCKEN (Montgomery/7,589) Swedes settled at this site shortly after William Penn received a deed from the Indians in 1683. By the 1800s, the Philadelphia, Germantown and Norristown Railroad had laid its tracks through the area, and the Schuylkill Canal began operations in 1824. Since limestone was available for the iron and steel industry, numerous rolling mills and furnaces were established. Conshohocken is derived from the Lenape word, kanshihaking, meaning "elegant land."

COPLAY (Lehigh/3,387) This borough was settled about 1740 by John Schreiber, and known as Schrieber's. It was predominantly a farming community inhabited by Pennsylvania Dutch and Germans. The name was changed to Lehigh Valley after the Lehigh Valley Iron Furnace was established about 1853, and later the Thomas Iron Company. The advent of the iron industry brought in Irish immigrants. Immigration was further intensified with the establishment of cement and silk mills, and cigar factories. In 1869, the name was changed to Coplay, derived from Kolapechka, who was the son of Shawanese Chief Paxanosa. It was interpreted as "fine running stream."

ERIE (Erie/103,717) This town was named for the Eriez Indians, whose name means "at the place of the panther," or "it is long tailed." Because the Indians resisted colonization, Erie didn't show much growth until about 1795. The salt trade was an important commodity that was transshipped from here. Erie developed rapidly after the Erie and Pittsburgh Canal opened in 1844, in addition to the building of railroads. It was also one of the Underground Railroads, enabling the slaves to escape to Canada.

HOKENDAUQUA (Northampton/3,411) This town took its name from the Hokendauqua Creek and was settled about 1854 with the arrival of the Thomas Iron Company, which purchased the land, and the first general store was built in 1856. Located near Hokendauqua Creek, the site was named Hockyondocquay in the 1700s. The spelling was changed to Hockendauqua, a Delaware expression meaning "searching for land," and may have signified negotiations the colonists made for the site.

KITTANNING (Armstrong/4,787) Owing to boundary disputes with the state of Virginia, Arthur St. Clair suggested building a fort and establishing a town, which was accomplished in 1778. It was after 1796 that the first permanent settlers came, the majority Germans and the Scotch-Irish. The Great Western Iron Works was established in 1839 and manufactured the first "T" rail west of the Allegheny Mountains. Kittanning may be derived from kit-anne, Delaware for "at the great stream," or "greatest river."

MAHANOY CITY (Schuylkill/4,647) The first person to claim the land was a German named John Riesch in 1791. It was known simply as the "hills" until the site was laid out by Frank Carter. Coal was the town's lifeblood, and numerous collieries were established in the 1800s. Derived from the Delaware word, maghonioy (or mahoni), Mahanoy means "lick," descriptive of the saline deposits frequented by wild game.

MAXATAWNY (Berks/5,982) Much of the land was purchased from the Indians in 1732 by John, Thomas and Richard Penn. In 1742, the townsite was surveyed and named Maxatawny, derived from machksit-hanne, a Delaware word meaning "bear path stream." It wasn't until about the 1860s that the first general store was established, and the post office opened in 1895. Maxatawny was once a thriving industrial town of foundries and coal mines.

MONONGAHELA (Greene/4,761) Located at the mouth of Pigeon Creek, the site was called Parkinson's Ferry during the 1770s. The 1800s brought the majority of businesses: boat building, grist mill, brewery, paper mill, and glass factory. The name was changed to Williamsport, but when the post office was established, duplication caused it to be given the Delaware name of Monongahela. It was derived from menaongihela, meaning "where the land erodes, referring to riverfront land that would collapsed during floods.

NANTICOKE (Luzerne/10,955) Located between the Blue Ridge Mountains and Susquehanna River, this was home to the Nentego Tribe of Delawares who were removed from their lands in Maryland. Permanent white settlement occurred in the early 1800s. John Alden, John Oint and Nat Chapman established grist mills and forges powered by the Nanticoke Falls. The town later became a terminal point for the North Branch Canal which shipped massive amounts of coal to the large cities. Nanticoke is derived from Nentego, and in turn is a variation of unechtgo or unalachtgo, for "tidewater people."

NESQUEHONING (Carbon/3,288) This village is located at the foot of Nesquehoning Mountain. It was originally laid out as a mining town by the Lehigh Coal & Navigation Company (LC&N) in 1831 and surveyed by Enoch Lewis. A smallpox epidemic hit the town in 1850, who some thought was brought in by, of all things, a bag of feathers. First called "Hell's Kitchen," the LC&N renamed it Nesquehoning, after a creek the Delaware Indians called neskahoni, which means "black" or "dirty lick," because the stream was black. The color came from the hemlock that seeped out of the roots of the trees.

OHIOPYLE (Fayette/77) Ohiopyle was made a borough in 1901 and is situated on the Youghiogheny River. It is now the Ohiopyle State Park. Andrew Stewart donated land for a church and also gave the village square to residents. The Kendall Lumber Company was established in 1906, in addition to a hydroelectric power plant. Ohiopyle was quite prosperous until the depression hit in the 1930s, and residents turned to making moonshine for their survival. The name may be derived from ohiopehelle, a Delaware word meaning "water whitened by froth," referring to the water hitting the rocks at the falls.

OSWAYO (Potter/159) This region attracted many settlers because of the white pine forest. Numerous sawmills and a tannery were established The site was named Brindleville because one of the settlers had a team of brindle oxen. It was changed in the 1840s to Oswayo when the post office was established. The name is derived from the Seneca word o-sa-ayeh, interpreted as "pine forest." By 1889, the lumber had been depleted and agriculture became a prime resource.

PERKASIE (Bucks/4,358) This site was settled about 1708 and known as the Manor of Perkasie, owned by William Penn's daughter. The North Pennsylvania Railroad Company was established in the 1850s. First known as Comleysville, it was changed to Perkasie, a Delaware word for "hickory nuts cracked at." The post office began operating in 1871. Perkasie became very prosperous after numerous cigar factories were established, the first in 1892. One of the larger factories, Boltz, Clymer & Company, was producing more than 150,000 cigars a month destined for consumers in Hawaii.

PUNXSUTAWNEY (Jefferson/6,271) The "Legendary Weather Capital of the World," Punxsutawney was originally an Indian camp site. The town was laid out and platted in 1821 by Reverend Barclay. Its economy was dependent on agriculture. Development of the surrounding coal fields also spurred the town's growth, in addition to building of the Buffalo, Rochester and Pittsburgh Railway in 1883. The Indians called their village Ponksad-uteney, from where Punxsutawney is derived, a Delaware word for "town of sandflies."

SHAMOKIN (Northumberland/8,009) This Indian village was the largest in the state until 1756, when they were removed to a place called Big Island. Bits of coal in Shamokin Creek discovered by John Boyd would turn Shamokin into a coal mining town. In 1836, the Shamokin Coal Company was formed, and a few years later opened the first colliery. This town was founded by Boyd in 1825, and known as Boyd's Stone-coal Quarry. Shamokin was interpreted from the Delaware word, schahamoki, for "place of eels," "place where gun barrels are straightened," and "where antlers are plenty."

SHESHEQUIN (Bradford/1,300) Before the area was settled, it was nothing but forests of pine and oak trees. Sheshequin was once part of the Susquehanna Company's townships of Ulster and Claverack. The year 1783 was the beginning of this settlement when General Simon Spalding arrived. Sheshequin is derived from tschetschequannink, signifying "the place of a rattle," or taken from sheshekan, meaning "a gourd rattle."

SHOHOLA (Pike/2,088) In 1751, Samuel Wares established the Shohola House (a hotel) which would be the only business until 1815. Since this site was a major crossing point on the Delaware River, a ferry business began operating in 1829 when the Erie and Hudson Canal was built. Establishment of the Erie Railroad brought added stability to Shohola. It is a Lenape word that means "place of peace," or "distressed."

SINNAMAHONING (Cameron) Located deep in the Allegheny Mountains, Sinnamahoning was created in the 1860s because of timber. Its economy was spurred when the Philadelphia and Erie, and the Buffalo and Susquehanna Railroads built their tracks through the region. Later, establishment of dynamite plants supplanted the logging industry. Sinnamahoning took its name from the river, a derivation of the Delaware expression, achsinni-mahoni, defined as "stony lick."

TAMAQUA (Schuylkill/7,174) Originally home to the Iroquois, Tamaqua was occupied by Burkhardt Moser, who was given 6,000 acres of land because of his participation in the Boston Tea Party. After he accidentally found a vein of coal while erecting a sawmill, land developers and coal companies moved in. In 1817, the Little Schuylkill Navigation, Railroad and Coal Company purchased most of the land for coal development. The townsite was laid out in 1829 by railroad engineers. Tamaqua is a Delaware word meaning "home of the beaver," or "land of running water."

TIDIOUTE (Warren/792) Located along the Allegheny River, Tidioute is a Seneca word interpreted as "see far," "straight water," "cluster of islands," and "protrusion of land." With the water power from the river, numerous sawmill were established. One of the settlers was Samuel Hunter who established the Hunter Lumber Company. Tidioute became an oil center when oil was discovered in the region about 1859. It was here that Standard Oil was formed.

TINICUM (Delaware/4,353) An island on the Delaware River, Tinicum was the first permanent European community in the state, created in 1643 when Swedish Lt. Col. Johan Printz and his crew arrived and established a seat of government. Because part of the island was low and marshy, the Swedes built a system of dykes to reclaim the land. In addition to farming, boat-building was a big industry. The people later destroyed the dykes during the Revolution to deter the advancing British. Tinicum, an Algonquin word, means "at an island."

TIONESTA (Forest/615) Early people were the Munsee Wolf Clan, a branch of the Delaware Indians who lived at a village called Goshgoshing. After John Range's service during the Revolution, he was granted a tract of land in 1785, which was called Saqualinget ("place of council"). The timber industry began when John Middleton built mills near Tionesta, and the post office was established in 1866 (J.G. Dale, postmaster). Tionesta is derived from the Iroquois word, tiyohwenoisto," signifying "it penetrates the land." Others ascribe it to tigowanowisto, for "meeting of the waters."

TOUGHKENAMON (Chester/1,375) This town grew up around an inn that William Carpenter opened in 1738. The Philadelphia and Baltimore Central Railroad was built and completed to Toughkenamon about 1854. The post office was established in 1868 as Tough Kenamon (George C. Gallagher, postmaster). Toughkenamon is derived from the Algonquin word, doch-can-amon, which means "firebrand hill."

TOWANDA (Bradford/3,024) During 1710, many Palatines were induced to emigrate to New York. Dissatisfied with their location, they moved to Pennsylvania in 1727. The site was laid out by William Means in 1812 as Meansville. Towanda was selected in 1828 because Meansville caused some animosity. The name came from tawundeunk, for "where we bury the dead," referring to the place the Nanticoke Indians buried their dead. Another theory ascribed the name from ta-na-wun-da, which means "swift water," or "rapids."

TUNKHANNOCK (Wyoming/1,911) The Lenape, Mingo and Shawnee inhabited this region before white settlement. An early settler was Jeremiah Osterhout who was attracted by trading possibilities along an old Indian trail. Since the town was located at the confluence of Tunkhannock Creek and a branch of the Susquehanna River, a successful business was a shad fishery. During the early 1900s, part of the town's income came from witch hazel plants which manufactured extract. At that time there were only three of these plants in the U.S. Tunkahannock was derived from tankhanek, Lenape for "small creek."

VENANGO (Crawford/288) Originally home to the Seneca Indians, the majority of residents settled here during the 1790s. Solomon Walter and John Lasher purchased the land because they thought a turnpike would be built, and named their plot Strawsburg. When the road did not come through, the parcel was sold to John Kleckner, who had the site surveyed in 1838 and named it Klecknersville. When the town was incorporated in 1852, it was renamed Venango, derived from the Seneca word, onenge, thought to mean "mink," or "bull thistle." It may have come from innungah, which described something carved in a tree.

WYALUSING (Bradford/564) The Andaste Indians (or Susquehannocks) were here as early as 1620; not much is known about them except their camp was called Gohontoto ("village of the old man"). A Monsey chief named Papunhank brought a few families here in 1752 and established a village. After Moravian missionary Reverend Christian Post arrived in 1760, the name was changed to Friedenshuetten ("Tents of peace"). During the 1800s, the town was the center of shipping for logs down the Susquehanna River and later became a commercial center. Wyalusing is a corruption of the Delaware word, m'chwihilusing, for "the place of the old man."

WYOMISSING (Berks/8,587) This name was interpreted from Lenape as "place of many water falls," "place of long fish," and "place of flats." In 1685, the Indians conveyed their lands to William Penn. When the Reading Suburban Real Estate Company was established in 1896, it began developing the town and named it Wyomissing. The world's largest manufacturer of textile machinery was established in 1892. The Textile Machine Works produced the first braiding and knitting machines.

RHODE ISLAND

ASHAWAY (Washington, 1,537) This village was once called Cundall's Mills for Isaac Cundall, who built a mill in 1816. The first business was a blacksmith in 1750, and would be the only industry for about 50 years. During the early 1800s, trades included a factory that manufactured woolen goods and an iron forge. In 1825, Lester Crandall established a prosperous fishing business that served the New York Market. It was later taken over and became the Ashaway Line and Twine Manufacturing Company. Ashaway is an Algonquin word derived from asha and waugh, for "cold spring," descriptive of the water that stayed frigid during the summertime in the Ashaway River.

CHEPACHET (Providence) Chepachet is a small village within the town of Glocester. It was once a busy manufacturing village with a hat factory, grist mill, distillery, and the Chepachet Manufacturing Company, which spun cotton yarn. The name is derived from the Narragansett expression, chepuck and chack, meaning "devil bag." It was thought that a wallet or bag was found here, and an Indian said it was the devil. Some theorized the name meant "place of separation," designating a division of rivers.

CONIMICUT (Kent) Sam Gorton and his followers settled here about 1862. They were each allotted a one-third section of a point of land that jutted into Narragansett Bay. Fencing was installed in order to allow the settlers' cattle and horses to pasture. The Warwick Railroad came through during the1870s. Steamers coming down the bay to the Warwick coast began stopping here, with the result that Conimicut became a resort town. The hurricanes of 1938 and 1954 almost devastated the village. Conimicut is a Narragansett word, possibly meaning "shallow place for boats," and may have designated the numerous coves that were used for coastal trade.

NARRAGANSETT (Washington/16,361) This site was part of a larger area purchased from the Indians in the 1600s. During King Philip's War, the Narragansetts gave refuge to the Wampanoag Indians. Although Sachem Canochet tried to remain neutral, he refused to turn them over to the English, and as a result the colonists attacked. Canochet and his warriors attacked Providence and the surrounding area. He was captured in 1767 and executed. The region's biggest industry was shipbuilding, but by the 1880s the town was better known as a summer resort for the wealthy. Narragansett means "at the small narrow point," or "island."

PAWTUCKET (Providence/72,958) This town grew up around an iron forge established by Joseph Jenks, Jr. shortly after King Philip's War in 1671. Pawtucket became the "Birthplace of the American Industrial Revolution" after Samuel Slater built a successful cotton mill in 1793. He duplicated the British water-powered spinning, picking and carding machines, and created the first water-powered factory in America. The town no longer dominates the textile industry, although there are specialty textile workers. Pawtucket has been interpreted as Narragansett for "a waterfall place," or "falls of the water."

QUIDNICK (Kent) Located in the town Coventry, this village was named Greeneville for the Greene family. In 1823, it was changed to Taftville, and finally Quidnick. The Sprague family began the textile industry in 1811, expanded their business, and became the largest mill owners in the state. During the Civil War, the town prospered because of the great demand for material for the soldiers. Quidnick means "place at the end of the hill," derived from acqueedenuck in the Narragansett language.

SACONNET (Newport) During the 1660s, the Saconet Indians were made offers for purchase of their land, which they refused. Believing the Indians were going to side with King Phillip, the General Court negotiated with the Indians to lay down their arms and cede their land in 1671. The tract was surveyed three years later, Saconnet has many interpretations: "wild goose," "widening of the stream," "where the black goose flies," "haunt of the black goose," "at the outlet," and "third conquered territory."

WOONSOCKET (Providence/43,224) Before settlement, this region was home to the Nipmuc, Wampanoag and Narragansett Indians. In 1810, the first textile mill was established, and by 1842 there were numerous villages with cotton mills that dotted the Blackstone River. Woonsocket was formed from six of these villages in 1888 since it had the largest mills. The town became one of the largest manufacturing centers in the U.S. It was named for Woonsocket Falls, which may come from the Nipmuc Indians, meaning "thunder mist," and described the noise and spray from the waterfalls. Other definitions were "place of steep ascent," and "two brook place."

SOUTH CAROLINA

CATEECHEE (Pickens) Founder of Cateechee was Colonel D.K. Norris, a planter who moved here in 1895 and established a cotton mill on Twelve Mile River. Opening of the mill brought employment for people who came from the Blue Ridge Mountain area. Cateechee means "deer's head," and denotes grace and beauty. It was the name of a Creek maiden who fell in love with a white man named Allen Francis. When the Cherokee War broke out in 1760, she warned Francis of a pending attack on the fort at the town of Ninety Six.

CHERAW (Chesterfield/5,742) Named for the Cheraw Indians, the town was settled about 1752 by the Welsh who migrated from Pennsylvania. The Cheraws were first mentioned by DeSoto in 1540, whom he called Xuala. After the Yamassee War in 1716, the Indians were removed from the Carolinas. Later settlers were James Gillespie and Thomas Ellerbe who started a trading center in 1740. Ten years later, Joseph and Eli Kershaw received a land grant and platted the town. The place was first called Chatham, and officially became Cheraw in 1820, meaning "sparkling waters," or "fire."

CONESTEE (Greenville) Vardry McBee was a founder of the town of Greenville. He needed a place to build a mill and selected the Reedy River for construction of a dam which, in turn, created Lake Conestee About 1835, the mill began manufacturing paper, and later cotton textiles. A town was founded specifically for mill workers and named Conestee, a Cherokee word for "land of beautiful waters." Over the years waste from the mills at Greenville polluted the lake, which is still heavily polluted. The Conestee mills took Greenville to court and the South Carolina Supreme court ruled in favor of Conestee. It wasn't until after 1972 that any upgrades were made.

COOSAWHATCHIE (Jasper) Once home to the Coosaw Indians, the site was settled by Henry DeSaussure in the 1740s when he established an inn and trading post. During the Revolution, Coosawhatchie was besieged by the British, most of the town was burned, and half of the Continental Army was killed. In 1860, the Charleston and Savannah Railroad was completed. Robert E. Lee made the town his headquarters just before the onset of the Civil War. The name has been interpreted as "city of refuge."

EDISTO (Colleton/2,632) The Edistow Indians met their first white man when explorer Robert Sandford stopped at the island in 1666. Paul Grimball and his family settled here after he received a land grant about 1674. One of the biggest industries was the cultivation of indigo. After the Depression two millionaires purchased substantial land that was transformed into a hunting preserve. The community was named for the Edistow Indians, meaning "water sprinkler," for a ceremony the warriors performed by taking water from the river and sprinkling it about, signifying blood showered upon their enemies.

ELLOREE (Orangeburg/742) Founder William Snider moved here in the early 1800s. Transportation was via Hagues

Landing a few miles from town which brought barges and boats shipping supplies and cotton. During the war, residents took up arms with Francis Marion and joined the Confederacy. The town was laid out in 1886 as Harlin City for General John Hardin who promised the town a new railroad. When he failed to do so, the name was changed to Elloree, which may come from the Siouan stock, meaning "the home I love."

HONEA PATH (Anderson/3,504) Arriving from Ireland about 1794, David Greer moved to this site and called it Greerton, and the Columbia and Greenville Railroad made it a terminus in 1852. The origin of Honea is uncertain. It was thought to mean "path," giving the town a double name. The local Indian trail was known to contain numerous bee trees, from which the Cherokee Indians gathered honey. Their word for honey sounded much like path, so Honea Path may have meant "honey path."

OKATIE (Beaufort) Okatie is not classified as a town, but is a populated place. It may have originally been a tidewater crossing at which Charles Purry established a store in the 1740s. This crossing provided direct access from the mainland to the inland passage to Beaufort and Charleston. Okatie (or Okeetee) may be a Choctaw word for "water." Another interpretation was "place of bright waters." (Much of the documentation on this area was destroyed when Sherman's troops burned their way across parts of the county.)

YEMASSEE (Hampden/807) In 1707, the General Assembly gave the Yamassee Indians exclusive use of this land. Because of the white man's dishonesty toward the Indians, the Yamassee War broke out in 1715 and the Indians were driven out. A tavern was built along the Pocotaligo River, which played a major role during the Revolution when Fort Balfour was captured. Plantations later dotted the landscape. Yamasee has a number of interpretations: from the Catawba word, yamusane ("fire") or Muskokee, yumuse (or yamasi), for "kind" or "gentle." Other definitions are "singer" and "bluebird."

SOUTH DAKOTA

AKASKA (Walworth/*52*) Singleton Smith was an early homesteaders in 1888, but it wasn't until the spring of 1907 that the town of Akaska was established. The Sioux name was interpreted as "to eat up," and "woman who lives with several men." It may be a derivation of akastaka, meaning "smear." The Dakota, Minnesota and Pacific Railroad was built in 1907 and continued operating until 1941. The second year of settlement, a fire destroyed many of the business structures.

CANISTOTA (McCook/700) When the Northwestern Railroad bypassed the community of Cameron, a new town was laid out near the tracks and named Canastota. Major Free named it for his home in

Canastota, New York. The name is derived from Iroquois words, knista and stoat for "pine tree standing alone," or "silent cluster of pines." Another theory was "board on the water." In 1883, the Western Town Lot Company platted the town. When the post office was established there was a clerical error with the name was spelled Canistota. Attempts to have it changed came to naught.

KADOKA (Jackson/706) Located about two miles from the Badlands, Kadoka had its beginnings in 1906 after the Milwaukee Railroad extended its line past the site. The post office was established the same year (Lenore McCarthy, postmaster) Kadoka is Sioux for "hole in the wall," or "opening," referring to the entrance into the Badlands just west of the town. Settlers found the region had good loamy soil and sufficient water for their farming needs. In 1914, Kadoka became the county seat.

KENNEBEC (Lyman/286) Established in the early 1900s, Kennebec got its start when the first railroad came through in 1905. Charley Warner was an early settler who established a general store. By 1907, a hardware store and the Prairie Sun newspaper had been established. Kennebec's economy was based on cattle, sheep and hogs which were shipped out to various destinations. An early settler may have moved from the east to Kennebec, since it was the name of a place in Maine, an Algonquin word for "river god," or "long lake."

OACOMA (Lyman/390) Once home to the Sioux Indians and the Lower Brule Indian Agency, the region was open for settlement in 1890. This same year the town was established as Nobleton, and later changed to Gladstone. Building of the railroad opened the way west for settlers and merchants. Oacoma became county seat in 1894, until it was given to Kennebec in 1922. As a result, many businesses moved, causing a decline in Oacoma's population. The post office was established in August, 1890, as Oacoma, a Sioux word for "in between," descriptive of the town's location between the bluffs and the Missouri River.

ONAKA (Faulk/30) This region was home to the buffalo and a favorite hunting ground of the Arikara Indians. Onaka is from the Dakota word, oyanke, meaning "place," or "meeting place," an apt name for the numerous Indian hunting camps. Onaka was born in the early 1900s when the Minneapolis and St. Louis Railroad came through and brought an influx of settlers. Cattle ranching was a big industry until 1902, when a treacherous blizzard arrived, wiping out much of the cattle business. People turned to agriculture for their economy, and resumed cattle ranching in later years.

ONIDA (Sully/740) Onida was platted in 1883 by surveyor H.C. Alexander who named the town after his former home in Oneida, New York, for the Oneida Indians, which means "people of the living stone." The post office opened in the general store on May 2, 1883 (B.F. Brier, postmaster). When Onida was made county seat, it brought settlers from the nearby town of Clinton. It was 1910 before a railroad came through. Farmers dealt primarily in raising wheat. During 1899, a disastrous prairie fire started near Fort Sully, narrowly missing Onida.

PUKWANA (Brule/287) Pukwana was surveyed in 1882, and named by a woman visiting the site who was related to a railroad official with the Milwaukee Railroad. The name was taken from the poem "Hiawatha" and means "smoke of the peace pipe." One of the moving forces in developing the town was a land dealer, John

Stansky. His promotion of the area brought settlers in from the east. The early economy was tied to shipping sheep to the Sioux City markets. Pukwana was famous for being the smallest town in the U.S. to acquire a first-class post office.

SISSETON (Roberts/2,572) Authorities believe that the Sisseton-Wahpeton were originally comprised of the early Santee Dakota Indians. When the Sisseton-Wahpeton Indian Reservation was open for settlement in 1892, the rush was on. The Reservation Land Improvement Company claimed a piece of land for the townsite and the post office was established this same year (W.B. Wampler, postmaster). By the early 1900s, the agency for the reservation and a trading center were established. The name may be a shortened version of Sisi-oton-we, for "fish village," or "dwellers among the fish scales." Since the Indians once lived near the lakes where fish was plentiful, their camps were always full of fish scales.

SIOUX FALLS (Minnehaha/123,975) In 1856, the Dakota Land Company was chartered, which named the site Sioux Falls for the Sioux Indians, defined as "snake-like," or "enemy." The Western Town Company built a sawmill and general store. Indian uprisings forced residents to leave, and it wasn't until 1865 that permanent settlement occurred. The Morrell Packing Plant was established in 1909 and developed into a large meat-packing company. The State Penitentiary was also located here, built in 1881.

WASTA (Pennington/75) During the 1880s, this site was used as grazing range for cattle ranchers, as well as a trading center for them. Located at the foot of bluffs near the Cheyenne River, Wasta is derived from the Sioux word, wasto (or wastah) and means "good." It was named by Donne Robinson, the first State Historian. The town is part of the Rapid City metro area.

WAUBAY (Day/662) An Indian trader named Francis Rondelle settled along Waubay Lake. In 1880, the Chicago, Milwaukee & St. Paul Railroad came through the region, bringing in settlers. This white settlement was one of the few towns where a number of Sioux Indians actually lived. The name may be a corruption of the Sioux words, wahohipi or wahopkoza, meaning "where wild fowl build their nests," or "where wild fowl congregate."

WETONKA (McPherson/12) Wetonka was born in 1906 when a branch of the Minneapolis, St. Louis Railroad established stations along its route. Two sites between Aberdeen and Leola were selected: Richmond and Wetonka. George and Matilda Kernon originally owned the land of the future townsite. Grain elevators and stock yards were soon built along the tracks. Wetonka is a Sioux word derived from witanka, for "great," or "big sun," and was also the name of a Sioux chief.

YANKTON (Yankton/13,528) This site was selected in 1858 because of a steamboat landing on the Missouri River. The town was surveyed a year later and named after the Yankton Indians, a corruption of a Sioux word, thanktonwan, meaning "end village," or "at the end." It may have been derived from ihanktonwan for "people of the end." In 1875, the Frost-Todd Trading Company was established, which dealt in furs in addition to regular trade items. Yankton was an important transportation center with river traffic until the Great Northern Railroad was built, which supplanted the steamboats. Yankton was the campground of the 7th U.S. Cavalry in 1873, just before the Battle of the Little Big Horn.

TENNESSEE

CHATTANOOGA (Hamilton/155,554) The first record of white men through this region was in 1540 with Hernando De Soto's Spanish Expedition. The site was established on a former Cherokee outpost as Ross's Landing in 1816. Rail service precipitated the development of timber resources in the region. During the Civil War, the Battle of Chickamauga near Chattanooga occurred, which sealed the fate of the Confederacy. In 1838, the name was changed to Chattanooga, a Cherokee word, tsatanugi, translated as "rock that comes (or rises) to a point," describing Lookout Rock that stands like a sentinel over the city.

OOLTEWAH (Hamilton/5,681) When DeSoto and his men came through the region, their field notes recorded the site as Ooltewah Gap. Located in the base of White Oak Mountain, Ooltewah was claimed by Major Finley P. Watkins and William Stone about 1856. The townsite was laid out when the Hiwassee Railroad completed it line to the site. The depot that was built in 1882 was closed permanently in 1976. Ooltewah was considered a citadel of temperance because it had no saloons. It is a Cherokee word meaning "resting place," or "owls nest."

SEWANEE (Franklin/2,361) Sewanee is home to the University of the South, founded in 1857. Coal interests brought in the Tennessee Coal, Iron and Railroad. Early homesteaders sold their land to the Sewanee Mining Company, but with little coal to be found, the company later donated part of the land for a university. Jabez Hays was a moving force in the community, building the first free school, a sawmill and fruit orchard. Sewanee is a Shawnee word meaning "southern" or "south," and designated the direction the Indians took during their migrations to middle Tennessee and the Cumberland Plateau regions.

TULLAHOMA (Coffee/17,994) The springs in the area provided a generous water supply and attracted the Cherokee Indians. In the early 1800s, white settlers of Scot and Irish stock migrated here from East Tennessee. The site was not very suitable for agriculture, and so Tullahoma was sparsely populated until about 1852 when the Nashville, Chattanooga & St. Louis Railway made the site a railroad labor camp. The town developed as a railroad and manufacturing center. Tullahoma is interpreted as "a land of golden flowers," and "land of red clay." It may be a Muskogean word for "red town."

TEXAS

ANAHUAC (Chambers/2,210) The Attakapas Indians were here when French explorer Jean Baptiste de La Harpe visited in 1721. Established before 1745 by the Karankawa Indians, the earliest record of a postmaster at Anahuac was in 1816. It was called Perry's Point, then changed to Anahuac in 1831, derived from an Aztec word, anahuacalli, which may signify "land by the water." Today, Anahuac's economy is tied to oil and cattle. In 1989, the Texas Legislature named Anahuac the "Alligator Capital of Texas" because it had more alligators than people.

CAYUGA (Anderson/*55*) Early settlers were Reverend West Jackson and a man named Cox who arrived about 1846. Originally located at a place called Wild Cat Bluff until the Trinity River became unnavigatable, another settlement began to grow nearby. The town was named Judson, and changed to Cayuga in 1898 when the post office was established. Taken from the Cayuga Indians in New York, the name was defined as "long lake," "mucky land," or "canoes pulled out of the water."

CHENANGO (Brazoria) This place began as a cotton-producer known as the Chenango Plantation. It was later purchased by Benjamin Smith who converted it to a sugarcane plantation in 1836. For a few years, the site was named Parker's Point. In 1890, International-Great Northern Railroad came through and made Chenango one of its stations. It was named for a town in New York, an Iroquois word meaning "bull thistles." Chenango did not grow much, and by 1947 there was only one business in town. Later records showed only a small church left.

CHICOTA (Lamar/*130*) First known as Center Springs, the site was a trading center for the French and Indians as early as 1805. Located just south of Red River, it was also a popular stopping place for travelers because of the abundant water. A few immigrants stayed, and were followed by others after the Civil War. Some homesteaded on the lower bottom lands, but came down with what they called swamp fever, (malaria), causing the people to move their homes to higher ground. The post office was established in 1879, and the name was changed to Chicota, for Samuel Checote, a full-blood Creek chief, but his name origin is unknown.

KEECHI (Leon/*67*) Keechi was named for the Kichai Indians, a subtribe of the Wichitas or Caddoes who had their camps in the region in the early 1700s. The Missouri Pacific Railroad laid its tracks through town in 1884. It wasn't until 1890 that substantial businesses had been established. The post office opened in 1872 (Francis Eldridge, postmaster). Today, Keechi is a bedroom community. The name means "peaceful."

KEMAH (Galveston/2,330) Kemah is situated on Galveston Bay. In 1824, Michael Gouldrich received a Mexican land grant and his daughter, Elizabeth Kipp, acquired the balance of the grant in the early 1890s. After Texas and New Orleans Railroad extended its line, the Kipp family established the town in 1904, naming it Evergreen. When the post office opened in 1907, its name was changed to Kemah, meaning "facing the wind," a descriptive name since the town faces the bay. In 1915, a devastating hurricane hit Kemah, creating a 15-foot tidal surge; it took five years to rebuild the town.

KIOMATIA (Red River/*61*) Located on the shore of the Red River near an old buffalo crossing, Kiomatia was named after the river, which is a Muscogee word for "clear water." Its post office was established in 1850 (Travis Write, postmaster), but discontinued in 1859. It was reopened and went through a number of name changes: from Kiomatia to Flintham's Tanyard, Milton, back to Kiomatia, then Hooks Ferry, and reverted to Kiomatia. The post office finally closed its door in the 1950s. The Kiomatia Mounds are located on the south side of the Red River, and are a group of Caddoan ceremonial mounds. In recent years, artifacts have been found, but their history and significance will not be known until more excavations are conducted.

MOBEETIE (Wheeler/107) This town developed from a buffalo hunter's camp called Hide Town, and then established as a trading post in 1875. Bat Masterson surveyed the site. The name was changed to Sweetwater, but postal officials turned it down because of duplication. So it was renamed Mobeetie, an Indian word for "sweet water." The town was a trade center for the panhandle until a tornado hit in 1898 and destroyed many of the buildings. That, plus the fact that Mobeetie was unable to secure a railroad, caused the town to move to its present site where the Santa Fe Railroad extended its line.

NACOGDOCHES (Nacogdoches/29,914) The region was home to the Nacogdoches Indians, part of the Caddoan Tribe. Tradition says a Caddo Chief sent his twin sons to found villages (Nacogdoches and Natchitoches in Louisiana). Claiming to be the oldest town in Texas, Nacogdoches' permanent settlement began when Antonio Gil Ybarbo and about 300 Adaesanos (people from Los Adaes) moved here. Many borderline disputes occurred because of the town's location on the eastern border of Texas Territory. Nacogdoches had the first newspaper in the state, and the first ceiling fans that were powered by a mule-drawn treadmill. Nacogdoches was interpreted as "persimmons."

NOCONA (Montague/3,198) Comanche Chief Pete Nocona (origin unknown) was head of the Kwahadi band of Indians, from whom the town takes its name. Nocona was also the husband of Cynthia Ann Parker and the father of Quanah Parker. In the 1870s, William Broaddus and D.C. Jordan started a ranch with more than 15,000 head of cattle. Jordan donated some of his land for a townsite when he found out the Gainesville, Henrietta and Western Railway was bringing its line through. Nocona grew up around the Red River and became a shipping center for drovers on the Chisholm Trail.

PALO PINTO (Palo Pinto) Situated in the Brazos River Valley, Palo Pinto means "painted post," for the varicolored petrified wood found in the region. The fertile soil attracted the pioneers and by 1858 the town had a solid foundation. The post office was established in 1858 as Golconda, but changed to Palo Pinto shortly thereafter. The town was a stop on the stage line that had its route between Fort Worth and Fort Griffin. After the Civil War, Palo Pinto became a ranching trade center, and then in 1915 a high-producing oil well was struck near town.

PONTOTOC (Mason/*206*) Named for a town in Mississippi, Benjamin Willis was the earliest settler, arriving in 1859. M.R. Kidd named the town Pontotoc, which could be derived from the Muskogean word, ponti-tokali, meaning "upper end of the cattail," or paki-takali, for "hanging grapes," or "grapes on the vine." The post office was established in 1880 (B. Willis, postmaster). A typhoid epidemic nearly wiped the town out in 1887. When the hoped-for railroad failed to materialize, Pontotoc went into decline, and people moved away.

QUANAH (Hardeman/3,022) Comanche Chief Nocona and captive Cynthia Ann Parker had a son named Quanah who was born in 1845. His name means "fragrant." When it was learned the Fort Worth and Denver City Railway was building west into the county, townsite officials had a general store and saloon built on the site. Quanah experienced an upswing in its economy as a cattle shipping point because the railroad made the town its western terminus for about two years before pushing on. One of the first purebred cattle auctions in the state was conducted at Quanah in 1898.

QUITAQUE (Briscoe/432) A trading post was built in 1865, operated by Jose Tafoya. In addition to stock trading, he also supplied the Comanche Indians with ammunition. The Lazy F Ranch was established in 1878 by George and Jim Baker, and sold to Charles Goodnight in 1880. It is believed that Goodnight named the town Quitaque, interpreted as "end of the trail." Settlers translated Quitaque as "whatever one steals," but it is not known if it was actually the Indian word, or the whites' name for the Quitaca Indians. Another theory is that the name means "horse manure," because two buttes in the region resembled piles of manure.

TAHOKA (Lynn/2,910) This site was used by military expeditions as a campground while pursuing the Comanche and Kiowa Indians. Later, it was a stopping place for cattle drives and freighters. The town was established in 1903 by the Tahoka Townsite Company, and its growth was ensured by cattle ranching and cotton farming. The post office opened on April 30, 1903. Tahoka took its name from Tahoka Lake, which may be a Comanche word for "clear (or fresh) water," because of the lake's clarity. Seedsmen found pastures that were abundant with a type of daisy and were given permission to harvest the seeds. Resembling a lavender daisy, the flower was sold commercially as the Tahoka Daisy.

TEHUACANA (Limestone/307) Explorer Philip Nolan was here as early as 1797 while he was on a mapping expedition and came across the Tehuacana (or Tawakoni) Indians, who were part of the Wichita tribe. Major John Boyd was given a land grant by Mexico about 1835 which included this site. In 1847, a post office was established as Tewockony Springs until the Civil War when the post office closed. When it reopened in 1869, the name was changed to Tehuacana, meaning "the three canes." Most of the businesses closed their doors during the 1980s, and today there is only a post office and small store.

TENAHA (Shelby/1,046) The year 1886 was the establishment of Tenaha. A family of lumberman named Hicks originally owned the townsite and gave the railroad land so it would built a depot. They also named the town, Comanche for "muddy water." This same year the post office was established (James Woodfin, postmaster). Tenaha became an important shipping center for the farmers when the Houston, East and West Texas Railway came through. This was a big tomato raising area, with a large canning factory and tomato sheds that lined the railroad tracks.

WAKA (Ochiltree/55) Waka was an Indian camp as shown by Alibates flint found in a local farmer's field. In 1902, a post office was opened as Wawaka. When the Santa Fe Railroad built its line in 1919, the post office moved to be closer to the tracks. The railroad refused to accept Wawaka because it was too long, but it wasn't until 1927 that the name was shortened to Waka, which means "marshy" or "swampy." It was a booming town in the 1920s and early 1930s, with its grain elevators and cattle that were shipped by rail. Today, the people rely on agriculture.

WACO (McLennan/113,726) Named for the Waco Indians who were a Caddoan-speaking branch of the Wichitas, the town was first visited in 1541 by the Luis Moscoso de Alvarado Expedition. Written on their maps was the name Guasco, which would become Waco Village. General Thomas Chambers owned the land that surrounded Waco Village and sold it to a group of businessmen in 1848. The following year the town was laid out as Lamartine, and later changed to Waco. A ferry business on the Brazos River caused Waco to became a trade and distribution center, in addition to a cotton-producing community. Waco was interpreted as "river bend in a sandy place."

WATAUGA (Tarrant/21,908) The first settlers arrived about 1843. When the railroad came through in 1876, it brought great prosperity to Watauga until 1930, when the Texas and Pacific Railway moved its depot to another town. Watauga then became a way station for moving cattle into Fort Worth and points east. The name may come from the Cherokee for "village (or land) of many springs." Watauga didn't grow much because it had no tax base or major source of revenue. Up until 1959, it didn't even have sewer lines or natural gas service. Watauga was almost annexed to the community of Haltom City, but managed to incorporate itself despite opposition. Residents didn't think the town was going anywhere, but now boasts a population of more than 20,000.

WAXAHACHIE (Ellis/21,426) The first white settler was Emory Rogers in 1846 who donated some of his land for the townsite, which was founded in 1851. Located about 25 miles south of Dallas, the town received its name from the creek, a Tonkawa word that means "cow creek." Waxahachie was a watering point for the big cattle drives that went via the Shawnee Trail from Texas to Kansas. It also gained significance as a commerce and trading center when a military road was built, and then a stagecoach route was established.

UTAH

GOSHUTE (Tooele) Goshute today is an Indian community on the Goshute Indian Reservation. A treaty was signed in 1863 which stipulated that the Indians not cede their land, but allowed routes through their land for the whites. It also permitted stagecoaches and railroad to come through, in addition to some ranches being established. But by the early 1900s, most of the Goshutes had been moved to reservations. Part of the Shoshonean-speaking Native Americans, Goshute is a Ute word that means "dust (or desert) people."

HALCHITA (San Juan/270) Situated near the San Juan River, Halchita was originally part of the town of Mexican Hat. There were two Mexican Hats: one on the Navajo Reservation and one off. This community was once a uranium mining town run by the Vandium Corporation. When mining came to an end in the 1960s, the Utah Navajo Development Council took over ownership and sold the homes to the Navajo Indians. Some of the people got ill and died from the effects of radiation. In 1975, the Navajo chapter separated part of the land from Mexican Hat that was non-reservation and formed the community of Halchita, which means "red sand."

HIAWATHA (Carbon/*43*) Hiawatha was a coal community, located at the foot of Gentry Mountain. An Austrian named Smith was the first settler when he started a ranch on the future townsite. When F.E. Sweet opened a mine in 1908, he called his camp Hiawatha, an Iroquois word that means "prophet" or "teacher." Another mine began operating at Camp Black Hawk. In 1912, the U.S. Fuel Company bought and consolidated the two mines, with its headquarters at Black Hawk. The company also built the first railroad to Hiawatha, with the engine maintenance shops at East Hiawatha. The last mine closed in 1991.

IBAPAH (Tooele/*400*) A Mormon missionary moved to Ibapah in 1859 and established a farm in order to teach agriculture to the Indians. First called Deep Creek Station, it began as a Pony Express station about 1860. Trading stores established were used mainly by miners prospecting in the nearby mountains. The post office opened in 1883. The Lincoln Highway was built near town, but when the Wendover cutoff was built, people no longer used the highway on their way further west, and Ibapah became a small bedroom community. Edward Ferguson selected the name, derived from a Goshute word, ai-bim-pa, meaning "white clay water," because the water contained fine, white, clay particles.

KAMAS (Summit/1,274) In 1859, Brigham Young gave Thomas Rhodes permission to move to the site he named Rhodes Valley. It was later changed to Kamas, which may be a Ute word designating a type of tuber the Indians used as a staple diet. Because of the excellent soil, agricultural products were grown and many of the farmers went into the dairy industry, which is still ongoing. Today, Kamas is headquarters for the Wasatch National Forest.

KANAB (Kane/3,564) Mormons made their home at Kanab about 1870 under the direction of Brigham Young who wanted to expand his domain. They built Fort

Kanab for protection, which also became a trading post and a base of operations for the Geological Survey. Kanab is Paiute word that means "place of the willows," or describes an edible tuber. The townsite was laid out in characteristic Mormon fashion, with all the streets leading to the center of the town square. Zane Grey lived here while he wrote his book *Riders of the Purple Sage.*

KANOSH (Millard/485) C-Nos was a Paiute Chief who lived near the Pahvant Mountains, but the white men called him Kanosh, derived from kan and oush, meaning "willow bowl." C-Nos was a peaceful man, preferring to negotiate with the white men rather than fight. In 1854, he represented the Pahvant Utes when he signed a treaty that ended the Walker War. First called Corn Creek, Mortimer Warner suggested the name Kanosh. The Kanosh Indian Reservation is located near town. In 1954, the tribal status was terminated because sponsors believed it would speed integration of the Indians into non-Indian society. But it did not occur, and their status was restored in 1980.

KOOSHAREM (Sevier/276) The region was once home to a small band of Paiute Indians who made their living farming and hunting. By 1880, most of them had left. People on their way to settle at a place called Payson ended up here about 1851. There were no problems with the Indians because one of the residents befriended Ute Chief Guffich. This lasted until the Walker War broke out in 1853, necessitating in the building of a fort. The community became known as Summit Creek and later renamed Koosharem, which means "red clover," or a type of edible root.

LEOTA (Uintah) A former town, Leota ("maiden") was settled in 1912 by William Ellsworth and his family. Settlers had to build canals for needed irrigation, which were completed about 1916. Vern Collett and William Smart are credited with selecting the name for the town. When a severe drought occurred, many of the residents left for other, more prosperous towns. Agriculture proved futile because the land was too alkaline, and by 1947 Leota ceased to exist.

OLJETO (San Juan/864) Oljeto became a chapter community on the Navajo Reservation by executive order of President Arthur in 1884. Despite this order, white men continued trespassing to search for silver. In 1906, John and Louisa Wetherill were the only white people here and opened a trading post, providing services for the Navajo people. The Wetherills left in 1910 to open another post at Kayenta, Arizona. In 1921, another trading post was opened by Joseph Heffernan, and later taken over by Harry Goulding (still in operation). Oljeto is a Navajo word for "moon water," or "moonlight."

PANGUITCH (Garfield/1,623) In 1864, Jens Nielsen brought 54 Mormons into the valley from their home in Parowan and built a fort. The first year they experienced a severe winter and ended up eating frozen wheat and beef fat. When the food ran out, some of the settlers started out for the town of Parowan. The snow was so deep they could not make their way until someone put one quilt down in front of another, creating a walkable path to Parowan. This became known as the "Panguitch Quilt Walk." Panguitch comes from a Paiute word that means "big fish," descriptive of the fish in Panguitch Lake.

PARAGONAH (Iron/470) While on an expedition heading to Manti in 1849, a group of Mormons reported this site would be suitable for settlement. Two years later Job and Charles Hall laid out the town. First named Red Creek, it was changed to Paragonah, from the Paiute word, paragoonah, meaning "many water holes (or springs)," or "marsh land." Because of later problems with the Indians, Brigham Young ordered his people to go to the town of Parowan. They stayed there until 1855 when Young told them it was safe to return.

PAROWAN (Iron/*2,565*) The Fremont and Anasazi Indians were the region's first inhabitants. Parowan was established in 1851 by Apostle George Smith for the purpose of manufacturing iron implements. It was the first settlement in Southern Utah, considered the Mother Town of the Southwest, because it was from here that Mormon pioneers left to start other settlements. The name means "evil waters," and refers to a Paiute legend that says while the Indians were camped along the Little Salt Lake, a monster arose from the lake, grabbed an Indian maiden and took her beneath the lake. She was never seen again. The name was also interpreted as "bad water," and "marsh people."

SANTAQUIN (Utah/4,834) Located between the Utah and Juab valleys, the town was established in 1851 as Summit City. Settlers came to the region to found the town of Payson, and while doing so also began the community of Santaquin (origin unknown), named for the son of Ute Chief Guffich. They were forced to leave during outbreak of the Walker War and did not return until 1855. Earlier, the settlers had befriended Chief Guffich, and when the Walker War started, Guffich alerted the settlers. When the Indians found the place deserted, Guffich told them the Great Spirit had told the Mormons about the raid, and the settlers were never bothered again.

TABIONA (Duchesne/149) A fort was built on this site about 1860, and the town was established in 1902 on land owned by Ute Indians. Tabiona became predominantly an agricultural community. It was named for Ute Chief Tabby-to-kwanah, interpreted as "child of the sun." He was instrumental as a peacekeeper between the settlers and Indians, even through the Black Hawk War of 1865–1868. Tabby died at the age of 104 in 1903, and was buried at the White Rocks Indian Agency.

TOOELE (Tooele/22,502) Tooele Valley was originally home to the Goshute Indians. Settlement began in 1849 with the arrival of three Mormon families. In 1852, a mail route was established, with John Roland as postmaster, and the following year the town was surveyed. Tooele was mainly a farming and ranching community, but by the 1900s it turned to industry with the opening of the Tooele Smelter and Combined Metals Flotation Mill. Tooele may have been the name of Chief Tuilla, or taken from tule, which is an abundant weed in the region. It was also defined as a Goshute word for "bear."

UINTAH (Weber/794) Shoshone Indians used this site as a camping spot while they hunted. The first settlers came to what was East Weber in 1850. When the town became too populated to support them, people moved on. Residents who remained changed the name to Easton. When a train depot was built, it was renamed Deseret, then Unitah, derived from the Ute word, uintaugump, for "at the edge of the pine." After the Utah Central Railroad built its line to Salt Lake City, Unitah became a quiet farming community.

WANSHIP (Summit). This community was settled in 1859 by a family who moved here from Provo. It is located at the junction of Silver Creek and the Weber River.

Wanship became an important stage station on the Overland route. Frequent Indian visitors were friendly to the whites at the station. Originally the county seat, about 1870 it was moved to the town of Coalville. Wanship was named for a Ute chief, which means "good man."

VERMONT

ASCUTNEY (Windsor) A village in the town of Weathersfield, Ascutney began as The Corners in the early 1800s. The center of social life for the community was a hotel built by a man named Colston. In 1763, Benjamin Allen had a road built from The Corners into the Marsh district. The post office was established in 1830 as Corners, and changed to Ascutneyville in 1851 (the "ville" was dropped in 1925). It is an old Abnaki name for the mountain, interpreted as "at the end of the river fork." Others ascribe the name from cascadnack, which means "bald or peaked with steep sides."

PASSUMPSIC (Caledonia) Taking its name from the river, Passumpsic is Abnaki for "flowing over clear, sandy bottom," or "much clear water." The town was originally land that was granted to Joseph Stevens. It was called Kendall's Mills after William Kendall purchased the property. When the post office opened in 1825, it was spelled Passumsic, but not corrected until 1850. When the Passumpsic Turnpike was built, it further lent to the town's economy which brought teamsters who frequented the taverns in town.

QUECHEE (Windsor) One of five villages in the town of Hartford, Quechee was settled in 1768. The name is derived from the Ottauquechee River, an Abnaki word defined as "swift mountain stream," or "swiftly running water." Quechee became a town of woolen mills, the first built in 1883 by J.C. Parker. After the Francis K. Nichols & Co. was established, it introduced "shoddy" fabric (reworked rags and new wool) which revolutionalized the industry. Quechee was also home to breeders of Hambletonian horses.

WINOOSKI (Chittenden/6,561) Winooski was founded in 1787 by Ira Allen and Remember Baker, who saw great potential in the water power at the falls of the Winooski River. Famous for its woolen mills, the largest (Champlain) was built in 1912. Development of these mills was directly responsible for the town's growth. Rapid expansion of the industry after the Civil War brought French Canadians from Quebec to work. Winooski is an Abnaki word derived from winoskietew, which means "onion land river," or "the wild onion river."

VIRGINIA

APPOMATTOX (Appomattox/1,761) This site was named for the Appomattox Indians. They may have been from the Powatan confederacy, but were extinct by the 1700s. This is the place where General Lee surrendered to General Grant and ended the Civil War. The final blow came when General George Custer confiscated Lee's train loaded with critical food and supplies on April 8, 1865. Appomattox means "tobacco plant country."

AQUIA (Stafford/7,856) In 1640, the Woodstock Plantation was built by Giles Brent, who lived here with his Indian wife and established massive tobacco fields. The community later became a trading village and shipping point because of its deep-water harbor. Aquia was established as a Catholic community after the Indian wars of 1767 and became the first English-speaking colony in the state. During the Civil War, the Union army had its quartermaster based here, used for transfer of war supplies. Aquia is Algonquin for "bush nut," or "seagull."

ACCOMACK (Accomack/470) Governor Dale sent an expedition to the eastern shore in 1614 for the purpose of establishing a salt works, which turned out to be an unsatisfactory venture. The site was called Kingdome of Accawmacke in 1620. The name was taken from the peaceful Accawmacke Indians, interpreted as "across the water place," or "otherside place." The post office was established in 1792 as Accomack Court House, and later changed to Accomack.

CHINCOTEAGUE ISLAND (Accomack/4,317) The island was granted to Captain William Whitington in 1662 by king of the Gingoteague tribe. Chincoteague is derived from gingoteague, which means "beautiful island across the water." The island's early economy was primarily farming and livestock. The post office was established in 1856, (John Corbin, postmaster). The famous pony penning began about 1835 and today the tradition continues. The ponies are owned by the Chincoteague Volunteer Fire Department, rounded up from Assateague each year, and brought to Chincoteague to preserve the balance of nature.

MOBJACK (Matthews) Hezekiah Philpotts (also known as Captain Thornton) purchased the site in 1871. By 1910, Mobjack was a bustling community and its economy was based on agricultural products shipped by steamboat, in addition to oystering and crabbing. During the 1950s, the packing houses closed down after the oysters succumbed to diseases. Known as Mobjack in the Virginia General Assembly since 1652, the name may be a corruption of an Algonquin word for "bad land."

OCCOQUAN (Prince William/759) The Dogue Indians were resident here because of the abundance of fish at the headwaters of Occoquan River. Occoquan is an Algonquin word that means "end of the waters." John Ballendine founded the settlement in 1750. Industry came with the building of a grist mill (the first automated one in the U.S.), sawmills, and forges (that may have produced cannon balls for the American Revolution). Occoquan began to decline when it suffered a fire in 1916, destroying most of the town. Then Route 1 and the railroad bypassed the town, and the river silted up. When Hurricane Agnes hit in 1972, its floodwaters damaged much of Occoquan.

ONANCOCK (Accomack/1,525) This site was once an Indian village ruled by Ekeeks, King of the Onancocks in 1621. Daniel Jenifer was paid 540 pounds of tobacco for the land in 1680 and the site was called Port Scarburgh. It was later changed to Onancock, meaning "foggy place." Quakers were some of the early settlers, followed by the founder of Presbyterism in America in 1699. During the Revolution, Onancock was headquarters for General John Cropper.

POQUOSON (York/11,566) This name may have been taken from an Algonquin word descriptive of boundaries between elevated tracts of land, or may have designated something swampy or shallow. It was also interpreted as "flat land." Poquoson was formed when the first land patents were issued about 1631. Most of the colonists engaged in agriculture raising tobacco. The majority of permanent settlers arrived during the War of 1812 and supported themselves by establishing the seafood industry. With its proximity to the Poquoson River, the town enjoyed a brisk economy as a shipping port for produce and seafood.

PUNGOTEAGUE (Accomack) Located at the head of Pungoteague Creek, this site was patented by Nichola Waddilow about 1655. The same year the town hosted the first theatrical performance held in the United States. "Ye Bare and Ye Cubb" prompted the court to ask for a script of the play because of immorality charges, and were found innocent. The post office was established in 1816. The name was interpreted as "sand fly river," or "place of fine sand," an Algonquin expression descriptive of the soil in the region.

QUANTICO (Prince William/561) This site began as a government reservation along the Potomac River. Its purpose was to service the ships of the Potomac Navy during the Revolution. The land was sold to the Marine Corps in 1917 for a training camp. During World War II, Quantico was the place that amphibious warfare was conceived, and the first helicopter troop was created in 1947. The name has been interpreted as an Algonquin word for as "by the large stream," descriptive of the Potomac River.

ROANOKE (Roanoke/94,911) The Indians favored this region because of abundant game and salt licks. Roanoke got its start about 1852 as Big Lick, and was laid out two years later. The town became a junction point and repair shop for the Shenandoah Valley and Norfolk and Western Railroads. The name was changed to Roanoke in 1882, derived from the Algonquin words, rawrenock or rawranoke, meaning "shell money." Roanoke was once home to the American Viscose Corporation, one of the largest artificial silk factories in the world.

SHENANDOAH (Page/1,878) This town was once known as Forrers' Iron Works, named for the foundry built because of the extensive iron ore resources. The site was purchased by a group of men from Pennsylvania in 1865. When the post office was established in 1838, the name was changed to Shenandoah Iron Works, and later shortened. Shenandoah is an Algonquin word that means "spruce stream." Another theory was "daughter of the stars." During the Civil War, the Confederacy maintained a gun powder plant here. When the Shenandoah Valley Railroad was built in 1881, it made the town one of its train repair shops.

TAPPAHANNOCK (Essex/2,086) The land of the Rappahannocks was visited by Captain John Smith in 1608 while exploring the Chickahominy River. When tobacco became popular and prices soared, tobacco plantations were built along the James River and flourished until the 1630s, when the product's prices declined. The town was established about 1680. John Stone and a group of men acquired land at what was called "Hobses Hole" It was named New Plymouth until the early 1700s, then changed to Tappahannock, which means "on the rising water" in the Algonquin language.

WACHAPREAGUE (Accomack/236) Located on the Eastern Shore, this fishing village was inhabited by Chief Wachiwampe and his tribe. When he died, his will stated that his reservation have no leader, his daughter was to succeed him and take title to either a place called Ockahannock or Wachapreague. Edward Revell and Jonah Jackson later obtained the property. Known as Teackle's Landing, the name was changed to Locust Mount in the 1800s, then Powellton, and finally Wachapreague, Algonquin for "little town by the sea." In the late 1800s, Wachapreague was turned into a resort area.

WEYANOKE (Charles City) Originally home to the Weyanoke Indians who were ruled by Chief Powhaten, this site was used in the early 1600s for growing tobacco by the Smith's Hundred Company. The same year, Henry Wriothesley received a land grant from Chief Powhaten. After his death, his successor, Chief Opechancanough attacked the settlers. Continued uprising resulted in a garrison being built. The site went through succeeding titles passed down through the generations, and today is owned by the descendants of Louise Moon. Weyanoke was interpreted as "land of the sassafrass."

WASHINGTON

AHTANUM (Yakima/4,181) This community is located on the edge of the Yakima Indian Reservation. The name means "creek by the long mountain," an apt name since the site was near the Ahtanum Ridge. It was also interpreted as "people of the water by the long hill," derived from ahtanumlema. The town was once supported by farming and the dairy industry, and the Old Woodcock Academy was established in 1892.

ANATONE (Asotin) Originally a trading post, Anatone became part of the gold trail to the Salmon River area of Idaho in the 1860s. The post supplied the gold fields of the Imnaha and Snake River mining districts. The post office opened in 1878 (Charles Isecke, postmaster). Anatone was platted in 1902, but it never developed much and remained a bedroom community. It was thought the name came from a town in Greece, there is no record of an Anatone there. It was actually named for a

Nez Perce woman named Anatone (origin unknown).

ASOTIN (Asotin/1,095) Asotin was once a Nez Perce Indian camp because the high bluffs afforded them shelter during the winters. They called the creek Has-shu-tin, which means "eel," for the species of fish prevalent in the region. A.F. Beall surveyed the town. The fertile land was used by farmers for raising wheat, which was shipped out of Asotin by steamboats on the Snake River. Asotin became a river-freighting town and, along with wheat, farmers established orchards and vineyards.

CAMAS (Clark/12,534) The site was known as LaCamas when the LaCamas Colony Company established the town in 1883, followed the next year by a post office. A lake in the region was used by the Oregonian newspaper which supplied the company with the needed water for its paper-making machines. In the 1920s, Crown-Zellerbach Corporation was formed, and during World War II it manufactured ship rudders for Liberty ships. The name was changed to Camas, which is a bulb not unlike an onion. It may have been derived from the Nootka word chamass, which means "sweet fruit."

CATHLAMET (Wahkiakum/565) The Cathlamet Indians were a branch of the Chinook Tribe who originally lived on the Columbia River in Oregon. The town was named for them, and means "stone," descriptive of the rocky course of the Columbia River. About 1846, James Birnie opened a trading post and called the site Birnie's Retreat. Timber was an important industry, since the area was heavily forested with hemlock and yellow fir trees. Misappropriated money and destroyed paperwork caused a survey to be redone in 1923. As a result, Cathlamet was one of the last towns in Washington to get a road built.

CHEHALIS (Lewis/7,057) Said by a prominent judge to be "fit only for a frog pond," this community was known as Saunder's Bottom, an apt name, since the place was swampy. The Chehalis, Chinook, and Cowlitz Indians lived here before they were removed to the Chehalis Reservation at Oakville. When the post office was established on May 8, 1858, it was renamed Saundersville, and later changed to Chehalis, meaning "shifting sands," referring to the sandy banks of the Chehalis River.

CHELAN (Chelan/3,522) Alexander Ross and David Thompson were the first explorers to pass this way about 1811 looking for a place to establish a trading post. They met friendly Indians who called the river Tsill-ane, from which Chelan is derived, interpreted from a Chinook word meaning "land of bubbling water." A military post was built in 1879 at Chelan to protect the settlers from Indians, but it didn't last long because of the expense and the steep terrain. Chelan's most prosperous business was apples, and today continues to produce some of the best apples in the world.

CHEWELAH (Stevens/2,186) The Chewelah Indians were an offshoot of the Pend Oreilles, a tribe that was part of the plateau Indians in Montana. Father Desmet established a mission in 1845, naming it Saint Francis Regis. Tom Brown and his family were permanent settlers in the 1850s, and their place became a rendezvous point for travelers. The post office was established in 1878 as Chewelah, derived from s che weeleh, for as "water" or "garter snake." The motion of the water in a spring gave the illusion of snakes moving in the water.

CHIMACUM (Jefferson) This town was named for the Chimacum Indians (origin unknown) who may have been a remnant of the Quileute band of Indians. Supposedly an aggressive and warlike tribe, they may have died out because they were killed by their enemies, or from a smallpox epidemic. Others think they were annihilated by the Snohomish and Barkley Sound Indians in 1857. Reuben Robinson and his wife settled at Chimacum in 1855. The Chimacum Trading Company was established and also served as the post office, which opened June 17, 1878 (Joseph Cargon, postmaster).

CLALLAM BAY (Clallam) This site is along the Strait of Juan De Fuca, and was once home to the Klallam Indians. The name was derived from the Klallam's word for themselves, Nu'sklaim, which means "strong people." The site was platted as East Clallam in 1890 by Dave Kellogg, and the post office opened two years later. The name was changed to Clallam Bay in 1907. A weather station was established that had contact by telegraph with Tatoosh Island. This early forecast system allowed the ship captains to go to the station and get a weather report before sailing out to sea.

CLAQUATO (Lewis) Claquato was one of the earliest settlements in the region. In the Salish language, it is translated to "high land." Claquato was founded by Lewis Hawkins Davis, who took a donation claim on Claquato Hill in 1852. He donated part of his land for a right of way that would bring in a road. He was also postmaster in 1858 and named the town Davis Prairie. It was changed to Claquato on September 15, 1858. Northern Pacific Railroad built its line between Kalama and Tacoma in the 1870s and bypassed Claquato. As a result, the community lost its county-seat status which went to Chehalis; most of the residents relocated there. The only thing left is the oldest standing church in the state of Washington, and perhaps a few homes.

CLE ELUM (Kittitas/1,755) Walter Reed and his wife platted the town on July 26, 1886. When a coal outcrop was discovered in 1883 near Roslyn Canyon, Northern Pacific Railroad surveyors came to the territory and extended its line. The name Cle Elum was chosen, defined as "swift water." Coal mining began in earnest with the beginning of the Roslyn beds in the 1880s. Timber was also a big industry for the county. The post office opened on January 13, 1887.

CONCONULLY (Okanogan/185) Located on a branch of the Salmon River, this town was established as Salmon City, then renamed Conconully, meaning "cloudy," or "evil spirit." The Indians believed a monster lived in the small lake nearby. Another interpretation comes from conconulp, from a tribe who called themselves Konekonl'p, meaning "money hole," a place where the beaver were in great numbers and used as money by the Indians. The year 1886 brought prospectors to the Salmon River when word got out about gold and silver in the region. Timber later supplanted gold mining.

DEWATTO (Mason) Although this Hood Canal hamlet is considered a ghost town, there are still a few people living here. The 1860s brought in the timbermen to glean the wealth of trees in the region. About ten years later, settlement began with the arrival of Jack Wilson and Alexander Dillman. The post office began operating in 1889. Dewatto was derived from du-a-to, for "home of evil spirits who make men crazy." This stemmed from a legend that wicked Indian spirits came up from the ground and tried to enter the men's bodies.

ENTIAT (Chelan/957) Entiat was about a year old when the first steamboat came up the Columbia River in 1888. The name is derived from entiatqua, signifying "rushing water," appropriate for one of the major rapids of the Columbia River. An early settler was James C. Bonar in 1887, who was instrumental in building a road. Entiat moved a number of times. In 1896 it was located about one-half mile west of the Entiat River. When the railroad were built, the town relocated to the tracks in 1914. It had to move again when the Rocky Reach Dam was filled in 1960. It is now located along Highway 97A.

ENUMCLAW (King/11,116) Named for the mountain, Enumclaw was established in 1885. Definitions of the name vary: "place of the evil spirits," "thundering mountain," or "loud, rattling noise." A band of Duwamish Indians were camped at the base of the mountain when a terrific thunder storm came through. The Indians thought the sound came from spirits inside the mountain, and were so frightened they called it Enumclaw. About 1883, a hotel was built in anticipation of growth, and completion of the Northern Pacific Railroad linked Enumclaw to Seattle and Tacoma.

HOQUIAM (Grays Harbor/9,097) Situated at the mouth of the Hoquiam River, James Karr and his family made their home on the banks of the river in 1859. When the post office was established it was named Hoquiam. It may be derived from ho-qui-umpts, which means "hungry for wood," referring to the driftwood at the mouth of the river. Timber was a big industry until the lumber played itself out and bottomed out with the Depression.

HUMPTULIPS (Grays Harabor/216) A small ranching community, Humptulips was once a prosperous logging town and boasted the greatest stand of Douglas fir trees in the entire Northwest. It was said that the trees were so dense they all had to be felled in the same direction. Humptulips is derived from ho-to-la-bixh, a Quinault word for "hard to pole," descriptive of the Indians who poled their canoes down the river.

ILWACO (Pacific/950) Ilwaco was initially called Unity to show its devotion to the Union during the Civil War. It was later named for a Chinook Indian named Elowahka Jim (unknown origin). James Holman platted the town in 1850, built a hotel and purchased interest in a sawmill. Lewis Loomis and a group of men founded the Ilwaco Wharf Company in 1874, and Loomis later organized a stage line and railroad called the "Clamshell" because it ran along the beach. Ilwaco was a stopping point on the expanding stagecoach and steamer ferry route between Astoria, Oregon, and the Puget Sound country.

INCHELIUM (Ferry/389) Once called Buffalo and Troy, this community was originally about a mile from its present site. The town was moved when it was flooded by creation of a lake behind Grand Coulee Dam, which angered the Salish Indians because it wiped out all the fish. Inchelium is an Indian sub-agency, and was derived from the Salish word, en-charlay-um (or en-ch'lay-um), which could mean "where big water meets little water," "meeting place among three waters," or "surrounded by water," designating the merging of Hall and Stranger Creeks.

ISSAQUAH (King/11,212) In a valley between the Squak and Tiger Mountains lies the historic mining town of Issaquah. This area was the fishing and hunting ground of the Snoqualmie Indian Tribe before white settlers arrived in the 1800s. The Indians called it Ishquoh, but the white man could not pronounce the word and it came out "Squak." It may have been derived from isquoah, meaning "the sound of the birds," or it could refer to a snake or a river. A huge coal seam was discovered in the region in the 1870s. By the 1930s, the coal mining industry dwindled, and residents turned to agriculture and dairy farming.

KAHLOTUS (Franklin/214) Kahlotus is located on the west side of Lake Kahlotus. Henry Villard, president of the Oregon-Washington River & Navigation Co. Railroad, extended a branch line to Kahlotus in 1883. On July 24, 1886, the post office was established (Thomas Winn, postmaster). Kahlotus shipped vast amounts of wheat and was considered the largest shipping point for the product. The town was platted in 1902 by the Hardersburg Townsite and Improvement Company. A surveyor platted the town in 1902 and named it Hardersburg. It was later changed to Kahlotus, for a Palouse Indian, whose name means "hole in the ground."

KAPOWSIN (Pierce/*150*) This was home to a tribe of Indians led by Chief Kapowsin (or Kapowsen). There were no white men here until 1888, when F.W. Hilgert claimed the land and subsequently planted orchards. The Tacoma Eastern Railroad had built its tracks through town, which connected it to Tacoma. When the post office opened in 1890, it was named for the Chief, whose name means "shallow," referring to the shallow end of the lake. The post office closed its door in 1899, and reopened in 1901 as Hall (Charles Fix, postmaster).

KENNEWICK (Benton/54,693) Kennewick may have been taken from the Chemnapam Indians who called this place "winter haven." Civil engineer H.S. Huson wrote in 1883, "...They called this place 'Kone Wack,' meaning a grassy place or glade ... I wrote underneath 'Kennewick.'"[35] Other sources interpreted it as "winter paradise. C.J. Beach worked on construction of the Northern Pacific Railroad and founded Kennewick. Most of early residents were railroad workers until the tracks were completed. In July 1996, a skeleton dubbed "Kennewick Man" was found at the edge of the Columbia River near town by two college students. It is still being studied.

KITTITAS (Kittitas/1,105) The Pschwan-wap-pam Indians lived in the region, early forerunners of the Yakima Nation. The only record to show the early settlement of Kittitas is the building of a school in 1893. The Milwaukee Land Company from Seattle built the Milwaukee Railroad in 1906 and platted the town of Kittitas two years later. Kittitas comes from various derivations, and all may be correct depending on the dialects. It could mean "shale rock," "white chalk," "land of plenty," or "shoal people."

KLICKITAT (Klickitat/417) The Klickitats were a Shahaptian tribe originally from the Cowlitz River area. They joined with the Yakima Indians in the Treaty of 1855 when they ceded their land. The post office was established on May 20, 1872. Timber initially brought interest to this area. The site was called Wright for Edgar Wright who settled here in 1889. About 1902, the Columbia River and Northern Railroad came through. The name was changed to Klickitat in 1910. It has several meanings: "beyond" and "robber." "Beyond" is the accepted version as it applies to the Indians' reference to the Cascade Mountains.

KOOSKOOSKIE (Walla Walla) Not much history is available for this tiny community situated on Mill Creek, which may have originated as a summer retreat. When explorers came through, they mistook the Indians' explanation of the river which they called koos, koos, a Nez Perce word for "water, water," and somehow the name ended up Kooskooskie. The Indians had names for localities and not the rivers themselves, and were probably simply telling the explorers here was water.

LATAH (Spokane/151) Latah takes its name from Latah Creek and was platted in 1886. Originally called Alpha, the name Latah may have its origins from a number of definitions. The Indians dug up the plentiful camas roots that were a staple food. They called the river Lahtoo, a Nez Perce word meaning "the place of pine trees and pestle." It was also translated from la-koh for "white pine" and tah-ol for "pestle." Latah could also mean "stream where little fish are caught, "camping ground" or "place well supplied with food."

LILLIWAUP (Mason) Once the center of activity as an outfitting point for prospectors, Lilliwaup is located on Lilliwaup Bay, three miles north of Hoodsport. The name has been translated as "inlet," derived from a Twana word, lil-la-wop. The post office opened on September 6, 1895 (Spiro Bisazza, postmaster). Encouraging settlement was the anticipated arrival of the Union Pacific Railroad. The Lilliwaup Land and Resort Company built a trail to Lilliwaup Falls, hoping to create a vacation resort. The company eventually folded and Lilliwaup reverted to a sleepy little town.

LUMMI ISLAND (Whatcom) The ancient name for this island was Skallaham, so called by the Lummi Indians. It was charted by Spanish explorers in 1792 and named Isle de Pacheco. Lummi was interpreted as "the people who repelled," or "capable of being repelled; that is, they did not mix with other people. In the mid 1800s, many of the Lummis died from diseases and Indian raiding parties. Captain Christian Tuttle, a gold miner and whaler, was the first permanent settler on the island in 1871. There was some logging, but biggest economy to the island was sport fishing. By the 1960s, Lummi Island had become more or less a retirement community.

MATTAWA (Grant/2,609) This region was once occupied by the Wanapum Indians, who were hunter-gatherers, and today there are but a few of them left. Traders observed the Indians' religious rites and called the site Priest Rapids. Settlers attempted farming, but lack of water prevented any successful crops. It wasn't until 1955 that the current town was established, and the name changed to Mattawa, which means "Where is it?" There is no explanation for this interesting definition, although the town cannot be seen from the highway. When the Priest Rapids and Wanapum Dam were built, local farmers used the irrigation for vineyards.

MEMALOOSE ISLAND (Klickitat) One of the largest funeral islands in the Columbia River Gorge, Memaloose means "dead," or "place of the dead," and was used by the Klickitat Indians as their burial ground. The only white man to be buried on this island was Victor Trevitt. He had more Indian friends that he did the whites, and wanted to be buried on the island with his Indian friends. When the Bonneville Dam was built in 1937, the bodies were moved to a higher part of the island because the dam was going to submerge the lower section.

METHOW (Okanogan) First known as Squaw Creek, the site was originally a mining camp. During the gold rush a 5-stamp mill was built. The miners later held a meeting to create a town. A hunting and gathering place for the Methow Indians, their name means as "sun" or "sunflower seeds," derived from smeetheowe. The post office was established on November 8, 1894, and a weekly stage line began its run that went from Chelan to Methow. The town went into decline after the depression of 1893.

MOCLIPS (Grays Harbor/615) Moclips sits on a bluff that overlooks the Pacific Ocean, and was a thriving summer town. It is a Quinault expression that designates the site where young Indian maidens underwent their puberty rites; that is, they were not allowed near the rivers full of salmon during menstruation. In the early 1900s, a hotel concern built the 300-room Moclips Hotel that fronted the ocean. A huge storm hit the Pacific coast in 1913 and seas hit the hotel, destroying it. A second hotel was constructed further back from the beach on a site believed to be an old Quinault village.

MOXEE CITY (Yakima/821) Fielding M. Thorp was an early settler about 1860. He brought numerous Durham cattle with him because of the wealth of bunchgrass. The Moxie Company was established and owned by founder of the National Geographic Society, Gardiner Hubbard. Moxie may mean "whirlwinds," because the region was known for its dust devils during certain times of the year.

MUKILTEO (Snohomish/18,019) This is the site where the Indians signed the Point Everett Treaty of 1855 and ceded the land of today's Seattle. Once an Indian ceremony and council ground, the settlement was named Mukilteo, meaning "good camping (or hunting) ground." Early development began in 1858 along the shoreline with the establishment of cannery and lumber mill. Town founders were Jacob Fowler and Morris Frost. The Mukilteo Lumber Company built its plant in 1903, and in the early 1900s Crown Lumber took over until it closed in 1930.

NACHES (Yakima/643) Situated at the foot of Mt. Cleman, Naches was settled by Harry Painter in 1898 and laid out in 1905 by the West and Wheel Land Company. The post office was established the following year. Naches became firmly established when reclamation projects began with the Bumping Dam and Yakima Tieton Reservoir, which supplied water to the valley. First called Natchez, the name was later spelled Naches. The Indians called the site Natcheez, interpreted as "turbulent waters," referring to the swift moving river. It was also defined as "oh water!" and "one water." Another interpretation is from nahchess, for "plenty of water."

NAHCOTTA (Pacific) Located on the Long Beach Peninsula, Nahcotta was an important oystering center. Named for an old Chinook Chief Nahcati (origin obscure) who became friends with the settlers, the town was established in 1888 as the terminus of a narrow-gauge railroad. In addition to oysters, there was also a growing timber trade out of Willapa Bay. During the early 1900s, the oyster population severely declined because of over-harvesting. In an attempt to replenish them, Eastern oysters were brought here, but they refused to propagate. Pacific oyster seeds were introduced in 1929 which proved successful.

NAPAVINE (Lewis/1,361) The site was settled in 1872 by John Cutting who called it Napawyna, presumably for an Indian princess. The word was translated to "small prairie." Horace H. Pinto may have named the town. He and a band of emigrants were bound for the Dalles in 1850, but Pinto decided to stay here. James

Urquhart platted the town in 1863 and anglicized the name to Napavine. Urquhart was very active in public affairs and went on to serve two terms in the Territorial Legislature in 1863 and 1865. Supported in the early days by sawmills, today Napavine is a bedroom community.

NASELLE (Pacific/377) This was home to a branch of the Chinook Indians who called themselves Na-sil. A smallpox epidemic hit the region in the early 1800s, almost decimating the tribe. There were about six families left who settled at what they called the Na-sil River. William Whealdon and two Indian guides stopped at Naselle to visit a family in 1862. He wrote of this visit, and since he was an expert in the pure Chinook language, it is believed his account of the name origin is accurate. When asked what Na-sil meant, he was told it was an old Chinook word that meant "protection" and "shelter."

NEAH BAY (Clallam/794) Neah Bay is home to the Makah Indians, and named for Makah Chief Dee-ah (origin unknown). Neah Bay was discovered by navigator Apostolos Valerianus (Juan de Fuca) in 1592. Captain Henry Kellett landed in 1828 for fresh water and met Chief Dee-ah. Unable to pronounce the name, he called the site Neah. Fur-trading was a big part of the Indians' lives until the otters were almost extinct. Governor Isaac Stevens convinced the Makahs to sell their land, but they stipulated they still be able to fish and hunt on the land. In 1875, the Makah Treaty was ratified and is still in effect today. Makah itself translates to "generous with food."

NESPELEM (Okanogan/290) Nespelem is located on a portion of the Colville Indian Reservation. Before settlement, the Indians camped along the Columbia River, following the salmon migration. The Colville Reservation was established when a treaty was signed in 1855. One of the early settlers was Francis Daugherty, who was postmaster when the office opened on November 20, 1899. Leader of the Nez Perce, Chief Joseph, is buried near town. Nespelem may have been derived from nespilim, which means "flat land." It has also been translated as "large meadow beside a stream."

NEWAUKUM (Lewis) The town took its name from the Newaukum River, which means "gently flowing water." There were settlers in the early 1800s, but it wasn't until 1873 that General Sprague arrived and built up the town. The post office had been established in 1856 (discontinued in 1863). Sprague opened another post office in 1873, built the train depot, side track and water tank. When the Northern Pacific Railway offered to build a courthouse if Newaukum would become county seat, residents said no, and the seat was moved to Chehalis.

NEWHALEM (Whatcom) Newhalem is a small mountain community situated on the Skagit River and headquarters for the Seattle Light Operation, which gave the town its name. Built as a company town, employees maintained a series of dams that produced power for Seattle. The name means "goat snare," designating a goat trail upstream from town. The region was a center of mining activity in 1878, but the mines failed to produce enough gold to make it worthwhile.

NOOKSACK (Whatcom/851) The Nooksack Indians gave their name to the river, which means "fern-eating people," because they ate the roots of the ferns. The town experienced some growth after the Whatcom Trail was built in 1858, and later in anticipation of Northern Pacific establishing a junction here (which never occurred). When W.R. Moultray arrived, he and M.J. Heney created the Nooksack Improvement Company, which laid out the town in 1890. Today, the town serves a rural area which is predominantly dairy farms and raspberry production.

OKANOGAN (Okanogan/2,484) Located about 40 miles south of the Canadian border, the community was called Alma, for the daughter of a Prussian who was an ex-Indian fighter and construction worker. The post office was established on May 26, 1889. The name was changed to Pogue in 1905, in honor of Dr. J.I. Pogue, an orchardist. It was renamed Okanogan in 1907, and means "rendezvous," which may come from the Salish word, okanagen, an appropriate word as the Indians used this site for their potlatches.

OLEMA (Okanogan/*245*) Settled in 1890, Olema became a terminus when a road was built between the settlement of Brewster and into the Methow Valley. One of the early residents was Charles McFarlane, who was postmaster when the office opened on November 17, 1896. Drought destroyed most of the farms, and before long most of the farmers had left the area. With the decrease in population, the post office closed its doors in 1924. Olema was translated from Salish as "big hole above a creek."

OLLALA (Kitsap) Situated on Puget Sound, Olalla was settled about 1880 when pioneers discovered a creek that went into the sound, enabling them to reach the shoreline with ease. After Charles Nelson made his fortune in real estate and the Yukon gold rush, he came to Olema and opened a general store. Local farmers were primarily Scandinavians who grew strawberries Before any roads were built, Ollala was a stop for the steamboats and a shipping point for the fruit. The name was derived from olallie, a Chinook word for "many berries," or just "berries."

OMAK (Okanogan/4,721) In 1906, surveyor Ben Ross laid out lots for a community. The post office opened on June 4, 1907 (Rebecca Lucas, postmaster). J.C. Biles purchased a sawmill and box manufacturing factory in the 1920s, and built a five-mile-long, narrow-gauge railroad on Omak Mountain. Biles also purchased a stand of timber that held more than a half-billion board feet, and established a sawmill at Omak in 1924. Omak was named for a nearby lake, and may have been derived from omache, which means "great medicine," because the lake was thought to have medicinal powers.

ORTING (Pierce/3,760) In 1854, William H. Whitesell filed a claim at Orting. Coal was discovered near the Puyallup River, and as a result the Northern Pacific Railroad built its tracks in 1877. Hops was an important industry until the plants were destroyed by the hops louse. In addition to coal, the advent of the timber industry in the 1880s brought added wealth. The post office was established in 1878 (Henry Whitesel, postmaster). The 1920s brought in the daffodil industry. Orting was interpreted a "a prairie in the woods." An old map shows it as a Chinook word for "valley glade," or "opening between hills."

PALOUSE (Whitman/1,011) Palouse could be of Indian or French origin. The tribe's original name may have been Palus, Palloatpallah or Pelusha. French-Canadians probably translated it to pelouse, which described the area as a grassy expanse. Some scholars think the Indians were the Palloatpallahs, close relatives of the Nez Perce Indians. The Palouse Indians were not resident in the region because it presented no shelter and the winters were severe, but they did visit occasionally. When gold was discovered in Idaho at its Gold Hill and Hoodoo Districts, Palouse became a trading post and outfitter for the miners, and later a wheat and timber producing town.

PATAHA (Garfield) In 1861, James Bowers was the first settler. Angevine Favor acquired the property a few years later, and the town was laid out in 1882. J.N. Bowman and George Snyder built a flour mill. Born in Pataha, Snyder was a grain dealer who shipped flour to San Francisco with wheat grown in the Pataha Valley that was very high in gluten, and in great demand for the manufacture of macaroni. Once known as Waterstown and Favorsburg, the settlement was renamed Pataha. It means "brush," a Nez Perce term for the brush growing along a creek.

PESHASHTIN (Chelan) Robert and William Tandy settled at Peshashtin in 1890. Mail was delivered by the Great Northern Railroad until the post office was established on May 22, 1890. The Indians' name for the community was retained. Peshashtin was pronounced as pish-pish-astin, which meant "broad bottom canyon." With the building of irrigation canals, Peshashtin became known for its pear and apple orchards.

PUYALLUP (Pierce/33,011) Although Ezra Meeker was here in 1851, the first people to actually build their homes were men who worked for the Hudson Bay Company. Puyallup was ceded by the Indians after the treaty at Medicine Creek in 1854. The name may be a Salish word meaning "generous people," or "shadows," descriptive of the shade made by the forest. When the post office opened, it was named Franklin. Ezra Meeker returned in 1877, platted the town and renamed it Puyallup. He later rued the day he gave it such an unpronounceable name. During the 1920s, Puyallup's cash crop was daffodils and tulips after bulbs from Holland were banned because of disease and foreign insects.

PYSHT (Clallam) This former community was located about 10 miles southeast of Clallam Bay, and started out as a logging camp. Pysht is a Chinook word that means "fish." The post office was established on January 15, 1878 (David Brownfield, postmaster). In 1890, a road was opened up that went from here to Clallam Bay. Before that time, cattlemen had to drive their herds from Pysht to Port Angeles along the beach. A timber camp was built at Pysht and began logging in 1916, and continued for more than 35 years. By 1958, most of the buildings had completely deteriorated.

QUEETS (Jefferson) The 1850 Donation Claim Act opened the area for settlement. The post office was established on June 2, 1900, and served the Quinault Reservation. Queets corridor became part of the national park, and by 1953 the families living within its boundaries had to give up their land. Queets is derived from the Quiatso Indian Tribe. The word is thought to literally mean "out of the dirt of the skin." Legend says when the Great Spirit crossed a cold river, he rubbed his legs together to warm them and came up with a handful of dirt. He tossed the dirt into the river and a man and woman arose from the dirt which created the Quiatso Tribe.

QUILCENE (Jefferson/591) Once the home of the Twana Indians, the area was explored by the Wilkes Expedition in 1841, where they noted on their charts the name "Kwil-sid." Quilcene is located at the mouth of the Quilcene River, and the name may signify "salt water people." The post office opened on March 16, 1881 (James Haradan, postmaster). In 1902, the Tubal Cain Mining Company opened after gold and manganese were found, but there was never much ore taken out. Quilcene's economy was later tied to logging and oystering.

SALKUM (Lewis) Salem Plant was an early settler, perhaps the first, who came here about 1827 and began growing hops. Much of the area trade was by river steamboats. On October 10, 1882, the post office opened (Jacob Beusch, postmaster). Salkum is interpreted as "boiling up," referring to a section on the Cowlitz River where the falls were located. As the water hit a deep hole at the bottom, the Indians thought it looked like it was boiling up. When the Mayfield Dam was constructed, rocks were blasted to change the channel and adversely affected the waterfall.

SEATTLE (King/563,374) Chief Sealth was born to the Suquamish Tribe between 1786 and 1790, from whom the city got its name. Seattle was as close as the white men could get to pronouncing his name (origin unknown). In 1851, Arthur Denny brought in a group of settlers to Alki Point. Residents later moved the settlement closer to Elliott Bay because of the timber forests and natural harbor. Seattle's population boomed when gold was discovered in Canada, bringing miners who stopped here on their way to the gold fields. The year 1889 brought the great Seattle fire, which destroyed more then 50 blocks of the business district.

SEQUIM (Clallam/4,334) Sequim is located on the north coast of the Olympic Peninsula, and was once home to the Klallam Indian Tribe. John Bell homesteaded the site in 1854. The post office opened on August 13, 1879 as Seguin, and renamed Sequim in 1907. A California-based company built a tanbark factory where bark was made into tannic acid and shipped out to tanneries. In the early 1890s, James Grant and a group of men formed the Sequim Prairie Ditch Company, bringing irrigation to the farmers. The Klallam Indians called the bay such-e-kwai-ing or suxtcikwi'in, meaning "quiet water."

SKAMANIA (Skamania) Skamania was once called Butler and Mendota. It was later named Skamania, meaning "swift water." The Indians may have been of the Shahala Tribe. Below a landmark called Beacon Rock was the Wahclellah tribe of a Shahala village, which was probably used as a winter camp. William Butler and his family came from England about 1892 and moved to Skamania. At first there was just a small country road that went from the schoolhouse to a dock in the early 1900s. Eventually a railroad came through.

SKAMOKAWA (Wahkiakum/*400*) Skamokawa was established at the junction of three sloughs, which became highways of commerce and communication until roads were built. Scandinavians moved here in the 1870s and established the first cooperative creamery in the state. When the Northern Pacific Railroad was being constructed, a local sawmill supplied ties to the railroad. The name came from Chinook Chief Skamokawa, interpreted as "smoke over the water," because of early morning fog that settled over the town.

SKYKOMISH (King/214) The Skykomish Indians were once considered by the U.S. government an offshoot of the Snohomish Tribe. When the Treaty of Point Elliott was signed in 1855, the Skykomish Indians left the area and went to the Tulalip Reservation. Skykomish is derived from skaikh and mish, meaning "inland people." The town got its start with the building of the Great Northern Railroad. In 1890, John Maloney settled at a site he called Maloney's Siding (later changed to Skykomish), which became a switching yard that maintained a roundhouse for helper engines used through the Cascade Tunnel.

SNOHOMISH (Snohomish/8,494) The Snohomish Indians were a relatively peaceful tribe who were not nomadic and engaged in agriculture. Snohomish has a number of possible meanings, derived from sdah-hob-mish: "tidewater people," "the men," "the warriors," or "the braves." Emory Ferguson took up residence in 1860 when he found out a military road was going to be built. The road was never completed, but Ferguson went on to became a prominent businessman and politician.

SNOQUALMIE (King/1,631) The Snoqualmie Indians historically lived in the Puget Sound area, and made first contact with the white man about 1833 when Fort Nisqually was built. The Snoqualmie Tribe has been classified as part of the Coast Salish Indians. When the Treaty of Point Elliott was signed, some of the natives relocated to the Tulalip Reservation. Snoqualmie may be derived from sdoh-kwahlb, which means "moon people," or just "moon." The Indians believed this is where their ancestors originated; the place where their life source came from. Snoqualmie was born during the prosperous days of lumbering and milling.

SPANAWAY (Pierce/21,588) Spanaway was one of the first settlements in the county. Thought to be an Indian word, local tradition says yawanaps, backwards for Spanaway, meant "beautiful water." The Old Military Road was built in the 1850s near Spanaway. The first immigrant train over the Naches Pass brought the Wright family here in 1853. Hops was an important crop that was grown in the bottom lands. Some logging was also conducted.

SPOKANE (Spokane/195,629) Acting for the North West Fur Company, Finan McDonald and Joco Finlay built a trading post called Spokane House in 1810. They took the name from the Spokane Indians, which signified "children of the sun," or "sun people." The chief called himself Illim-Spokane, "Chief of the sun people." Settlement near the falls started in 1871 when J.J. Downing and his family homesteaded on the banks of the river. A plat was filed in 1871 and the site named Spokane Falls. Encouraging settlement was the discovery of silver and lead deposits in Idaho and British Columbia. In 1891, Spokane Falls became Spokane by popular vote.

STEHEKIN (Chelan/*100*) Stehekin was once part of the Columbia Indian Reservation, which was later disbanded. When traveling through the Cascade Mountains, nomadic Indians camped at this site situated at the head of Lake Chelan and called it Stehekin, meaning "the way through," signifying a pass through the mountains. Civil War veteran John Horton built his home at the mouth of the Stehekin River in the 1890s. Although Stehekin was isolated, it still drew homesteaders who practiced subsistence farming. In 1892, Merritt Field bought a partially finished hotel and eventually turned it into a resort.

STEILACOOM (Pierce/6,049) This site was originally a Salish Indian village called tchil-ac-cum, which means "pink flower," descriptive of the pink flowers that grew in the region. The arrival of a sea captain named Lafayette Balch in 1851 was the beginning of Steilacoom when he claimed land and named the site. The town grew considerably after gold was discovered on the Thompson and Fraser rivers. Businesses capitalized on this opportunity and Steilacoom became an outfitting center for the miners. When the Northern Pacific Railroad Company bypassed the town, its importance declined and many residents moved to Tacoma.

SUMAS (Whatcom/960) Sumas means "land without trees," and signifies the flat prairie in the immediate region. The Sumas Indians had their camp near the confluence of the Sumas and Fraser rivers. Sumas began as a railroad town with three direct lines to Whatcom, Seattle and Vancouver, British Columbia. Because of the massive timber resources, lumber was a big industry. In 1897, gold was discovered on Mount Baker and Sumas became an outfitting center. The town's location on the American/Canadian border made it an ideal route for smugglers.

SQUAXIN ISLAND (Mason) The Indians who called themselves Skwaks-namish were removed in 1854 when the Medicine Creek was signed on December 26. Located on Puget Sound, part of this island was later designated as a state park. The name comes from skwaks-namish, which means "silent," or "alone," descriptive of a small, isolated creek on North Bay.

TACOMA (Pierce/193,556) Tacoma was first known by the Chelaulip Indians as shubahlup or chelaulip ("the sheltered place"). A Swede named Nicholas De Lin moved to Tacoma and developed a lumber business in 1852. General Morton McCarver later purchased the townsite, naming it Tacoma, derived from takhoma or tayma, meaning "mountain that is god," in reference to Mt. Rainier. Other definitions have included "frozen waters," "nourishing breast," and "near to heaven." Tacoma experienced phenomenal growth when the Stampede Pass Tunnel was built and a switchback was constructed over the summit of the Cascades, bringing direct transcontinental rail service to the region.

TAHUYA (Mason) Rufus Moang, Franklin C. Purdy and Charles Wiggins were early settlers in the 1850s. There were only about 6–7 families living here by 1915. The post office was established the same year on August 2 (John Rolie, postmaster). Most of the people living in the region were engaged in farming, fishing or lumbering. Tahuya was named for the Tahuya Indians, derived from tehuyeh, meaning "oldest people," or "oldest settlers." It may also be from Twana words, ta and ho-I, defined as "that done," and referred to some event that occurred in earlier days.

TATOOSH ISLAND (Clallam) This bean-shaped island is situated off the extreme northwestern point of the state near the Makah Indian Reservation, and traditionally a summer fishing village for the Makahs. John Meares named the island in 1788 to commemorate a Nootka chief named Tatoochatticus, interpreted as "milk" or "breasts." A similar Nootkan word, tatootshe, means "thunder," "fire from thunder," or "thunder bird." Not much importance was given to the island until a lighthouse was built by the Federal Government in 1857. Today, the island is a meteorological station.

TENINO (Thurston/1,447) This site was once an Indian meeting ground and trading spot. Stephen Hodgden was the first settler to file a donation claim in 1851. The Tenino post office was established in 1860 as Hodgden's Station (Stephen Hodgden, postmaster). Northern Pacific built its tracks to the station, where it constructed a roundhouse, and Tenino grew up around the railroad building. Tenino is a Chinook word that could mean "meeting ground," "ford in the road," or "junction"; all referring to the Indian trail crossings.

TILLICUM (Pierce) Very little is known about Tillicum's history and it is not known when the site was founded. Built around American Lake, which is one of the state's largest and deepest lakes, the community was originally called American Lake South. One of the first stores was owned by N.B. Henderson. Jessi West helped name the town Tillicum in 1920, Chinook for "friend." Tillicum became a favorite swimming area in the early 1900s, and during World War I, the lake was used as an Army training facility.

TOKELAND (Pacific/194) Located on north Willapa Bay, Tokeland saw its first settler in 1854 when J.F. Barrows settled at what was called Toke Point. Chief Toke, who may have been of the Chehalis Tribe, was living here when the Barrows arrived. In the 1890s, the Kindred Inn was opened, and the post office was established in 1894. The name was changed from Toke Point to Tokeland (unknown origin). The Tokeland Hotel was built in 1910, but over time the sea began to erode the shoreline. A rock wall was built, which helped until 1973 when a monster storm hit. Today, Tokeland is mainly a resort town.

TONASKET (Okanogan/994) Tonasket is an old Indian camp site where trappers hunted in the early 1800s. The town was named for Chief Tonasket of the Okanogan Tribe, which may have been a branch of the Colville Indians. Its name origin is uncertain. The town got its start when Watkins Parry came to the Okanogan Valley in 1888 and called his site Parry's Landing. The post office was established on December 30, 1892 (Charles A. Thompson, postmaster). When there was the possibility of a railroad, a banker named Arthur Lund decided this site, rather than Parry's section, would be just the place for a town if the railroad from Wenatchee were constructed, which occurred in 1914.

TOPPENISH (Yakima/8,946) Toppenish is situated on the 1,000,000-acre Yakima Indian Reservation. The Yakima Indians have reverted to the original spelling of their tribe, Yakama, as signed on a Treaty of 1855. The Northern Pacific Railway laid its tracks in 1884 and Toppenish was the halfway point where a substation was established. A sugar processing plant was built in 1918, but after the leaf hoppers invaded all the crops the company closed down. Toppenish is derived from thap-pahn-ish, for "people of the trail which comes from the foot of the hills." Others think the word came from qapuishlema, "people from the foot of the hills;" or a Yakima word meaning "sloping and spreading land."

TUKWILA (King/17,181) This was home to the Duwamish who lived along the rivers. Because of the abundance of hazelnut trees, they named the region Tukwila ("land of hazelnuts"). The 1850s brought in the first homesteaders. Goods such as produce and coal from the local mines were shipped by flatboats on the Duwamish and Green and Black rivers. Because of its location near rivers, trails and railroads, Tukwila became a commerce center. First known as Garden City, the name was changed in 1905.

TUMWATER (Thurston/12,698) Growth of this community began about 1845, which was originally British Territory, and became the first America settlement in the Puget Sound region. Located on the Deschutes River, the town's history and economy was tied to the river. The Chinook Indians called the river Tum Chuk, describing the falls that sounded like the beating of a heart, and meant "throbbing (or noisy) water." First called New Market, the town's name was changed to Tumwater in 1857. Leopold Schmidt was the founder of the first brewery in Tumwater which would go on to become the Olympia Brewing Company.

TWISP (Okanogan/938) Twisp is a modification of t-wapsp, meaning "yellow jacket." Another derivation is from twistsp, an imitation of a yellow jacket's buzzing. It was also suggested it was a Chinook word designating the forks of two rivers. H.C. Glover named the first site Gloversville, and platted the town in 1897. When Amanda Burgar purchased land adjacent to Gloversville, she built a hotel and named that section Twisp. The town's main source of income was gold mining which started in the 1890s and a number of mining districts were established. Livestock, dairy farming and agriculture later supplanted mining.

WAIILATPU (8 miles west of Walla Walla) This former community was settled by Dr. Marcus Whitman and his wife when they established a mission and taught the Indians Christianity. Their home also became a stopping place for immigrants along the Oregon Trail. Sickness that Whitman could not cure, plus the influx of immigrants, angered the Cayuse Indians who massacred the Whitmans and burned the mission. Waiilatpu means "place of the rye grass."

WALLA WALLA (Walla Walla/29,686) This is the place where Governor Isaac Stevens and Joel Palmer with Indian Affairs for Oregon held a council in 1855 with more than 5,000 Indians to convince them to move onto reservations. As a result, three treaties were signed. Factors that contributed to Walla Walla's growth were the lifting of a ban on immigration into the territory, and construction of the Mullan Military Road. First called Steptoeville, the name was changed to Walla Walla in 1858, derived from a Nez Perce word, walastu, meaning either "running water," or "small, rapid streams."

WALLULA (Walla Walla/197) Wallula is a Nez Perce word meaning "abundance of water," descriptive of the site's proximity to the confluence of the Columbia and Walla Walla rivers. When Hudson's Bay Company abandoned Fort Walla Walla, it was turned into a townsite. Wallulla Landing was built in 1859, and a railroad later linked Wallula with the town of Touchet. J.M. Vansycle and S.W. Tatem laid out the town in 1882. When the McNary Dam began rising, the town moved to its present location in 1953.

WAPATO (Yakima/4,582) Wapato started out as a blind siding for the Northern Pacific Railroad. Settlers had been here since 1885, but the majority of businesses were not established until about 1904. Wapato was located on the Yakima Indian Reservation, and Alex McCredy was appointed the Indian post trader who later developed the townsite. First called Simcoe, it was changed to Wapato about 1903, from the Chinook word, wapatoo, meaning "potato, or "big potato," designating the Camas root the Indians dug up for their food.

WASHOUGAL (Clark/8,598) In 1844, settlers led by Michael Simmons and George Bush came here and called the site Parker's Landing. Washougal is considered the first American settlement in Washington north of the Columbia River. In addition to farming, logging camps and copper mines helped the town's economy. The Washougal Woolen Mill was established in 1910. What started with 450 head of sheep became the home industry of making wool socks. Washougal could mean "between two rivers," "laughing waters," "running (or rushing) water," or "land of plenty and pleasant."

WASHTUCNA (Adams/260) Washtucna was founded in 1878 by George W. Bassett. The post office opened in 1882, and Bassett was postmaster. He also named the town Washtucna for an old Palouse Indian chief. When Bassett asked an Indians what the word meant, all they would tell him was "Big Chief named Washtucna in the long ago." He never learned the definition. Another theory is that Washtucna was a Palouse word that meant "many waters." In 1886, the Oregon Improvement Company arranged to have a railroad built. By 1891, Washtucna was shipping out extraordinary amounts of wheat. In 1902, the Palouse River was dammed up, supporting irrigation of the west.

WELLPINIT (Stevens) A Presbyterian mission was once located on the Spokane Indian Reservation. It was first named Germmania, and later changed to Wellpinit, which may be a Nez Perce word that means "water gushing," referring to an artesian spring. It has also been defined as "two small creeks in a valley."

WENATCHEE (Chelan/27,856) Wenatchee sits at the foothills of the Cascade Mountains, a favorite spot for many of the Northwest tribes who used it as a council ground and camp. The name was interpreted from a Yakima word for "robe of the rainbow," "good place," or "boiling waters." Ingraham and McBride opened a trading post in 1867 to sell supplies to the Indians. Construction of the Highline Canal in 1903 brought water to the Wenatchee region. Farmers started apple orchards, and by the 1920s Wenatchee became one of the important apple-producing regions in the world.

WISHRAM (Klickitat/324) This community is located along the Columbia River. Wishram means "flea" or "louse," and was originally a Chinook Indian village. Most of the Indians were relocated to the Yakima Reservation. F.G. Bunn was a merchandiser from The Dalles who moved here in 1911 and drew up a plat for a town he called Fallbridge. The post office opened on May 9, 1911 (Josephine Gates, postmaster), and the name was changed to Wishram in 1926. The Spokane, Portland and Seattle Railroad built and maintained a roundhouse and train yard. Wishram was an important railroad terminus during World War II.

YACOLT (Clark/1,055) Yacolt is derived from yolicolb, meaning something analogous to "haunted valley," "place abounding in evil spirits," or valley of the demons." The Indians became fearful of this place when their children came to pick berries and never returned home, causing the Indians to believe a demon had taken them. Charley Landon filed on a section of land and had it surveyed. The Yacolt Burn of September, 1902, destroyed more than 250,000 acres of forest, and was the worst fire to hit Washington. It may have started from sparks from logging trains or donkey engines. After the great fire, Weyerhaeuser came in to start clean-up operations, which were not completed until 1924.

YAKIMA (Yakima/71,845) Yakima was settled about 1858 after the Yakima Indians signed a treaty putting them on a reservation. The first permanent residents were Fielding Thorpe and his family. Growth of Yakima was slow until irrigation was brought to the arid valley. About 1893, the Northern Pacific Railway built its station a few miles from town. The entire town was moved on rollers and skids in 1884 to be closer to the tracks. When the Reclamation Service unified its irrigation efforts in 1902, Yakima's population tripled, and the people began to grow hops, in addition to fruit and vegetables. Yakima has been defined as "big belly, "pregnant one," "runaway," or "bountiful."

YELM (Thurston/3,289) Yelm is located on the Yelm prairie that stretches to the foothills of Mount Rainier. James Longmire brought the first immigrant train over the Cascades in 1853 and arrived at Yelm Prairie, where he purchased a home. In 1873, Tacoma became the terminus of the Northern Pacific Railroad, which then extended its line to this area. Residents didn't benefit much from the railroad because Yelm was just a flag station. The railroad named this site Yelm Prairie, but it was later shortened to Yelm. It may be a Salish word, shelm or chelm, which described the heat waves that emanated from the ground during the hot summers. The Indians believed that it was a manifestation of their Great Spirit.

WEST VIRGINIA

BUCKHANNON (Upshur/5,725) One of the first permanent settlements between Fort Pitt and the Gulf of Mexico, this townsite was purchased by Elizabeth Jackson. Her son, Colonel Edward Jackson, platted the town in 1806. The post office had been established two years earlier. During the Civil War, Buckhannon was pillaged by the Confederacy. Buckhannon's origins are in dispute. Some believe it was not an Indian name, but a Colonel named Buchanan. Others have attached its origin to a band of Delaware Indians with a chief named Buckongehanon. It was also defined as "brick river," and "breaker in pieces."

MATOAKA (Mercer/317) Pocahontas gave herself the secret name of Matoaka, which was derived from the Algonquin word, metawake, meaning "she amuses herself." Matoaka is located along Widemouth Creek and was named by Captain D.H. Barger in 1903. Coal mining and timber were the main industries, which brought in the Norfolk and Western Railway. Matoaka also became a trading and banking center for the surrounding coal towns and lumber camps. At one time, Matoaka was shipping out more than 8,000,000 tons of coal per year.

MONONGAH (Marion/939) Nathanial Cochran and his wife were the first settlers at Monongah in 1789. James Watkins hired a surveyor in 1850 to survey the townsite. Called Briartown, it was changed to Camdenburg in 1890. A short period of time later, it was renamed Clarkson, and finally Monongah, for the Monongahela Coal and Coke Company. The name is derived from the Monongahela River, derived from the Lenape word, menaonginela, meaning "where the land erodes." In 1907, the worst coal mine explosion to date occurred here, killing more than 350 men.

WISCONSIN

ANTIGO (Langlade/1,487) Settlers were attracted to this region because of its vast stands of timber and the exceptionally rich soil. Francis Deleglise staked out the town, and took the name from a Chippewa word, nequi-antigo-seebah, which signified the balsam evergreens prevalent in the region. When the timber declined, residents turned to agriculture.

CHETEK (Barron/2,180) Lakes flooded this area which once held rice beds for the Chippewa Indians. A trading post was opened in 1836 by Joe Trepannier. Knapp Stout & Co. purchased about 115,000 acres of the land in the 1870s, and established one of its lumber camps and built a dam at Chetek. The name was derived from sheetak, an Ojibway word that means "little pelican." Another interpretation was from sagaigan, meaning "island lake." When the post office was established in 1872, it was spelled Sheteack and later evolved to Chetek.

KAUKAUNA (Outagamie/1,142) When the Treaty of the Cedars was signed in 1836, this region was opened for settlement. The town was platted by George Lawe in 1850. The Milwaukee Lake-Shore and Western Railroad moved its district office to Kaukauna in 1881. Along with railroad development came power canals, which brought in the paper industry. Kaukauna is derived from ogag-kane, an Ojibway word meaning "place of the pike," or from o-gau-gau-ning, meaning "stopping place of the pickerel."

KENOSHA (Kenosha/90,352) In 1834, John Bullen and a group of people created the Western Emigrating Company for the purpose of founding a town in the West. They arrived in 1835 at the shores of Lake Michigan, but finding the cost of land too prohibitive, they purchased property at this site and named it Pike. Before white settlement, the Algonquin Indians caught fish they called kenozia ("pike fish"). The town was renamed Southport about 1842, and changed to Kenosha in 1850, which is derived from kenozia.

KEWAUNEE (Kewaunee/2,806) Potawatomi Chief Simon Kahquados and his descendants had their principal village here for more than 600 years. A trading post was established at the mouth of the Kewaunee River in 1796 by Jacques Veau, agent for the North West Fur Company. Kewaunee is a Potawatomi word that means "we are lost." Indians canoeing on Lake Michigan would occasionally find themselves shrouded in fog and lose their way. Crying, "Kewaunee," the Indians on the shore would respond so the canoers could find their way to land. Others believe the word means "go around," or "wild duck."

MANAWA (Waupaca/1,169) Located along Little Wolf River, Manawa began its development in the 1840s as Centerville. The region was conducive to dairies and agriculture, in addition to potatoes and timber harvesting. The post office opened in 1853 (A.P. Jones, postmaster). Manawa was an Anishinabe Indian, and his name was interpreted as "having no tobacco," from his habit of trading for the item. It may have been derived from manawakaranianaga, for "he took his bow and arrows."

MANITOWOC (Manitowoc/1,073) The Northwest Fur Company established a trading post in 1795. Manitowoc was established in the 1830s with the arrival of timber men and land speculators. Benjamin Jones purchased the site in 1836. Manitowoc became a lumber town until all the timber had been depleted, and the community turned to agriculture, in addition to shipbuilding. Manitowoc is derived from mundeowk, Ojibway for "home of the good spirit."

MAZOMANIE (Dane/1,185) Settlement began with three members of the British Temperance Emigration Society in 1843. Under the auspices of the society, Irish, Scots and Germans settled here between 1843 and 1850. Edward Brodhead, superintendent of the Milwaukee and Mississippi Railroad, name the town after a Winnebago chief, which means "iron that walks."

MENASHA (Winnebago/154,689) "The Paper City of Wisconsin" was settled by Curtis Reed in 1848 and the post office opened the next year (James Lush, postmaster). By 1862, Menasha was a station on the Chicago, St. Paul and Fond du Lac Railroad. The town came into prominence in the 1880s when William Gilbert started a one-machine paper mill that manufactured bond paper. The Walter Bros. Brewing Company, founded in 1888, further lent to Menasha's prosperity. The name is Algonquin for "island."

MENOMONIE (Dunn/14,937) The Menominee tribe who lived here were visited by Nicolet in 1634. This tribe was generally at peace with the white men, but they disappeared from history. The Knapp, Stout & Company had its headquarters here and became the largest lumber company in the world. Captain William Wilson was founder of Menomonie and had the town platted in 1859. When the timber had been depleted by 1910, residents developed dairy and cheese industries. Menomonie means "wild rice."

METOMEN (Fond du Lac/761) The town was named by F.D. Bowman in the 1840s, taken from the Menominee word for "a grain of corn." Early industries were a wagon factory, and a sash, door and blind establishment. A flour mill was established on a branch of the Grand River. Sheep raising later came into prominence. The Milwaukee and Horicon Railroad made the town one of its stations, and Metomen acquired its post office in 1873.

MILWAUKEE (Milwaukee/596,974) French traders and trappers were the first immigrants to Milwaukee, which was an early campsite between Chicago and Green Bay. The city was founded by Solomon Juneau. By 1833, the settlement had grown significantly with an influx of Germans, Scandinavians, Dutch and Irish. The Potawatomi Indians called the site mahn-ah-wauk, which means "council grounds." Others believe it came from millocki, defined as "gathering place by the waters," or from milioke, for "good earth."

MINOCQUA ISLAND (Oneida/4,859) This island became a natural logging center when the Chicago, Milwaukee, St. Paul and Pacific Railroads came through in 1887. Viewed as an inexhaustible forest, loggers came to harvest the timber, but by the early 1900s the timber was gone. Early settler Stiles Ray said the town was named in 1888 for Chief Nocwib. Missionary Francis Spees thought it was called menocuay, which meant a bad woman was located here. Another believed it came from the Potawatomi word, nin-oco-qua, meaning "noon-day" or "mid-day rest." Other interpretations were "good woman," or "fair maiden."

MINONG (Washburn/*761*) Minong started its life as a trading post about 1867. The stands of white pine lured timbermen to the region in the 1880s. The Chicago, St. Paul, Minnesota and Omaha Railroad came through in 1883, and the village was platted in 1891 by Josiah Bond. First called O'Brien's Landing, it was later changed to Minong, a Chippewa word for "pleasant valley." The Indians lived here because the ranges of hills sheltered them from the elements.

MISHICOT (Manitowoc/1,422) Before settlement, the region was a fur-trading post operated by Jacques Vieux in 1795, the first European settler. Daniel Smith was an early resident who built a sawmill in 1844. The town was founded three years later by Ira Clark and Alfred Smith as Mishicot. It was changed to Saxonburgh in 1853, but reverted to Mishicot in 1855. It is an Ottawa word for "hairy legs." Other interpretations were "turtle," and "covered by clouds." The town's economy was tied to agriculture, as it is today.

MOQUAH (Bayfield) The town's name was born from legend about a trapper who came to the region with his sled for pelts, but got lost. He met an Indian who was willing to help him, but told the trapper to leave his sled and he could come back for it later. When he returned, the sled's contents had been strewn about and much of his food was gone. When the Indian saw tracks in the snow, he pointed to them and said "moquah," an Algonquin word for "big bear."

MOSINEE (Maratahon/4,063) The Potawatomi and Menominee Indians farmed and hunted in this area before the white man arrived. When the region was opened for settlement in the 1830s, it was called Little Bull Falls. Because of the vast amount of timber in the region, Mosinee prospered. When a post office was established in 1857, postmaster Truman Keeler didn't like Little Bull Falls because he thought is was too vulgar for women. It was renamed for Algonquin Chief Mosinee, meaning "moose." Mosinee went on to become one of the biggest manufacturers of Kraft paper.

MUKWONAGO (Waukesha/6,868) This was the capital village of the Potawatomi Tribe. Sewall Andrews left Vermont to visit Wisconsin in 1835 in order to found a town. After the Treaty of Chicago was signed, the Indians still refused to leave. Andrews negotiated with them, and eventually the Indians left the region but came back periodically to trade. The name was derived from mequanego, meaning "place of the bears."

MUSKEGO (Waukesha/21,397) The town's first settler was a Yankee named Luther Parker in 1836, followed by others who went into agriculture. What product they had left over was sold to Milwaukee, the principal market for Muskego, and the town's economic backbone. The post office was established in 1848. Muskego is an Algonquin word interpreted as "swamp," "cranberry bog," "fishing place," or "sunfish."

NASHOTAH (Waukesha/1,266) This site was first occupied by the Reverends Adams and Breck who opened the Nashotah Theological Seminary in 1842, and is the oldest Episcopal seminary in the Middle West. It was established to serve the Indians and settlers, and also to train candidates for priesthood. The community itself was called Pine Lake Station and settled in the 1840s. Francis Schraudenbach purchased 40 acres in 1847 and built an inn that also served as a stagecoach stop. The name was changed about 1875 and renamed Nashotah, an Algonquin word which means "twin lakes."

NEENAH (Winnebago/2,657) Menominee, Winnebago and Fox Indians occupied this region when French missionaries and traders arrived. In 1835, the U.S. government built a sawmill, gristmill, and homes for the Indians in an attempt to educate them, but the Indians weren't interested. They left the region after they ceded their land to the Government in 1836. Harrison Reed purchased land and water rights in 1846. When the post office was established, Reed named it Neenah, a Winnebago word for "water," or "running water."

NESHKORO (Marquette/453) Neshkoro saw its first resident with the arrival of Eben Dakin in 1848. Because of the wealth of trees, he built a sawmill which brought others to settle here. Other prosperous industries were foundries, woolen mills and a distillery. William Clay opened a general mercantile in 1852, followed by the first hotel. Part of Neshkoro is Winnebago for "water," but the rest of the word is unknown.

OCONOMOWOC (Waukesha/7,451) Settlers were drawn to this region because of the Oconomowoc River's water power. Oconomowoc started in 1844 and was platted about 1849. It became an established community when the Milwaukee-Watertown Railroad was built. Settlers thought the word meant "the place of the beavers." Another authority believed it meant "the river of lakes." A French trader named Vieu said that the word was derived from con-n-mo-wauk, an Algonquin word defined as "place where the river falls," or "home of the beaver."

OCONTO (Oconto/4,708) The Menominee Indians called the site oak-a-toe, which means "river plentiful with fish," from where Oconto was derived. Father Allouez established the Mission of St. Francis Xavier at Oconto in 1669 to protect the Indians against European fur traders. John Stein came from Norway and started a business of building sailboats and setting nets, which began the commercial fishing industry for the town. Oconto's economy was later tied to the manufacture of plywood and the Bond Pickle Company, which became the largest pickle company in the world.

ODANAH (Ashland/254) Odanah was founded in the 1840s by Leonard and Harriet Wheeler, missionaries to the Ojibway Indians. Odanah is one of northern Wisconsin's most populous villages on the Bad River Indian Reservation, and is the seat of the Chippewa Tribal Government. This region was once heavily wooded, bringing in the lumber mills, but once the timber was depleted the whites left the barren land for the Indians. Near the village were the Kakagan Sloughs which provided the Chippewas with wild rice. Odanah is a Chippewa word for "town" or "village."

OSHKOSH (Winnebago/62,916) On his way to the upper Fox River in 1634, Frenchman Jean Nicolet was probably the first white man to see this region. In 1818, Augustin Grignon and James Porlier built a trading post near town. The settlement was originally named Athens. During a meeting to select a permanent name for the village, someone suggested Oshkosh, for a Menominee chief, meaning "brave." Other authorities believe it meant "nail (or claw)," or the thorny part of the foot of a beast.

PACKWAUKEE (Marquette/2,574) Settlers moved to the north side of Buffalo Lake, which became Packwaukee, a Winnebago expression for 'where the water is shallow" or "forest spring." The town was platted in 1853 by Ira Reed and Sam McCracken, who named it for a Winnebago chief. When the Wisconsin Improvement Company had the Fox River dredged, it opened the way for river traffic, and Packwaukee became a principal trading center.

PEWAUKEE (Waukesha/8,170) This was the hunting ground of the Menomonee and Potawatomi Indian tribes. In 1836, Deacon Asa Clark purchased a quarter section of land and established a sawmill, in addition to building a dam. George P. Peffer started a nursery and fruit farm, and went on to develop the Pewaukee Apple. When William Caldwall arrived in 1843, he established a general store. The Bolles family moved here the following year, and established the beginning of the lime and stone business in town. Pewaukee is Algonquin for "swampy," or "lake of shells."

POY SIPPI (Waushara/972) George Hawley came to Poy Sippi in 1856 and is considered the father of the town. He became its first postmaster, and later manufactured lumber wagons and sleighs. Local folklore says that the name Poy Sippi came about when a friendly Indian met one of the first exploring parties who asked the Indian the name of this site. The Algonquin Indian answered that sippi meant "river," and poy was from "poygan," designating the river flowing into Lake Poygan.

SHAWANO (Shawano/8,298) Shawano was located near the Menominee Indian Reservation. Jean Nicolet came from Canada to negotiate a peace treaty at Shawano between the Winnebago and Huron Tribes. Timber brought settlers to the area, and in 1843 Samuel Farnsworth and Charles Westcott established a sawmill. A military road went through Shawano in 1853 which served as a supply route for rivermen and lumbermen. When the timber was gone, the town turned to making paper and woodworking. The Ojibway Indians called the lake sha-wa-nah-pay-sa ("lake to the south"), from which Shawano was derived, and means "to the south."

SHEBOYGAN (Sheboygan/50,792) Sheboygan was once a Potawatomi Indian village called Shab-wa-wa-go-ning, which meant "rumbling waters," or "waters disappearing underground." German immigrants settled at Sheboygan fleeing religious persecution from their homelands. The town became a port of call for the schooners plying Lake Michigan. During the 1880's, phenomenal growth occurred in the area due to large-scale industry.

SHIOCTON (Outagamie/954) This territory was claimed by the French in 1618 which was home to the Outagamie Indians until they were driven away by the French. The Menominees then became the dominant tribe in the area. Numerous interpretations have been made for Shiocton. Some think it is a Chippewa word that means "floats upstream by force of wind," or "place of flowing water." Another authority believes it was the name of a Menominee Chief named Shioc. Other historians think it was derived from saiak, meaning "wild rice along the banks."

TAYCHEEDAH (Fond du Lac/3,666) Before establishment as a town, this site was home to Chief Sar-ro-chau of the Winnebago tribe. Francis McCarty founded the town in 1839, with great hopes to build an industrial city, since the Military Road that went to Green Bay and Prairie du Chien was a junction point here. Taycheedah became a gateway for people traveling from Green Bay to the open prairies. In 1868, the Sheboygan and Fond du Lac Railway laid its tracks. James Doty named the site, which was derived from tee-char-rah, a Winnebago word, meaning "camping place." The town went into decline as the city of Fond du Lac began to grow.

WABENO (Forest/1,264) Wabeno was opened for settlement after the Civil War when the U.S. government deeded this region to the State of Wisconsin. It was once used by the Chippewa Indians as their hunting ground. In 1896, the site was surveyed by the Chicago & Northwestern Railroad. Wabeno began its life as a logging town with the establishment of five lumber companies; by 1936, all of them had closed down because of overharvesting the timber. Wabeno is a Chippewa word for "wild swan," which were once prevalent in the region.

WAUKAU (Winnebago) This village was established in 1820. The first person to permanently settle in Waukau was Morton Parsons in 1846. When the Preemption Act was passed, it opened up the Menominee Indian land for settlement. The name may have originally been spelled Wacquau, and named for the son of the Waukau clan of Indians. Another theory was a Menominee word for "going around," or "heap crooked." Others believed it meant "winding" "zig-zag," and "often."

WAUKESHA (Waukesha/64,825) Known as Prairie Village, the first people through the area were the Cutler brothers in 1834. The town was known as "that abolition hole," because it was an important station in the Underground Railroad. Col. Richard Dunbar visited in 1868 and discovered the curative properties from one of the mineral springs. As word spread, tourists flocked to town and hotels were built to accommodate them. Eventually the resorts faded away. Waukesha is a Potawatomi word defined as "burnt prairie (or land)," or derived from wauk-tsha, for "fox."

WAUNAKEE (Dane/8,995) This village was settled after the Winnebago ceded their lands when the Rock Island Treaty was signed on September 15, 1832, after the Black Hawk War. Timber and agriculture (corn, grain and hay) were important to Waunakee's stability. Surveyors came through in 1869 so the Chicago and Northwestern Railroad could extend its line. The site was laid out in 1870, and the railroad made it one of its stations. Waunakee is an Ojibway word that means "good earth," or "peaceful place." In the Chippewa language, it means "he lies in peace."

WAUPACA (Waupaca/5,676) A group of men from Vermont settled at Waupaca and surveyed the townsite. In 1852, the post office was established and the town was officially named Waupaca for an old chief named Wa-Puka, which means "watching." Most early historians, however, believe the word comes from a Menominee word, waubeck-seba, defined as "pale or clear water." While other northern frontier towns were occupied with the timber industry, Waupaca became the center of Wisconsin's potato production.

WAUPUN (Fond du Lac/1,385) Seymour Wilcox arrived in the autumn of 1838 and selected this site for his home. John Fairbanks was to later write, "It was in the summer of 1844 that I, for the first time, set my eyes ... on Waupun ... what rapture and delight I gazed on the lovely scene...."[36] This was the region of the Winnebago Indians, who jealously guarded their Indian trail. In February of 1856, the Milwaukee and Horicon Railroad came to Waupun, enabling settlers to ship out their grain instead of hauling it to Milwaukee by wagons. The Wisconsin State Prison was established here in 1851. Waupun may be a Winnebago word for "early dawn," or "early light of day." The name was actually Waubun, but postal error caused it to be Waupun.

WAUSAU (Marathon/38,426) Originally called Big Bull Falls because the first white men thought the Wisconsin River sounded like the "gentle lowing of a bull." Settlement began when George Stevens claimed property in 1837 and built a sawmill a few years later because of the large stands of white pines. Wausau's name origin was explained in the Wausau Record of February 17, 1908: "In the early days the Chippewa Indians were very numerous ... they would remain in this vicinity several days, hold their pow wows, medicine dances, etc. When they were asked where they were going and how far, their reply was always with uplifted hands, 'Wittie Wausau' meaning a long distance, a long way off..."[37]

WAUWATOSA (Milwaukee/47,271) French territory until the British defeated them in 1760, this location drew settlers in the 1730s. Charles Hart built a sawmill and grist mill in 1835 along the Menomonee River and called it Hart's Mills. During 1838, U.S. Topographical engineers built the United States Road through town. When streetcar service was begun in 1892, it turned Wauwatosa from a little crossroads village to a suburban community. In 1842, the name was changed to Wauwatosa, from the Algonquin word, wau-wau-tae-sie, meaning "firefly," descriptive of the fireflies prevalent in the area.

WONEWOC (Juneau/871) About 1852, Delando Pratt purchased the site and laid out the town. The dense hardwood forest brought in scores of people to establish sawmills and flour mills. The post office was opened in 1856 (J. Clement, postmaster). Hops was a major industry until the market crashed in 1868, ruining many of the farmers. The Wonewoc Wagon Company revived the village when it was established in 1877, and Wonewoc became known as "The Wagon City." The name was thought to mean "they howl," from wonowag, in the Chippewa language. However, the Chippewa never lived in the region. The Ho-Chunk Indians were resident and their word, wo-woc, meant "you are naughty." The Indians may have been indulging in some type of humor when someone asked them what the area was called.

WYOMING

CHEYENNE (Laramie/53,011) Named for the Cheyenne Indians ("aliens" or "people of a foreign language,"), the town was known as the "Magic City of the Plains," because it grew so fast, a result of Union Pacific Railroads' arrival in 1867. Cheyenne later became the center for powerful cattlemen. Cheyenne was one of the towns nicknamed "hell on wheels" because of the hundreds of gamblers that followed the building of the railroads. These were railroad cars that sprang up as temporary tent camps and would move on as the tracks were extended.

CHUGWATER (Platte/244) This interesting name came about because of legend. An old Mandan chief's son was known as "The Dreamer," because he was lazy. He came up with the idea of stampeding the buffalo over the chalk cliffs, which would break away abruptly and the buffalo would fall down the cliff. Chugwater referred to the sound the buffalo made, "chug, chug" when their stomachs burst from impact. The first settlers were in the range cattle business. An important company was the Swan Land and Cattle Company that had much influence on the developing community.

MEETEETSE (Park/351) The earliest ranch in the area was established by Otto Franc in 1879 who brought thousands of head of cattle in from Texas. It was believed that Franc bankrolled the Cattlemen's Association during their conflict with the sheepmen. Settlers began arriving in the 1880s and the town became a supply center for the Montana and Wyoming ranches. The post office was established in 1883 (Margaret Wilson, postmaster). When the town of Arland began to decline (1896), most of the people moved their buildings to Meeteetse. It is Shoshone word that means "the meeting place," or "nearby place."

OSHOTO (Crook) Oshoto is situated at the headwaters of the Little Missouri River. While a group of residents were discussing a name for their town, a blizzard came up. Samuel E. Rathburn, a former Indian scout with General Custer, suggested Oshoto, which is Arapaho for "blizzard" or some type of bad weather. The post office was established in 1911. Close to the town was a bentonite processing plant, which was the first in the world.

SHOSHONI (Fremont/635) This region is occupied jointly by the Shoshone and Northern Arapaho Tribes. Shoshoni occupies part of the Wind River Reservation. In 1904, the Pioneer Townsite Company laid out the town and the Chicago & Northwestern Railroad platted Shoshoni. The Indians opened part of their land on the Wind River Reservation for homesteading in 1905. The town had a population of 2,000 people and more than 25 bars. Residents thought Shoshoni would be a crossroads town for five proposed railroads, but it never happened. Shoshoni means "abundance of grass," or "grass lodge people."

TEN SLEEP (Washakie/304) The Indians' method for measuring time gave Ten Sleep its name. They measured days (or sleeps) from place to place. This mountain town was a ten day's walk from the Crow Reservation in Montana and to the Shoshone Reservation. Ten Sleep had irrigation to the settlers' farms as early as 1885. It was first named Sacket's Fork, and later changed to Ten Sleep. The first hotel was built in 1900, and the Ten Sleep Sheep Company was organized in 1917. Just south of Ten Sleep occurred the Bates Battle, where the Arapahos were defeated by U.S. Army Troops.

Notes

1. Donna MacAlpine, Anvik Historical Society. Letter to author, July 13, 1999.

2. Daniel Nelson, City of Napakiak. Letter to author, July 8, 1999.

3. Douglas Preston. *Cities of Gold*. Simon & Schuster, 1992, p. 360.

4. Dave Shaul. "Tubac Name Origin," Internet: www.tubacaz.com/history.

5. Dan Garate, Chief of Interpretation, National Park Service. Email to author, October 5, 2000.

6. Alfred L. Kroeber. *California Place Names of Indian Origin*. University of California Press, 1916, p. 54.

7. Judy Barras. *Tehachapi: The Formative Years*. Reed Pub., 1973, p. 75.

8. Doug Kyle, Tehama County Historical Society. Letter to author, March 9, 1999.

9. Deborah Roy & Gloria Stuart. *Norwalk: Being an Historical Account of That Connecticut Town*, 1979, p. 6.

10. Marion County History, *Star-Banner*, 1997, p. 35.

11. Sister Alfreda Elsensohn. *Pioneer Days in Idaho County*, Vol. 1. Idaho Corp. of Benedictine Sisters, 1978, p. 396.

12. Douglas Jones. *The News Journal*, May 15, 1991, p. 1.

13. "Howard County History," Kokomo-Howard County Library vertical files.

14. *History of Jones County*. Western Historical Co., 1879, p. 293.

15. John Rydjord. *Indian Place Names*, Univ. Oklahoma Press, 1968, pp. 150–157.

16. Tangipahoa Parrish Centennial, 1969.

17. Harriet Chadbourne. *Maine Place Names and the Peopling of Its Towns*. 1955, p. 39.

18. Robert E.T. Pogue. *Old Maryland Landmarks*, Bushwood, MD, 1972, p. 42.

19. Dot Clark. "Cecil's Lost Town," *Cecil Whig*, Feb. 3, 1971.

20. R.A. Lovell, Jr. *Sandwich: A Cape Cod Town*. Sandwich Archives and Hist. Center, 1984, p. 109.

21. Charles E. Banks, M.D. *The History of Martha's Vineyard*, Vol. I. Dukes County Hist. Soc., 1966, p. 347.

22. Russell H. Gardner. Letter to author, January 15, 1999.

23. Dave Hagen. *Kalamazoo Gazette* Supplement. July 16, 1978.

24. "How Did Newago Get Its Name?" Newaygo Carnegie Library vertical files.

25. *The Story of Wabasso*, 1899–1934, p. 8.

26. Samuel McKinney III. *St. Teresa of Avila Catholic Church, 1868–1993: A History*, p. 2.

27. *Tekamah Centennial, 1854–1954*, p. 14.

28. Herbert C. Kraft. *The Lenape or Delaware Indians*, p. 57. n.d.

29. Donald W. Becker. *Indian Place-*

Names in New Jersey. Phillips-Campbell Pub., 1964, p. 37.

30. Austin A. Yates. *Schenectady County, New York: Its History to the Close of the Nineteenth Century*. New York History Co., 1902, p. 412.

31. R.G. Robertson. *Rotting Face: Smallpox and the American Indian*. Caxton Press, 2001, p. 90.

32. Allen Raymond, Ochelata. Letter to author, Aug. 20, 1999.

33. Darrell Rice. "The Origin of Watonga's Name." Blaine County vertical files.

34. George P. Donehoo. *History of the Indian Place Names of Pennsylvania*. Telegraph Press, 1928, p. 45.

35. Federal Writer's Project, *Washington: The Evergreen State*. Binfords & Mort, 1941, p. 370.

36. *A History of Waupun: 1839 to 1939*. Waupun Centennial Celebration, 1939, p. 5.

37. "Origin of Wausau," *Wausau Record*, Feb. 17, 1908.

Bibliography

Alabama

"Autaugaville, Alabama: The Story of a Southern Town." Autaugaville-Prattville Public Library vertical files.

Brewer, Rev. George E. "History of Coosa County, Alabama." *Alabama Historical Quarterly*. Vol. 4, Nos. 1 & 2. Spring/Summer, 1942.

"City of Attalla." City of Attalla. n.d.

Enslen, John. "City's Name Didn't Come From Indians." *Journal-Advertiser*. Sept. 2, 1964: 12f.

_____. "Settlers Hesitated to Make Homesteads Because of Indians." *Alabama Journal-Montgomery Advertiser*. Sept. 2, 1964.

Federal Writers' Project. *Alabama: A Guide to the Deep South*. New York: Richard R. Smith, Pub., 1941.

Foscue, Virginia O. *Place Names in Alabama*. Tuscaloosa: University of Alabama Press, 1989.

"History of Eufaula." Eufaula/Barbour County Chamber of Commerce, n.d.

Jemison, Grace. *Historic Tales of Talledega*. Montgomery: Paragon Press, 1959.

"Koasati/Coosada." Autauga-Prattville Public Library vertical files.

McMillan, James B. (ed.). *Dictionary of Place Names in Talladega County, Alabama*. Tuscaloosa: James B. McMillan, 1985.

Mizzell, Philip G. *A History of Sylacauga*. Sylacauga: First National Bank, 1986.

Nunn, Alexander (ed.). *Lee County and Her Forebears*. Opelika Commissioners, 1983.

Pierce, Donna G. "It All Started With a Giant of a Man." *Alabama West*. 1994: 29.

"Pilot Who Flew Original Tuskegee Airmen Missions Dead of Cancer." *Mail Tribune*. Aug. 16, 2001: 2b.

Read, William A. *Indian Place-Names in Alabama*. Tuscaloosa: University of Alabama Press, 1984.

"Town of Loachapoka." Loachapoka Historian's (Dr. Elizabeth Schafer) vertical files.

"Tuskegee, Alabama: Pride of the Swift Growing South." Tuskegee Municipal Complex, 1980.

Walker, George P., III. "History of Attalla." Gadsden Public Library vertical files.

Alaska

"Angoon: Its History, Population and Economy." Bureau of Indian Affairs Village Study. June, 1975.

Becker, Ethel A. *A Treasury of Alaskana*. Seattle: Superior Pub., 1969.

Brown, Dale. *Wild Alaska*. New York: Time, Inc., 5th Printing, 1976.

Cantwell, Sister Margaret, S. S. A., and Sister Mary George Edmond, S. S. A. *North to Share: The Sisters of St. Ann in Alaska and the Yukon Territory*. Victoria, British Columbia: Sisters of Saint Ann, 1992.

Chandonnet, Ann. *On the Trail of Eklutna*. Anchorage: User-Friendly Press, 1985.

Cochrane, Marjorie. *Between Two Rivers: The Growth of Chugiak-Eagle River*. Alaska State Library in conjunction with Chugiak-Eagle River Chamber of Commerce, 1983.

Dmytryshyn, Basil, and E. A. P. Crownhart-Vaughn (transl.). *Civil and Savage Encounters: The Worldly Travel Letters of an Imperial Russian Navy Officer, 1860–1861*. Portland: Western Imprints, Press of the Oregon Historical Society, 1983.

_____, and E. A. P. Crownhart-Vaughn (transl.). *Colonial Russian America: Kyrill T. Khlebnikov's Reports, 1817–1832*. Portland: Oregon Historical Society, 1976.

Dodd, Dr. John M. "Salmon - Alaska's Real Gold." *Alaska Life*. Vol. IX, No. 4. April, 1946: 42–43.

Doward, Jan S. *They Came to Wrong Way Home*. Mountain View, California: Pacific Press, 1961.

"Egegik, Alaska." Bureau of Indian Affairs Village Study. June 1966.

Ekstrom, Robert J. "Ugashik — Our History." *Riverbank Chatter*. Vol. 1, Issue 1. Spring 1997.

Eppenbach, Sarah. *Alaska's Southeast*. Seattle: Pacific Search Press, 1983.

Federal Writers' Project. *Alaska: Last American Frontier*. New York: Macmillan Co., 1943.

"Hoonah History." Hoonah High School. Alaska History Class, 1973.

Hrdlika, Ales. *Alaska Diary: 1926–1931*. Lancaster, Pennsylvania: Jaques Cattell Press, 1943.

Ivanoff, Doris. Unalakleet. Letter to author, April 1999.

John, Betty. *Libby: The Alaskan Diaries & Letters of Libby Beaman, 1879–1880*. Boston: Houghton Mifflin, 1989.

Karamanski, Theodore J. *Fur Trade and Exploration: Opening the Far Northwest, 1821–1852*. Norman: University of Oklahoma Press, 1983.

Krieger, Herbert W. *Indian Villages of Southeast Alaska* (facsimile). Seattle: Shorey Pub., 1966.

"Lake Clark-Iliamna County." *Alaska Geographic Quarterly*. Vol. 8, No. 3. 1981: 136, 142.

MacAlpine, Donna. "A Brief History of the Anvik Mission." *Anvik Historical Society*. June 1987.

_____. Letter to author, July 13, 1999.

"Manokotak, Alaska." Bureau of Indian Affairs Village Study. June 1966.

Molvar, Erik. *Scenic Driving: Alaska and the Yukon*. Helena, Montana: Falcon Press, 1996.

"Naknek and South Naknek." Bureau of Indian Affairs Village Study. June 1966.

"Native Village of Tyonek: A Review of Our Athabascan Heritage." Tyonek: E. L. Bartlett High School, 1983.

Nelson, Daniel. Napakiak. Letter to author, July 1999.

Oswalt, Wendell. *Napaskiak: An Alaskan Eskimo Community*. Tucson: University of Arizona Press, 1963.

Pederson, Elsa, and Walt Pedersen (eds.). *A Larger History of the Kenai Peninsula*. Chicago: Adams Press, 1963.

Phillips, James W. *Alaska-Yukon Place Names*. Seattle: University of Washington Press, 1973.

Simmerman, Nancy L. *Wild Alaska*. Seattle: The Mountaineers, 1999.

Stein, Gary C. "Uprooted: Native Casualities of the Aleutian Campaign of World War II." Alaska State Library archives.

Thompson, Paul E. "Alaska Villages." Unpublished manuscript No. 4, 1937. Alaska State Library archives.

"Togiak, Alaska." Bureau of Indian Affairs Village Study. June 1966.

"Traditional Council Report." *Quinhagak Village Tribal Council*, 1990.

"Ugashik, Alaska." Bureau of Indian Affairs Village Study. June 1966.

Vick, Ann. *The Cama-i Book*. Garden City, New York: Anchor Books, 1983.

Wade, Patricia. Chicaloon Village Traditional

Council. Email to author, December 1998.

Wayburn, Peggy. *Adventuring in Alaska*. San Francisco: Sierra Club Books, 1994.

Wharton, David. *They Don't Speak Russian in Sitka: A New Look at the History of Southern Alaska*. Menlo Park, California: Markgrat Pub., 1991.

Wilson, William H. *Railroad in the Clouds: The Alaska Railroad in the Age of Steam. 1914–1945*. Boulder, Colorado: Pruett Pub., 1977.

Winslow, Kathryn. *Alaska Bound*. New York: Dodd, Mead & Co., 1960.

Wright, Sam. *Koviashuvik: A Time and Place of Joy*. San Francisco: Sierra Club Books, 1988.

Arizona

Barnes, Will C. *Arizona Place Names*. Introduction by Bernard L. Fontana. Tucson: University of Arizona Press, 1988.

Bawaya, Michael. "Ancient Settlement Found in Arizona." *American Archaeology*. Summer 2002: 9.

Casey, Robert L. *Journey to the High Southwest*. Seattle: Pacific Search Press, 1983.

"Community Profile: Apache Junction." Arizona Department of Commerce, n.d.

Corley, Arthur. *Old Post: Fort Huachuca, Arizona*. Fort Huachuca Historical Museum, 1976.

Dary, David. *Seeking Pleasures in the Old West*. New York: Alfred A. Knopf, 1991.

Dillon, Richard. *Arizona's Amazing Towns*. Tempe: Four Peaks Press, 1992.

Dobyns, Henry F. "Tubac: Where Some Enemies Rotted." *Arizona Quarterly*. Vol. 19, No. 3. Autumn 1963: 229.

Dutton, Bertha P. *The Pueblos*. Englewood Cliffs, New Jersey: Prentice-Hall, 1976.

Father Max, San Solano Mission, Topawa. Letter to author, January 15, 2001.

Federal Writers' Project. *Arizona: A State Guide*. New York: Hastings House, 1940.

Ferguson, William M., and Arthur H. Rohn. *Anasazi Ruins of the Southwest in Color*. Albuquerque: University of New Mexico Press, 1987.

Fireman, Bert M. *Arizona: Historic Land*. New York: Alfred A. Knopf, 1982.

Garate, Don, Chief of Interpretation, Tumacacori Historical Park. Email to author, October 5, 2000.

Hegemann, Elizabeth C. *Navajo Trading Days*. Albuquerque: University of New Mexico Press, 1963.

Hendricks, Jennifer, College of Education, Arizona State University (Cibeque). Email to author, June 14, 2001.

Hillerman, Tony. "A Museum Etched in Stone." *National Geographic Traveler*. Vol. X, No. 3. May/June 1993: 69.

Hirst, Stephen, and Terry Eiler. *Life in a Narrow Place*. New York: David McKay Co., 1976.

Howard, Enid C. "An Historic Landmark— The Cochise Hotel." *The Cochise Quarterly*. Vol. 14, No. 3. Fall 1984: 19.

Kaplan, Robert D. *An Empire Wilderness: Travels Into America's Future*. New York: Random House, 1998.

Kosik, Fran. *Native Roads*. Flagstaff: Creative Solutions Pub., 1996.

Lichtenstein, Grace. "Downtown Digs." *Smithsonian*. May 2002: 24.

Linford, Laurance D. *Navajo Places: History, Legend, Landscape*. Salt Lake City: University of Utah Press, 2000.

Mays, Buddy. *Indian Villages of the Southwest: A Practical Guide to the Pueblo Indian Villages of New Mexico and Arizona*. San Francisco: Chronicle Books, 1985.

Newton, Charles H. *Place Names in Arizona*. Phoenix: Primer Pub., 1954.

Patera, Alan H., and John S. Gallagher. *Arizona Post Offices*. Lake Grove, Oregon: The Depot, 1988.

Preston, Douglas. *Cities of Gold*. New York: Simon & Schuster, 1992.

Richardson, Cecil C. "The Navajo Way." *Arizona Highways*. April 1995: 2–4.

Rohder, Father Regis. *Padre to the Papagos: Father Bonaventura Oblasser*. Tucson: Oblasser Library, San Xavier Mission, 1982.

Rolak, Bruno J. "History of Fort Huachuca, 1877–1890." *The Smoke Signal*. Spring 1974: 206.

Rose, Dan. *The Ancient Mines of Ajo*. Tucson: Mission Pub., 1936.

Rushlo, Michelle. "Neither Rain, Sleet nor Balky Mule: Supai Gets Its Mail the Old-Fashioned Way." *Mail Tribune*. July 30, 2000: 2a.

"Sacaton." Gila River Indian Reservation Public Relations vertical files.

Shaul, David. "Tubac Name Origin." www.tubacz.com/history.

Shearer, Frederick. *The Pacific Tourist: Illustrated Trans-Continental Guide of Travel from the Atlantic to the Pacific Ocean*. New York: Adams & Bishop, 1884.

Sheridan, Thomas E. *Arizona: A History*. Tucson: University of Arizona Press, 1995.

Smith, Cornelius C., Jr. *Fort Huachuca: The Story of a Frontier Post*. Washington D.C.: Dept. of the Army, 1981.

Theobald, John, and Lillian Theobald. *Arizona Territory Post Offices & Postmasters*. Phoenix: Arizona Historical Foundation, 1961.

Trimble, Marshall. *Roadside History of Arizona*. Missoula, Montana: Mountain Press, 1986.

Vannoy, Vernon. "Buried Treasure at Arivaca." *Treasure World*. June 1977: 40.

Varney, Philip. *Arizona's Best Ghost Towns*. Flagstaff: Northland Press. 1980.

Weir, Bill. *Arizona Traveler's Handbook*. Chico, California: Moon Pub., 1992.

Arkansas

Allsopp, Fred W. "Solgohachia." *The Gorlier Society*. Vol. 1, 1931: 126.

Biographical and Historical Memoirs of Western Arkansas. Chicago: Goodspeed Pub., 1890.

Deane, Ernie. *Arkansas Place Names*. Branson, Missouri: Ozarks Mountaineer, 1986.

Federal Writers' Project. *Arkansas: A Guide to the State*. New York: Hastings House, 1941.

Snowden, Deanna (comp.). *Mississippi County, Arkansas: Appreciating the Past, Anticipating the Future*. Blytheville: August House, 1986.

Thompson, Glynda, Osceola, Mississippi County Historical & Geneological Society. Letter to author, February 4, 2000.

California

As We Were Told. Coarsegold: Coarsegold Historical Society, 1990.

"Azusa History." Azusa City Library vertical files.

Bahti, Tom. *Southwest Indian Tribes*. Flagstaff: KC Pub., 1973.

Barras, Judy. *Long Road to Tehachapi*. Tehachapi Heritage League, 1976.

Bergman, Coral R. Aguanga. Letter to author, July 19, 1999.

Brigandi, Phil. *Temecula, the Crossroads of History*. Encinitas: Heritage Media, 1998.

Clough, Charles W. *Madera: The Rich, Colorful and Exciting Historical Heritage of that Area Now Known as Madera County, California*. Madera: Madera County Historical Society, 1968.

Coburn, Jesse L. *Letters of Gold: California Postal History Through 1869*. New York: U.S. Philatelic Classics Society, 1984.

Delay, Peer J. *History of Yuba and Sutter Counties, California with Biographical Sketches, etc*. Los Angeles: Historic Record Co., 1924.

Detzer, Jordan E. *Exploring Behind San Diego: Bibles, Bullets, & Bullion on the Border*. San Diego: Jordan E. Detzer, 1980.

Doud, Jess. "California Historic Landmarks of Napa County." *Napa County Historical Society*. March 1988.

Draper, Prue. "The Cotati Scene in the Early 1900s." *Rohnert-Park-Cotati Clarion*. July 13, 1983.

Encyclopedia of California. New York: Somerset Pub., 2nd Edition, 1944.

Farquhar, Francis. *History of the Sierra Nevada*. Berkeley: University of California, 1966.

Federal Writers' Project. *California: A Guide to the Golden State*. New York: Hastings House. 4th Printing, 1945.

Fradkin, Phillip. *Seven States of California*. Berkeley: University of California, 1977.

Gordon, Marjorie. *Changes in Harmony: An Illustrated History of Yuba & Sutter Counties*. Northridge: Windsor Pub., 1988.

Greenland, Powell. *Port Hueneme: A History*. Ventura: Ventura County Maritime Museum, 1994.

Gudde, Erwin G. *1000 California Place Names*. Berkeley: University of California Press, 1959.

Hall-Patton, Mark P. *Memories of the Land: Placenames of San Luis Obispo County*. San Luis Obispo: EZ Nature Books, 1994.

Hanna, Phil T. *The Dictionary of California Land Names*. Los Angeles: Automobile Club of Southern California, 1946.

Hassan, Louhelen E. *Paguay*. Poway: Poway Historical & Memorial Society, 1993.

Heig, Adair. *History of Petaluma: A California River Town*. Petaluma: Scottwall Associates, 1982.

Hisken, Clara H. *Tehama: Little City of the Big Trees*. New York: Exposition Press, 1948.

Historical Guide to the Back Country. Campo: Mountain Empire Historical Society, 1990.

"History of Lompoc." Lompoc Public Library vertical files.

History of Placer County, California, with Illustrations & Biographical Sketches of Its Prominent Men & Places. Oakland: Thompson & West, 1882.

"History of Simi Valley." Simi Valley Unified School District & Simi Valley Historical Society vertical files.

History of Siskiyou County, California. Oakland: D. J. Stewart & Co., 1881.

"History of the Ojai Valley." www.weinman.com/don/html/ojai_history.

Hoover, Mildred Brooke, Hero E. Rensch, and Ethel G. Rensch. *Historic Spots in California*. Stanford: Stanford University Press. 3rd Edition, 1990.

Hudson, Tom. *A Thousand Years in Temecula*. Temecula Chamber of Commerce, 1981.

Hughe, Ralph. "Town of Requa Constructed on Site of Indian Village on Klamath River." Del Norte County Public Library vertical files.

Kroeber, Alfred L. *California Place Names of Indian Origin*. Berkeley: University of California Press, 1916.

Kuhn, Mike. "What Does Simi Mean?" Simi Valley Public Library vertical files.

Kyle, Doug, Tehama County Historical Society. Letter to author, March 1999.

Larkey, Joann, and Shipley Walters. *Yolo County: Land of Changing Patterns*. Northridge: Windsor Pub., 1987.

Lawson, Faerie R. *A History of Lake Riverside Estates*. Aguanga: Lake Riverside Mountain Ears, 1995.

Lucas, Pete E. "County of Yolo." Yolo County Archives/Records Center vertical files.

Madera County: 1883–1993. Madera: Madera Newspapers, Inc., 1993.

McKenzie, Bob. "Early Research Toward Finding Roots of Napa." *The Napa Valley Register*. Napa Public Library vertical files.

Meschery, Joanne. *Truckee: An Illustrated History of the Town and Its Surroundings*. Truckee: Rocking Stone Press, 1978.

Morrison, Annie L., and John H. Haydon. *History of San Luis Obispo County and Environs*. Los Angeles: Historic Record Co., 1917.

Nielsen, Valentino. "Geographical Features of Tehama County." *Wagon Wheels*. Colusa County Historical Society. Feb. 1956: 5.

"On the History of Jacumba." *San Diego Herald*. June 10, 1851.

Ormsby, Waterman L. *The Butterfield Overland Mail*. San Marino: Huntington Public Library, 1991.

Orr, Elizabeth L., and William N. Orr. *Rivers of the West: A Guide to the Geology and History*. Eugene, Oregon: Eagle Web Press, 1985.

Palmer, L. L. *History of Mendocino County, California*. San Francisco: Alley, Bowen & Co., 1880.

Parks, Annette W. *g^hawála li, "Water Coming Down Place": A History of Gualala, Mendicino County, California*. Ukiah: Freshcut Press, 1980.

Pittman, Ruth. *Roadside History of California*. Missoula, Montana: Mountain Press, 1995.

Poway: A Pictorial History. Poway Historical Society, 1995.

Prusinskas, Kay. "Homesteading and the First American Settlers." *Poway Progress*. Vol. V, No. 1. July-Oct., 1998.

Reed, Anna M. "Cotati Past and Present." *The Northern Crown*. Vol. V, No. 1. Nov. 1911.

Rogers, Justus H. *Colusa County: Its History Traced from a State of Nature Through the Early Period of Settlement and Development to the Present Day*. Orland: Justus H. Rogers, 1891.

Sanchez, Nellie Van De Grift. *Spanish and Indian Place Names of California*. San Francisco: A. M. Robertson, 1930.

Sell, William Martin, Jr. "Autobiography and Reminiscences Related by Mr. Sell on a Tape Recording." *The Madera County Historian*. Vol. VII, No. 3. July 1967: 1–6.

Settle, Glen, and Kathy Hansen. *Mojave—A Rich History of Rails, Mines and Flight*. Bakersfield: Kern-Antelope Historical Society, 1996.

Sowaal, Marguerite. "Tecopa and Tecopa Hot Springs." Tecopa Public Library vertical files.

Tehama County Memories. Tehama: Tehama County Genealogical and Historical Society, 1984.

"Temecula: History of the Temecula Valley." Temecula Public Library vertical files.

"Tiny Cotati Has Expansive History." *Rohnert Park-Cotati Clarion*. February 27, 1991: 5a.

Washburn, Ian. "Early Days in Cotati Area, 1844–1900." *Rohnert Park-Cotati Clarion*. July 13, 1983: 4a.

White, Katherine (comp.). *A Yankee Trader in the Gold Rush: The Letters of Franklin A. Buck*. Boston: Houghton Mifflin, 1930.

Willits, O. W. *The Story of Oak Glen and the Yucaipa Valley*. O.W. Willits, 1971.

"Yucaipa Valley History." *The Sun*. March 15, 1997.

Yeadon, David. *Exploring Small Towns: Southern California*. Los Angeles: Ward Ritchie Press, 1973.

Colorado

Arps, Louisa W., and Elinor E. Kingery. *High Country Names*. Boulder: Johnson Books, 1994.

Bauer, William H., James L. Ozment, and John H. Willard. *Colorado Postal History: The Post Offices*. Crete, Nebraska: J-B Pub., 1971.

Benson, Maxine. *1001 Colorado Place Names*. Lawrence: University Press of Kansas, 1994.

Black, Robert C., III. *Island in the Rockies: The History of Grand County, Colorado, to 1930*. Boulder: Pruett Pub., 1969.

Bright, William. *Colorado Place Names*. Boulder: Johnson Books, 1993.

"Cheyenne Wells." Colorado State University Cooperative Extension Library vertical files.

Collins, Judith K., Deputy Town Clerk, Saguache. Letter to author, October 8, 1996.

Corbett, Ethel R. *Western Pioneer Days*. Denver: Ethel R. Corbett, 1974.

Cunningham, Sharon A. *Manitou: Saratoga of the West*. Colorado Springs: Gowdy-Printcraft Press, 1980.

Eberhart, Perry. *Ghosts of the Colorado Plains*. Athens: Ohio University Press, 1986.

Federal Writers' Project. *Colorado: A Guide to the Highest State*. New York: Hastings House. 4th Printing, 1946.

_____. *Ghost Towns of Colorado*. New York: Hastings House, 1947.

Flanders, Lea. "Dodds Among Original Settlers in Niwot." *Longmont Daily Times Call*. March 6–7, 1982: 14.

Greever, William S. *Bonanza West: The Story of the Western Mining Rushes, 1848–1900*. Norman: University of Oklahoma Press, 1963.

"Hornbaker Has Fond Memories of Old Niwot." *The Recorder*. Nov. 21, 1985: 1.

Keck, E. Frances. *Conquistadors to the 21st Century: A History of Otero and Crowley Counties, Colorado*. La Junta: Otero Press, 1999.

Manning, Barbralu C. "Niwot Struggles for the Right Flavor." *The Sunday Camera's Focus*. June 19, 1983.

Matthews, Carl F. *Early Days Around the Divide.* St. Louis: Sign Book Co., 1969.

McTighe, James. *Roadside History of Colorado.* Boulder: Johnson Books, 1989.

Miller, Jean, and Jim Wier (eds.). "Ranch Creek and Its Tributaries from the Divide." *Grand County Historical Association Journal.* Vol. VIII, No. 1. Nov. 1988: 9–11.

"Niwot Named After Indian Chief." *The Sunday Camera's Focus.* Aug. 1, 1964.

"Niwot. Colorado." *Niwot Business Association.* n.d.

Ormes, Robert. *Tracking Ghost Railroads in Colorado.* Colorado Springs: Century One Press. 2nd Printing, 1975.

Pelton, A. R. *The San Luis Valley with Illustrations.* Denver: Carson, Hurst & Harper Pub., 1891.

Peterson, Frank K. *Frazer Valley Memoirs.* Hot Sulphur Springs: Frank K. Peterson, 1999.

"Saguache (Sa-Watch)." Saguache County Museum vertical files.

Shaffer, Ray. *A Guide to Places on the Colorado Prairie: 1540–1975.* Boulder: Pruett Pub., 1978.

Stark, P. Fulton. "Niwot's History Full of Color and Myths." *The Recorder.* June 20, 1985:1.

Ubbelohde, Carl, Maxine Benson, and Duane A. Smith. *A Colorado History.* Boulder: Pruett Pub., 1965.

Ute Mountain Ute Tribe. *Ute Mountain Utes: A History Text.* Salt Lake City: University of Utah Printing, 1985.

Vandenbusche, Duane. *The Gunnison Country.* Gunnison: B & B Printers. 4th Printing, 1992.

Connecticut

"A Brief History of Mystic." Mystic Celebration booklet, 1976.

Bayles, Richard M. *History of Windham County, Connecticut.* New York: W. W. Preston & Co., 1889.

Beardsley, Thomas R. *Willimantic Industry and Community: The Rise and Decline of a Connecticut Textile City.* Willimantic: Windham Textile & Historical Museum, 1993.

Bedine, Silvio A. *Ridgefield in Review.* Ridgefield 250th Anniversary Committee, 1958.

Caffrey, Bartlett. "Attawaugan Reminiscences." *Windham County Transcript.* March 18, 1943.

"Charles J. Norris Gives Account of Old Wequetequock Chapel and Opening of Its Cornerstone." *Mirror.* Dec. 2, 1938.

Chendali, Olive Tubbs. *East Lyme: Our Town and How It Grew.* Mystic: Mystic Pub., 1989.

Crandall, Katharine B. *The Fine Old Town of Stonington: A Historical Tribute to the Founders and Their Descendants.* Watch Hill, Rhode Island: The Book & Tackle Shop, 1962.

Crofut, Florence S. *Guide to the History and the Historic Sites of Connecticut.* New Haven: Yale University Press, 1937.

Danenberg, Elsie N. *The Romance of Norwalk.* New York: The States History Company, 1929.

Federal Writers' Project. *Connecticut: A Guide to Its Roads, Lore, and People.* Boston: Houghton Mifflin, 1938.

Frank, Judith. "The Mianus River." *Link Magazine.* Mid-Winter, 1962: 12.

Hughes, Arthur H., and Morse S. Allen. *Connecticut Place Names.* Hartford: Connecticut Historical Society, 1976.

Hughes, Scran. *History of East Haven.* New Haven: Tuttle, Morehouse & Taylor Press, 1908.

"Indian Tribes Named This River Area, 'Squag'." *Naugatuck Daily News.* June 17, 1944.

Kimball, Carol. *The Poquonnock Bridge Story.* Groton: Groton Public Library, 1984.

Mosey, Rick. "Steeped in History, Taconic Remains Quiet County Haven;" "Taconic in the Town of Salisbury, The Lure of the Litchfield Hills." Misc. material from Norman Sills, Volunteer Town Historian. n.d.

"Naugatuck." Howard Whittemore Memorial Library vertical files.

Nipmuc Place Names of New England. Historical Series No. 3. 1st Edition. Thompson:

Nipmuc Indian Association of Connecticut, 1995.

Noank: From the Papers of Clazude M. Chester. Essex: Pequot Press, 1970.

"Plymouth Connecticut: 1776–1976." Terryville Public Library vertical files.

Ray, Deborah W., and Gloria P. Stewart. *Norwalk: Being an Historical Account of That Connecticut Town*. Canaan, New Hampshire: Phoenix Pub., 1979.

Roads Lead Back to Glory: The History of Sterling, CT. Sterling Historical Society, 1982.

Rockey, J. L. *History of New Haven County, Connecticut*. New York: W. W. Preston & Co., 1892.

Rockwell, George L. *The History of Ridgefield*. Harrison, New York: Harbor Hill Books, 1979.

Seder, Eugene. "Mamauguin." *The New Haven Register*. Sept. 19, 1971.

"So Where Did the Moose in Moosup Come From?" Aldrich Public Library vertical files.

Teller, Daniel W. *The History of Ridgefield, Conn*. Danbury: T. Donovan, 1878.

Trumbull, J. Hammond. *Indian Names of Places Etc. and on the Borders of Connecticut*. Hartford: Press of the Case, Lockwood & Brainard Co., 1881.

U. S. Rubber Co. "Varied Opinions on the Meaning of Naugatuck." *Naugatuck Daily News*. June 17, 1944.

Zaravella, Mario. *Windsor 350: 1633–1983*. Windsor: Windsor Historical Survey, 1981.

Delaware

Dunlap, A. R., and C. A. Weslager. *Indian Place-Names in Delaware*. Wilmington: Archaeological Society of Delaware, 1950.

Federal Writers' Project. *Delaware: A Guide to the First State*. New York: Viking Press, 1938.

Hoffecker, Carol E. *Delaware: A Bicentennial History*. New York: Norton Pub., 1977.

Miller, Beth. "Discovering Delaware: Hockessin." *The News Journal*. May 21, 2001. Online edition. www.delawareonline.com/newsjournal/local/2001/05/21hockessin.

Neuenschwander, John A. *The Middle Colonies and the Coming of the American Revolution*. Port Washington, New York: Kennikat Press, 1977.

Florida

Bowman, Lila, Aripeka Public Library. Email to author, March 29, 1999.

Bush, Edna. Alachua. Letter to author, March 3, 2002.

Chapel, George L. "A Brief History of the Apalachicola Area." *Apalachicola Area Historical Society*. n.d.

Chase, Frank. "Yalaha Named for Mule, a Seminole Term." *The Daily Commercial*. April 13, 1991: A2.

"Early History of Wewahitchka." www.wewahitchka.com/wewa/history.

Ellis, Mary L., and William W. Rogers. *Tallahassee, Leon County: A History and Bibliography*. Tallahassee: Historical Tallahassee Preservation Board, 1986.

Federal Writers' Project. *Florida: A Guide to the Southernmost State*. New York: Oxford University Press, 1939.

Fish, Steven. "The Casino Was Center of Dance, Sport & Fun!" *The Compass*. May 20, 1981: 23.

Gregware, Bill, and Carol Gregware. *Guide to Lake Okeechobee Area*. Sarasota: Pineapple Press, 1997.

Hendricks, Norma. "Monument Touches History of Yalaha." *Leesburg Commercial*. Jan. 11, 1989: A3.

History of Lake County, Florida. Tavares: Lake County Historical Society, 2002.

"History of Weeki Wachee." *Hernando Today*. March 28, 1997: 9.

"Hypoluxo History." www.hypoluxo.org/about/history.

Jones, John P. "Gem City of the St. Johns." *Guide to North Florida Living*. Jan./Feb. 1983: 10–11.

"Letters from Our Readers: Interesting Article on Palataka and Palatkans of the Long Ago." *Palatka Times-Herald*. Jan. 20, 1933.

Lewis, Doris M. "Immokalee: Formerly Gopher Ridge." Collier County Public Library vertical files.

"Marion County History." *Star-Banner Supplement* [Ocala]. 1997.

Morris, Allen. *Florida Place Names.* Sarasota: Pineapple Press, 1995.

Robinson, Ernest L. *History of Hillsborough County, Florida.* St. Augustine: The Record Company, 1928.

Shofner, Jerrell H. *History of Brevard County.* Melbourne: Brevard County Historical Society, 1995.

Smith, Ryan, and Richard Staehler. "A History of Yalaha's Past and A Look Into Its Future." Tavares High School Final Project Report. May 24, 2002.

Stanaback, Richard J. *A History of Hernando County: 1840–1976.* Brooksville: Action '76 Steering Committee, 1976.

"Steinhatchee: Brimming with History, Brimming with Fish." *Progress '89.* Feb. 24, 1989: 19.

Stone, Maria. *The End of the Oxcart Trail.* Naples: Stone Enterprises, 1989.

Valentine, Doris. *Looking Back, Sumter County: A Photographic Essay.* Sumterville: Sumter County Historical Society, 1981.

"Vignettes of Palatka and Putnam County History Taken From the Newspapers." Palatka Public Library vertical files.

Watkins, Caroline. *The Story of Historic Micanopy.* Micanopy Historical Society, 1991.

Welch, Michael W. Ocoee. Email to author, 1998.

Westerlin, Tom. "Aripeka: A Small Florida Fishing Village Where Change is Not Welcome." *Ford Times.* Nov. 1976: 5–7.

Will, Lawrence E. *Cracker History of Okeechobee.* Palm Beach: Glades Historical Society, 1977.

Georgia

"Attapulgus." City of Attapulgus. n.d.

Brinkley, Hal E. *How Georgia Got Her Name.* Lakemont: CSA Printing, 1967.

"Chattahoochee County History." Chattahoochee County Public Library vertical files.

"Ellijay in the 1800s." *Times-Courier.* Dec. 3, 1982: 23b.

Federal Writers' Project. *Georgia: A Guide to Its Towns and Countryside.*" Atlanta: Tupper & Love, 1954.

Flanigan, James C. *History of Gwinnett County, Georgia: 1818–1943.* Vol. I. Lawrenceville: Gwinnett Historical Society, 1943.

Garrett, Franklin M. *Atlanta and Environs: A Chronicle of Its People and Events.* New York: Lewis Historical Pub. Co., 1954.

Godley, Margaret. *Historic Tybee Island.* Savannah Beach Chamber of Commerce, 1958.

"History of Willacoochee." City of Willacoochee, 2001.

Kirby, Bill. *Dynamic Gwinnett: Legacy, Life and Vision.* Atlanta: Longstreet Press, 1993.

Krakow, Kenneth K. *Georgia Place Names.* Macon: Winship Press, 1975.

"Our Roots on Tybee." Chatham-Effingham Regional Library vertical files.

Rogers, Norma K. *History of Chattahoochee County, Georgia.* Columbus: Columbus Office Supply Co., 1933.

Smith, George G. *The Story of Georgia and the Georgia People: 1732–1860.* Atlanta: Franklin Printing & Pub., 1900.

Tallapoosa Centennial: September 2, 3, 4, 1960. Tallapoosa Centennial Committee, 1960.

Towns County: A Pictorial History. Hiawassee: Towns County Chamber of Commerce. 1992.

Trefftz, Roy W., and Lillian Heinsohn. *Heritage of Thomas County, Georgia.* Thomasville: Bicentennial/Sesquicentennial Committee, 1975.

Trogdon, Kathryn C. (ed.). *The History of Stephens County, Georgia.* Toccoa Woman's Club, 1973.

Ward, George Gordon. *The Annals of Upper Georgia Centered in Gilmer County.* Carrollton: Thomasson Print & Office Equipment Co., 196.

Williams, B. "Where, Oh Where is Ty Ty?" Tifton-Tift County Public Library vertical files.

White, George. *Statistics of the State of Georgia.* Savannah: W. Thorne Williams, 1849.

Wood, G. G. *Heritage of Gilmer County and Its People.* Carrollton: Thomasson Printing, 1965.

Idaho

"A Brief History of Arimo." Pocatello Public Library vertical files.

Albertson, Herma G. "History of Blackfoot and Vicinity." Term paper, 1923. University of Idaho.

Ashlock, Herb. "North Fork Presbyterian Church for Indians Holds 75th Anniversary at Ahsahka Today." *Lewiston Morning Tribune.* July 26, 1959.

Barber, Floyd R., and Dan W. Martin. *Idaho in the Pacific Northwest.* Caldwell: Caxton Printers, 1956.

Bonner County Historical Commission. *Beautiful Bonner: The History of Bonner County, Idaho.* Dallas: Curtis Media Corp., 1991.

Boone, Lalila. *Idaho Place Names.* Moscow: University of Idaho Press, 1988.

Conley, Cort. *Idaho for the Curious.* Riggins: Backeddy Books, 1982.

Derig, Betty. *Roadside History of Idaho.* Missoula: Mountain Press, 1996.

Elsensohn, Sister M. Alfreda. *Pioneer Days in Idaho County.* Vol. 1. Cottonwood: Idaho Corporation of Benedictine Sisters, 1978.

Federal Writers' Project. *Idaho: A Guide in Word and Pictures.* Caldwell: Caxton Printers, 1937.

_____. *The Idaho Encyclopedia.* Caldwell: Caxton Printers, 1983.

Friedman, Ralph. *Tracking Down Idaho.* Caldwell: Caxton Printers, 1978.

Greever, William S. *Bonanza West: The Story of the Western Mining Rushes, 1848–1900.* Moscow: University of Idaho Press, 1963.

History of Minidoka County and Its People. Rupert: Minidoka County Historical Society, 1985.

"Indian Leader Lauds Hatchery." *Spokesman-Review.* Aug. 24, 1969.

Kuna Joint School District. *The Settlement of the Kuna Region, 1900–1925.* Caldwell: Caxton Printers, 1983.

"Land of Sunshine, Land of Promise." *Rupert Record.* Sept. 28, 1905.

Morgan, Clay, and Steve Mitchell. *Idaho unBound.* Ketchum: West Bound Books, 1995.

Peterson, Keith C. *Company Town: Potlatch, Idaho, and the Potlatch Lumber Company.* Seattle: Washington State University, 1987.

Pethtel, Lillian. Kamiah. Letter to author, July, 2000.

Poole, Elaine, and Gwen Fillmore. *Menan: 1879–1986.* Menan: Elaine Poole, 1986.

Pratt, Grace R. "History of the Beautiful Cocolalla Valley: Part One." *Sandpoint News-Bulletin.* July 20, 1968.

Wanner, Marcell, and Julie Miller. *Ingacom: A History of the Inkom Area.* Inkom: Mike Boyce Pub., 1989.

Wrigley, Robert L., Jr. "The Early History of Pocatello, Idaho." *Pacific Northwest Quarterly.* Vol. 34, No. 4. Oct., 1943: 362.

Illinois

Adams, James N. *Illinois Place Names.* Springfield: Illinois State Historical Society, 1989.

A History of Somonauk: 1843–1970. Somonauk Junior Women's Club, 1985.

Annals of Knox County: Commemorating Centennial of Admission of Illinois as a State of the Union in 1818. Galesburg: Knox County Board of Supervisors. n.d.

Arrowheads to Aerojets: Monroe County, Illinois. Valmeyer: Myron Roever Associates, 1967.

Batemen, Newton, and Paul Selby. *Historical Encyclopedia of Illinois and History of Livingston County.* Chicago: Munsell Pub., 1909.

Beckwith, H. W. *History of Iroquois County, Together with Historic Notes on the Northwest.* Chicago: H. H. Hill and Co., 1880.

Dickinson, Lora T. *The Story of Winnetka.* Winnetka: Winnetka Historical Society, 1956.

Encyclopedia of Illinois. New York: Somerset Publishers, 1996–1997.

Federal Writers' Project. *Illinois: A Descriptive and Historical Guide.* Chicago: A.C. McClurg & Co., 1939.

Fridlund, John. *Centennial: History of Itasca.* Itasca Historical Society, 2nd Edition, 1990.

Garst, Gladys (ed.). *Mackinaw Remembers: 1827–1977, Mackinaw Sesquicentennial.* Mackinaw Historical Society, 1977.

Gregg, Thomas. *History of Hancock County, Together with an Outline History of the State, and a Digest of State laws.* Chicago: C.C. Chapman, 1880.

History of Lee County, Together with Biographical Matter, Statistics, etc. Chicago: H. H. Hill & Co., 1881.

History of Livingston County, Illinois, Containing a History of the County, Its Cities, Towns, etc. Chicago: Wm. Le Baron, Jr. & Co., 1878.

History of Maquon and Vicinity: 1827–1976. Maquon Historical Association, 1976.

History of Nokomis, Illinois: 1856–1956. Nokomis Centennial Committee, 1956.

History of Peoria County, Illinois, Containing a History of the Northwest — History of Illinois — History of the County, Its Early Settlement, Growth, Development, Resources, etc. Chicago: Johnson & Co., 1880.

It Seems Like Only Yesterday: From Stagecoach to Monorail. Pecatonica Centennial Committee, 1969.

Lill, Peter W. "100 Years Ago, or How Mascoutah Had Its Start." Mascoutah Public Library vertical files.

Magnificent Whistle Stop: The 100 Year Story of Mendota, Ill. Mendota Centennial Committee, 1953.

"Minonk." miscellaneous articles from old newspaper accounts. Filger Library vertical files.

Mokena Memorabilia: 1832–1945. Mokena Village Board, 1945.

Morrison, Elizabeth B. *History of Maquon and Vicinity: 1827–1976.* Maquon Historical Society, 1976.

"Otisco." Charleston Public Library vertical files.

Past and Present of Woodford County, Illinois. Chicago: Wm. LeBaron, Jr. & Co., 1878.

Polson, Terry E. *Corn, Commerce and Country Living: A History of Henry County, Illinois.* Moline: Desaulniers & Co., 1968.

"Shabbona: A Friend of the White Men." *Nature Bulletin.* No. 748. March 21, 1964.

Shabbona Centennial: 1872–1971. Shabbona Centennial Committee, 1972.

Steimle, Mary B. *When Tiskilwa Was Young..* Tiskilwa: Mary B. Steimle, 1985.

Stevens, Frank E. *History of Lee County, Illinois.* Chicago: S. J. Clark Pub., 1914.

Temple, Wayne C. "Indian Villages of the Illinois Country." Illinois State Museum, Scientific Papers. Vol. II, Part 2. 1977: 165.

Tiskilwa History. Tiskilwa Township Library vertical files.

Trebe, Patricia. "Planned Progress, Pleasant Living." *Lincoln-Way Sun.* May 28, 1998.

Vogel, Virgil J. *Indian Place Names in Illinois.* Springfield: Illinois State Historical Society, 1963.

"Wauponsee Station." *Morris Daily Herald.* Oct. 6, 1916:4.

Whittingham. Richard. *Skokie: 1888–1988, A Centennial History.* Village of Skokie, 1988.

Woodford County History. Bloomington: Woodford County Sesquicentennial History Committee, 1968.

Zeman, Alice F. *Wabansi: Fiend or Friend?* Henry: M and D Printers, 1991.

Indiana

Ashkum Quasquicentennial. Village of Ashkum, 1981.

Baker, J. David, and Leonard H. Hartmann. *The Postal History of Indiana.* Vol. II. Louisville, Kentucky: Philatelic Bibliopole, 1976.

Baker, Ronald L. *From Needmore to Prosperity: Hoosier Place Names in Folklore His-*

tory. Bloomington: Indiana University Press, 1995.

_____. *Indiana Place Names*. Bloomington: Indiana University Press, 1975.

Bartholomew, Henry S. *Pioneer History of Elkhart County, Indiana, with Sketches and Stories*. Goshen: Goshen Printery, 1930.

Blanchard, Charles. *Counties of Howard and Tipton, Indiana, Historical and Biographical*. Chicago: F. A. Battey & Co., 1883.

Centennial Anniversary of Pulaski County, Indiana and of the Town of Winamac. Waynesville: Pulaski County Centennial Association, 1939.

Counties of White and Pulaski, Indiana. Chicago: F. A. Battey & Co., 1883.

Dice, Mrs. Lewis. "Denver Visitors to Honor Indian Chief (Ashkum)." *Peru Daily Tribune*. Aug. 6, 1981.

"Did Winamac's Chief Winamac Rate Even a Footnote in History?" *Pulaski County Journal*. Nov. 16, 1961.

Eisen, David (ed.). *A Mishawaka Mosaic*. Elkhart: Bethel Pub., 1983.

Farlow, Arlene. "Majenica: Thanks to Planks." *Huntington Herald-Press*. Jan. 29, 1979.

Federal Writers' Project. *Indiana: A Guide to the Hoosier State*. New York: Hastings House, 1941.

Hanan, John W. *LaGrange County Centennial History, 1828–1928*. LaGrange: LaGrange Pub., 1929.

History of Huntington County, Indiana, From the Earliest Time to the Present, with Biographical Sketches, Notes, etc. Chicago: Brant & Fuller, 1887.

"History of Lake Maxinkuckee." Culver-Union Township Public Library vertical files.

"Howard County History." Kokomo-Howard County vertical files.

Howard County, Indiana Family History: 1844–1994. Oakford: Howard County Genealogical Society, 1994.

Johnson, Margaret. *A History of Patoka: Written During This Bicentennial Year of Our Country (1776–1976)*. Patoka: Patoka National Bank, 1976.

Kewanna Centennial, Harvest Festival: 1871–1971. Kewanna Centennial Committee, 1971.

Lyons, James. "Waupecong." Peru Public Library vertical files.

"Majenica Tile Plant Dates Back to 1870s." *Huntington Herald-Press*. July 3, 1969.

Notastine, Ilah. Mongo. Letter to author, November, 1996.

"Roads Opened Way to Development." *Huntington Herald-Press*. July 3, 1969.

Taylor, Robert M., Jr., *et al*. *Indiana: A New Historical Guide*. Bloomington: Indiana Historical Society, 1989.

"The Wabash Light." *Wabash Rotary Club*. n.d.

They Called It Napanee: A History, 1874–1974. Nappanee: Nappanee Centennial Committee, 1974.

"Wakarusa History." Wakarusa Public Library vertical files.

Wanatah Centennial, Wanatah Centennial Committee, 1965.

"Waupecong, The Village that Never Grew Beyond Its Original Platting." *Miami County Historical Society History Bulletin*. Vol. XII, No. 9. Sept. 1986.

Weesner, Clarkson. *History of Wabash County*. Chicago: Lewis Pub., 1914.

Iowa

Bohrofen, Alva. *Koeta Centennial History: 1873–1973*. Keota: Iowa Centennial Committee, 1973.

Boyken, Clarine. *Whistle and a Spur: A History of Titonka, Jubilee Book*. Lake Mills: Graphic Pub. Co., 1973.

Chapman, Samuel D. *History of Tama County, Iowa*. Toledo: Toledo Times, 1879.

"Death of a Pioneer." *Muscatine Daily Journal*. Jan. 17, 1857.

Dilts, Harold, Kathleen A. Dilts, and Linda J. Dilts. *From Ackley to Zwingle: A Collection of the Origins of Iowa Place Names*. Ames: Iowa State University Press, 1993.

Encyclopedia of Iowa. New York: Somerset Publications, 1995.

Federal Writers' Project. *Iowa: A Guide to the Hawkeye State*. New York: Viking Press, 1938.

Fulton, Alexander R. *The Red Men of Iowa*. Des Moines: Mills & Co., 1882.

Hart, William H. *History of Sac County*. Indianapolis: B. F. Bowen & Co., 1914.

Hedge, Manoah. *Past and Present of Mahaska County, Iowa*. Chicago: S. J. Clarke Pub., 1906.

"Historical Walking Tour of Sac City, Iowa." Sac City Chamber of Commerce, 1977.

"History of Fayette County Towns." *Daily Register*. Oct. 31, 1996: 22b.

History of Jones County, Iowa, Containing a History of the County, Its Cities, Towns, etc. Chicago: Western Historical Co., 1879.

History of Kossuth County. Lake Mills: Graphic Pub., 1976.

History of Monona County, Iowa, Containing Full-Page Portraits and Biographical Sketches of Prominent and Representative Citizens, etc. Chicago: National Pub. Co., 1890.

History of Muscatine County, Iowa, Containing a History of the County, Its Cities, Towns, etc. Chicago: Western Historical Co., 1879.

Huffman, L.A. *The Frontier Years*. New York: Henry Holt & Co., 1955.

"Keokuk." Keokuk Public Library vertical files.

"Keosauqua — Its Early History." www.showcase.netins.net/web/villages/koe/history.

"Maquoketa, No Other Town Like It." *Explore Jackson County*. 1996: 9.

McCulla, Thomas. *History of Cherokee County, Iowa*. Vol. I. Chicago: S. J. Clarke Pub., 1914.

Ocheyedan, A Centennial. Ocheyedan Centennial Steering Committee, 1991.

Ocheyedan Mound. Ocheyedan Commercial Club, 1979.

"Onawa." Onawa Public Library vertical files.

"Our Town: Keota Formerly Was Named Keoton." *Keota Eagle*. June 1998: 8.

Petersen, William J. "Land of the Fire Makers." *The Palimpsest*. Vol. XLV, No. 9. Sept. 1964. 321–343.

Quasqueton. Iowa: 1842–1967. Quasqueton Quasquicentennial Committee, 1967.

Ramsey, Guy R. *Postmarked Iowa*. Crete, Nebraska: J-B Pub., 1976.

Reflections: Sac City Quasquicentennial Book, 1855–1980. Odebolt: Odebolt Chronicle Print, 1980.

"Story of Washta and Its People." Washta Public Library vertical files.

Tama Centennial Book: 1862–1962. Tama Centennial Committee, 1962.

There Grew a Timber City. Maquoketa: Jackson State Bank, 1996.

Vogel, Virgil J. *Iowa Place Names of Indian Origin*. Iowa City: University of Iowa Press, 1983.

"Waukon's History." Robey Memorial Library vertical files.

Weaver, William O. *Hail to the Chief: True Tales of Old Wapello*. Wapello: Louisa Pub., 1974.

Who's Who in Iowa. Des Moines: Iowa Press Association, 1940.

Wilhelm, Lana. "They Came and Settled Along the Corn." Sac City vertical files.

Kansas

"A Look Back at Kechi's Early Families." *The Ark Valley News*. Aug. 18, 1988.

Barnes, Elizabeth E. *Historic Johnson County: A Bird's Eye View of the Development of the Area*. Mission: Neff Printing, 1969.

Barry, Louise. *The Beginning of the West: Annals of the Kansas Gateway to the American West, 1540–1894*. Topeka: Kansas State Historical Society, 1972.

Caldwell, Messenger. *The History of Sumner County, Kansas*. Dallas: Curtis Media Corp., 1987.

"Chautauqua." Chautauqua County Historical & Geneological Society vertical files.

Cutler, William. *History of Kansas*. Chicago: A. T. Andreas, 1883.

Dunn, J. W. "Historical Sketch of Onaga City." *Onaga Herald*. May 8, 1947.

Federal Writers' Project. *Kansas: A Guide to the Sunflower State*. New York: Viking Press, 1939.

Gray, J. Rufus. "Pioneer Saints and Sinners." *Pratt Rotary Club,* 1968.

Guise, Byron E., and Edalia T. Guise. *An Affair with the Past: From the Otoes to the Astronauts.* Marysville, Byron & Edalia Guise, 1970.

History of Neosho and Wilson Counties, Kansas, Containing Sketches of Our Pioneers, etc. Fort Scott: L. Wallace Duncan, 1902.

History of Onaga. Onaga Historical Society, n.d.

"How Wamego Was Named." *The Wamego Reporter.* May 20, 1954.

"Illustrated Doniphan County: 1837–1916." *Weekly Kansas Chief Supplement,* April 6, 1916.

Ingalls, Sheffield. *History of Atchison County.* Lawrence: Lawrence Standard Pub., 1916.

LaFlesche, Francis. *A Dictionary of the Osage Language.* Washington, D. C.: U.S. Government Printing Office, 1932.

Mahaska History Bicentennial. Mahaska Bicentennial Book Committee, 1976.

McCoy, Sandra V., and Jan Hults. *1001 Kansas Place Names.* Lawrence: University of Kansas, 1989.

Mooney, V. P. *History of Butler County, Kansas.* Lawrence: Lawrence Standard Pub., 1916.

Natoma History: 1888–1988. Natoma Centennial Book Committee, 1988.

"Neosho Falls." Yates Center Public Library vertical files.

Olathe, The City Beautiful, Arrows to Atoms: 1857–1957. Baldwin: Baldwin Ledger, 1957.

Quenemo History: 1870–1970. Quenemo: Sunflower-Fidelis Club, 1970.

Rydjord, John. *Kansas Place-Names.* Norman: University of Oklahoma Press, 1979.

Seneca 125 Years Ago: A Souvenir Collection of Seneca's History Regarding Its 1870 Incorporation as a 3rd Class Town. Seneca: G & R Printing, 1995.

Smith, Nathaniel E. "History of Penokee." Graham County Library vertical files.

Starr, Dorothy. *The Mooney Memorial Christian Church.* Newton: Mennonite Press, 1978.

Steffey, Erma, Delvis Steffey, and Fern Vanderpool. *Ozawkie on the Delaware: 1854–1976.* Pleasant View Grange #1459, 1976.

Tennal, Ralph. *History of Nemaha County, Kansas.* Lawrence: Lawrence Standard Pub., 1916.

Tindle, Lela J. *Wilson County, Kansas: People of the South Wind.* Dallas: Curtis Media Corp., 1988.

Veach, Mrs. W. R. "History of Chetopa." *Advance-Clipper.* February 1, 1934

"Wamego, Kansas." Wamego Public Library vertical files.

Kentucky

Dysan, John P. "The Naming of Paducah." *Register of the Kentucky Historical Society.* Vol. 92, No. 2. Spring 1994.

Federal Writers' Project. *Kentucky: A Guide to the Bluegrass State.* New York: Harcourt. Brace and Co., 1939.

Rennick, Robert M. *Kentucky Place Names.* Lexington: University Press of Kentucky, 1984.

Robertson, John E. L. *Paducah, 1830–1980: A Sesquicentennial History.* John E. L. Robertson, 1980.

Talley, Dr. William M. "Kinniconick Creek: A Natural and historic Treasure of Lewis County: Part I." *Lewis County Herald.* May 12, 1998.

_____. "Kinniconick Creek: A Natural and Historic Treasure of Lewis County: Part II." *Lewis County Herald.* May 19, 1998.

Walker, Odell. *Profiles of the Past.* Kuttawa: McClanahan Pub., 1994.

Louisiana

"A Walking Tour of Opelousas, Louisiana." *Rotary Club of Opelousas.* n.d.

Amite City: 1861–1961. Amite City Centennial Celebration, 1961.

Bogalusa Silver Jubilee Celebration, 1914–1939. Official Souvenir Program. Bogalusa Silver Jubilee, Inc., 1939.

DeBlieux, Robert B. "Natchitoches: A Guide

to the Historically and Architectually Important Buildings in the Historic District, A Walking Tour." *Natchitoches Times*, 1989.

Centennial Celebration, Houma, Louisiana, May 10–13, 1934. Morgan City: King-Hannaford Co., 1934.

Ellis, Frederick S. *St. Tammany Parish*. Gretna: Pelican Pub., 1981.

"Farm Corner [Anacoco]." *Beaumont Enterprise*. Feb. 9, 1971.

Federal Writers' Project. *Louisiana: A Guide to the State*. New York: Hastings House, 1941.

"History of Iberville Parish." Iberville Parish Library vertical files.

"History of Maringouin." Maringouin Branch Library vertical files.

Hughes, C.M. "Some Parish Sketches." *Leesville Leader*. July 3, 1947.

Hymal, Diane. "Natalbany: There's No Whistle Anymore." *Gumbo Magazine*. May 31, 1987.

Jagneaux, Charles, Clerk of Court, Opelousas. Letter to author, Oct. 9, 1997.

Leeper, Clare D. *Louisiana Places: A Collection of the Columns from the Baton Rouge Sunday Advocate, 1960–1974*. Baton Rouge: Legacy Pub., 1976.

Pigno, Sam J., former Mayor of Tickfaw. Letter to author, 1997.

Read, William A. "Louisiana Place-Names of Indian Origin." *University Bulletin*. Baton Rouge: Louisiana State University. Vol. XIX. Feb., 1927, No. 2.

Souvenir of Centennial Celebration, Houma, Louisiana, May 10–13, 1934. Friends of the Terrebonne Public Library and the Terrebonne Historical and Cultural Society, 1984.

Tangipahoa Parish: 1869–1969. Official Souvenir Program, 1969.

Maine

Albert, Julie D. *Madawaska: 1869–1969*. Town of Madawaska, 1969.

Attwood, Stanley B. *The Length and Breadth of Maine*. Augusta: Kennebec Journal Print Shop, 1946.

"Bits and Pieces of Allagash History." *Allagash Historical Society*, 1976.

Chadbourne, Ava H. *Maine Place Names and the Peopling of Its Towns*. Portland: Farbush-Roberts Printing, 1955.

Chase, Fannie. *Wiscasset in Pownalborough*. Wiscasset: The Southworth-Anthoensen Press, 1941.

Eckstrom, Fannie H. *Indian Place-Names of the Penobscot Valley and the Maine Coast*. Orono: University of Maine, 1978.

Federal Writers' Project. *Maine: A Guide to Down East*. Boston: Houghton Mifflin, 1937.

Historical Sketch of Town of Orono, Orono Sesquicentennial. Clarence A. Day, 1956.

History of Penobscot County, Maine, with Illustrations and Biographical Sketches, etc. Cleveland: Williams, Chase & Co., 1882.

"History of the Town of Meddybemps, Maine." Meddybemps Historical Society vertical files.

Laverty, Dorothy B. *Millinocket: Magic City of Maine's Wilderness*. Freeport: Bond Wheelwright Co., 1973.

Long Search of the Katahdin Area. Penobscot Times, Inc., 1979.

Norridgewock, 200 Years: 1788–1988. Norridgewock Bicentennial Book Committee, 1988.

"Ogunquit Then and Now." Ogunquit Memorial Library vertical files.

Parker, Arlita D. *A History of Pemaquid with Sketches of Monhegan, Popham, Castine*. Boston: MacDonald & Evans, 1925.

Penobscot Bicentennial: 1787–1987. Penobscot Historical Society, 1987.

Perkins, Esselyn G. *History of Ogunquit Village*. Portland: Falmouth Pub., 1951.

Rich, Louise D. *State O' Maine*. New York: Harper & Row, 1964.

Rutherford, Phillip R. *The Dictionary of Maine Place-Names*. Freeport: Bond Wheelright Co., 1970.

"Saco History." Dyer Library vertical files.

Simpson, Dorothy. *The Maine Islands in Story and Legend*. Philadelphia: J. B. Lippincott Co., 1960.

Strong, Jean, *et al.* (eds.). *Oyster Shells and

Sailing Ships: Damariscotta, Maine Sesquicentennial. New Castle: Lincoln County Pub., 1998.

Sweetser, Phyllis S. *Cumberland, Maine, in Four Centuries.* Town of Cumberland, 1976.

Varney, George J. *A Gazetteer of the State of Maine.* Boston: B. B. Russell, 1886.

Maryland

Antunes, Clicia. "What's In a Name?" *Discover Charles County.* Oct. 24, 1990: 3.

Arnett, Earl, *et al. A New Guide to the Old Line State.* Baltimore: Johns Hopkins University Press, 1999.

Brown, Robin. "Conowingo's Not the Town It Used to Be." *Compass.* March 13, 1980.

"Cities, Villages, and Towns of Allegany County, Maryland, and How They Got Their Names." Cumberland: *Allegany County Historical Society.* n.d.

Clark, Dot. "Cecil's Lost Town." *Cecil Whig.* Feb. 3, 1971.

Diggs, Louis S. *In Our Voices.* Chattalonee: Louis S. Diggs, 1999.

Federal Writers' Project. *Maryland: A Guide to the Old Line State.* New York: Oxford University Press, 1941.

Harris, Ann P. *The Potomac Adventure.* Potomac: Jantron, Inc., 1978.

Jacob, John E., Jr. *Salisbury and Wicomico County: A Pictorial History.* Norfolk, Virginia: Donning Co., 1981.

Kaminkow, Marion J. *Maryland A to Z: A Topographical Dictionary.* Baltimore: Magna Carter Book Co., 1985.

Keatley, J. Kenneth. *Place Names of the Eastern Shore of Maryland.* Queenstown: Queen Anne Press, 1987.

Kenny, Hammil. *The Placenames of Maryland, Their Origin and Meaning.* Baltimore: Maryland Historical Society, 1984.

McBee, Avery. "An End to Isolation in Nanjemoy." Charles County Library vertical files.

"Old Conowingo Span Wrecked by Explosives." *Baltimore Sun.* Nov. 29, 1927.

Pogue, Robert E. T. *Old Maryland and Landmarks.* Bushwoood: Robert E. T. Pogue, 1972.

_____. *Yesterday in Old St. Mary's County.* New York: Carlton Press. Inc., 1968.

Rollo, Vera F. *Your Maryland.* Lanham: Maryland Historical Press. 2nd Edition, 1971.

Rountree, Helen C., and Thomas E. Davidson. *Eastern Shore Indians of Virginia and Maryland.* Charlottesville: University Press of Virginia, 1997.

Smith, Jane O. *One-Day Trips through History: 200 Excursions Within 150 Miles of Washington. D.C.* McLean, Virginia: EPM Pub., 1982.

Stegmaier, Harry L., Jr., *et al. Allegany County: A History.* Parsons, West Virginia: McClain Printing, 1976.

Truitt, Dr. Reginald V., and Dr. Millard G. Les Callette. *Worcester County, Maryland's Arcadia.* Snow Hill: Worcester County Historical Society, 1977.

Turner, Tessa G. "You'd Never Know There Was a Conowingo Village." *The Record.* Sept. 11, 1974.

Massachusetts

"A Brief History of Seekonk, Massachusetts: 1636–1967." *Seekonk Historical Society.* Pub. No. 5, 1967.

Acushnet Centennial. Acushnet Centennial Committee, 1960.

Agawam. Massachusetts: Over the Span of a Century, 1855–1955. Town of Agawam, 1955.

"Aquinnah." Martha's Vineyard Chamber of Commerce. n.d.

Atherton, Horace H., Jr. *History of Saugus, Massachusetts.* Citizens Committee of the Saugus Board of Trade, 1916.

Baldwin, Henry S. "Swampscott — Past and Present." *Massachusetts Selectman.* Summer, 1944.

Banks, Dr. Charles E. *The History of Martha's Vineyard.* Vol. II. Edgartown: Dukes County Historical Society, 1966.

Barnes, Margaret F. *Sconset Heyday.* Nantucket: Inquirer & Mirror, 1979.

Benedict, Rev. William A., and Rev. Hiram A. Trace. *History of the Town of Sutton, Massachusetts, from 1704 to 1876.* Worcester, Pennsylvania: Sanford & Co., 1878.

Bigelow, E. Victor. *Narrative History of the Town of Cohasset, Massachusetts.* Cohasset: Committee on Town History, 1898.

Brooks, Tom. "Annis Squam Important Port Before Gloucester." *Gloucester Daily Times.* Aug. 16, 1956.

Canton Comes of Age, 1979–1997: A History of the Town of Canton, Massachusetts. Town of Canton, 1997.

Carlson, Stephen P. *First Iron World: A History of the First Iron Works Association.* Saugus Historical Society, 1991.

Cotuit—Some Notes on Her History. Hyannis: F. B. & F. P. Goss, 1939.

Damon, Samuel C. *History of Holden, 1667–1841.* Worcester: Wallace and Ripley, 1841.

Dean, Samuel. *History of Scituate Massachusetts, From Its First Settlement to 1831.* Boston: J. Loring, 1831.

Federal Writers' Project. *The Origin of Massachusetts Place Names of the State, Counties, Cities, and Towns.* New York: Harian Pub., 1941.

_____. *Massachusetts: A Guide to Its Places and People.* Boston: Houghton Mifflin Co., 1937.

Fitzgerald, Jared E. "Josias Wampatuck Sold Scituate for 14 Pounds." *Heritage Days.* Aug. 1993.

Freeman, Frederick. *The History of Cape Cod: The Annals of the Thirteen Towns of Barnstable County.* Vol. II. Boston: Geo. C. Rand & Avery, 1862.

Harrington, Joe. "Swampscott Prefers to Spell It R-e-s-i-d-e-n-t." *Boston Globe Magazine.* Oct. 20, 1963: 48, 49.

"History of Chicopee." Chicopee Public Library vertical files.

"History of Seekonk." Seekonk Public Library vertical files.

History of the Town of Freetown, Massachusetts. Fall River: J. H. Franklin & Co., 1902.

Hodgman, Edwin R. *History of the Town of Westford, in the County of Middlesex, Massachusetts, 1659–1883.* Lowell: Morning Mail Co., 1883.

Huntoon, Daniel T.V. *History of the Town of Canton, Norfolk County, Massachusetts.* Cambridge: John Wilson & Son, 1893.

Karbott, Grace E. "A Brief History of Manomet"; "Lest We Forget." Plymouth Public Library vertical files.

Keene, Betsey. *History of Bourne from 1622 to 1937.* Bourne Historical Society, 1975.

Kennedy, June W. *Westford Recollections: 1729–1979.* Westford: Murray Printing Co., 1979.

Kenyon, Paul. "Annisquam's History Glimpsed at Fair." *Gloucester Daily Times.* Aug. 7, 1981: A4.

Kerr, Bessie Warner. "History of Chicopee: Early History, 1641 to 1848." Chicopee Public Library vertical files.

LaFrancis, Edith. *Agawam, Massachusetts: A Town History.* Springfield: Pond-Ekberg Co., 1980.

Lindner, Constance P. "Cohasset—The Long, Rocky Place." South Shore Area Community Guide. Oct. 1998: 12, 13.

Lovell, R.A., Jr. *Sandwich: A Cape Cod Town.* Town of Sandwich, 1984.

Mattapoisett and Old Rochester, Massachusetts; Being a History of These Towns and Also in Part of Marion and a Portion of Wareham, etc. New York: The Grafton Press, 1907.

"Mattapoisett. Know Your Town." *Marion Area League of Women Voters.* n.d.

Merritt, Joseph F. *History of South Scituate-Norwell, Massachusetts.* Rockland: Rockland Standard Pub., 1938.

Murphy, Barbara. *Scituate: The Coming of Age of a Plymouth Colony Town.* Barbara Murphy, 1985.

Nason, Elias. *A Gazetteer of Massachusetts.* Boston: B. B. Russell, 1874.

O'Brien, Greg. *O'Brien's Original Guide to Cape Cod and the Islands.* Hyannis: Parnassus Imprints, 1996.

Pratt, Harvey H. *The Early Planters of Scituate; A History of the Town of Scituate, Massachusetts, from Its Establishment to the End of the Revolutionary War.* Scituate Historical Society, 1929.

"Prof. Norton Tells of Early Squam at Historical Meeting." *Gloucester Daily Times.* Sept. 17, 1966.

Sawyer, Richard P. (ed.). *From Pocasset to Cataumet.* Bourne Historic Commission, 1988.

Stuart, Anne. "Manomet: Life Remains Shore-Focused." *Patriot Ledger.* Aug. 3, 1988.

Taylor, Charles J. *History of Great Barrington (Berkshire), Massachusetts.* Town of Barrington, 1928.

"The Tranquil Peninsula." *Gloucester Daily News.* Aug. 29, 1980: 4.

Todd, Charles B. *In Olde Massachusetts, Sketches of Old Times and Places During the Early Days of the Commonwealth.* New York: The Grafton Press, 1907.

Tougias, Michael J. *A Taunton River Journey.* Bridgewater: Taunton River Watershed Alliance, 1996.

Vuilleumier, Marion. *Indians on Olde Cape Cod.* Taunton: Wm. S. Sullwold Pub., 1970.

Wilson, Fred A. *Some Annals of Nahant, Massachusetts.* Boston: Old Corner Book Store, 1928.

Zimiles, Martha, and Murray Zimiles. *Early American Mills.* New York: Bramhall House, 1973.

Zook, Nicholas. *Holden, The Evolution of a Town.* Holden Bicentennial Commission, 1976.

Michigan

Arndt, Leslie E. *The Bay County Story: Memoirs of the County's 125 Years.* Linwood: Huron News Service, 1982.

Ball, Adele. *Early History of Owosso.* East Lansing: Michigan Historical Society, 1944.

Boulton, William. *Complete History, Alpena County, Michigan.* Alpena: Argus Book and Job Rooms, 1876.

Ceasar, Ford. *The Bicentennial History of Ingham County, Michigan.* Ann Arbor: Braun-Brumfield, 1976.

Chaney, Elsket B. *The Story of Portage.* Onekama: Elsket B. Chaney, 1960.

Durant, Samuel W. *History of Ingham and Eaton Counties, Michigan.* Philadelphia: D. W. Ensign & Co., 1880.

Encyclopedia of Michigan. New York: Somerset Publishers, 1981.

Federal Writers' Project. *Michigan: A Guide to the Wolverine State.* New York: Oxford University Press, 1941.

First Hundred Years — Newaygo, Michigan, 1853–1953. Newaygo Centennial Commission, 1953.

Gansser, Capt. Augustus H. *History of Bay County, Michigan and Representative Citizens.* Chicago: Richmond & Arnold, 1905.

Hagen, Dave. *Kalazamoo Gazette Supplement.* July 16, 1978.

History and Directory of Kent County, Michigan, Containing a History of Each Township and the City of Grand Rapids. Grand Rapids: Daily Eagle Steam Printing House, 1870.

History of Iosco County, Michigan. East Tawas: Iosco County Historical Society. n.d.

History of Lake Huron Shore, With Illustrations and Biographical Sketches of Some of Its Prominent Men and Pioneers. Chicago: H. R. Page & Co., 1883.

History of Manistee County, Michigan, With Illustrations and Biographical Sketches of Some of Its Prominent Men and Pioneers. Chicago: H. R. Page & Co., 1882.

History of Muskegon County, Michigan, With Illustrations and Biographical Sketches of Some of Its Prominent Men and Pioneers. Chicago: H. R. Page & Co., 1882.

History of the City of Menominee, Michigan: The Past with Remembrance, the Future with Longing, 1883–1983. Menominee Centennial Corp., 1983.

"History of Negaunee." *Negaunee Irontown Association.* 1979.

History of the Upper Peninsula of Michigan. Chicago: Western Historical Co., 1883.

Ireland, Mark L., and Irma Thompson Ireland. *Place of the Big Rock, Chesaning, Michigan: 1842–1950.* Mark L. Ireland and Irma Thompson Ireland, 1950.

Kilar, Jeremy. *Saginaw's Changeable Past: An Illustrated History.* St. Louis: G. Bradley Pub., 1994

Little Traverse Bay: Historical Review. Petoskey Junior Chamber of Commerce, 1967.

Morris, Betty. "History of Manistee County." Manistee County Public Library vertical files.

"Newaygo's Origin"; "Village of Newaygo, 1953–1888: How Did Newaygo Get Its Name." Newaygo Carnegie Public Library vertical files.

Onaway, Michigan: 1899–1974. Onaway Jubilee Book Committee, 1974.

Owosso, Dream City of the Indians. Owosso: Argus Press, 1936.

Pinconning, Place Where Wild Potatoes Grow: Its Centennial Year. Pinconning Centennial Committee, 1972.

Romig, Walter. *Michigan Place Names.* Grosse Pointe: Walter Romig, 1972.

Seely, Charles J. *Souvenir of Owosso.* Belding, 1908 (reprinted in *Souvenir of Owosso. Michigan: 1836–1986. 150 Years of Owosso Highlights,* 1986).

Stillman, Ruth. *How Okemos Began: A Short History.* Friends of Okemos Library, 1956.

Symon, Charles A. (ed.). *Alger County: A Centennial History, 1885–1985.* Munising: Alger County Historical Society, 1985.

The Traverse Region, Historical and Descriptive, with Illustrations of Scenery. Chicago: H. R. Page & Co., 1884.

Trumble, Hazel A. (ed.). *Sanilac County History, 1834–1984.* Sesquicentennial Celebration, 1984.

Vanderburg, Berenice E. *A Dowagaic Collection.* Berrien Springs: Hardscrabble Books, 1982.

Minnesota

100 Year History of the City of Osseo: September 6–7, 1975. Osseo Lionelles Club, 1975.

Bauer, Arnold J. *Story of Wabasso: 1899–1934.* Wabasso: Arnold J. Bauer, 1934.

Bemidji, First City on the Mississippi: Bemediji Centennial, 1896–1996. Bemidji Book Committee, 1994.

"Biwabik History." Aurora Public Library vertical files.

Blegen, Theodore C. *Minnesota: A History of the State.* Minneapolis: University of Minnesota Press, 1963.

Boucher, Colleen. *Jackson County History.* Vol. II. Jackson: Jackson County Historical Society, 1979.

Bryant, Charles S. *History of the Minnesota Valley, Including the Explorers and Pioneers of Minnesota.* Minneapolis: North Star Pub., 1882.

Centennial, July 16, 17, 18, Anoka, Minnesota. Anoka Centennial Committee, 1947.

Curtiss-Wedge, Franklyn. *History of Wabasha County, Minnesota.* Winona: H. C. Cooper, Jr., & Co., 1920.

Edelman, Carol. Ah-Gwah-Ching Center. Letter to author, March 13, 1999.

Federal Writers' Project. *The WPA Guide to Minnesota.* St. Paul: Minnesota Historical Society Press, 1985.

Goorich, Albert M. *History of Anoka County.* Minneapolis: Hennepin Pub., 1905.

History of Mower County, Together with Sketches of Its Towns, Villages and Townships, Educational, Civil, Military and Political History, etc. Mankato: Free Press Pub,. 1884.

"History of Naytahwaush." Mahnomen High School Library vertical files.

History of Olmsted County, Together With Biographical Matter, Statistics, etc. Chicago: H. H. Hill and Co,. 1883.

History of Rock County from 1911 to 1976. Luverne: Rock County Historical Society, 1977.

Jones, Thelma. *Once Upon a Lake: A History of Lake Minnetonka and Its People.* Minneapolis: Ross and Haines, 1969.

Keewatin, From Timber to Iron in Fifty Years. Keewatin: The Committee, 1956.

Lee, Carlton R. *Cokato's First Century: 1878–1978.* Cokato Centennial Committee, 1979.

Leonard, Joseph A. *History of Olmsted County, Minnesota, Together with Sketches of Many of Its Pioneers, Citizens, Families and Institutions, etc.* Chicago: Goodspeed Pub., 1910.

Mill on the Willow: History of Mower County. Lake Mills: Graphic Pub. Co., 1984.

"Minnetonka History." Minnetonka Manager's Office. n.d.

Nashwauk, "From Timber to Taconite," The Story of Nashwauk, Minnesota. Compiled by the Seventy-Fifth Anniversary Book Committee. Nashwauk: The Eastern Itascan, 1978.

Neill, Rev. Edward D., and Charles S. Bryant. *History of the Minnesota Valley.* Minneapolis: North Star Pub., 1882.

Nichols, Mrs. Carl. "What's in a Name?— Settlers of Eyota Used Indian Word to Designate Young Town." *Post-Bulletin.* Sept. 19, 1961.

O'Connell, Ella. "Early History of Keewatin. Minnesota, 1938." Keewatin Public Library vertical files.

Rose, Arthur P. *An Illustrated History of the Counties of Rock and Pipestone Counties.* Luverne: Northern Minnesota Pub. Co., 1911.

Rose, Arthur P. *History of Jackson County.* Marshall: Northern History Pub., 1910.

Rutledge, Carol. *The Streets are Wider Now: A History of the City of Waseca, Minnesota. Written in Celebration of One Hundred Twenty Years.* Waseca: Master Graphics, 1988.

Upham, Warren. *Minnesota Geographic Names.* St. Paul: Minnesota Historical Society, 1969.

Wesley, Edgar B. *Owatonna: The Social Development of a Minnesota Community.* Minneapolis: University of Minnesota Press, 1938.

Ziegler, Frank. *Ken-A-Big— The Story of Kanabec County: An Illustrated History of Kanabec County, Its Early Years.* Mora: B & W Pub., 1977.

Mississippi

Bellar, George W. (ed.). *Itta Bena, Miss: "Homeseeker's Paradise."* Itta Bena Business League, 1912.

Brieger, James F. *Hometown Mississippi.* Jackson: Town Square Books, 1997.

Brown, A. J. *History of Newton County, Mississippi, from 1834 to 1894.* Jackson: Clarion-Ledger Co., 1894.

Byrd, Anne. "History of Iuka." Iuka Chamber of Commerce, 1963.

Cain, Cyril E. *Four Centuries on the Pascagoula.* Vol. I. State College, 1953.

Chastain, Rosiland. "Talowah." Lamar County Library vertical files.

"Early History of Okolona." Okolona Chamber of Commerce, 1961.

Federal Writers' Project. *Mississippi: A Guide to the Magnolia State.* New York: Viking Press, 1938.

"Following the Chickasaw Trail." *Northeast Mississippi Daily Journal.* March 12–18, 1983.

Henderson, R. B. "Town of Byhalia Rich in Historical Interest." *South Report.* Oct. 4, 1971: 36.

Higginbotham, Jay. *Pascagoula: Singing River City.* Mobile: Gill Press, 1967.

History of Rankin County, Mississippi. Vol. II. Brandon: Rankin County Historical Society, 1988.

"Hometown Names Carry Own Tale." *Northeast Mississippi Daily Journal.* March 6–12, 1982.

"How Scooba Received Its Name." Kemper County Historical Society vertical files.

Irvine, Keith (ed.). *Encyclopedia of Indians of the Americas.* Vol. 2. St. Clair Shores, Michigan: Scholarly Press, 1974.

McKinney, Samuel M., Jr. *St. Teresa of Avila Catholic Church, A History: 1868–1993.* Chatawa: Samuel M. McKinney, Jr., 1993.

Pelahatchie, Mississippi, 1981 Annual Report. Town of Pelahatchie, 1981.

Reed, Rad H. *Houlka, Yesterday, Today.* Memphis: Press of S. C. Toof & Co., 1914.

"Shuqualak Anniversary Looms, Noxubee Town has Scenic Past." *Jackson Daily News.* March 11, 1964.

Sumners, Cecil L. *Chief Tishomingo: A History of the Chickasaw Indians, and Some Historical Events of Their Era (1737–1839).* Amory: Amory Advertiser, 1974.

Varner. Janet, "Pelahatchie — A Never-Ending Town of Progress." *Morton-Pelahatchie Advertiser.* Aug. 27, 1974:1.

Walker, Durr., Jr. *Lincoln County, Mississippi: A Pictorial History.* Norfolk, Virginia: Donning Co. Pub., 1998.

Ward, Dorothy. "Byhalia is Coming Back

Strong." *Memphis Press-Scimitar*. Jan. 17, 1980.

Wayman, Norbury L. *Life on the River: A Pictorial History of the Mississippi, the Missouri, and the Western River System*. New York: Bonanza Books, 1962.

Weeks, Linton. *Clarksdale & Coahoma County: A History*. Clarksdale: Carnegie Public Library, 1982.

Winston, J. "Okolona." Sept. 14, 1935. Okolona Carnegie Public Library vertical files.

Yates, Jenelle B., and Theresa T. Ridout. *Red Clay Hills of Neshoba*. Neshoba County Historical Society, 1992.

"Yazoo—What Does It Mean?"; "A Brief History of the County." Yazoo City Public Library vertical files.

Missouri

Alexander, Wanda. Monegaw Springs. Letter to author, January 25, 2000.

Cramer, Rose. F. *Wayne County, Missouri*. Cape Girardeau: Ramfre Press, 1972.

Federal Writers' Project. *Missouri: A Guide to the "Show Me" State*. New York: Duell, Sloan and Pearce, 1941.

History of Clark County, Missouri, Bicentennial, Kahoka, 1976.

Kenoma, Lakeside Hamlet: 1880–1983. Town of Kenoma, 1983.

"Location of Neosho"; "Beautiful Neosho." Newton County Historical Society vertical files.

McMillen, Margot F. *A to Z Missouri: The Dictionary of Missouri Place Names*. Columbia: Pebble Pub., 1996.

Oregon County, Missouri. Alton: Oregon County Historical Society, 1992.

Ramsey, Robert L. *Our Storehouse of Missouri Place Names*. Columbia: University of Missouri, 1952.

Watters, George F. *History of Webster County, 1855–1955*. Springfield: George F. Watters, 1955.

Montana

Annin, Jim. *They Gazed on the Beartooth Mountains*. Billings: Reporter Printing & Supply Co., 1964.

Armstrong, J. B. *Bedding the Drags*. Missoula: University of Montana, 1972.

Cheney, Roberta C. *Names on the Face of Montana: The Story of Montana's Place Names*. Missoula: University of Montana, 1971.

Chinook: The First 100 Years, Centennial. Great Falls: VisYuill Enterprises, 1989.

McAlear, J. F. *The Fabulous Flathead*. Polson: Treasure State Pub., 1962.

Merrill, Andrea, and Judy Jacobson. *Montana Almanac*. Helena: Falcon Press, 1997.

Paul, Rodman W. *Mining Frontiers of the Far West: 1848–1880*. New York: Holt. Rinehart and Winston, 1963.

Reflections of the Past. Bozeman: Montana Ghost Town Preservation Society, 1983.

VanWest, Carroll. *A Traveler's Companion to Montana History*. Helena: Montana Historical Society, 1986.

Wetzel, Betty. *Missoula: The Town and the People*. Montana Magazine, 1987.

Wright, John B. *Montana Places: Exploring Big Sky Country*. Mesilla: New Mexico Geographical Society, 2000.

Nebraska

"A Jaunt Through Our Lively Town." *Dakota City Mail*. Feb. 16, 1872.

Bull, Mrs. H. H. "Mrs. H. H. Bull Writes of Early Pawnee City History." *The Pawnee Republican*. April 2, 1966.

Butcher, Solomon. *Pioneer History of Custer County, Nebraska*. Denver, Colorado: Sage Books, 1965.

Creigh, Dorothy W. *Adams County: The Story, 1872–1972*. Hastings: Adams County-Hastings Centennial Commission, 1972.

Federal Writers' Project. *Nebraska: A Guide to the Cornhusker State*. New York: Viking Press, 1939.

Fitzpatrick, Lilian L. *Nebraska Place-Names*.

Lincoln: University of Nebraska Press, 1960.

Gaston, William. *History of Custer County, Nebraska.* Lincoln: Western Pub. & Engraving Co., 1919.

Giago, Tim. "From Lakota Country to Land of Dakota." *Lakota Times.* n.d.

History of the State of Nebraska. Chicago: Western Historical Co., 1882.

Huse, William. *The History of Dixon County, Nebraska.* Norfolk: Press of the Daily News, 1896.

Kolar, Anna. Monowi. Letter to author, June 25, 1999.

Lee, Wayne. *Wild Towns of Nebraska.* Caldwell, Idaho: Caxton Printers, 1988.

"Minatare." Minatare Public Library vertical files.

Moulton, Candy. *Roadside History of Nebraska.* Missoula, Montana: Mountain Press, 1997.

"Nemaha City." *Nebraska State Journal.* June 1887: 15.

Niobrara Centennial Book. Niobrara Centennial Committee, 1958.

Perkey, Elton A. *Perkey's Nebraska Place-Names.* Lincoln: Nebraska State Historical Society, 1995.

Rapp, William F. *Postal History of Nebraska: Part 2.* Crete: J-B Pub., 1985.

Rodaway, Norman. *Unadilla. the First 100 Years: 1871–1971.* Unadilla: Norman Rodaway, 1971.

Sheldon, Ruth A. "Newhawka's 100th Birthday Based on Faith in Area." *Plattsmouth Journal.* July 23, 1987.

Silverberg, Robert. *Ghost Towns of the American West.* New York: Thomas Y. Crowell Co., 1968.

Tekamah: 1854–1954. Tekamah Chamber of Commerce, 1954

"The Dakota Country, As Seen in 1857 by the Editor of the *Omaha Nebraskian.*" *Eagle.* July 15, 1857.

Vandenack, Marjorie B. "Yutan Woman Researches Chief Ietan." *Wahoo Newspaper.* Aug. 8, 1991: 7A.

Wahoo's Century Roundup. Wahoo Centennial Committee, 1970.

"Yutan History." Yutan Public Library vertical files.

Nevada

Ashbaugh, Don. *Nevada's Turbulent Yesterday: A Study in Ghost Towns.* Los Angeles: Westernlore Press, 1963.

Carlson, Helen S. *Nevada Place Names: A Geographical Dictionary.* Reno: University of Nevada Press, 1974.

Elliott, Russell R. *History of Nevada.* Reno: University of Nebraska Press, 1987.

Federal Writers' Project. *Nevada: A Guide to the Silver State.* Portland: Binfords & Mort, 1940.

_____. *Origin of Place Names: Nevada.* Reno: Nevada State Dept. of Highways and State Dept. of Education, 1941.

Gamett, James, and Stanley W. Paher. *Nevada Post Offices.* Las Vegas: Nevada Pub., 1983.

Hall, Shawn. *Romancing Nevada's Past.* Reno: University of Nevada, 1994.

Hulse, James W. *The Silver State.* Reno: University of Nevada, 1998.

Leigh, Rufus W. *Nevada Place Names: Their Origin and Significance.* Salt Lake City: Deseret Press, 1964.

McCracken, Robert D. *A History of Pahrump, Nevada.* Tonopah: Nye County Press, 1990.

Paher, Stanley. *Nevada Ghost Towns & Mining Camps.* Berkeley: Howell-North Books, 1970.

Patterson, Edna. *Who Named It? History of Elko County Place Names.* Elko: Warren & Mary Monroe, Pub., 1964.

Reproduction of Thompson and West's History of Humboldt County, 1881, With Illustrations and Biographical Sketches of Its Prominent Men and Pioneers. Berkeley: Howell-North Books, 1958.

Toll, David W. *The Complete Nevada Traveler: A Guide to the State.* Reno: University of Nevada Press, 1976.

"Tuscarora, Nevada." Tuscarora Branch Library vertical files.

Williams, Brad, and Choral Pepper. *Lost Treasures of the West.* New York: Holt, Rinehart and Winston, 1975.

New Hampshire

Arrett, Albert, and Alice E. Ledtiver. *Jaffrey History: Narrative*. Vol. 1. Town of Jaffrey, 1937.

Bartlett, John H. *The Story of Sunapee*. Washington. D.C.: Byron S. Adams, 1941.

"Chocorua and His Mountain." *Weirs Times*. Vol. 5, No. 52. Dec. 26, 1996.

Cook, Edward M., Jr. *Ossipee, New Hampshire: 1785–1985, A History*. New Hampshire: Peter Randall, Pub., 1989.

Doolittle, Dorothy. Ashuelot. Letter to author, February 10, 1999.

Federal Writers' Project. *New Hampshire: A Guide to the Granite State*. Boston: Houghton Mifflin, 1938.

History of Merrimack, New Hampshire. Vol. 1. Merrimack Historical Society, 1976.

Hunt, Elmer M. *New Hampshire Town Names and Whence They Came*. Peterborough: Noone House, 1970.

Life and Times in Hopkinton, 1735–1970. Hopkinton: New Hampshire Antiquarian Society, 1970.

Manoian, Alan S. "The Enduring Power of the Mills." *The Nashua Century*, 1997.

McDuffee, Franklin. *The History of Rochester, New Hampshire*. Manchester: J.B. Clarke Co., 1892.

Scales, John. *History of Strafford County, New Hampshire, and Representative Citizens*. Chicago: Richmond-Arnold Pub., 1914.

"Stagecoaches and Roads to Nashua." *The Nashua Century*, 1997.

New Jersey

"Abescon Has Colorful and Moving History." *Atlantic City Press*. June 12, 1960: 5.

Alotta, Robert I. *Signposts & Settlers: The History of Place Names in the Middle Atlantic States*. Chicago: Bonus Books, 1992.

Atkins, George F. "Historical Background — Shamong." *Indian Mills Historical Society*. n.d.

Becker, Donald W. *Indian Place-Names in New Jersey*. Cedar Grove: Phillips-Campbell Pub., 1964.

Bisbee, Henry H. *Sign Posts: Place Names and History of Burlington County, New Jersey*. Willingboro: Alexia Press, 1971.

Bogert, Frederick W. *Paramus: A Chronicle of Four Centuries*. Paramus Free Library, 1961.

Brescia, Louis A., and Lillias F. Brescia. *Stafford Township — A Pictorial Review*, Louis A. and Lillias F. Brescia, 1964.

Brown, James S. *Manalapan in Three Centuries*. Township of Manalapan, 1991.

Chesterfield Township Heritage. Chesterfield Township Tercentenary Committee, 1964.

Edwards, Carl I. *Pequannock Township: 1740–1956, A Town's Growth in Words and Pictures*. Pequannock Township: Carlton & Smith Print Co., 1956.

Federal Writers' Project. *Matawan, 1686–1936*. Newark: Brown Pub. & Printing, 1936.

_____. *New Jersey: A Guide to Its Present and Past*. New York: Hastings House, 1939.

Fichter, Jack. *The Pennsauken Story*. Pennsauken Township Committee, 1991.

Griscom, Lloyd. *Tales of Three Towns: Cinnaminson, Palmyra, Riverton*. Riverton: Lloyd Griscom, 1981.

"History of Paramus." *Paramus Chamber of Commerce Directory*, 1995–1996.

"Hoboken, The Mile Square City." *Hoboken Historical Museum*. n.d

Ho-Ho-Kus: 1908–1958. Ho-Ho-Kus 50th Anniversary Committee, 1958.

Izon, Michelle. "Remembering Old Absecon." *South Jersey Advisor*. Oct. 23–29, 1992: 4.

Know Your Town: Pequannock Township, New Jersey. Pequannock League of Women Voters, 1969.

Kraft, Herbert C. *The Lenape or Delaware Indians*. South Orange: Seton Hall University Museum, 1996.

"New Jersey Historic Sites Inventory." Prepared by Acroterion, Historic Preservation Consultants. *Morris County Heritage Commission*, 1987.

None Outside Parsippany. Parsippany: *Daily Record*, 1976.

Potter, Ginny. "Netcong, 1900." *Sunday Daily Record*. May 25, 1975.

"Remembering Old Abescon." *South Jersey Advisor*. Oct. 16–22, 1992.
Salvini, Emil R. *Historic Pequannock Township*. Lyndhurst: Wheal Grace Corporation Historical Pub., 1987.
Struble, Evelin A. *In the Ramapos*. Patterson: Rocco Press, 1966.
Sullivan, Elizabeth A., and Dorothy H. Voorhees. "The History of Watchung, New Jersey, 1934." Watchung Public Library vertical files.
Taylor, Mildred. *The History of Teaneck*. Teaneck American Revolution Bicentennial Committee, 1977.
Township of Ocean Monmouth County, New Jersey, Commemorative Book Published for the Centennial. Ocean Township Centennial Corporation, 1949.

New Mexico

Casey, Robert L. *Journey to the High Southwest*. Seattle: Pacific Search Press, 1983.
Clark, Mary Grooms. *A History of New Mexico: A Mark of Time*. Canyon, Texas: Staked Plains Press, 1983.
Dutton, Bertha. *Indians of the American Southwest*. Englewood Cliffs: Prentice-Hall, Inc., 1975.
Federal Writers' Project. *New Mexico: A Guide to the Colorful State*. New York: Hastings House, 1940.
Fugate, Francis L., and Roberta B. Fugate. *Roadside History of New Mexico*. Missoula, Montana: Mountain Press, 1989.
Gregg, Andrew. *New Mexico in the 19th Century*. Albuquerque: University of New Mexico, 1968.
Helbock, Richard W. *Post Offices of New Mexico*. Las Cruces: Richard W. Helbock, 1981.
Hillerman, Tony. *New Mexico, Rio Grande, and Other Essays*. Portland, Oregon: Graphic Arts Center Pub., 1974.
Hinshaw, Gil. *Tucumcari: Gateway to the West*. Hobbs: Gil Hinshaw, 1997.
Kosik, Fran. *Native Roads*. Flagstaff: Creative Solutions Pub., 1996.
Linford, Laurance D. *Navajo Places: History, Legend, Landscape*. Logan: University of Utah Press, 2000.
Ludmer, Larry H. *New Mexico Guide: Be a Traveler, Not a Tourist*. Cold Spring Harbor, New York: Open Road Pub., 1999.
Mays, Buddy. *Indian Villages of the Southwest: A Practical Guide to the Pueblo Indian Villages of New Mexico and Arizona*. San Francisco: Chronicle Books, 1985.
Pearce, T. M. *New Mexico Place Names: A Geographical Dictionary*. Albuquerque: University of New Mexico Press, 1965.
Poling-Kempes, Lesley. *Valley of Shining Stone: The Story of Abiquiu*. Tucson: University of Arizona Press, 1997.
Quay County: 1903–1985. Tucumcari: Quay County Book Committee, 1985.
White, Leslie. A. *The Acoma Indians, Forty-Seventh Annual Report of the Bureau of American Ethnology to the Secretary of the Smithsonian Institution, 1929–1930*. Glorietta: Rio Grande Press, 1973.
Whittington, Debra A. *In the Shadow of the Mountain: Living in Tucumcari*, Amarillo, Texas: Copperleaf Press, 1997.

New York

"A Short History of Wantagh." Wantagh Public Library vertical files.
An Illustrated History of Massapequa. Massapequa Post, 1968.
An Informal History of Richmond, New York, For the Settlements of Honeoye, Allen's Hill, Richmond Mills, Richmond Center and Dennison's Corners. Honeoye Senior Citizens' Bicentennial Committee of Honeoye, 1976.
Barker, Ruth F. *Quogue Through the Centuries*. Quogue: Ruth F. Barker, 1955.
Bayles, Thomas R. "Mills of Yaphank." *Patchogue Advance*. December 6, 1956.
Beauchamp, William M. *Aboriginal Place Names of New York*. New York State Education Dept. Detroit: Grand River Books, 1971.
Brown, John M. *Brief Sketch of First Settlement of the County of Schoharie by the Germans*. Schoharie: L. Cuthbert, 1823.

Carman, Russell V. *Quogue, 1659–1984: The 325th Anniversary of the Purchase of the Lands From the Shinnecock Indians.* Quogue: Quogue Historical Society, 1984.

Celebrate Clarkstown: 1791–1991. Clarkstown Bicentennial Commission, 1991.

Child, Hamilton. *Gazetteer and Business Directory for Rensselaer County, N.Y.* New York: Journal Office, 1870.

Conover, George S., and Lewis C. Aldrich. *History of Ontario County, New York.* Syracuse: D. Mason & Co., 1893.

Coxsackie Declaration Bicentennial, May 17–24, 1975. Hillcrest Press, 1975.

Coxsackie On the Hudson, New York, 1776–1976. Town of Coxsackie Bicentennial Committee, 1976.

Craven, Charles E. *A History of Mattituck, Long Island, N.Y.* Mattituck: Amereon House, 1906.

DeGraff, Lee S. (ed.). *Post Offices of New York State: 1792–1969.* Ballston Spa: Empire State Postal History Society, 1969.

DeLancey, Edward F. *Mamaroneck From Colonial Times Through the First Century of the Republic.* Mamaroneck: American Revolution Bicentennial Committee, 1976.

Douglas, Sandra, and Jean Meyers. "Early History of Syosset." Syosset Public Library vertical files.

Duncombe, Frances E. "Katonah: 1878–1987." Katonah Village Improvement Society, 1978.

"Early Caneadea." Town of Caneadea. n.d.

"Early Skaneatles." Skaneatles Public Library vertical files.

Eide, Elizabeth. *Copiague— Your Town and Mine.* Copiague: Board of Education, 1971.

Everts, L. H. *History of Cattaraugus Co., New York, with Illustrations and Biographical Sketches of Some of Its Prominent Men and Pioneers.* Philadelphia: J. B. Lippincott, 1879.

Federal Writers Project. *New York City Guide.* New York: Random House, 1939.

_____. *New York: A Guide to the Empire State.* New York: Oxford University Press, 1940.

Frost, James A. *Life On the Upper Susquehanna, 1783–1860.* New York: Columbia University, 1951.

Frost, Marjorie. *From Early Years, Town of Nunda, 1808–1983.* Dalton: Burt's Printing Service, 1983.

Fulcher, William G. *Mamaroneck Through the Years.* Larchmont: Larchmont Times. n.d.

Gleason, Gene. "A History of Commack." Commack Branch Library vertical files.

Gordon, H. W. "History of Patchogue." Patchogue Public Library vertical files.

Gordon, Thomas. *Gazetteer of the State of New York.* Philadelphia: T. K. & P. G. Collins Printers, 1836.

Greene, Nelson. *The Old Mohawk Turnpike Book.* Fort Plain: Press of Journal & Courier, 1924.

Groves, Helen. Otego. Letter to author, March 15, 1999.

Herrick, Margaret. *Early Settlements in Dutchess County, NY.* Rhinebeck: Kinship, 1994.

Historical Gazetteer and Biographical Memorial of Cattaraugus County, New York. New York: Lyman, Horton & Cox. Ltd., 1983.

History of Montgomery and Fulton Counties, N.Y., with Illustrations Descriptive of Scenery, Private Residences, Public Buildings, Fine Blocks, etc. New York: F. W. Beers & Co. 1878.

History of Queens County, New York, With Illustrations, Portraits, & Sketches of Prominent Families and Individuals, etc. Albany: W. W. Munsell & Co., 1882.

Howell, George R. *The Early History of Southampton, L.I., New York, with Genealogies.* New York: J. N. Hallock, 1866.

Klein, Howard. *Three Village Guidebook: The Setaukets, Poquott, Old Field & Stony Brook.* East Setauket: Three Village Historical Society, 1986.

Lawson, Dorris. "A Short History of Canastota for Young People." Dorris Lawson, Lenox Historian. n.d.

"Nesconset, Creating a Street to Reach Their Land." *Newsday.* Feb. 22, 1998.

Nichols, Claude A. *Sullivan in History, Interesting People and Events, etc.* Chittenango: McHenry Press, Inc., 1939.

Nundarama: A Sesquicentennial Souvenir: 1808–1958. Nunda Sesquicentennial Committee, 1958.

"Patchogue, Product of a Lottery." *Long Island Forum.* Aug. 1947: 145.

"Patchogue of Indian Derivation." *Long Island Advance.* Dec. 5, 1946.

Post, Richard H. *Notes on Quogue: 1659–1959. East Hampston Star,* 1959.

Reinstein, Julya B. *A History of the Town of Cheektowaga.* Buffalo: Buffalo & Erie County Historical Society, 1971.

Reynolds, Helen W. *Poughkeepsie: The Origin and Meaning of the Word.* Dutchess County Historical Society, 1924.

Sedore, Emma, Town Historian, Owego. Letter to author, March 18, 1999.

Shandaken Bicentennial. Town of Shandaken Bicentennial Commission, 1976.

Sherwin, Mark. "Jamaica Owes Name to Indians' Beaver." *Daily News.* Feb. 9, 1936.

Smith, Philip H. *General History of Duchess County: 1609–1876.* Pawling: Philip H. Smith, 1877.

Southold Town, 350th Anniversary: 1640–1990. Southold Celebration Journal, 1990.

Strong, John A. *The Algonquian Peoples of Long Island from Earliest Times to 1900.* Interlaken: Empire State Books, 1997.

Sullivan, Dr. James. *The History of New York State.* Book V, Chapter III. New York: Lewis Historical Pub., 1927.

"Syosset, For Centuries, A Land of Plenty." *Newsday.* Feb. 22, 1998: 67.

Terwilliger, Katharine T. *Napanoch, Land Overflowed by Water.* Ellenville Library and Museum, 1982.

"The Town of Owego, Including the Village of Owego, Tioga County." *NY Socio-Economic Profile,* 1993.

Tooker, William W. *The Indian Place-Names on Long Island and Islands Adjacent, with Their Probable Significations.* New York: G. P. Putnam's Sons, 1911.

Town of Canisteo History to 1873. Canisteo Centennial Committee, 1973.

"Tuckahoe Hills." *Eastchester Record.* Nov. 27, 1977.

"Village of Tuckahoe." *The Villager.* Nov., 1985: 42.

West, Maude I. *Irondequoit Story.* Town of Irondequoit, 1957.

Wyld, Lionel D. *Canastota and Chittenango: Two Historic Canal Towns.* Charleston, South Carolina: Arcadia Pub., 1998.

"Yaphank. Community Took Off with Railroad's Arrival." www.lihistory.com/spectown/hist0069.

Yates, Austin A. *Schenectady County: Its History to the Close of the Nineteenth Century.* New York Historical Co., 1902.

North Carolina

Bishop, Bonnie. "Toxaway in Cherokee Language: Red Bird." *Translyvania Times.* Jan. 28, 1976.

"Catawba is Believed County's Oldest Settlement." *Observer-News Enterprise.* Jan., 1969.

Durschlag, Dr. Richard, Director, Museum of the Waxhaws. Letter to author, July 9, 2000.

Federal Writers' Project. *North Carolina: A Guide to the Old North State.* Chapel Hill: University of North Carolina Press, 1939.

Goerch, Carl. *Ocracoke.* Winston-Salem: John F. Blair, 1956.

Heritage of Transylvania County, North Carolina. Heritage Book Committee, 1995.

"History of Pace's Gap." Polk County Library vertical files.

Lassiter, Mable S. "Tradition Says Saxapahaw Named by Newlin." *N.C. Times-News.* June 1, 1991.

"More on Cooleemee's Indian Connections." *Cooleemee History Loom.* No. 17. Fall 1994: 1, 9.

Payne, Roger L. *Place Names of the Outer Banks.* Washington: Thomas A. Williams, 1985.

Plemmons, Jan C. *Treasures of Toxaway.* Jacksonville, Florida: J. C. Plemmons, 1984.

Powell, William S. *The North Carolina Gazetteer: A Dictionary of Tar Heel Places.* Chapel Hill: University of North Carolina Press, 1968.

Preslar, Charles J., Jr. *A History of Catawba*

County, Salisbury: Rowan Printing, 1954.

Rights, Douglas L. *The American Indian in North Carolina.* Winston-Salem: John F. Blair, 1957.

Ross, Thomas E. *American Indians in North Carolina: Geographic Interpretations.* Southern Pines: Karo Hollow Press, 1999.

Simmons, Geitner. "Catawba Links the County to Its Past." *Observer-News-Enterprise.* Dec. 8, 1986.

Stick, David. *An Outer Banks Reader.* Chapel Hill: University of North Carolina Press, 1998.

_____. *The Outer Banks of North Carolina: 1584–1958.* Chapel Hill: University of North Carolina Press, 1958.

North Dakota

Federal Writers' Project. *North Dakota: A Guide to the Northern Prairie State.* New York: Oxford University Press, 1950.

Fristad, Palma. *Historic Mandan and Morton County: Early Days to 1970.* Mandan: Palma Fristad, 1970.

Lakota's 75 Years: Lakota Diamond Jubilee, June 18, 19, 20, 1950. Lakota Diamond Jubilee Committee, 1950.

Makoti Diamond Jubilee: 1911–1986. Makoti Diamond Jubilee Committee, 1958.

"On-a-Slant, Mandan Village." North Dakota Parks & Recreation Dept., Bismarck, 1990.

Peterson, Marion P. *Morton Prairie Roots, American Revolution Bicentennial Heritage Project: 1776–1976.* Dallas: Taylor Pub., 1976.

"Proudly We Speak." Neche Methodist Church files.

Tostevin, Sarah. "Mantin: A History of Mandan-Morton County." *Mandan Chamber of Commerce,* 1964.

"Wahpeton, North Dakota." Leach Public Library vertical files.

Wick, Douglas A. *North Dakota Place Names.* Fargo: Prairie House, 1989.

Williams, Mary Ann B. *Origins of North Dakota Place Names.* Bismarck: Bismarck Tribune, 1966.

Ohio

"A Brief History of Piqua." *Piqua Historical Museum.* n.d.

Aldrich, Lewis C. (ed.). *History of Erie County, Ohio: with Illustrations and Biographical Sketches of Some of Its Prominent Men and Pioneers.* Syracuse: D. Mason, 1889

Hurt, R. Douglas. *The Ohio Frontier: Crucible of the Old Northwest, 1720–1830.* Bloomington: Indiana University Press, 1996.

Large, Moina W. *History of Ashtabula County, Ohio.* Vol. I. Topeka: Historical Pub. Co., 1924.

Miller, Larry L. *Ohio Place Names.* Bloomington: Indiana University Press, 1996.

Newman, Frank J. (ed.). *Portraits from the Past, Souvenir Book.* Sandusky Area Sesquicentennial, Inc., 1968.

Overman, William D. *Ohio Town Names.* Akron: Atlantic Press, 1958.

Peeke, Hewson. *A Standard History of Erie County, Ohio.* New York: Lewis Pub. Co., 1916.

Reinhart, Paul F., and Barbara Vogel (comp.). *A Brief History of Auglaise County.* Wapakoneta: A Sesquicentennial Publication, 1998.

Sandusky Area Sesquincentennial: 1818–1968. Sandusky Sesquincentennial Committee, 1968.

Tontogany Times, Story of of Tontogany, Ohio: 1875–1975. Tontogany History Committee, 1975.

"Welcome to Wapakoneta." Wapakoneta Area Chamber of Commerce. n.d.

Williams, William W. *History of Ashtabula County, Ohio.* Philadelphia: Williams Bros., 1878.

Oklahoma

Allen, Raymond. Ochelata. Letter to author, Aug. 20, 1999.

Atoka County Heritage. Atoka: Atoka County Historical Society, 1983.

Benedict, John D. *Muskogee and Northeastern Oklahoma.* Vol. I. Chicago: S. J. Clark Pub., 1922.

Cannon, Phil., and Glen D. Carter. *Tecumseh, Oklahoma: An Illustrated History of Its First Century*. Inola: Evans Pub., 1991.

"Catoosa." Catoosa Public Library vertical files.

Clubb, Ike. "My Early Days in Kaw City." *The Kaw City News*. Jan. 15, 1942.

Corbett, William P. "Peerless Princess of the Best Country: The Early Years of Tonkawa." Reprint from the *Chronicles of Oklahoma*. Vol. LXIII, No. 4. Winter 1984–85.

Cox, Pauline. "Lucy Tayiah Eads." *Wind People*. No. 002. Spring 1997: 7.

Ellis, Doris F (comp.). *Choctaw, Oklahoma and Eastern Oklahoma County: A History, A Centennial Celebration of People, Places, and Times: 1893–1993*. Harrah: Eagle Printing, 1993.

Federal Writers' Project. *The WPA Guide to 1930s Oklahoma*. Lawrence: University Press of Kansas, 1986.

Fugate, Francis L., and Roberta B. Fugate. *Roadside History of Oklahoma*. Missoula, Montana: Mountain Press, 1991.

Gamblin, Yvonne. *Checotah Historical Highlights: 1890–1990*. Marcelene, Missouri: Heritage House, 1990.

Gibson, Arrell M. *Oklahoma: A History of Five Centuries*. Norman: University of Oklahoma Press, 1965.

Gideon, D.C. *Indian Territory, Descriptive Biographical and Genealogical, Including the Landed Estates, County Seats, etc.* New York: Lewis Pub., 1901.

Gould, Charles N. *Oklahoma Place Names*. Norman: University of Oklahoma Press, 1933.

Harper, Sharron. Talala. Letter to author, December 6, 1999.

Harper, W. R. "Musical Indian Names." *The Claremore Weekly Progress*. Nov. 1930: 8.

"Historical Significance of Waynoka and Its Depot and Harvey House." Waynoka Historical Society vertical files.

"History of Tahlequah." Northeastern State University vertical files.

"History of the Kaw City Depot." *Kaw City Museum News*. Spring 1994: 1.

Jackson, Pauline P. "The Sapulpa Story to 1929." Thesis submitted in partial fulfillment of Master of Arts, University of Tulsa, 1956.

"Ka-Na-Wa, 'String of Beads'." Konawa Historical Society vertical files.

Keneda, Scott. Skedee. Email to author, February 8, 2002.

Martin, Baird. *Industrial and Civic Survey of Okmulgee and Okmulgee County*, 1936. Okmulgee Public Library vertical files.

McReynolds, Edwin C. *Oklahoma: A History of the Sooner State*. Norman: University of Oklahoma Press, 1964.

Methvin, Rev. J.J. *In the Limelight or History of Anadarko (Caddo County) and Vicinity From the Earliest Days*. Oklahoma City: Walker-Wilson Titles Co., 1926.

"Ochelata." Bartlesville Public Library vertical files.

Okema Remembered: A Brief History of Okemah, Oklahoma. Okfuskee: Okfuskee County Historical Board. n.d.

Okmulgee Historical Society. *History of Okmulgee County, Oklahoma*. Tulsa: Historical Enterprises, Inc., 1985.

"Our Name." *Konawa Chief-Leader*. March 8, 1912.

Peck, Henry. *Proud Heritage of LeFlore County*. Muscogee: Hoffman Printing, 1967.

Pioneering in Kiowa County. Hobart: Kiowa County Historical Society, 1978.

Raymond, Allen. Ochelata. Letter to author, August, 1999.

Rice, Darrell. "The Origin of Watonga's Name." Blaine County Vertical files.

Shirk, George H. *Oklahoma Place Names*. Norman: University of Oklahoma, 1965.

Tanner, Fred. "Skedee: Why Did They Ever Build a Town There and Why Did It Die?" 1978. Unpublished manuscript. (Text emailed to author by Scott Keneda, Skedee.)

The Last Run: Kay County, Oklahoma, 1893. Ponca Chapter, Daughters of the American Revolution. Ponca City: Courier Printing, 1939.

Their Story: A Pioneer Days Album of the Blaine County Area. Watonga Heritage Book Committee, 1977.

Thoburn, Joseph B., and Isaac Holcomb. *History of Oklahoma*. San Francisco: Doub & Co., 1908.

Webb, Guy P. *History of Grant County, Oklahoma, 1811–1970*. North Newton, Kansas: Grant County Historical Society, 1971.

"Yesterday and Today." *Skiatook Journal*. 1998: 4.

Oregon

Associated Press. "Run to the Rogue Recalls Indians' Forced March." *Mail Tribune*. Sept. 16, 2000: 3A.

Barklow, Irene. *History of the Post Offices of Wallowa County, Oregon*. Taylor Pub., 1983.

Battaile, Connie H. *The Oregon Book*. Missoula, Montana: Mountain Press, 1998.

Beckham, Stephen D. *Land of the Umpqua: A History of Douglas County, Oregon*. Roseburg: Douglas County Commissioners, 1986.

Catholic Encyclopedia. "Siletz Indians." Vol. 12. Robert Appleton Co., 1912. 791–792.

"Come to the Molalla River." *Molalla Area Historical Society*. n.d.

Federal Writers' Project. *Oregon: End of the Trail*. Portland: Binfords & Mort, 1940.

Fosmark, Jack. "Herman Ahlers, Fireweed Honey Man of Push." Email to author, February, 2000.

Gaston, Joseph. *Centennial History of Oregon*. Chicago: S. J. Clark. Pub., 1912.

"General History of the Town of Netarts." *Netarts Steering Committee*. n.d.

Gibson, Betty, Yoncala. Letter to author, January 30, 1999.

Hanson, Inez. *Life on Clatsop*. Astoria: Astoria Printing, 1977.

Harrison, Ruth. "Ever Wonder Where 'Yachats' Got Its Name?" *South Lincoln News*. n.d.

_____. "The Little Log Church By the Sea." *Yachats Museum*, 1994.

Hays, Marjorie H. *The Land That Kept Its Promise: A History of South Lincoln County*. Newport: Lincoln County Historical Society, 1976.

Lockley, Fred. *History of the Columbia River: From the Dalles to the Sea*. Vol. 1. Chicago: S. J. Clark Pub., 1928.

Mallory, Clark. "Little Known About Native Americans Who Gave Name to Clatskanie." *Clatskanie Chief*. Nov. 25, 1999: 11.

McArthur, Lewis L. *Oregon Geographic Names*. Portland: Oregon Historical Society, 1974.

Powers, Alfred. *Little Known Tales from Oregon History*. Vol. 1. Geoff Hill (ed.). Bend: Sun Pub., 1988.

Rock, Alexandria. *Short History of the Little Nestucca River Valley*. Unpublished manuscript. Tillamook, 1949.

Ruby, Robert, and John A. Brown. *Indians of the Pacific Northwest*. Norman: University of Oklahoma Press, 1981.

Todd, John. "History of Clatskanie Indians Discussed." *Clatskanie Chief*. Dec. 30, 1999: 9.

Wiederhold, Kathleen. *Exploring Oregon's Historic Courthouses*. Corvallis: Oregon State University Press, 1998.

Pennsylvania

Anderson, Bill. *Groundhog Day: 1886 to 1992*. Punxsutawney: Spirit Publishing, 1992.

Ashman, George, Aquashicola. Letter to author, June 29, 1999.

Battle, J. H. *The History of Columbia and Montour Counties, Pennsylvania*. Chicago: A. Warner & Co., 1887.

Bradsby, H.C. *History of Bradford County, Pennsylvania, with Biographical Selections*. Chicago: S. B. Nelson & Co., 1891.

Brenckman, Frederick. *History of Carbon County, Pennsylvania, Also Containing a Separate Account of the Several Boroughs and Townships in the County*. Harrisburg: J. J. Nungessen, 1913.

Catasauqua, North Catasauqua: A Profile of the Boroughs. Historic Catasauqua Preservation Association, 1991.

Craft, David. *History of Bradford County, Pennsylvania, with Illustrations of Some of Its Prominent Men and Pioneers*. Philadelphia: L.H. Everts, 1878.

Davis, W. W. H. *History of Bucks County, Pennsylvania, from the Discovery of the Delaware to the Present Time.* Doylestown: Democrat Book & Job Office Printing, 1876.

Delany, Leslie L. *Search for Friedenshutten, 1772–1971.* Wyoming: Cro Woods Pub., 1973.

Donehoo. Dr. George P. *A History of the Indian Villages and Place Names in Pennsylvania.* Harrisburg: Telegraph Press, 1928.

"East Monterey: Maxatawny Section of the Easton Road." *Kutztown Area Historical Society.* Vol. 9, No. 1. Feb. 1986.

Federal Writers' Project. *Pennsylvania: A Guide to the Keystone State.* New York: Oxford University Press. 3rd Printing, 1947.

Gottlund, Jane. "Maxatawny." *Along the Saucony.* Kutztown Area Historical Society. V. 15, No. 4. Nov. 1992.

Greater Shamokin Centennial: 1864–1964. Greater Shamokin Centennial Committee, 1964.

Hazen, Hon. Aaron L. *20th Century History of New Castle and Lawrence County, Pennsylvania, and Representative Citizens.* Chicago: Richmond-Arnold Pub., 1908.

Heverly, Clement F. *History of Sheshequin, Including Hartley's and Sullivan's Expedition, Yankees and Pennamites, Sketches of All the Pioneer Families, etc.* Towanda: Bradford Star Printing, 1902.

_____. *History of the Towandas: 1770–1886, Including the Aborigines, Pennamites, and Yankees, etc.* Towanda: Report-Journal Printing, 1886.

History of Butler County, Pennsylvania: Embracing Its Physical Features, Aborigines and Explorers, Public Lands and Surveys, Pioneers, Early Settlement, etc. Chicago: R. C. Brown & Co., 1895.

History of Monroe County, Pennsylvania: 1725–1976. Stroudsburg: Bicentennial Project of the Pocono Hospital Auxiliary, 1976.

History of Tinicum Township: The First Permanent European Settlement in Pennsylvania, 1643–1993. Tinicum Township Historical Society, 1993.

History of Tioga County, Pennsylvania, With Sketches of Prominent Families and Individuals. New York: W. W. Munsell & Co., 1883.

Jones, Robert J. *Place Names of Monroe County, Pennsylvania.* Apollo: Closson Press, 1993.

Juniata: A County for All Seasons: Sesquicentennial Year. Mifflintown: Juniata County Historical Society, 1981.

Koch, Carol C. "The Maxatawny Farm." *Along the Saucony.* Kutztown Area Historical Society. Vol. 14, No. 3. Sept. 1991.

Korcheck, Robert A. *Nemacolin. The Mine — The Community: 1917–1950,* 1950.

Bicentennial Conshohocken: March to Valley Forge Under General George Washington, 1776–1976. Conshohocken Bicentennial Committee, 1976.

Mathews, Alfred. *History of Wayne, Pike and Monroe Counties, Pennsylvania.* Philadelphia: R. T. Peck & Co., 1886.

"Monongahela Marks Its 200th Anniversary." *PG Washington.* Jan. 28, 1996: W6.

Nanticoke City: Proud of our Heritage, 1798–1993, 200th Anniversary. Town of Nanticoke, 1993.

Pinkowskie, Edward. *Chester County Place Names.* Philadelphia: Sunshine Press, 1962.

Serfass, Donald R. *Iron Steps: Illustrated History of Tamaqua, Pennsylvania.* Tamaqua: Donald R. Surfass, 1995.

Smith, Chester M., Jr. *Pennsylvania Postal History.* Lawrence, Massachusetts: Quarterman Pub., 1976.

Smith, Helene, and George Swetnam. *A Guidebook to Historic Western Pennsylvania.* Pittsburgh: University of Pittsburgh, 1991.

Smith, Robert W. *History of Armstrong County, Pennsylvania.* Chicago: Waterman. Watkins & Co., 1883.

Thomas, Thomas L. "Collieries Around Mahanoy City, PA." Mahanoy City Public Library vertical files.

"Tionesta Fact Sheet, Indian History, and Origin of Name." Sara Bovard Memorial Library vertical files.

Watson, John F. *Annals of Philadelphia and*

Pennsylvania in the Older Time. Philadelphia. J. H. Stoddart & Co., 1877.
Wyomissing Bicentennial. Wyomissing Bicentennial Committee, March 1976.
Yesteryear in Ohiopyle and Surrounding Mountain Communities. Vol. I. Backwoods Books Pub., 1993.

Rhode Island

Boucher, Susan M. *The History of Pawtucket: 1935–1986.* Pawtucket Public Library & Pawtucket Centennial Committee, 1986.
Brown, Henry. Conimicut. Letter to author, February 22, 1999.
Carter, Virginia (ed.). *Reflections of Coventry's Yesterdays.* Coventry Public Library, 1976.
Cole, J.R. *History of Washington and Kent Counties.* New York: W. W. Preston & Co., 1889.
D'Amato, Donald. Conimicut. Letter to author, February 16, 1999.
_____. *Coventry Celebration: A Pictorial History.* Norfolk, Virginia: Donning Co. Pub., 1991.
Federal Writers' Project. *Rhode Island: A Guide to the Smallest State.* Boston: Houghton Mifflin, 1937.
Goodrich, Rev. Massena. *Historical Sketch of the Town of Pawtucket.* Pawtucket: Nickerson. Sibley & Co., 1876.
Historic and Architectural Resources of Little Compton, Rhode Island. Providence: Rhode Island Historical Preservation Commission, 1990.
History of Rhode Island: 1636–1878. Philadelphia: Hoag, Wade & Co., 1878.
History of the Town of Hopkinton, Rhode Island: 1757–1976. Hopkinton Bicentennial Commission, 1976.
Pawtucket: Past and Present. Pawtucket: Slater Trust Co., 1917.
Stretch, George E. (ed.). *Three Centuries, Little Compton: 1675–1975.* George E. Stretch, 1975.
"Walk Woonsocket." Blackstone Valley Tourism Council. n.d.
Wright, Marion, and Robert J. Sullivan. *The Rhode Island Atlas.* Providence: Rhode Island Publications Society, 1982.

South Carolina

Abate, Frank R. (ed.). *Omni Gazetteer of the United States of America.* Detroit: Omnigraphics, Inc., 1991.
Alexander, Jerry. *A Little Place Called Cateechee.* Cateechee: Jerry Alexander, 1981.
Both Sides of the Swamp, Hampton County. Hampton: Hampton County Tricentennial Commission, 1970.
Brown, Douglas S. *The Catawba Indians: The People of the River.* Columbia: University of South Carolina, 1966.
"Cateechee Mill Village Was County's First." *Pickens County Heritage,* 1995.
Cordial, Grace. Okatie. Letter to author, July 20, 2000.
Federal Writers' Project. *Palmetto Place Names.* Columbia: Sloan Printing, 1941.
_____. *South Carolina: A Guide to the Palmetto State.* New York: Oxford University Press. 3rd Printing. 1946.
Honea Path Milestones. Misc. files, town of Honea Path.
Lewis, Catherine H. *Horry County, South Carolina: 1730–1993.* Columbia: University of South Carolina Press, 1998.
Malone, George W. *An Attractive New Book Describing the Principal Towns of Lancaster County, South Carolina.* Enterprise Pub., 1900.
Neuffer, Claude H. (ed.). *Names in South Carolina.* Vols. I-XII. 1954–1965. Columbia: University of South Carolina, 1965.
Pluckette, Clara C., and Clara Childs Mackenzie. *Edisto: A Sea Island Principality.* Cleveland, Ohio: Seaforth Pub., 1978.
Rowland, Lawrence S., Alexander Moore, and George C. Rogers, Jr. *The History of Beaufort County, South Carolina, Vol. 1, 1514–1861.* Columbia: University of South Carolina Press, 1996.

South Dakota

Black Thunder, Elijah, *et al. Ehanna Woyakapi, History and Culture of the Sisseton-Wahpeton Sioux Tribe of South Dakota*. Sisseton: Sisseton-Wahpeton Sioux Tribe, 1975.

Brule County History. Pukwana: Brule County Historical Society, 1977.

Federal Writers' Project. *A South Dakota Guide*. Pierre: State Pub. Co., 1938.

_____. *South Dakota Place Names*. Vermillion: University of South Dakota, 1941.

Jackson-Washabaugh Counties: 1915–1965. Kadoka: Jackson-Washabaugh County Historical Society, 1965.

Remembrances, Onaka, S.D. Onaka Diamond Jubilee Committee, 1982.

Schlueter, John H. *History of Canistota from 1878 to 1959*. Canistota: Canistota Clipper, 1959.

Snever, Virginia Driving Hawk. *Dakota's Heritage: A Compilation of Indian Place Names in South Dakota*. Sioux Falls: Brevet Press, 1973.

Thompson, E. L. (ed.). *75 Years of Sully County History: 1883–1958*. Onida: Onida Watchman, 1958.

"Yankton's Rich History." *Yankton Magazine*. Summer 1998: 23.

Tennessee

Chitty, Arthur B. *Sewanee Sampler*. New Orleans: University Press of the South, 1978.

Cities of the United States. Vol. 1. Detroit: Gale Research, 1994.

Donnelly, Polly W. (ed.). *James County: A Lost County of Tennessee, Old James Chapter*. Knoxville: East Tennessee Historical Society, 1983.

Federal Writers' Project. *Tennessee: A Guide to the State*. New York: Hastings House, 1949.

History of Coffee County. Chicago: Goodspeed Pub., 1887.

Livingood, James W. *A History of Hamilton County, Tennessee*. Memphis: Memphis State University Press, 1981.

Miller, Larry L. *Tennessee Place Names*. Bloomington: Indiana University Press, 2001.

People's History of Claiborne County, Tennessee: 1801–1988. Claiborne County Historical Society, 1988.

"Tullahoma History." City of Tullahoma. n.d.

Tullahoma, 1851. Historic Preservation Society of Tullahoma, 1986.

Texas

Baker, T. Lindsay. *Building the Lone Star*. College Station: Texas A & M, 1986.

Bicentennial Commemorative History of Nacogdoches. Nacogdoches Jaycees, 1976.

Braake, Alex L. *Texas: A Drama of Its Postal Past*. State College, Pennsylvania: American Philatelic Society, 1970.

"Cayuga Settled in 1846: Originally Called Judson." *Athens Review*. March 15, 1951.

Drake, Sandy. Waka. Email to author, February 29, 2000.

Dunlop, Richard. *Great Trails of the West*. Nashville: Abingdon Press, 1971.

Federal Writers' Project. *Texas: A Guide to the Lone Star State*. New York: Hastings House, 1940.

Gallaway, Alecya. "Coast Country Memories." *Bay Watcher*. Vol. 2, No. 4. Jan. 26, 1995: 1.

Handbook of Texas. Vol. II. Austin: Texas State Historical Association, 1952.

Hanna, Betty E. *Doodle Bugs and Cactus Berries: A Historical Sketch of Stephens County*. Burnet: Nortex Press, 1975.

Henson, Margaret, and Kevin Ladd. *Chambers County: A Pictorial History*. Norfolk, Virginia: Donning Co. ,1988.

Johnson, Michael G. *The Native Tribes of North America: A Concise Encyclopedia*. New York: MacMillan Pub., 1994.

Mason County Historical Book. Mason: Mason County Historical Commission, 1976.

Memorial and Biographical History of Navarro, Henderson, Anderson, Limestone, Freestone and Leon Counties, Texas. Chicago: Lewis Pub., 1893.

Metz, Leon C. *Roadside History of Texas.* Missoula, Montana: Mountain Press, 1994.

New Handbook of Texas. Vol. I. Austin: Texas State Historical Association, 1996.

Newcomb, W. W. *The Indians of Texas from Prehistoric to Modern Times.* Austin: University of Texas Press, 1961.

Polk, Dorothy. "Pontotoc Once Had Movie Theater and Newspaper." *Mason County News.* July 15, 1976: Sec. 4. 6.

Pruett, Jakie L., and Everett B. Cole. *The History & Heritage of Goliad County.* Austin: Eakin Pub., 1983.

Quanah: 1884–1984. Quanah Centennial Committee, 1984.

Robertson, Pauline, and R. L. Robertson. *Panhandle Pilgrimage: Illustrated Tales Tracing History on the Texas Panhandle.* Canyon: Staked Plains Press, 1976.

Sowell, Mel. *A Short History of Watauga.* Watauga History Committee, 1990.

St. Clair, Kathleen E., and Clifton R. St. Clair. *Little Towns of Texas.* Jacksonville: Jayroe Graphic Arts, 1982.

Tarpley, Fred. *1001 Texas Place Names.* Austin: University of Texas Press, 1980.

Tehuacana: A Collection of Recollections. Tehuacana Anniversary Celebration History Committee, 1990.

"Waxahatchie History." Nicholas P. Sims Library vertical files.

Utah

Allred, Mildred M. *History of Tooele County.* Salt Lake City: Tooele Company, Daughters of Utah Pioneers, 1961.

Bancroft, Hubert H. *History of Utah.* San Francisco: The History Co., 1890.

Bennett, Cynthia L. *Roadside History of Utah.* Missoula. Montana: Mountain Press, 1999.

Camp, Betsy T. (comp.). *A Memory Bank for Paragonah: 1851–1990.* Daughters of the Utah Pioneers. Provo: Community Press, 1990.

Day, Stella H., and Sebrina C. Ekins (eds.). *100 Years of History of Millard County.* Springville: Art City Pub. Co., 1951.

Federal Writers' Project. *Utah: A Guide to the State.* New York: Hastings House, 1941.

Fowler, Don D. (ed.). *Photographed All the Best Scenery: Jack Hillers' Diary of the Powell Expeditions, 1871–1875.* Salt Lake City: University of Utah Press, 1972.

Kane County History. Daughters of Utah Pioneers. Utah Printing Co., 1960.

Miller, Orrin P. *History of Tooele County.* Vol. II. Tooele: Tooele Transcript Bulletin, 1990.

"Parowan. Southern Utah's First Settlement." Town of Parowan. n.d.

Powell, Allan K. *The Utah Guide.* Boulder, Colorado: Fulcrum Pub., 1998.

Uintah County Company, Builders of Uintah: A Centennial History of Uintah County, 1872–1947. Daughters of Utah Pioneers, Uintah County. Springville: Art City Pub. Co., 1947.

Van Cott, John W. *Utah Place Names.* Salt Lake City: University of Utah Press, 1990.

Vermont

"By the Old Mill Stream: An Architectural and Historical Walking Tour of Quechee, Vermont." Quechee Chamber of Commerce. n.d.

Croix, John W. *Historical Highlights of the Town of Hartford, Vermont: 1761–1974.* Hartford, Connecticut: Imperial Co., 1974.

Federal Writers' Project. *Vermont: A Guide to the Green Mountain State.* Boston: Houghton Mifflin Co., 1937.

Hunter, Edith F. *A History of Weathersfield, Vermont.* Weathersfield Historical Society, n.d.

Paulsen, Ruth W. *Colchester, Vermont: From Ice Cap to Interstate.* Colchester: Ruth W. Paulsen, 1963.

Swift, Esther. M. *Vermont Place-Names: Footprints of History.* Brattleboro: S. Greene Press, 1977.

Wells, Frederic P. *History of Barnet, Vermont, From the Outbreak of the French and Indian War to the Present Time.* Burlington: Free Press Printing, 1923.

Virginia

Crist, Charlotte. "Mobjack, Despite Many Changes, Keeps Its Family Feeling." *Gloucester-Mathews Gazette-Journal.* Jan. 15, 1987: 14A.

Federal Writers' Project. *Virginia: A Guide to the Old Dominion.* New York: Oxford University Press, 1940.

Hagemann, James A. *The Heritage of Virginia: The Story of Place Names in the Old Dominion.* Norfolk: Donning Co., 1986.

Hanson, Raus M. *Virginia Place Names.* Verona: McClure Press, 1969.

"Historical Background." Town of Occoquan vertical files.

"Poquoson Historical Trail." City of Poquoson, 1990.

Reps, John W. *Tidewater Towns.* Williamsburg: Colonial Williamsburg Foundation, 1972.

Slaughter, James B. *Settlers, Southerners, Americans: The History of Essex County, Virginia. 1608–1984.* Salem, West Virginia: Don Mills. Inc., 1985.

Watkins, Thomas V. *A History of Poquoson, Virginia, Poquoson Handbook.* Poquoson: T. V. Watkins, 1988.

Washington

Adams County Historical Society. *A Pictorial History of Adams County, Washington.* Dallas: Taylor Pub., 1986.

Adams, Kramer A. *Logging Railroads of the West.* Seattle: Superior Pub. Co., 1961.

An Illustrated History of Southeastern Washington. Chicago: Western Historical Pub., 1906.

Bagley, Clarence B. *History of King County, Washington.* Chicago: S. J. Clark Pub., 1929.

Binns, Archie. *Sea in the Forest.* New York: Doubleday & Co., 1953.

Brands, Aviva L., Associated Press. "Feds: Send Kennewick Man Back to Tribes." *Mail Tribune.* Sept. 26, 2000: 1.

Butler, John W. "Butler's Landing on the Columbia." *Skamania County Heritage.* Vol. 9, No. 2. Oct. 1980: 3, 7.

Capoeman, Pauline K. (ed.). *Land of the Quinault.* Seattle: Continental Printing, 1990.

Chehalis Community Development Program. Chehalis Community Development Program History Committee, 1954.

Cle Elum Community Development Study, History Report: Operation Cooperation. Town of Cle Elum, 1955.

Culp, Edwin D. *Stations West.* Caldwell, Idaho: Caxton Printers, 1972.

Davenport, Marge. *Best of the Old Northwest.* Tigard, Oregon: Paddlewheel Press, 1980.

Dow, Edson. *Passes to the North.* Wenatchee: Wenatchee Bindery & Printing, 1963.

Dwelley, Art. *Tenino: The First Hundred Years.* Tenino: Tenino Independent, 1971.

Edwards, Jonathan. *History of Spokane County.* San Francisco: W. H. Lever. Pub., 1900.

Eells, Rev. Myron. *The Twana, Chemakum, and Klallam Indians of Washington Territory.* Fairfield: Ye Galleon Press, 1996.

Elyea, Winifred. "The History of Tatoosh Island." *Washington Historical Quarterly.* Vol. 20, No. 3. July 1929. 223–224.

"Enumclaw." *The Buckley News Banner.* May 20, 1998.

Estes, George. *The Rawhide Railroad.* Canby: George Estes' Pub., 1924.

Feagans, Raymond J. *The Railroad That Ran By the Tide.* Berkeley: Howell-North Books, 1972.

Federal Writers' Project. *Washington: A Guide to the Evergreen State.* Portland: Binfords & Mort, 1941.

Felt, Margaret. *Rivers to Reckon With.* Forks: Gockerell & Fletcher Pub., 1985.

"First Inhabitants of Naselle." *The Sou'wester.* Pacific County Historical Society. Vol. X, No. 1. Spring, 1975. 3.

Fish, Harriet J. "Name Game — What to Call the City?" *The Issaquah Press.* Online edition. www.isspress.com/archive/name/name/.

Florin, Lambert. *Historic Western Churches.* Seattle: Superior Pub., 1969.

Gaston, Joseph. *Centennial History of Oregon.* Chicago: S. J. Clark Pub., 1912.

Goodman, Walt E. *Chewelah and Vicinity Before 1971.* Chewelah: Walt E. Goodman, n.d.

Gossett, Greta. *A History of the Nile Valley in Washington State*. Fairfield: Ye Galleon Press, 1979.

Griffith, Phyllis. "The Entiat Rapids." *Entiat Valley Explorer*. Sept. 2, 1998: 4.

Harder, John. Kahlotus. Letter to author, March 6, 1999.

Harvey, Paul W. "Steilacoom Boomed Decade Before Tacoma Became Town." *Tacoma News Tribune*. June 27, 1969.

Helm, Elva. *All Roads Lead to Tonasket*. Colville: Statesman-Examiner, 1985.

Hermanson, James. "Chimacum Trading Co. Was Community Center." *Port Townsend Jefferson County Leader*. Jan. 6, 1993: A7.

Hiler, Mike. "Naches in a Nutshell." *Naches Basin Community History*, 1988.

Historical Building Survey, Mukilteo, Washington. Prepared for City of Mukilteo. Historical Research Associates, 1994.

"Historically Speaking." Town of Skykomish. n.d.

Hitchman, Robert. *Place Names of Washington*. Tacoma: Washington State Historical Society, 1985.

Hull, Lindley. *A History of Central Washington*. Spokane: Shaw & Borden, 1929.

Hult, Ruby E. *The Untamed Olympics*. Portland: Binfords & Mort, 1954.

With Pride in Heritage, History of Jefferson County. Port Townsend: Jefferson County Historical Society, 1966.

Jones, Aiden H. "Yacolt." *Ft. Vancouver Historical Society*. Vol. 16. 1975. 59–60.

Jones, Roy F. *Boundary Town*. Vancouver: Fleet Printing, 1985.

Kirk, Ruth, and Carmela Alexander. *Exploring Washington's Past*. Seattle: University Washington Press, 1990.

Kuykendall, Elgin V. *History of Garfield County*. Fairfield: Ye Galleon Press, 1984.

Lewis, William S. *The Story of Early Days in the Big Bend Country* (facsimile). Seattle: Shorey Book Store, 1965.

Lockley, Fred. *History of the Columbia River Valley: From the Dalles to the Sea*. Vol. 1. Chicago: S. J. Clark Pub., 1928.

Lyman, W.D. *Lyman's History of Old Walla Walla County*. Chicago: S. J. Clark Pub., 1918.

Martin, Irene. *Skamokawa: Sad Years, Glad Years*. Skamokawa: Irene Martin, 1985.

May, Pete (ed.). *History of Klickitat County*. Goldendale: Klickiat County Historical Society, 1982.

McCausland, Ruth. "Tokeland: Alive and Well." *The Sou'wester*. Pacific County Historical Society.Vol. 12, No. 2. Summer 1987.

McDonald, Lucile S. *Making History: The People Who Shaped the San Juan Islands*. Friday Harbor: Harbor Press, 1990.

Meany, Edmond S. *Origin of Washington Geographic Names*. Seattle: University Washington Press, 1923.

Miller, Emma G. *Clatsop County, Oregon, Its History, Legends and Industries*. Portland: Binfords & Mort, 1958.

Morgan, Murry, and Rosa Morgan. *South on the Sound: An Illustrated History of Tacoma and Pierce County*. Woodland Hills. California: Windsor Pub., 1984.

Mottishaw, Marjorie P. "Quiet, Peaceful, Old Steilacoom." *Pacific Northwest Quarterly*. Vol. 46, No. 1. Jan. 1955. 1.

"Naches, A Valley Town With a Long Past." *Yakima Valley Sun*. Oct. 28, 1976: 28.

Nasel 1878– Naselle 1978: The Centennial Book. Naselle Centennial Committee, 1978.

"Origin and Meaning of the Geographic Name Palouse." *Washington Historical Quarterly*. Vol. 24, No. 3. July 1933: 190–191.

Palmer, Gayle (ed.). *City of Tumwater, The River Remembers: A History of Tumwater, 1845–1995*. Norfolk, Virginia: Donning Co., 1995.

_____, and Shanna Stevenson (eds.). *Thurston County Place Names: A Heritage Guide*. Olympia: Thurston County Historic Committee, 1992.

Patty, Stanton H. "Oyster Port Showcases History on the Half Shell." *The Seattle Times/Seattle Post-Intelligencer*. Jan. 6, 1991: J2–3.

Peterson, Keith C. *Company Town: Potlatch, Idaho, and the Potlatch Lumber Company*. Seattle: Washington State University Press, 1987.

Phillippay, Minola. *Kahlotus is Home*. Steamboat Springs, Colorado: Steamboat Pilot, 1973.

Phillips, James W. *Washington State Place Names.* Seattle: University Washington Press, 1971.

Poppleton, Lois R. *There is Only One Enumclaw.* Enumclaw: Lois R. Poppleton, 1985.

Portman, Sally. *The Smiling Country: A History of the Methow Valley.* Winthrop: Sun Mountain Resorts, 1993.

Prescott, Edgar. *Early Yelm.* Tacoma: The Folly Press, 1979.

Ramsey, Guy. *Postmarked Washington: Pierce County.* Tacoma: Washington State Historical Society, 1981.

Reese, Gary F. *Origins of Pierce County Place Names.* Tacoma: R & M Press, 1989.

Riley, Elizabeth F. *Still Strong Beats the Heart.* Chewelah: Elizabeth F. Riley, 1985.

River Reflections: Snohomish City—1859 to 1910. Snohomish Historical Society, 1975.

Robertson, Gay. *Stehekin Remembered.* Seattle: Pacific Northwest National Parks & Forests Association, 1987.

Roe, Joann. *Stevens Pass: The Story of Railroading and Recreation in the North Cascades.* Seattle: The Mountaineers, 1995.

Rushton, Alice. *The History of the Town of Orting.* Olympia: Warren's Printing & Graphics, 1981.

Russel, Jervis (ed.). *Jimmy Come Lately: History of Clallam County.* Port Angeles: Clallam County Historical Society, 1971.

Speidel, Bill. *The Wet Side of the Mountain (Or Prowling Western Washington).* Seattle: Nettle Creek Pub., 1981.

Steele, Richard F. *An Illustrated History of Stevens, Ferry, Okanogan and Chelen Counties, State of Washington.* Spokane: Western Heritage Pub., 1904.

Stevenson, Kathleen. *History of Washougal.* Federal Writer's Project Manuscript. Washougal Public Library vertical files.

Swan, James. *The Northwest Coast.* Introduction by W. A. Katy. Fairfield: Ye Galleon Press, 1966.

Swart, Phillip. *Hole in the Ground: Tales of Kahlotus.* Seattle: Sand Hill Books, 1997.

Timmon, Fritz. *Blow for the Landing: A Hundred Years of Steam Navigation on the Waters of the West.* Caldwell, Idaho: Caxton Printers, 1973.

Wapato History and Heritage. Wapato: Wapato Historical Committee, 1978.

Warren, Cindy. "Naches is the town that (Painter's) Butter Built." *Yakima Valley Sun.* May 26, 1977: 24.

Welsh, William D. *Brief Historical Sketch of Grays Harbor, Washington. Produced by William D. Welsh. from the Splendid Manuscript of Ed. Van Syckle.* Jointly presented by the chambers of commerce of Hoquiam and Aberdeen. Belleview: Rayonier. Inc. 1942

Wilson, Bruce. *Late Frontier: A History of Okanogan County, Washington.* Okanogan: Okanogan County Historical Society, 1990.

Winston, Dorothy E. *Early Spanaway.* Tacoma: Graphic Press, 1976.

Wuerthner, George. *Olympic, A Visitor's Companion.* Mechanicsburg, Pennsylvania: Stackpole Books, 1999.

West Virginia

Federal Writers' Project. *West Virginia: A Guide to the Mountain State.* New York: Oxford University Press, 1946.

Kenny, Hamill. *West Virginia Place Names.* Piedmont: The Place Name Press, 1945.

Koon, Thomas J. *Marion County, West Virginia: A Pictorial History.* Norfolk, Virginia: Donning Co., Pub. 1995

Leeper, Thomas. *Monongah.* Unpublished manuscript, July 1949. Town of Monongah files.

Ralston, R. H., Sr. "Who Put the K in Buckhannon." *Record Delta.* Dec. 5, 1986: 5.

_____. "Spelling Mystery." *Record Delta.* Mar. 30, 1987:1.

Wisconsin

A History of Waupun: 1839 to 1939. Waupun Centennial Celebration, 1939.

Auer, James M. *Centennial Memories: A Brief History of Menasha, Wisconsin.* Menasha: James M. Auer, 1953.

Carter, Byron. "Early History of Chetek." *Chetek Alert,* 1936.

"Centuries Passing in Review." *Wisconsin Magazine* (Oshkosh Edition). Dec. 1950.

"Chetek History." Chetek Public Library vertical files.

Corrigan, Walter D. *History of the Town of Mequon, Ozaukee County, Wisconsin, Brought Down to About 1870.* Mequon: Cederburg Newsprint, 1950.

Egar, Rev. John H. *The Story of Nashotah.* Milwaukee: Burdick & Armitage Printers, 1874.

Federal Writers' Project. *Wisconsin: A Guide to the Badger State.* New York: Duell, Sloan and Pearce, 1941.

Gard, Robert, and L. G. Sorden. *The Romance of Wisconsin Place Names.* New York: October House, Inc., 1968.

Goc, Michael J. *Land Rich Enough: An Illustrated History of Oshkosh and Winnebago County.* Northridge, California: Windsor Pub., 1988.

Griffin, Fern. "Echoes of a Boardwalk." *Washburn County Register.* Aug. 30, 1979.

Hallock, Rev. Donald H. V. "The Story of Nashotah." *Historical Magazine of the Protestant Episcopal Church.* Vol. XI, No. 1. March 1942.

Hanold, Darrel. "Brief History of Wonewoc, Wisconsin." *Wonewoc History Project,* 1998.

Hardy, Tom A. "Nekoosa." High school term paper, 1957. Charles and Jo Ann Lester Library vertical files.

"History of City of Wausau." *Wausau News.* Mar. 8, 1905.

History of Fond du Lac County, Wisconsin , Containing an Account of Its Settlement, Growth, Development and Resources, Biographical Sketches, etc. Chicago: Western Historical Co., 1880.

"History of Packwaukee Goes Back to Early Pioneer Days." *The Tribune.* Dec. 16, 1955.

History of Washington and Ozaukee Counties, Wisconsin, Containing an Account of Its Settlement, Growth, Development and Resource, etc. Chicago: Western Historical Co., 1881.

History of Waukesha County, Wisconsin, Containing an Account of Its Settlement, Growth, Development and Resources, etc. Chicago: Western Historical Co., 1880.

"History of Wausau." Wausau Area Chamber of Commerce. n.d.

Illustrated Waupaca, Containing a Brief Historical Sketch; a Complete List of Incorporations and Societies, with Their Present Officers, etc. Waupaca: D. I. Stinchfield, Pub., 1888.

"Indians Inhabited Area Before White Settlers." *Mukwonago Chief.* July 30, 1986: 7.

Jones, Mrs. Jessie. "History of Packwaukee Goes Back to Early Pioneer Days." *The Tribune.* Dec. 16, 1965.

Kewaunee Centennial, A Harbor Community: Centennial, 1883–1983. Kewaunee Chamber of Commerce Centennial Book Committee, 1983.

Langill, Ellen D., and Jean P. Loerke (eds.). *From Farmland to Freeways, A History of Waukesha County, Wisconsin.* Waukesha County Historical Society, 1984.

McMurray, William J. (ed.). *History of Auglaize County, Ohio.* Indianapolis: Historical Pub. Co., 1923.

"Minong." Miscellaneous publications. Wisconsin Historical Society vertical files.

Mosinee Centennial, August 9, 10, 11: 1857–1957. Mosinee Centennial Brochure Committee, 1957.

Mundstock, Jeannette, and Tom Stoker (eds.). *Footsteps Through the Past: A Short History of Monona, Town of Blooming Grove and East Madison.* Monona: Community Herald Newspaper. Inc., 1976.

"Muskego, Wisconsin." *Encyclopedia of Wisconsin* Questionnaire. Submitted to Somerset Pub., New York, 1993.

"Naming of Wausau." *Rhinelander Herald.* Jan. 7, 1905.

Neuman, Ted. "A History of the City of Kewaunee." *Press Gazette.* July 1934.

"Origin of Wausau." *Wausau Record.* Feb. 17, 1908.

Oshkosh, One Hundred Years a City: 1853–1953. Oshkosh: Castle-Pierce Printing, 1953.

Our 100th Year, The State Bank of Wonewoc: 1887–1987. Wonewoc: The Bank, 1987.

Redfield, Lorraine C. *A History of the Settlement and Progress of Pewaukee, Wisconsin, Published in honor of The Nation's Bicentennial and the 100th Anniversary of the Incorporation of the Village*: 1836–1976.

Reetz, Elaine. *Come Back in Time: Communities*. Vol. I. Princeton: Fox River Pub., 1981.

Schlies, Suzan. "H. P. Bird: A Man and His Town." 1995. Wausaukee Public Library vertical files.

Shadows on the Wolf. Shiocton History Project Committee, 1987.

Shattuck, S. F. (comp.). *A History of Neenah*. Neenah Historical Society, 1958.

Shawano Story—100 Years of History, Shawano Centennial, 1874–1974. Shawano County Historical Society, 1974.

Sprain, Fran. *Places and Faces in Marquette County, Wisconsin*. Vol. I. Westfield: Isabella Press, 1991.

Stark, William. *Pine Lake*. Sheboygan: Zimmerman Press, 1971.

Tammen, Howard N. *Spring City's Past: A Thematic History of Waukesha and the Final Report of Waukesha's Intensive Historic Resources Survey*. City of Waukesha Planning Department, 1982.

The First 100 Years, Minocqua-Woodruff: 1888–1988. Minocqua: Lakeland Times, 1988.

The First 100 Years, A History of Waupum. Waupum Centennial Celebration, 1939.

Trask, Kerry A. "Early Manitowoc and a Sense of Place." *Manitowoc County Historical Society*. Occupational Monograph 66, 1989.

Vogel, Virgil. *Indian Names on Wisconsin's Map*. Madison: University of Wisconsin, 1991.

Ware, John M. *A Standard History of Waupaca County, Wisconsin*. Vol. I. New York: Lewis Pub., 1917.

Waupaca Centennial Book: 1857–1957. Waupaca Centennial Corporation, 1957.

Waupaca Post. Waupaca Semi-Centennial Souvenir Edition, 1898.

"Wauwatosa is You." *League of Women Voters of Wauwatosa*. May 1970.

Westover, Ruth. *Waukau in History*. Berlin: The Print Shop, 1979.

Where the Wild Rice Grows: A Portrait of Menomonie. Menomonie Sesquentennial Commission, 1996.

Wolf, Frank E. "Mazomanie." *Mazomanie Historical Society*, 1998.

Wright, D. E. *A Chronicle of Mukwonago History*. Mukwonago: Mukwonago Historical Society, 1990.

Zehfus, Mark J. "Sheboygan, Wisconsin." Mead Public Library vertical files.

Wyoming

Barnhart, Bill. *The Northfork Trail: Guide and Pictorial History of Cody, Wyoming & Yellowstone Park*. Wapiti: Elkhorn Pub., 1982.

Campbell County: The Treasured Years. Gillette: Campbell County Historical Society, 1991.

Federal Writers' Project. *Wyoming: A Guide to Its History. Highways and People*. New York: Oxford University Press, 1941.

Field, Sharon L. (ed.). *History of Cheyenne, Wyoming, Laramie County*. Vol. 2. Dallas: Curtis Media Corp., 1989.

Hodgson, Don. *Chugwater: A Centennial History*. Chugwater: Don Hodgson, 1986.

"Meeteetse, Wyoming." Meeteetse Museum vertical files.

Pictorial History of Fremont County, Wyoming's Diamond Jubilee of Statehood: 1890–1965. Crossroads of the West, 1965.

Urbanek, Mae. *Wyoming Place Names*. Missoula, Montana: Mountain Press, 1988.

Wilson, Rufus R. *Out of the West*. New York: Wilson-Erickson. Inc., 1936.

Wyoming: Platt County Heritage. Platte County Extension Homemakers Council, 1981.

Wyoming's Diamond Jubilee of Statehood: 1890–1965. Crossroads of the West, Inc., 1965.

General References

Adams, Kramer A. *Logging Railroads of the West*. Seattle: Superior Pub. Co., 1961.

Armstrong, J. B. *Bedding the Drags.* Missoula: University of Montana, 1972.

Barr, Tom. *Unique Washington.* Santa Fe, New Mexico: John Muir Pub., 1995.

Beebe, Lucius, and Charles Clegg. *The American West.* New York: E. P. Dutton & Co., 1955.

Bennett, Robert A. *We'll All Go Home in the Spring: Personal Accounts and Adventures As Told By the Pioneers of the West.* Walla Walla: Pioneer Press, 1984.

Bower, Donald E. *Roaming the American West.* Mechanicsburg, Pennsylvania: Stackpole Books, 1971.

Brown, Dee. *Wondrous Times on the Frontier.* New York: Harper Perennial, 1991.

Casey, Robert L. *Journey to the High Southwest.* Seattle: Pacific Search Press, 1983.

Clark, Ella E. *Indian Legends of the Pacific Northwest.* Berkeley: University of California Press, 1953.

Crosby, Katharine. *Blue-Water Men and Other Cape Codders.* New York: MacMillan Co., 1946.

Culp, Edwin D. *Stations West.* Caldwell, Idaho: Caxton Printers, 1972.

Dary, David. *Entrepreneurs of the Old West.* New York: Alfred A. Knopf, 1986.

_____. *Seeking Pleasures in the Old West.* New York: Alfred A. Knopf, 1991.

Davenport, Marge. *Best of the Old Northwest.* Tigard, Oregon: Paddlewheel Press, 1980.

_____. *Fabulous Folks of the Old Northwest.* Tigard, Oregon: Paddlewheel Press, 1986.

Dawson, Frank. *Place Names in Colorado.* Denver, Colorado: J. Frank Publishing, 1954.

Dow, Edson. *Passes to the North.* Wenatchee: Wenatchee Bindery Printing, 1963.

Dunlop, Richard. *Great Trails of the West.* Nashville, Tennessee: Abingdon Press. 1971.

Dutton, Bertha P. *Indians of the American Southwest.* Englewood Cliffs, New Jersey: Prentice-Hall. Inc., 1975.

Federal Writers' Project. *U.S. One: Maine to Florida.* New York: Modern Age Books, 1938.

Ferguson, William M., and Arthur H. Rohn. *Anasazi Ruins of the Southwest in Color.* Albuquerque: University of New Mexico Press, 1987.

Flanagan, Mike. *Out West.* New York: Harry N. Abrams. Inc., 1987.

Florin, Lambert. *Ghost Towns of the Southwest.* New York: Promontory Press, 1970.

Gannett, Henry. *The Origin of Certain Place Names in the United States.* Washington, D.C.: U.S. Government Printing Office, 1905.

Gibbs, James A. *Shipwrecks of the Pacific Coast.* Portland: Binfords & Mort, 1957.

_____. James A. *Pacific Graveyard.* Portland: Binfords & Mort, 1950.

Gideon, D.C. *Indian Territory.* New York: Lewis Pub., 1901.

Goode, William H. *Outposts of Zion.* Cincinnati. Poe & Hitchcock, 1863.

Greever, William S. *Bonanza West: The Story of the Western Mining Rushes, 1848–1900.* Moscow: University of Idaho Press, 1963.

Gutek, Gerald L. *Experiencing America's Past.* Hoboken, New Jersey: John Wiley & Sons, 1986.

Harder, Kelsie B. (ed.). *Illustrated Dictionary of Place Names: United States and Canada.* New York: Facts on File, 1976.

Hart, Herbert M. *Old Forts of the Northwest.* Seattle: Superior Pub., 1963.

Huden, John C. *Indian Place Names of New England.* New York: Museum of the American Indian Heye Foundation, 1962.

Huffman, L. A. *The Frontier Years.* New York: Henry Holt & Co., 1955.

Hult, Ruby E. *Lost Mines and Treasures of the Pacific Northwest.* Portland: Binfords & Mort, 1957.

_____, Ruby E. *The Untamed Olympics.* Portland: Binfords & Mort, 1954.

Hurt. R. Douglas. *The Ohio Frontier: Crucible of the Old Northwest: 1720–1830.* Bloomington: Indiana University Press. 1996.

Johnson, Michael G. *The Native Tribes of North America: A Concise Encyclopedia.* New York: MacMillan Pub., 1994.

Jones, Ray, and Bruce Roberts. *Pacific Northwest Lighthouses: Oregon to the Aleu-*

tians. Guilford, Connecticut: Globe Pequot Press, 1997.

Kaplan, Robert D. *An Empire Wilderness: Travels Into America's Future*. New York: Random House, 1998.

Kingery, Hugh E. *High Country Names*. Boulder, Colorado: Johnson Books, 1994.

Lind, Carol J. *Big Timber, Big Men*. Seattle: Hancock House. Pub., 1978.

Malachi, Roman. *Big Sandy Country*. Arizona Bicentennial Commission, 1975.

Malinowski, Sharon, *et al*. *The Gale Encyclopedia of Native American Tribes*. Detroit: Gale Research, 1998.

Mavor, James W., and Byron E. Dix. *Manitou: The Sacred Landscape of New England's Native Civilization*. Rochester: Inner Traditions International, Ltd., 1989.

Mundo, Anna. *Southern New England*. New York: Fodor's Travel, 1999.

Nestor, Sandy. *Our Native American Legacy*. Caldwell, Idaho: Caxton Press, 2001.

Olmsted, Gerald W. *Fielding's Lewis and Clark Trail*. New York: William Morrow & Co., Inc., 1986.

Orchard, Vance. *Life on the Dry Side: A Nostalgic Journey Down the Backroads of the Inland Northwest*. Walla Walla: Pioneer Press, 1984.

Ormes, Robert. *Tracking Ghost Railroads in Colorado*. Colorado Springs: Century One Press, 1975.

Orr, Elizabeth L., and William N. Orr. *Rivers of the West: A Guide to the Geology and History*. Salem: Eagle Web Press, 1985.

Oswalt, Wendell. *This Land Was Theirs: A Study or the North American Indian*. Hoboken: New Jersey: John Wiley & Sons. 2nd Edition, 1973.

Paul, Rodman W. *Mining Frontiers of the Far West, 1848–1880*. New York: Holt, Rinehart and Winston, 1963.

Pettit, Jan. Utes: *The Mountain People*. Boulder, Colorado: Johnson Books, 1990.

Preston, Douglas. *Cities of Gold*. New York: Simon & Schuster, 1992.

Quimby, Myron J. *Scratch Ankle, U.S.A.: American Place Names and Their Derivation*. New York: A.S. Barnes and Co., 1969.

Ruby, Robert, and John A. Brown. *Indians of the Pacific Northwest*. Norman: University of Oklahoma Press, 1981.

Sealock, Richard B., *et al*. *Bibliography of Place-Name Literature: United States and Canada*. Chicago: American Library Association, 3rd Edition, 1982.

Simpson, Dorothy. *The Maine Islands in Story and Legend*. New York: J. B. Lippincott, 1960.

Stadius, Martin. *Dreamers: On the Trail of the Nez Perce*. Caldwell, Idaho: Caxton Press, 1999.

Stewart, George R. *American Place Names*. New York: Oxford University Press, 1970.

Strong, John A. *The Algonquian Peoples of Long Island from Earliest Times to 1900*. Interlaken, New York: Empire State Books, 1997.

Swan, James. *The Northwest Coast*. Introduction by W. A. Katy. Fairfield: Ye Galleon Press, 1966.

Vokac, David. *The Great Towns of the West*. San Diego. California: West Press, 1985.

Walking Turtle, Eagle. *Indian America*. Santa Fe, New Mexico: John Muir Pubs. 4th Edition, 1995.

Wilson, Rufus R. *Out of the West*. New York: Press of the Pioneers, 1933.

Index